"The maws of the Nazi machine fed on children ⟨...⟩ is remarkable in itself. But that, instead of stunting him, his tragic experiences spurred him on to become a sage and a leader is a tribute not only to his own qualities but to the exceptional people with whom his life was bound up. This book is many things: survivor story, auto-biography, wisdom literature and an unabashed love letter to Israel, the home to which its subtitle alludes."—*Montreal Gazette*

"The Chief Rabbi of Israel recounts a harrowing journey from child prisoner in Buchenwald to champion of Holocaust survivors. . . . [An] uplifting story of peace, reconciliation and an incredible life's journey."—Kirkus

"In 3,000 years of Jewish literature in all its scope and variety, we have had very few rabbinic autobiographies. . . . Why then, did some rabbis write their own biographies? Perhaps because their lives were tumul-tuous and adventurous . . . but primarily because they felt that others might learn some important lessons from their lives. . . . *Out of the Depths* contains both these elements: an eventful and rich life and a unique perspective on its purpose and meaning."—*Jewish Home*

"Thanks to his mother's quick thinking (she sized up the situation as soon as she saw the Nazis sort the cattle cars by men, and women and children to different cars) she grabbed her seven-year-old son's back with both hands and shoved him in the direction of the men. . . . The story of how Napthali [Lau's brother] fought to stay near his little brother until the end of the war, and how the brothers finally reached Israel after Buchenwald was liberated in 1945, is a rich, beautifully told story."—Jewish Book Council

"[Rabbi Lau's] tale of triumph and faith as a young boy during the Holocaust provides us with a model of personal greatness in the face of unimaginable hardship. . . . *Out of the Depths* tells the story of his miraculous journey from an orphaned refugee to become one of the leaders of the Jewish people."—Aish.com

"In this riveting and emotionally charged memoir, the former Chief Ashkenazi Rabbi of Israel relates the turbulent yet hopeful story of his life with unfailing honesty. . . . Rabbi Lau chronicles his life journey with ample detail to form vivid pictures and convey deep emotions. . . . The Holocaust comes alive with all its horrors, but so do the sparks of hope that emanate from his story."—Orthodox Union

OUT OF THE
DEPTHS

THE STORY OF A CHILD OF BUCHENWALD
WHO RETURNED HOME AT LAST

CHIEF RABBI
ISRAEL MEIR LAU

Forewords by
Shimon Peres
and
Elie Wiesel

Translated from the Hebrew by Jessica Setbon
and Shira Leibowitz Schmidt

OUPRESS

STERLING
New York

STERLING
New York

An Imprint of Sterling Publishing Co., Inc.
122 Fifth Avenue
New York, NY 10011

In conjunction with OU Press, an imprint of the Orthodox Union, www.ou.org

A note about the translation of Bible verses: The translators made every effort to ensure that the verses harmonize with and amplify the author's original Hebrew context, and at the same time that they are fluent and eloquent renditions of scripture. To that end, the translators consulted a variety of existing Bible translations, including the King James Version.

ISBN 978-1-4549-4263-4

Distributed in Canada by Sterling Publishing Co., Inc.
c/o Canadian Manda Group, 664 Annette Street
Toronto, Ontario M6S 2C8, Canada
Distributed in the United Kingdom by GMC Distribution Services
Castle Place, 166 High Street, Lewes, East Sussex BN7 1XU, England
Distributed in Australia by NewSouth Books
University of New South Wales, Sydney, NSW 2052, Australia

For information about custom editions, special sales, and premium and corporate purchases, please contact Sterling Special Sales at 800-805-5489 or specialsales@sterlingpublishing.com.

Manufactured in the United States of America

2 4 6 8 10 9 7 5 3

sterlingpublishing.com

Front cover design by The BookDesigners
Back cover design by David Ter-Avanesyan
Interior book design by Robin Arzt

Translation of Elie Wiesel foreword by Toula Ballas

This book is dedicated to the memory of my father, Rabbi Moshe Chaim Lau; to my mother, Rabbanit Chaya; to my brother Shmuel Yitzchak; to my grandfather Rabbi Simcha Frankel-Teomim; to my uncles and aunts; and to all my family who were taken away in the whirlwind together with the six million.

*Their blood cries out to us from the earth;
may the land not cover over their blood, and let there be
not space for their cries.
May the Lord avenge their blood.*

Contents

PART I The Knife, the Fire, and the Wood

OPPOSITE: With his coat and suitcase in hand, Israel Meir (Lulek) Lau,
a member of the Buchenwald children's transport, prepares to leave the
OSE children's home in Écouis, France, for the Land of Israel, 1945.

PART II The Ram's Horn

FOREWORD
by Shimon Peres

Before you is a book written by the most Jewish Jew of the last decades. This is a book on Judaism, its glory and ordeals, depicting a period that could possibly be judged as the hardest, bitterest, and darkest in the annals of the Jewish people. This is a book that portrays the persona of the writer alongside the traits of his Jewish people. This is a book whose every word has been inscribed in blood.

Inspired by the stirring words of our national poet, Chaim Nachman Bialik, "Should you wish to know the Source, / From which your brothers drew . . . / Their strength of soul . . . / Their comfort, courage, patience, trust, / And iron might to bear their hardships / And suffer without end or measure?" I conclude that *Out of the Depths* constitutes this very source.

As we read this book—in which the writer, Rabbi Israel Meir Lau, charts the twists and turns of his life in the Diaspora and in Israel—it is hard to make out the words, for our eyes have misted over, brimming with tears, as we are exposed to spine-chilling depictions, to words that hide a painful, soul-wrenching narrative. The silent words cry out to us. The probing questions remain unanswered to the bitter end.

In the words of King Solomon, I wish Rabbi Israel Meir Lau, the State of Israel, and the Jewish people "length of days, and long life, and peace, shall they add to thee" and all the house of Israel.

May this book serve as a pillar of fire for us all, whatever road we take.

—SHIMON PERES
PRESIDENT OF THE STATE OF ISRAEL

FOREWORD
by Elie Wiesel

A cry of despair? An act of faith? A heartrending echo of the Akedah, the eternal blight to which our people seem to have been subjected since the time of Abraham and his son?

This story, told by a child who became the chief rabbi of Israel, is all that—and much more.

Our paths crossed more than once. We were in Buchenwald together. We lived through its liberation together. We came to France together, with a group of four hundred young boys, led with unstinting devotion by the magnificent Oeuvre de Secours aux Enfants (Society for Rescuing Children). Lulek was the youngest—I would say the smallest among us.

But it was he who recalled our first true encounter.

We had come—he from Tel Aviv and I from New York—to participate in the annual ceremony of the March of the Living for the Yom HaShoah (Holocaust Remembrance Day) at Birkenau. In introducing me to a gathering of more than ten thousand people, he recalled that particular event. In May 1945 he had just learned—from his brother Naphtali—of the death of their mother. And it was you, said Lulek, the future chief rabbi of Israel, who taught me to recite the Kaddish.

I had forgotten it; he had as well because he did not mention it in his autobiography.

But in this book, so rich in dramatic memories that often extend beyond the personal, he sees himself as a child. In the ghetto of Piotrków Trybunalski. Cruel scenes in the synagogue. The selections later on. The overwhelming dread of successive separations. The scenes, each bloodier and more bruising, one after the other, all blending together.

He sees his father again, the chief rabbi of the city, humiliated and beaten by the SS because he refused to cut his beard. He remembers him telling the Jews to defend themselves by "tooth and nail." He recounts his father's final words about the martyrdom of Rabbi Akiva: his *Shema Yisrael* resounded to the heavens.

He evokes life with his mother in their attic hideout. The constant anguish. The daily miracles. Naphtali's escape from Auschwitz. Purim and Passover in the camp. The loss of their father's manuscript, which the elder brother always carried with him: a study on the sanctification of the Divine Name. The appearance of Feodor, the Russian sergeant from Rostov who became his guardian angel.

Like most memoirs written by survivors, each story is full of silent tears, of invisible wounds, of unfathomable gazes, but also of that which menaces life, hope, dignity. In this accursed place, the enemy has absolute power.

We were separated, Lulek and I, in Écouis, France. After several weeks, the first group left for Palestine, including the two brothers. In the Holy Land, they discovered that they had family there.

It's best if I stop now. Let the reader discover alone the intensity of this overwhelming journey that will describe how one can live with the dead or else join the dead. How one can cling, even in the deepest shadows, to the light of faith. And, above all, how one can build on ashes. And how a little boy from Piotrków and from Buchenwald succeeded in growing and blossoming under the radiance of the blue sky of the Jewish state. Did he know, could he know, what great joys awaited him there?

Me, I remained in France. And many years flowed by before we reunited.

To understand his well-deserved achievements—attained under the heavy burden of a nameless and limitless past that stretches from

Auschwitz to the Sinai—the reader also follows him from the depths of ultimate suffering to the summit of honors and victories. In the original Hebrew edition, the author sets his story in the shadow of the flames of Akedah.

Only this time, the father does not return from Mount Moriah.

—ELIE WIESEL

PREFACE TO THE
ENGLISH EDITION

ON JUNE 27, 2008, the telephone rang in my home in Tel Aviv. Naftali Menashe, news editor of one of the Israeli radio stations, was on the line. He asked whether the name Feodor meant anything to me, and, if so, who Feodor was and what I remembered about him. Surprised by the call, I replied that Feodor was a Russian taken captive by the Nazis and imprisoned in the Buchenwald concentration camp, in the same Block 8 where I was held toward the end of World War II. I did not know his last name, only that he came from the town of Rostov in Russia. "Why are you asking me about him?" I asked Mr. Menashe. He told me that the radio station had received information from the Associated Press news agency about a Professor Kenneth Waltzer of Michigan State University in the United States. After having recently studied Gestapo documents at the Bad Arolsen archives in Germany, Professor Waltzer discovered that the Gestapo had kept records of the Russian prisoner who had protected a Jewish child in the block, a boy named Lulek from Poland. Waltzer also found that Feodor's last name was Mikhailichenko, and that the boy was Israel Meir Lau, who eventually became chief rabbi of Israel.

That day, on Voice of Israel radio, I spoke of the great debt I owed Feodor. He had knitted me wool earmuffs so my ears would not freeze during the roll calls held in the morning, when we were forced to remove our caps. I recounted how he stole potatoes and made hot soup for me every day. With his body, he protected me from the hail of bullets shot at us from the guard towers on the day of liberation, April 11, 1945.

On the radio, I also spoke of my unsuccessful efforts over the decades to discover his whereabouts. I said that I would be happy to meet him, and would like to recommend to Yad Vashem in Jerusalem that he be granted the honorary title of Righteous Among the Nations. I contacted Chabad in Israel, and they put me in touch with their emissary in Rostov, Rabbi Chaim Friedman. He discovered, to my disappointment, that Feodor had died, but that he had two daughters in Rostov: Yulia Selutina and Yelena Belayaeva. They were thrilled to hear that the boy who had survived Buchenwald, of whom their father had spoken until his dying day, was alive in Israel, had become a well-known rabbi, and that, despite the more than sixty years that had passed, the rabbi still remembered their father and had been looking for him all that time. They gave the Chabad representative a copy of a film that Feodor had made for Russian television at the former Buchenwald site in 1992, one year before his death. In the film, Feodor recounts that, every day, the Jewish boy had to clean the entire block, the courtyard, and the toilets in order to earn his bread ration. Feodor and his companions used to get up at five every morning in order to do the boy's cleaning job. He explained, "The boy has no parents. At least he should have some time to play like a child."

On November 27, 2008, I was privileged to host Yulia and Yelena at my home in Tel Aviv. They had traveled to Israel from Russia, for the first time in their lives, to have dinner in our home and to visit Yad Vashem in Jerusalem. Rabbi Berel Lazar, chief rabbi of Russia, joined us that night and served as translator for Feodor's daughters. Also at dinner was my brother Naphtali and his wife Joan, who had come from Jerusalem to join us. He remembered Feodor well.

Toward the end of the meal, my sons and daughters arrived, along with their wives and husbands and our grandchildren, from all parts of Israel. I introduced them to Feodor's daughters and said that it was largely thanks to him that this entire tribe had been brought into existence. The next day, I accompanied them on a tour of Yad Vashem, and they were deeply moved.

This story is yet another testimonial to the fact that the Holocaust is not only the heritage of the past but also has many implications for the present and the future.

All recent attempts that we have witnessed to minimize the Holocaust and even to deny it will not stand the bitter test of the reality that has affected all of humanity. Its lessons must serve as a warning sign for generations to come.

I hope, dear readers, that this edition of my book will make a modest contribution to helping us remember the past and not forget it, and to ensuring that we maintain our hope and faith in a better future for all human beings.

Tel Aviv-Jaffa

INTRODUCTION

"WHAT DID YOU FEEL?" "What were you thinking about?" "Who came to mind?" These were just some of the questions members of the audience asked me after I had recited the Kaddish (mourners' prayer) and selected verses from Psalms. We were at Auschwitz-Birkenau, at a ceremony commemorating the sixtieth anniversary of the liberation of the camp. A heavy snow was falling in the freezing cold, and for the entire three hours, I pitied the thousands of participants, including the president of the State of Israel, the vice president of the United States, and the presidents and prime ministers of the major European countries.

With closed eyes, I recited from Psalms: *Yea, though I walk through the valley of the shadow of death, I will fear no evil, for thou art with me . . . and thou hast delivered my soul from death. . . . I will walk before the Lord in the land of the living.* I ended with the Kaddish: *Yitgadal ve-yitkadash shemeh rabbah*—Sanctified and magnified be Your great Name.

My eyes were closed, but I saw the victims clearly. In my mind's eye, they were getting off the train cars beside me. I saw them as they stood for the "selection," *those for death and those for life,* right at that very spot. I saw the shocked look in their eyes when they realized they had been deceived. I saw the Gestapo men and their Ukrainian henchmen beating

1

and pushing them, and with them the vicious dogs, cavernous mouths snarling. I saw the soldiers tearing children and babies from their parents' embrace. I saw families broken apart with savage cruelty. Three things linked to the nightmares of my childhood disturb me to this day: trains, boots, and dogs.

I heard the shouts: *"Schnell, schnell!"*—faster, faster! I heard the barks. I heard the screams of the children: *"Mameh! Tateh!"* I heard the bitter cries of the mothers and saw the bloody faces of the fathers beaten with rifle butts because they had tried to protect the children in their arms.

Although that recital of the Kaddish on January 27, 2005, was an isolated event, this book will act as an eternal light, an everlasting memorial that will tell the coming generations about the events in that dark tunnel, about the sparks of light that broke through it, and about the hope and faith that followed.

This book is not a conventional autobiography. You will not read here about the fifty-one years that I served in the rabbinate, at every stage from rabbi of a low-income neighborhood in Tel Aviv to chief rabbi of Israel. Instead, the stories here are about my personal memories of the Holocaust, my escape from its fiery furnace, its tortures of body and soul, and how I grew up without parents or a home. This book also tells about my acquaintance with some very special individuals, both Jews and non-Jews, who were instrumental in the national and personal miracle of rescue, the building of a national home in our native land, and the transition from Holocaust to revival.

Over time, the blazing flames of the survivors have died down to glowing embers, which by their very nature dwindle until they are extinguished. I am attempting to fan the flames of these embers so that they will never die out. I hope that my story will touch the consciousness of readers and bestir them to think again, to search their souls, and perhaps even to conclude that despite all the enigmas posed by the Holocaust, *I will walk before the Lord in the land of the living.*

When King Solomon dedicated the Temple, he announced, *The Lord said that He would dwell in thick darkness.* Sometimes, the Divine Presence rests within a domain that is hidden, concealed behind a screen of mystery. The great Chassidic teacher Rabbi Menachem Mendel of Kotsk used to say, "I am not capable of worshipping a God whose every path is clear to me." When everything is revealed and understood, that is friendship, not Divinity. When Joseph makes his enigmatic demand that his brothers bring Benjamin to him, he says, *By this you shall be tested*. Faith is tested through the unfathomable and the inexplicable.

I am a believer—and I will remain so until my dying day; *God has tried me with suffering, but He has not given me over to death*. I do not believe in coincidence, but in Divine Providence. The question for which I have not found an answer remains the question of why. Why did it have to happen? Why was my brother Milek, may God avenge his death, torn from our mother to go to his death, while I was separated from her and lived? I will never know, but this will not diminish my faith in the *One Who spoke and created the world*. As we repeat every morning in the prayer service, *into His hand I will entrust my spirit*.

I will pay my vows to the Lord, in the presence of all His people. Every day when I awake, I recite with complete conviction, *I gratefully thank You, O living and eternal King, for You have returned my soul to me with compassion*.

I CONCLUDE WITH A PRAYER to the Creator of the universe, that *nation shall not lift up sword against nation, neither shall they learn war any more*. I pray that no child in the entire world will ever have to traverse the tortured path my companions and I were forced to take until we arrived, like *children returning home*.

Tel Aviv-Jaffa

PART I

THE KNIFE, THE FIRE, AND THE WOOD

And [Isaac] said, "Here are the fire and the wood,
but where is the lamb for the offering?" . . .
Abraham stretched out his hand,
and took the knife.

GENESIS 22:7–9

CHAPTER 1

FIRST MEMORIES—
DEVASTATION NOW

*There is hope for your future, the word of God,
and your children will return home.*

JEREMIAH 31:16

MY FATHER STANDING at the deportation point—that is the first childhood memory engraved in my mind, and it is the image that accompanies me wherever I go. It is the autumn of 1942; I am five years old, short, and terrified. I stretch my neck as far as it will go in order to catch a glimpse of my father. He is standing in a crowd at the Umschlagplatz (assembly point for deportation), which is next to the Great Synagogue of our town, Piotrków, Poland. Father, with his impressive beard and black rabbi's suit, is in the center of the square surrounded by Jews, men on one side, women and children on the other.

I was there with my mother and my thirteen-year-old brother Shmuel, whom we called Milek. My older brother Naphtali, or Tulek, who was sixteen, lived at the Hortensia glass factory nearby, where he worked. The year before, the Nazis had taken him from our home and sent him to Auschwitz. Two SS officers who wore black uniforms and red armbands with swastikas emblazoned in their centers had burst through the front door of our house. They shouted at Naphtali, demanding to know where the rabbi was. Since they could not find Father, they dragged Naphtali with them and interrogated and tortured him in the basement of the Gestapo headquarters. On June 30, 1941, they put him on a truck straight to Auschwitz. Sent into forced labor, he planned his escape. On the fortieth day after his capture, he carried out his plan, escaped that hell, and returned home.

But the nightmare had begun to affect us in Piotrków as well. We felt the enormous tension that day as we stood in the assembly square. A menacing silence surrounded us. The captain of the Piotrków Gestapo approached my father, a deadly look in his eye. He stopped, and, pulling out his *maikeh*—a rubber club about three feet long—began to beat my father on the back with all his might. When the first blow struck my father from behind, the surprise and force of it made him stagger. His body bent forward as if he were about to topple over. And then, in a fraction of a second, he straightened up to his full height, stepped back, and returned to the place where he had been standing. There, he stood erect, making a supreme effort to hide his physical pain as well as his intense humiliation. I could see Father mustering all his strength to keep his balance and avoid collapsing at the German officer's feet. Father knew that if he fell, the spirit of the Jews in our town would break, and he was trying desperately to prevent that.

Everyone there knew why the German had beaten him. When the Nazis had ordered the Jews to shave off their beards, many Jews in Piotrków had come to ask Father whether they should follow this order. His answer was firm: do it in order to save yourselves from punishment. But he was stricter with himself; he kept his beard and *peyos* (sidelocks) intact, not only to safeguard tradition but also to preserve the honor of the town rabbinate. His defiance resulted in the *maikeh* on his back.

But the Gestapo captain had also singled out my father for abuse because he was the town's chief rabbi and because he spoke fluent German. Father was the highly respected representative of the Jews to the Germans; much of the Gestapo's interaction with Piotrków Jews took place through him, and vice versa. He was also a central figure in the Jewish community. Beating and humiliating him meant more to the Germans than beating just another Jew; it was an act of enormous symbolic meaning with a powerful effect on morale.

Perhaps there was another reason as well, or at least it was a remarkable coincidence. Many years later, I heard this story from Dr. Abraham

Greenberg, then the director of the Jewish hospital in Piotrków, who was saved from the inferno and later became a well-known gynecologist in Tel Aviv. He had been standing next to Father in the synagogue square, along with the town's Jewish council of elders, and heard him remark to the Jews next to him, "I don't know why we're standing here with our arms crossed. Even if we don't have weapons, we should attack them with our fingernails. I don't think this standing around can save any of us. We have nothing to lose by trying to fight them." Father had just finished his sentence when the captain's *maikeh* caught him on his back.

As a child, I did not really understand the issue of the beard or the significance of the order to shave it, but I did understand that they were beating my father. A son cannot bear to see his father shamed, as he identifies with his heroic image. I knew my father was the town's chief rabbi, admired and loved by all. I could not bear to see the beating and degradation.

Today, looking back on the six years of that war, I realize that the worst thing I endured in the Holocaust was not the hunger, the cold, or the beatings; it was the humiliation. It is almost impossible to bear the helplessness of unjustified humiliation. Helplessness becomes linked with that dishonor.

Throughout the war years, a Polish word went through my head—*dlaczego,* why? What did we do to you to make you crush our souls in this way? How great was our crime that this was our punishment? There was no answer, except this: we were Jews, and the Nazis saw us as the source of all evil in the world.

When a young boy sees his father beaten by a Gestapo captain with a *maikeh*, kicked with nailed boots, threatened by dogs, falter from the force of the blow, and suffer public shaming, he carries that terrible scene with him for the rest of his life. Yet I also carry the image of Father, with astonishing spiritual strength, bracing himself from falling, refusing to beg for his life, and standing tall once again before the Gestapo captain. For me, that image of his inner spiritual strength completely nullifies the helplessness that accompanied the humiliation.

At the end of that "selection," the guards separated the women and children from the men. They ordered Mother, Shmuel, and me into the

Great Synagogue, where we witnessed inhuman scenes. I remember an elderly woman of about eighty, stout and furrowed with wrinkles, sitting in the women's balcony. She grasped the wooden railing with both hands and revealed a particularly eye-catching ring on one of her fingers. One of the armed Ukrainian guards happened to glance up at the women's balcony and, out of the corner of his eye, caught sight of the jewel on the old lady's hand. He shouted to her in Russian, *"Davai, davai!"* (Give it to me, give it to me!) When the old woman did not respond, he raced upstairs, and, like a tiger attacking his prey, grabbed her shoulders with both hands and dragged her down to the floor. He stomped on her with his boots and tore the ring from her finger.

That was the atmosphere in the synagogue. Our lives were not worth a penny—a ring was worth much more than we were. Meanwhile, night fell, enveloping us in complete blackness. Hundreds of women and children were packed into the cramped synagogue hall. We were gripped by pure terror and feared for our lives.

Late that night, the synagogue door opened. Two Gestapo men lit a lamp, came inside, and stood in the doorway facing each other, leaving a narrow passage between them. In a thunderous voice, one declared, "I will now read a list of names. Everyone whose name I read will get up immediately, *schnell, schnell* [quickly, quickly], and go home." He began to read the list of those released. The first name he read was "Lau, Chaya"—my mother. She did not get up because she was waiting for him to read the names of her two sons, Shmuel and Israel, so that we could leave together. The German finished reading the list of names, but my brother and I were not on it. Everyone realized that those whose names he had not read would remain inside, their fate sealed.

As order and discipline were second nature to the Germans, one shouted, "One of the people whose names I called did not go out!" Then they both made an exact count of all those who had left, and checked their lists. One person had not left. My mother, her healthy maternal instinct aroused, scrutinized the narrow passage between the two guards at the door. She planned our moves quickly and precisely. She grabbed me with one hand, and Shmuel with the other. "Come here!" she ordered. We jumped to her.

We didn't need to be told that we must be completely silent, and, more important, keep as close as possible to Mother. The three of us had to meld together as one. She planned to smuggle us both out under cover of darkness, as if we were part of her body. To keep the Germans from closing the exit, she shouted toward the door, "I'm coming! I'm coming!"

Walking sideways as one body, we went out the door. But as close together as we might be, our group of three could not possibly pass through the narrow opening the Germans had left; they stood so that only one person at a time could pass through. I went out first, Mother was close behind me, and Shmuel behind her. But one German noticed a bit more movement than expected. Facing us, he raised both his arms together, palms facing the floor, and swung them down with all his might, one to the left and one to the right. Shmuel, who was on the left side, fell to the synagogue floor and had to go back inside. On the right side were my mother and myself. The force of the blow hurled us into a puddle in front of the synagogue. We were outside, but Shmuel remained inside. The two of us were saved, but we were separated from Shmuel, whom we never saw again. Later, we learned that he was sent to Treblinka the same day.

Mother understood that there was nothing she could do to bring back her son. The two of us walked in heavy silence to our home at 21 Pilsudski Street, near the synagogue. Our single-story, seven-room house was empty. Naphtali was working in the ghetto glass factory, Shmuel remained in the synagogue with those sentenced to death, and the Gestapo was holding Father. Only Mother and I remained, alone. Mother tried to get me to sleep but I could not close my eyes. The images of the day raced through my brain and gave me no rest.

A few hours later, I heard an earsplitting shriek on the street outside my bedroom window. I stood on my bed and looked out the window. A young woman was lying in a pool of blood, gripping a baby in her arms. A Gestapo man stood above her, kicking her body from side to side with his heavy boots, searching for any jewelry that might remain on her neck or fingers. I watched in horror, paralyzed. Suddenly, I felt the touch of my mother's hand on my shoulder. She, also unable to sleep, had heard the scream outside our house, and now tried to protect her son's innocence.

Mother gave me a loving hug, gently pulled me away from the window, and lay me in my bed.

Of course I still had trouble falling asleep. I turned from side to side, trying in vain not to think about that terrible day, about Shmuel, and about the woman and her baby. Then the door opened and someone came in. I jumped up. For the first few seconds we did not recognize Father, who had returned home beardless. This was the first time I had ever seen him that way, and it was a strange sight.

Father told Mother what had happened to him after she had left the synagogue with me. Behind his gold-rimmed eyeglasses, his blue eyes spilled tears. My father, who had always been strong as a rock and very reserved despite his sensitivity, was crying. He told us that when he had found out that Shmulek was in the synagogue by himself, separated from Mother and me, he realized that my brother was destined for death. Since Father was known to the Gestapo, he went to the captain in the office and begged him to release Shmulek. The captain offered to release the boy in exchange for my father's pocket watch, a valuable gold Schaffhausen on a gold chain. Father immediately pulled out his watch and gave it to the German officer. The German took the watch with great pleasure, but did not honor his promise to release Shmuel. He merely smiled and turned his back. "We'll never see Shmuel again," Father said in tears, and I understood that something terrible had happened to us and that there was nothing we could do about it.

Father told Mother about the rumor of a big *Aktion* (operation, or roundup of Jews) that was about to take place, and about the Nazis' thorough searches for the remaining Jews of Piotrków. He added that they were sending all the Jews to Treblinka. He whispered to Mother that in a certain house on Jerozolimska Street, we would find a better hiding place than in our own house. However, he told her, he himself did not intend to hide.

It was clear to him that the *Aktion* would entail rigorous searches, and that the Germans, who knew about him, would not leave the other Jews alone until they found him. "If I hide, they'll turn the ghetto upside down. They'll turn over every stone in the town until they find me. If I stand before them in the open, maybe their searches will be more superficial.

Maybe this will give other people a chance to remain in hiding," he explained to Mother, and his words remain ingrained in my memory.

Father said good-bye to us and returned to the synagogue, where he remained standing, the Torah scroll in his arms, until the Germans came and drove him out. Head held high, he walked to the train. It took him, along with about twenty-eight thousand other Jews of Piotrków, to Treblinka.

The day he arrived in Treblinka, a strange event occurred that I consider an act of Divine Providence. Another train had arrived there on that day, its cars packed with the Jews of Prešov, Slovakia. Eight years earlier, Father had finished his tenure as rabbi of that town, and Prešov had yet to elect another rabbi in his stead. Those two towns reflected two completely different worlds: the Jews of Prešov spoke German and Hungarian, whereas those of Piotrków spoke Yiddish and Polish. The only thing they had in common was that the last rabbi of Prešov was also the last rabbi of Piotrków—my father. The Jews of Prešov, the Jews of Piotrków, and their chief rabbi all met on the train platform of Treblinka on their way to the gas chambers.

Father addressed them by recounting the last speech of Rabbi Akiva, one of the Ten Martyrs of Israel. When the Romans raked the rabbi's flesh with iron combs, his disciples asked him how he could withstand the tortures. Rabbi Akiva replied by referring to the *Shema,* the declaration of faith, *Hear, O Israel, the Lord our God, the Lord is One.* "All my life I have wondered about the verse following the *Shema* prayer, *Love your God . . . with all your soul,*" mused Rabbi Akiva. "I understood this as meaning 'Love your God even if He takes your soul.' I asked myself, when will I have the opportunity to fulfill this commandment? Now that I have the opportunity, how can I not fulfill it?" Then Rabbi Akiva recited the *Shema*, prolonging the last word, *One,* as his soul departed.

"Jews!" Father shouted so that all present would hear his concluding words. "Of all the six hundred thirteen *mitzvot,* we have one remaining mitzvah to fulfill: *I should be sanctified among the Children of Israel* —to give up your life for bearing the name of God, for the name of God, *El,* is contained in the name of the People of Israel. Come, my brothers, let us fulfill this commandment in joy. The world is null and void, a boiling rain of hatred and bloodshed. The one mitzvah left for us is to sanctify God's name. Come, brothers, let us fulfill it joyfully. I repeat to you the words of Rabbi Simcha Bunim of Pshischa: 'For in joy you will go out—with the power of joy will we leave behind the troubles, the suffering, and the trials of this world.' " Then Father raised his voice and began to recite the *Vidui* prayer of confession: *For the sins we have sinned before you.* The crowd repeated it after him. The prayer began in a whisper and ended with the shout *"Shema Yisrael! Hear, O Israel, the Lord is our God, the Lord is One. God reigns, God has reigned, God will reign for all eternity."*[1]

I never saw Father again after that night at our house in Piotrków. My memories of him are few. In my earliest memory of him, from more distant and innocent days, when war had not yet come to the world, I am a little boy sitting on my father's knees and playing with his curly *peyos*. My next memory is completely different: people are gathered in our house, and my father is discussing the situation, his face furrowed in worry. The feeling of unease that dominated that day dwells inside me always.

My father accompanies me throughout my life, in whatever I do. I study the pictures of him that hang in my home and I think about him often. I miss him at every joyous or sad occasion in my life, at every crossroads I face. According to those who knew him, my father, Rabbi Moshe Chaim Lau, was a gifted speaker. Before every speech I make, I ask myself how he would have formulated it.

But Father was not with Mother and me when the two of us hid in the building at 12 Jerozolimska Street, near our house, where he had arranged a hiding place for us. This large building had once been filled with Jewish residents, but had been abandoned. The floor of one room in

---

1. I heard this description of Father's moving speech for the first time while still in the Piotrków ghetto, from a young man of our town, David (Dudek) Levkovitz; he had escaped from Treblinka, where he was during the fourth and last *Aktion,* when my father was taken, and had heard his address. Parts of the speech appeared during the war in Yiddish newspapers in the United States. In 1952, on the tenth anniversary of the massacre of Piotrków's Jews, my teacher, Rabbi Yosef Yehuda Reiner, who had been father's disciple and taught in the Kol Torah Yeshiva in Jerusalem, published the speech in the *She'arim* journal. He based the title of his article on David's lament for Jonathan (2 Samuel 1:23): *"Beloved and pleasant in their lives, Prešov and Piotrków, and in their death not parted."*

the top story was littered with wooden boards; the entry to the attic was through this room. Mother and I crowded into the attic along with about ten other Jews. They were constantly darting frightened looks at me, as if imploring me to keep silent, and at my mother, as if blaming her for bringing me to the hiding place and possibly endangering them. At least that is the way it seemed to me. I was barely five and a half, and they suspected I would cry noisily or else call out *"Mameh, Mameh,"* giving them all away to certain death. They were busily thinking how to make the child keep silent, but the child did not even open his mouth.

Before leaving our house, my mother had accurately foreseen what we might face, and baked my favorite honey cookies. She knew that when I ate them they would distract me. More important, they would fill up my mouth so I would be unable to make a sound.

Much later, I recounted this story to my father-in-law, Rabbi Yitzchak Yedidya Frankel. He drew my attention to the similarity between my hiding place and that of the infant Moses. *She took for him a wicker basket and smeared it with clay and pitch; she placed the child into it. . . . Pharaoh's daughter went down to bathe by the river. . . . She saw the basket among the reeds. . . . She opened it and saw him, the child, and behold! a youth was crying.* Even though Moses was only a three-month-old baby, he cried silently, as a young man would.

We went to hide in that attic in October 1942. The war had broken out more than three years earlier; we had been living through it and were well acquainted with its horrors. I could recognize the rumbling of the Gestapo motorcycles from afar. I knew well what a *maikeh* beating was and the reason for the voracious appetites of the Nazis' dogs, which were kept starved. Like an animal with an acute survival instinct, I understood that I had to keep quiet until the fury subsided, and I had no intention of behaving like a small child in our hideout.

Even today, many long years after those days of horror, I remember precisely the wonderful taste of Mother's honey cookies. The memory of them is my consolation in trying situations; they are the drop of honey with which I sweeten bitter days. But at the same time, I remember clearly that I would look at Mother, my mouth full of cookies, with a penetrating glance that seemed to say, "Mother, this whole business of using the cookies to silence me is unnecessary. I know I mustn't say a word, and therefore I intend to keep quiet. We have already been through all kinds of 'selections' and although I am a child, I understand exactly what's going on."

One day we heard the pounding of boots in the building—harsh and paralyzing; we knew the Germans were hunting for Jews. They searched through the building until they finally reached our room. Then, a miracle took place that was impossible to fathom. Normally, anyone entering the room would immediately notice the attic opening, but to our great luck, what attracted the attention of the German soldiers was the pile of boards lying on the floor. They were convinced that someone was hiding underneath them. They flipped the boards from side to side and stabbed their bayonets and rifle butts into the pile as if possessed by demons, hoping to spear people hiding between the planks. Miraculously, they did not even think to look up at the attic opening. They finished searching the pile of boards and left the building, and I allowed myself to breathe a slow sigh of relief. That night, the *Aktion* ended and the train left. The next day we left our hiding place.

Many years later, when I was serving as chief rabbi of Tel Aviv, in the late 1980s, a Jew from London came to visit me in my office unannounced. "An elderly man with a white beard," as my secretary described him. "His Hebrew is not native." I could not refuse my secretary's request and, despite my busy schedule, I received the visitor. He entered my office holding a package wrapped in a plastic bag. Inside it was a book—*Toward Evening*. "My name is Mordechai Kaminsky—Mottel," he said in Yiddish. I had not the faintest clue who this man was. "I've come to ask for your forgiveness. I was with you and your mother in the hideout in Piotrków," he continued, "and I stole an apple from you. You probably don't even know that I stole it, but the act has burdened me to this day." When he finished speaking, he gave me the book—his memoir, which included the story of the apple in the Piotrków attic hideout.

In the book, he describes how he hid in the attic without his family. He was a few years older than I was. My mother had brought along a bag of apples from home. At one point, Mottel Kaminsky saw that I looked away for a minute, and, unable to resist, he took an apple from my bag, then turned his back and bit into it. At that very moment, we heard the strides of the German searchers, and he stood with the bite of apple stuck in his mouth. The chunk was too large for him to swallow whole, but he did not dare chew, for fear of making noise and exposing us all. He was too embarrassed to return the apple.

For the entire hour that the Germans searched the building, that apple filled his mouth as regret filled his conscience for stealing it from the rabbi's son. He had lived with the guilt for forty-five years. I reassured him that I bore him no grudge; he accepted my forgiveness in the office of the chief rabbi of Tel Aviv, and returned to London to continue his life, finally relieved.

THE MORNING AFTER that incident with the boards, after an uneventful night, Mother and I climbed down from the attic together with the other Jews and returned home.

That evening, an indistinct figure carrying a satchel emerged from the shadows and appeared at the front door. When the figure heartily embraced Mother, I understood that it was Naphtali, my oldest brother, who had returned to us from the labor camp. I remember a quiet, tearful meeting, and he and Mother whispered together throughout the night. Naphtali refused to return to his work despite our mother's insistence that our lives depended on his job. He was torn; on the one hand, he saw that Mother was suffering from the loss of her husband and son, and wanted to be at her side. On the other, he felt that the fate of our family depended on his status as a factory worker, which granted us the right to live.

Naphtali recalled his last conversation with Father, in which Father had counted thirty-seven generations of rabbis on both his and my mother's sides of the family. He did this in order to demonstrate the great responsibility of whoever would be saved from the horror to continue the chain of our heritage. Father read verses from Jeremiah: *There is hope for your future, the word of God, and your children will return home.* He emphasized that if we escaped this inferno safely, we would know how to find our home, which was not this home or any other on this enemy land. "Your home will be in *Eretz Israel* [the Land of Israel], even if you have to acquire it through suffering," he said, and Naphtali and Father cried on each other's necks. After embracing each other tightly, Naphtali returned to his job in the ghetto. Father's words echoed in his ears: Father had believed that I, the youngest son of the Lau family, would escape the inferno safely and pass along the heritage that the Nazis were attempting to destroy.

Naphtali came to us as if from Heaven. *A generation goes and a generation comes.* Father goes, and my big brother, then sixteen and a half, comes and assumes responsibility for what is left of the family.

But the joy at his return did not last long. Two days later, the Germans took Mother, Naphtali, and me to the Piotrków ghetto, the first ghetto in Poland. We all felt the painful emptiness that penetrated our lives with the absence of Father and Shmulek; sometimes we discussed this, but mostly each of us bore the pain in silence.

In the ghetto, they placed me at the Hortensia glass factory along with my brother; I had to work to prove my right to live. The workers blew the glass in shifts, working alongside raging ovens that operated twenty-four hours a day. I was in charge of a wooden cart with iron wheels. It held some sixty bottles that I was supposed to fill with water from a tap outside the factory. After filling the bottles, I would push the cart into the factory, which itself was like a furnace. I would walk between the glassblowers and the ovens, and each worker would take a bottle of water to prevent dehydration from sweating so profusely in the intense heat.

After distributing the filled bottles, I went around again with the cart to collect the empties. Then I went back outside, filled them up with water, and began the rounds again. I did this for eight hours straight. While working at Hortensia, I contracted rheumatism due to my constant switching between the snow and intense cold outside to the fire inside. I went back and forth dozens of times a day. Only six years old, I toiled at that job for a year and a half. But thanks to my work in the glass factory, I remained alive and received a daily bread ration, as did all the other workers.

Along with my work as the water boy in Hortensia, I volunteered to help Mother, who had established a soup kitchen in the ghetto. She fed the sick, the elderly, and the handicapped, all of whom were unable to work and so did not receive a daily food ration. Mother called her soup kitchen *Beit Lechem,* a house of bread. The words are the root of the name

Bethlehem, the town in Eretz Israel, site of the burial place of the biblical Rachel, to whom God made the promise that her *children will return home*.

On Thursday nights after working in the glass factory, I would go to the kitchen. There, I helped Mother, mainly peeling potatoes and sometimes a few carrots so that she could finish all the necessary cooking before sunset on the next day, Friday, when Shabbat began. By then, Naphtali had begun working in the coal factory.

This routine continued until November 1944, two years after they took Father and Shmuel from us. For those two years in the ghetto, we were cut off from the world, with no idea what was going on outside. We did not know if the war was abating or escalating, what position the Germans were in, or whether the nations of the world were aware of our plight. The only thing we knew for certain was that in the Piotrków ghetto, the number of Jews was declining steadily. Jews died in the ghetto from beatings, diseases, weakness, and any number of calamities. The two Gestapo captains of the town, Herford and Willard, set records with their beatings of Jews. One of them, perhaps Willard, did not move without his fearsome dog. He addressed this dog with the bloodcurdling order, "Mensch, reiss dem Hund"—Man, tear up that dog. To him, a Jew was a dog, and a dog was a person.

In November 1944, Russian airplanes began to circle above our area. As soon as the Germans realized that the Russian army was approaching, they made it their first priority to prevent the rescue of Jews. All around, rumors began to fly that the ghetto would be liquidated. Mother began to prepare for the worst. She made rucksacks to hold our vital possessions. Then the rumors were confirmed; the Germans gave the ghetto Jews a few minutes to gather at the assembly point. Each of us came from his place of work to the train-station platform, where the Germans carried out a "selection." I clearly recall the shouts of *Schnell! Schnell!* as they packed us onto the platform.

Following orders, the women and children gathered on one side of the platform, and the men gathered on the other side. I was by then seven and a half years old, but I looked as though I were five. Naturally, I walked with Mother and stayed by her side, while Naphtali, who was almost eighteen, went with the men's group. Being separated on the train-station platform did not bode well for us.

Over the years, I occasionally have asked myself what my most vivid, distinct memories of the Holocaust are, and find myself singling out three things: dogs, boots, and trains. All three were there on the platform in Piotrków. The dogs ran amok, the German soldiers' boots thundered everywhere, and the trains filled with more and more Jews.

In the air we heard the constant shouts of *Schnell! Schnell!* and the people ran around in a panic, carrying their possessions. We had always known that our stay in the ghetto was only temporary, and that the day would come when they would expel us to an unknown destination. Each of us had an "expulsion package" that was kept ready and waiting for that bitter moment.

Mother had equipped me with a large down pillow on which she had sewn two straps. Because of my small size, this pillow would serve as a blanket that could cover almost my entire body. It was intended to save me from freezing to death. "Lulek, wherever you go, this will be your satchel," my mother said, hiding some food and clothing inside it. I treasured that pillow for a long time, holding on to it with all my might until I had no other choice but to give it up. Naphtali had a small kit bag. In it were his *tefillin*—the phylacteries that Mother had given him—and the sole remaining copy of a book manuscript our father had written.

Mother and I stood on the train platform, which was crowded with terrified Jews and shouting Germans. Before us was a freight car with a tiny hatch at the top, covered with barbed wire, and sliding doors that bolted shut. The Germans opened these doors in order to pack the people inside. Following their usual organized procedure, they directed men to one group of cars and women and children to another group of cars. The *maikeh* clubs, the whistles, and the dogs helped them carry out the operation.

Within a few short seconds, my mother realized what this separation meant. In another moment, I would be entering the car with her, so she made an instantaneous decision. With the pillow on my shoulders separating us, she grasped my back with both hands and shoved me in the direction of the men. I didn't understand what was going on. I only heard her say, "Tulek, take Lulek. Good-bye, Tulek; good-bye, Lulek," and I never saw her again.

Her maternal instinct was honed to its sharpest in those few seconds; she understood that women and children had less of a chance to survive. My guess is that she made this quick calculation based on her experience of the war. At that point, the war had been going on for five years. She must have understood that with the Russians about to invade, the Germans would need working hands for their war machine, and thus they would exploit us until our last breaths. She must have felt that it would be for my own good to go with Naphtali rather than with her, and so she pushed me toward him.

We did not have time for conversation or consultation, much less for saying good-bye. Naphtali caught me as she threw me to him; he grabbed me with both hands and shouted in Mother's direction, "What do I do?" She just waved her hand at us, and the Germans shoved her toward a car with the other women.

The moment was intensely traumatic for me. The Germans forced Naphtali and me into the men's car, and seconds later the doors locked behind us. I clearly recall Naphtali beating on the closing door with his fists and shouting in Polish, "There's been a mistake! There's a child here! You must take him back to his mother!" But no one listened to him. No one heard his plea.

I screamed in terror, and transferred all my rage at the separation to Naphtali, my brother. I beat my small fists against his chest unceasingly. He tried to hug me and calm me down, but I refused to be comforted. I kept hitting him and screaming, "What have you done to me? Why did you take me? I want to be with Mother!"

Several men joined Naphtali in his attempts to console me. Somehow I lay down on the floor of the crowded car and wept bitterly. I remember the biting cold that penetrated my body, the cold of November 1944. The men around me gave me hot black coffee to drink, but I spit it out and continued my cries of longing for Mother until I fell asleep on the floor.

In retrospect, this was clearly the hardest moment I experienced in the six years of the war. Never before and never since did I cry as I did on that day of my separation from Mother. To separate from your mother is inconceivable; it hurts your whole being all the years of your life. It took me a long time to understand that when Mother pushed me toward Naphtali, she saved my life.

Mother went her way, and we ours. We thought her way led her to Bergen-Belsen. Only when the war ended did we learn that on that day Mother was taken to the Ravensbrück concentration camp, where she was murdered. Naphtali and I got off the train at a labor camp in the Polish town of Częstochowa.

CHAPTER 2

FAMILY MATTERS

O Guardian of Israel . . . We know not what to do,
but our eyes are turned to You.

TAHANUN PRAYER OF SUPPLICATION

IN 1994, SOME TIME AFTER POLAND opened its borders to Israeli citizens, Naphtali and I went on a "back-to-our-roots" trip, along with nine other family members and a handful of friends. Naphtali acted as our guide.

Born in the city of Piotrków in central Poland, where Father was chief rabbi of the city, I was the third son of Rabbi Moshe Chaim Lau and his wife, Chaya, and am a member of the thirty-eighth generation of two rabbinic dynasties that have continued uninterrupted for more than one thousand years. Although I was too young during the war to appreciate this heritage, Naphtali was old enough to realize its weight. Thus he took to heart our father's parting words, instructing him to protect me so that I could carry on the family tradition. This was part of the drive that led him to push for our survival.

My father's first position was as the rabbi of the community of Schatz (present-day Suceava), Romania. Subsequently, he served in Prešov, Slovakia, and finally in Piotrków. His maternal grandfather was Rabbi Shmuel Yitzchak Schor, author of *Minchat Shai*, and one of the great responsa writers of his time.

Rabbi Schor's son Avraham Zvi, my father's uncle, was head of the Chassidic religious courts in Jerusalem. Rabbi Schor's only daughter,

Margala, married Rabbi Ya'akov Shimshon Shapira, and their son Rabbi Meir Shapira became well known as the rabbi of Lublin, founder of the Chachmei Lublin yeshiva, and, most important, founder of the *Daf Yomi* (daily page) system of Talmud study.

The Talmud comprises more than 2,700 pages of text and is divided into tractates, some of which are studied more frequently than others. In Vienna in 1923, at the second conference of Agudath Israel, an organization of Orthodox Jews, Rabbi Meir Shapira proposed that, just as Jewish communities throughout the world read the same exact portion of the Torah each week, thus completing the entire Torah in one year, so, too, should scholars and laymen in every community throughout the globe study the same page of Talmud daily. Thus everyone would complete the entire Talmud in seven and a half years. A wandering Jew could enter any synagogue in the world between the daily afternoon and evening services and would find the congregants tackling the same page as the one being studied back in his hometown synagogue.

Rabbi Shapira declared that the study cycle would begin on the upcoming Rosh Hashanah, but no one knew whether his idea would take off. On that Rosh Hashanah Eve, thousands of Jews stood in the court of the Rebbe of Gur in Gora Kalwaria, Poland, to receive their rabbi's blessing for the New Year. After a few hours, the rebbe stopped the flow of visitors, asked them to wait, and sat down to study the first page of the first tractate of the Talmud. The thousands awaiting his festival blessing joined in the study session, and so did the entire town. The day after the holiday, there was no more valuable commodity in Gora Kalwaria than a volume of that tractate of the Talmud, firm proof that the idea had taken hold.

Rabbi Meir Shapira was also one of the few Jews elected as a member of the Sejm, the Polish parliament, representing Agudath Israel. When he left Piotrków, Father replaced his friend and cousin as the rabbi of that city. They both served as members of the World Council of Torah Sages at a remarkably young age.

Rabbi Shmuel Yitzchak Schor's second daughter, Leah Hinda, married Rabbi Zvi Yehuda Lau, a leader in the Jewish community of Lvov, Poland (present-day Lviv, Ukraine), and raised a family of highly respected scholars. Their oldest son, Rabbi Yisrael Yosef Lau, was rabbi of the town of Kolomea in Galicia. When the war broke out, the Gestapo ordered Rabbi Yisrael Yosef to perform a particularly appalling task: to destroy the tombstones in the local Jewish cemetery. The Nazis would use the marble to pave highways.

The rabbi understood the gravity of the situation. He asked the members of his community to gather in the town's main synagogue for fasting and prayer. Then he led his congregation to the cemetery. Pickax in hand, he stood beside the tombstone of the town's previous leader, Rabbi Hillel Lichtenstein, and addressed those gathered. "If I could ask this great rabbi, and all your ancestors and family members resting here, whether I should carry out this decree, I have no doubt as to their reply. If it means gaining even one more day of life for each one of us—they would obligate us to obey it. Master of the Universe, Witness on High, know that we do this because we were forced to do it." Then, as he recited the *Tahanun* prayer of supplication to God, he raised his ax and dug up the rabbi's gravestone. The other community leaders followed suit, and after them, the community members dug up their own family tombstones.

My father was the second son of Rabbi Zvi Yehuda Lau and Leah Hinda. Their third son was Rabbi Ya'akov, also a leader of Lvov, who apparently met his death in the Belzec concentration camp. Their eldest sister, Chaya, my aunt, also died there. Another one of Father's sisters was Miriam-Ethel, Aunt Metta to us children. She managed to escape from the town of Brno, Czechoslovakia, along with her husband, my uncle Bruno-Berchiyahu Schounthal, and their two young children, Aviva and Uri. They made their way to Cuba, one of the few places in the world that opened its doors to Jews. From there, the Schounthal family moved to the United States, and then to Israel.

From an unusual request made by my Aunt Metta, I learned how strong the desire is to be a link in a family chain. Even though my uncle was buried in the Petach Tikva cemetery, my aunt asked to be buried among the tombs of the rebbes of the Rizhin dynasty in the old cemetery of Tiberias, overlooking the Sea of Galilee. In this way, she preserved her connection to her parents' membership in the Chassidic dynasty of Chortkov.

Father's younger sister Bella married the rabbi of Katowice, Morde-chai Vogelman. When the war began, they fled Poland with their young daughter and made *aliya*[1] to Eretz Israel, where my uncle served as rabbi of the Haifa coastal suburb Kiryat Motzkin for forty-five years. After the war ended, they welcomed me to their home and acted as my adoptive parents.

MY MOTHER, CHAYA, was the daughter of Rabbi Simcha Frankel-Teomim, better known as the rabbi of Skawina. He was a descendant of Rabbi Baruch Frankel-Teomim, one of the outstanding Torah scholars of the nineteenth century. My mother's parents, Rabbi Simcha and his wife, Miriam, née Halberstam, were cousins, and both were grandchildren of the founder of the Sanz Chassidic dynasty, Rebbe Chaim Halberstam (author of the *Divrei Chaim*, a collection of responsa).

A poignant tale is told about one ancestor of mine, Rabbi David Segal. Rabbi Segal had been the rabbi of the town of Provizne, Galicia, and, to my surprise, when I mentioned this to Mayor Reuben Kliegler of Netanya, Israel, to whom I presented my candidacy as chief rabbi of that city, Mayor Kliegler commented that he himself had been a native of Provizne. At this meeting, I had the opportunity to recount to him the tragicomic story of how Rabbi Segal had been expelled from the rabbinate of Provizne. "I very much hope, Mayor Kliegler, that whoever is chosen to head the Netanya rabbinate will enjoy more respectable treatment than my great-great-grandfather Rabbi Segal experienced in your hometown of Provizne."

Rabbi Segal was desperately poor because the town barely managed to support him as its rabbi, much less his wife and children. He was immersed, day and night, in Torah study, and was recognized as an out-standing scholar. One night as his family and the rest of the town slept, he was distracted from his studies by an excruciating toothache. It was three o'clock in the morning. Neither pills nor gargling eased the pain. He stopped studying and tried to sleep. "When I awaken," he thought, "I'll go for help." But he tossed and turned and could not sleep a wink.

---

1. *Aliya* (which literally means "ascending") is Hebrew for "immigrating to the Land of Israel."

Four in the morning arrived and outside it was freezing cold. The rabbi recalled that at the entrance to the town was a pub in an inn owned by Zelig the Jew. He would ask Zelig for some alcohol to ease his pain. He put on his patched coat and trudged through the snow in the dark toward the pub. When he opened the door, he saw that it was packed with Polish carters from the area who had stopped in at the bar to warm themselves with whiskey before going to work. The rabbi went up to Zelig at the bar, but his mouth was swollen so badly that he could not utter a word.

Zelig had noticed the door opening, and saw that this was no country carter but the town rabbi. Zelig shook in fear—what does the rabbi want from me? What have I done that the rabbi should come to me? The rabbi—in my pub, before sunrise? But the rabbi merely pointed to his mouth in silence. Zelig poured him a glass of whiskey. The rabbi gulped it down and sighed with relief. Finally, when he could breathe and speak again, he asked Zelig how much he owed.

The pub owner refused to take money from the town rabbi. "It's on me," he declared. The rabbi insisted, arguing, "I don't want free gifts from my employers. I get a salary from the community, and I want to pay. How much do I owe you for the glass of whiskey?"

"One kopeck," Zelig said in compromise. The rabbi rummaged through his pockets, but found not even one kopeck. "Write in your account book that I owe you a kopeck," the rabbi requested naively. Accordingly, Zelig wrote: "The rabbi, may he live a long life—one kopeck."

Meanwhile, the town's Jews awoke and went out to the synagogue. The cold was biting, so on the way they hurried to Zelig's to warm themselves with a glass of whiskey. When they approached the bar to pay, they were astonished to see that among the names of the debtors—Vassily, Gregory, Stefan—Zelig's account book also listed the name of the rabbi, who owed one kopeck. They continued on to the synagogue, where they murmured about what they had seen. "What kind of a rabbi have we chosen? Instead of sitting and studying Torah, he spends his nights in the pub with the hoi polloi!" they seethed. The three town leaders called a meeting and decided they had to dismiss the rabbi before he could cause them further embarrassment. They sent the beadle, the rabbi's right-hand man, to inform him of their decision.

The beadle arrived at the rabbi's house with an empty cart into which to load the rabbi, his wife and children, and their meager possessions, mostly books. The beadle meant to take him away from Provizne as quickly as possible. He entered the rabbi's house and found him seated at his desk, deep in study. The beadle could not work up the courage to inform the rabbi of his expulsion from the town. He shifted this way and that, gazing at the floor. From deep in his books, the rabbi sensed the unusual movement nearby. He glanced up from the page and asked, "Yankel, what are you looking for?"

The beadle answered, "I'm looking for the rabbinate of Provizne. It's been lost."

The rabbi needed no more hint than this. That very day, he left the town of Provizne.

ON OUR VISIT TO POLAND, we went to Piotrków, where the Great Synagogue still stands. This had been the site of the festivities surrounding my *bris* (circumcision ceremony), and the place where Naphtali and I had said good-bye to our brother Shmuel, may God avenge his death, when he was taken away to be murdered. After the war, the synagogue was divided into two stories (it is now a public library). The first floor holds study rooms, and the second floor was remade into a sizable library, packed with books from wall to wall and ceiling to floor. Rummaging through the books crammed into the bookcases, we discovered a seemingly useless curtain. Drawing it aside, we saw that it hid a carving of the two tablets of the covenant supported by a pair of lions. The words of the Ten Commandments, as well as the lions, were shot through with bullet holes.

The Poles tried to obliterate all signs of the Jews from the site, but they did not notice the Star of David, the six-pointed Jewish star, below the chandelier at the synagogue entrance. They also did not notice the lock on the door, which was also shaped like a Star of David. This door was the very one through which the Nazis pushed my mother and me out into the street while forcing my brother Shmuel back into the synagogue. The door brought back the memory of my mother's grip on my hand, and her terror upon discovering that Shmuel remained inside, sent to an unknown fate. The same door, the same lock, but everything else was so different.

The house where I was born, at 21 Pilsudski Street, was also still standing. Apparently, I bear a striking physical resemblance to my father, for when several elderly Christian residents of the building caught sight of me, they crossed themselves in shock. Pointing at me, they shouted, "The rabbi is back! *Naczelny rabin,* the chief rabbi, Mr. Lau is back!"

We traveled to the death camps at Majdanek and Treblinka, and then to Kraków. There we found our grandfather's home at 3 Jozefinska Street, a spacious house where his children and many of his grandchildren grew up. Of his forty-seven grandchildren, only five survived the Holocaust, among them Naphtali and myself.

On our way from Kraków to Auschwitz, we passed the town of Chrzanow. Naphtali said that inside the Jewish cemetery there was a structure that marked the burial plot of our family, the rabbis of the Halberstam lineage. We found the Polish man who kept the key, and he opened the gate for us. We entered a structure that covered nine graves. In the center lay Rabbi David Halberstam and his son Naphtali, the rabbi of Chrzanow, my mother's grandfather. Suddenly, my son David, rabbi of the town of Modi'in, cried out in excitement: "Look! Today [the twenty-ninth of Tammuz] is the memorial day of your great-grandfather, Rabbi Naphtali!" It was as if the man had invited his descendants to visit his grave on the anniversary of the day of his death—as if no fiery inferno had ever raged, no river of blood had ever flowed.

CHAPTER 3

A LIFESAVING SPEECH

Arise and depart from amid the upheaval;
Too long have you dwelled in the valley of weeping.
LECHA DODI, A SABBATH EVE HYMN

THE TRAIN CONTINUED ITS JOURNEY through the night while I remained pressed close to Naphtali inside the stiflingly crowded train car, crying incessantly. On Friday, November 26, 1944, the train stopped, the door opened with a mighty clang, and an SS officer shot a blinding flashlight beam at us. He stood inside the train car, pointing the barrel of his rifle at us.

We had arrived at a factory in the railway-stop town of Częstochowa, located near the industrial city of Łódź. After the Germans conquered Łódź, they commandeered all its factories to manufacture ammunition for their army. Częstochowa actually had four labor camps, one beside the other, each one built around a weapons factory. The one we stopped at was called Hasag.

A German soldier shouted for us to get off the freight train. Along with hundreds of other Piotrków Jews, Naphtali and I descended onto the platform. The first person we met was the camp commandant, an SS officer of daunting proportions who had the unforgettable name of Battenschlager (*schlager* in German means "one who hits"). In his threatening voice, he delivered a speech containing the usual message: If you behave, work properly, and follow discipline, you will stay alive. If not, you will be sentenced to death. Short and to the point, in the best Nazi tradition.

30

But at the height of his speech, Battenschlager's eyes picked out a young boy in the crowd of men standing before him. Astonishment registered on his face. It was a well-known rule that in the camps, the children went with the women, not with the men. His camp was for laborers. What could he get out of a skinny kid like me, who had no labor power to speak of?

He ordered me to step forward. Then his eyes shifted and he discovered Naphtali standing beside me. "Are you his father?" he asked. Without waiting for the answer, he added, "Since when do you have kids?" Naphtali was eighteen, as thin as everyone else, and did not look like the father of a child at all. "I'm his brother," he explained to the camp commandant. Battenschlager pushed me back into line. Luckily, he did not make an issue out of my presence, perhaps because of the busy day of arrival and sorting that awaited him.

The Nazis sent us to one of the miserable camp barracks. From then on, we were alone in the world, just the two of us. My older brother had sworn to protect me, taking upon himself a mission that was to prove incredibly difficult in that horrifying place. Naphtali spread a wool blanket on the ground and lay me down on it. I cried, missing my mother.

That was our first night in Częstochowa. It was a Friday night, the eve of the Shabbat. As Naphtali lay beside me, a familiar tune from far-off days reached our ears from the end of the barracks. Cantor Yosef Mandelbaum was singing the verse *Mikdash Melech* from *Lecha Dodi,* the traditional song for welcoming the Shabbat on Friday evenings. The tune, a distant reminder of home, allowed me to forget the events of the last few days and lulled me to sleep.

Rosenzweig, the Jewish camp commandant, ordered Naphtali to make sure I stayed inside the barracks, and that I allowed no one to see me. He explained that Ukrainians, not Germans, guarded the Jews. The Ukrainians walked around with the butts of their rifles pointed up and the barrels pointed down, so that they could use the butts on whomever they pleased. Therefore, he explained, it was better for me to stay inside the barracks and not show my face.

On the very first day, they took Naphtali to his assigned detail for forced labor. "Lulek, you stay here until I come back," he instructed me before leaving. He lay me down on the barracks floor, which was not a proper floor but damp, musty earth. I could not fall asleep. I had not yet recovered from the separation from Mother, but I knew I had to obey him.

The commandants harassed us often. During one of the lineups, the Gestapo commandant, Kiesling, shouted, "Children forward!" Not one of us moved. His voice thundered again, and this time he added, *"Schnell, schnell!"* We had no choice. The Jewish commandants, who were responsible for us to the Gestapo, pulled us out of the group and pushed us forward. "I want to see each child's father behind him," the commandant ordered.

Ten children stood with their fathers. Only I remained by myself. Out of the corner of my eye I glanced at Naphtali; I was afraid I might reveal him by looking at him. The Nazi camp commandant stood before me, his face frozen. I dragged my legs from side to side, scraping snow and mud right in front of the terror-inspiring Kiesling. In those few moments, I escaped into my imagination. In my mind, I formed a small mound from the mud and stood on top of it in order to make myself taller. To my dying day, I will not forget that mound.

Suddenly Naphtali moved to stand behind me. Rosenzweig, the Jew, explained to Kiesling, the German, that this was my brother. Kiesling listened, and his voice thundered in anger. "Wozu brauch ich diese dreckigen dicken Jungen, die sind nicht produktiv!"(What do I need these filthy kids for, they are totally useless!) "All they do here is eat!"

His words pounded in my head like hammers. I do not know exactly what came over me next, who gave me the courage to open my mouth, or who put the words into it. Apparently, the scorn the Nazi demonstrated with his pistol, *maikeh*, and dogs forced me to understand that life in Częstochowa was worth beans, maybe even less. It was exactly for that reason, that I—a boy no one there had any need for—had something to say to this commandant. In the muddy snow of Częstochowa, I gave the first speech I had ever given in my life, which was also the speech of my life, in the battle for my life. I spoke in Polish, the only language I knew fluently then, and Rosenzweig provided a simultaneous translation for Kiesling.

Why does the commandant say such things about us? That we are useless? That we are incapable? For twelve hours a day in Hortensia, the glass factory in Piotrków, I pushed a cart with sixty bottles of water among the furnaces of the glassblowers—into the fire, in and out, out and in. Fill, empty, fill—and that was already a year ago. Now I'm older and I can do more. I, the youngest, and my friends who are older than I am—we have a right to live, too.

Throughout my life, I have delivered thousands of speeches, but none has been comparable to this speech. Kiesling turned red with fury, and ordered that all eleven children should be brought immediately to the Gestapo headquarters. Spontaneously, the fathers and Naphtali moved to accompany us, but Kiesling pushed them back into the lineup, roaring that he wanted the children alone. Rosenzweig tried to calm the fathers. He ordered the adults to return to their barracks, assuring them that Kiesling had promised to discuss the children's fate with him personally.

After half an hour that seemed like an eternity, Rosenzweig returned to the fathers and Naphtali. He informed them that Kiesling was willing to give back the children, but in exchange for a very large sum of money: one thousand marks for the head of each child would ensure that child would remain alive—for the time being, until further notice. The evil Kiesling made it clear he was not promising this would be the last time.

Luckily, Mother had predicted just such a situation. While we were in the ghetto in Piotrków, she had equipped us with two diamonds and a gold watch. She sewed a pocket into the lining of Naphtali's coat, and inside it hid a two-carat diamond she removed from her ring. "This will help you keep your promise to Father, to take care of Lulek," she explained to Naphtali.

Naphtali went to the goldsmith who had come with us from Piotrków to Częstochowa, asking him to estimate the value of the diamond. The goldsmith determined that its value was far greater than one thousand marks. "It would be a shame to waste it—don't you have anything else with which to save the boy?" he asked.

We had another, smaller diamond, but it was much less accessible. Mother had asked Sigmund Rosenberg, a Jewish dentist, to use the diamond to fill a hole in one of Naphtali's back teeth. The doctor did so, hiding the diamond by covering it with a crown. Naphtali recalled the treasure buried in his tooth, and asked the goldsmith if he could remove the crown and extract the precious filling. The goldsmith broke the crown and removed the diamond. Rosenzweig, the Jewish commandant, presented it to Kiesling, and in exchange, I received my life.

Several months after this, Kiesling again plotted to eliminate the children. Naphtali had no other choice but to redeem my life with the large diamond our mother had sewn into his coat pocket. After that, all we had left was Father's gold watch, which was hidden in Naphtali's shoe, between the sole and the heel. He kept it on him constantly, knowing he would need it one day, for a new Kiesling might appear anytime, anywhere, with his own fanatic demands.

After the battle for my life, I continued to hide in the barracks most of the time, while Naphtali was forced to work as a mechanic in the phosphate factory. Occasionally, Gestapo men brought me their boots to polish, and this work granted me a meager subsistence ration. I stored a little food in the barracks, offering it to Naphtali when he returned at night after work. Sometimes, in order to escape the torments of the labor camp, I returned in my imagination to our first night in Częstochowa, that Shabbat eve when I had heard Yossel Mandelbaum singing a verse from *Lecha Dodi*.

Naphtali lay next to me on the cold, damp ground, trying to warm me, when suddenly we heard the Chassidic tune. Naphtali recalled this song from Kraków, the city of his birth. The memory of his childhood permeated the atmosphere, filling him with emotion, a vestige of vastly distant times. As a child, Naphtali had gone many times to visit Mother's cousin Rabbi Ben Zion Halberstam, the Admor of Bobov, a descendant of the Sanz dynasty, who died during the Holocaust, as we learned afterward. Yossel Mandelbaum, a Bobov Chassid, was the cantor of Kraków and one of the world's greatest cantors. The verse we heard him singing that night was:

O Sanctuary of the King [Mikdash Melech]*, royal city,*
Arise and depart from amid the upheaval.
Too long have you dwelled in the valley of weeping.
He will shower compassion upon you.

Naphtali crawled over the ground toward the singing voice. Yes, it was really Yossel Mandelbaum of Kraków, encircled by Chassidim. He saw not a trace of Mandelbaum's impressive beard, which Naphtali recalled from his childhood. Except for the hint of a mustache, Mandelbaum and all those surrounding him were clean-shaven. Only the cantor's marvelous voice remained—unmistakable, unique.

Naphtali was certain he had been granted a gift from Heaven. He sat down among the Chassidim and introduced himself as the son of Rabbi Lau of Piotrków. They all knew my father and his family, as well as my mother and her family. Indeed, they knew our family's genealogy better than Naphtali and I did. They smothered him with warmth and love that night, offering a ray of light within the darkness we inhabited.

As my brother later told me, Yossel Mandelbaum saw in us a reflection of his own sons, who were killed along with their mother. He took us under his wing, speaking to us and comforting us in our suffering during those first days of orphanhood.

Just as he remembered Shabbat eves in the labor camp, Yossel Mandelbaum also remembered the Jewish holidays. One December eve, he lit the first light of Hanukkah, fashioning an oil lamp from an empty bullet casing. He led a rousing version of *Ma'oz Tzur* ("Rock of Ages") inside the barracks, and we shared baked potatoes. We felt we were among close friends, like the friends who had known our family. We knew they would take care of us as best they could. But in January 1945, the Nazis sent Mandelbaum and his followers, who had come with him from Kraków, to Germany, and we lost contact with them. Before they left, Naphtali gave Mandelbaum a souvenir, a Bible that had belonged to our uncle Rabbi Mordechai Vogelman.

In 1940, Rabbi Vogelman had left Katowice, taking a circuitous route to Eretz Israel. He could not take his immense library with him, so he sent it to our home in Piotrków. When we left our home, Mother equipped Naphtali with this uncle's Bible, as well as his tefillin bag.

Later, as I will recount, we came to Buchenwald. When we entered the camp, they ordered all of us to throw our possessions into a pile for burning. Naphtali looked at the pile and saw our uncle's Bible poking out from among the heap. "Yossel Mandelbaum is here," he informed me.

"He arrived here before us." But we never saw him in the concentration camp and we assumed that, like most of those who arrived there, he was sent to his death.

Forty years later, Naphtali served as Israel's consul general in New York. For a family event, he went to Brooklyn, to the great *beit midrash* (study hall) of the then–Admor of Bobov, Rabbi Shlomo Halberstam. The rebbe treated Naphtali with the utmost respect, seating him on his right, to the great surprise of the crowd of Chassidim. Most of them were unaware of the family relationship between the Admor and Naphtali. They attributed the rebbe's warm hospitality to his respect for the official representative of the State of Israel. During the evening, the Admor and my brother conversed, and Naphtali told him about Yossel Mandelbaum, who had sung the verse from *Lecha Dodi* on Shabbat eve in Częstochowa, thus unwittingly making a valuable contribution to our spiritual lives.

Cantor Mandelbaum brought us back to the bosom of family despite the threatening conditions at the camp. "What a pity that we lost track of him in Buchenwald," Naphtali lamented. The rebbe whispered something in the ear of one of his assistants. A few minutes later, the assistant reappeared, holding the arm of a diminutive Jew with an impressive white beard. "Here is Yossel Mandelbaum!" announced the rebbe. He then asked the elderly man, who was more than eighty years old, to sing the *Mikdash Melech* verse from *Lecha Dodi*. Naphtali listened, astounded. Despite the forty years that had passed and his diminished height, Yossel Mandelbaum's voice had not changed, and remained as clear and strong as it was then.

As Yossel sang the phrase "Arise and depart from amid the upheaval," Naphtali no longer saw the Chassidim of the rebbe in Brooklyn but the miserable wretches who sat on the cold, damp ground of the barracks in Częstochowa that Shabbat eve in late November 1944.

IN MID-JANUARY 1945, we heard the sound of cannon fire surrounding the camp. The inmates began to argue among themselves about whether the cannons were Russian or German. No one had reliable information, but everyone argued heatedly. In retrospect, it seems apparent that both Russians and Germans were shooting.

The Nazis ordered us to evacuate the barracks immediately and to arrange ourselves in rows of five men each, as usual. Announcing that we were leaving the camp, but offering no details or explanations, they gave us one loaf of bread for every three people in line. Naphtali was on my left, and on my right walked David Feiner, who was also from Piotrków and was a student at the Chachmei Lublin yeshiva.[1]

While Naphtali carried our sack of belongings, I carried the bread. We trudged through the deep snow to an unknown destination. Ukrainians and Germans guarded us along the way. Suddenly, a terrifying volley of fire came at us. The guards took cover in the ditch at the side of the road, while we threw ourselves down into the snow. The bullets whistled above us. A few minutes later, the guards began to shoot in our direction from the ditch. The snow on my right reddened, and a puddle of blood formed within it. At the center of the puddle lay the body of David Feiner, an unbearable sight for me. Naphtali and I were unscathed, but our friend was dead. It was inconceivably painful.

We could not even allow ourselves to stop to mourn his death, because as soon as the volley ended, the guards forced us to get up and keep walking. We continued to walk like zombies until we reached a train station. There we stood in formation again, so that the guards could check who was missing and fill in the ranks. Then they loaded us onto the train cars in an organized manner, with true Nazi efficiency.

As we were boarding the train, the Gestapo commandant in charge fixed his eye on me, the little boy, although I tried to keep close to Naphtali. He thrust his stick into my face, grabbed me by the nape of my neck, and shouted, "Children with the mothers!" Then he threw me into a group of about fifty women and a few children. They had arrived from other camps near Częstochowa and were crowding into the first train car behind the engine. At a certain point, Naphtali realized, this car was to be detached from the other train cars, which held only men, and sent to another camp. Later, my brother told me that the last thing he saw, after I had already completely disappeared inside the car of women and

---

1. David Feiner was the cousin of Holocaust author Yehiel Dinur (see chapter 13), who wrote under the pen name Ka-Zetnik, camp slang for "inmate."

children, was the loaf of bread. I grasped it determinedly, holding my two hands above my head, guarding with my life the precious food I had been entrusted with. That is how Naphtali saw our separation.

Of the train car into which I was thrown, I recall mainly horrible smells, screams, and the sound of children crying. We often hear about the victims of the Nazi *Aktions,* but rarely do we hear about the days and nights, the hours and seconds, in which people drew their last breaths inside suffocating cattle cars, without water or bathrooms. These trains were in no way suitable for human beings. The souls of many women and children in that car returned to their Maker as a result of the inhuman conditions.

As I was being thrown into the first car, Naphtali was pushed along with the other men into one of the last cars of the same train. Thus we were on the same train, but at a great distance from each other. Naphtali was worried; he had no idea how many cars separated us, and the promise he had made to Father echoed through his head. In the stairwell of our home in Piotrków, he had sworn not to let me out of his sight, and to do anything in order to continue our family dynasty.

The train set out on its way, and Naphtali had an idea. He and two friends, who had been with him the whole way from Piotrków, began to manipulate the handle of the door of their train car until they managed to open it. But the train continued on its journey, and the open door did not advance the effort to rescue me at all. At the train's first stop, Naphtali and his friends slowly opened the door and looked around. Then Naphtali lowered himself underneath the car, aligned himself between the tracks, and crawled forward on his elbows to the door of the next car. He pounded on it and shouted my name: "Lulek! Lulek!" Meanwhile, the train whistled and shrieked, signaling that it was about to move. Naphtali quickly crawled back to the car he had just left. Because he had returned empty-handed, he repeated this operation at the next station, and the one after it, and so forth, four times, each time returning disappointed. He ignored those who complained of the freezing cold that penetrated the car through the open door, and insisted on continuing the mission to rescue me.

His next attempt was a success. When he reached the seventh car, the one just behind the engine, again he shouted my name. I was inside the car, wearing Mother's giant pillow and holding the bread, which had since hardened. One of the women had sprinkled a few fine sugar crystals on the bread, but they had slid off, scattering on the floor of the car, which was packed with bodies. I busied myself hunting for them, so longing to put something sweet into my mouth! Suddenly, as I was searching for the grains of sugar, I heard my name. I thought I was dreaming, but still, I moved in the direction of the voice. I climbed over and between the bodies, forging a path between the women and children, until I fell into the arms of my brother, Naphtali. He had managed to open the train car door using a pin he had modified.

I wanted to hug and kiss him, but he stopped me, demanding that I keep silent. He pulled me down under the car, and again signaled silence with his fingers over his mouth, in case a guard was posted on the roofs of the cars, or in case someone in the engine car noticed the movement on the tracks. It was night; thick darkness surrounded us and I could see only his eyes, but I understood the significance of what we were doing. Behaving with extreme caution, I imitated Naphtali's movements, crawling rhythmically on my elbows and knees. He counted seven cars, then stuck out his hands, pulling me after him. Two pairs of hands pulled him inside, and he pulled and lifted me into the car.

I remember his wisdom and common sense: a second before we squeezed into the car, he filled his hat with snow so that we could drink the pure water when it melted. Only after the two friends from Piotrków had closed the door did we allow ourselves to embrace each other tightly, with heartbreaking cries. After a seemingly final separation that we had thought impossible to overcome, we were together again.

In a few hours, Naphtali's intuition proved justified. At a certain point along the way, the train cars separated. The women and children's car continued to Bergen-Belsen or to Ravensbrück, I am not sure which, while we continued on a very long trip with countless stops. Quite a few of the men died in those freight cars. Those who survived the long journey found themselves, three days later, at the entrance to the Buchenwald concentration camp.

From the tiny train windows, the road to Buchenwald seemed completely unrelated to my life, as if it were in a film. The buildings stood intact and orderly, without any sign of the bombings. Those around me concluded we had crossed the border into Germany.

I noticed a sign announcing the city of Leipzig, and then someone said he saw a sign for Weimar, the cradle of German civilization, the birthplace of Goethe and Schiller. But the train did not stop; it continued on until before our eyes appeared the name Buchenwald, a name already familiar and weighted with meaning for many passengers. Its notoriety as the worst of all the concentration camps had spread throughout the Jewish community.

The Nazis had built Buchenwald in 1937 as a concentration camp for communists and other opponents of their regime. Later, they sent their most loathed enemies, the Jews, there as well. The crematorium there burned countless bodies. Buchenwald was a prototype for other concentration camps that the Nazis built, such as Majdanek.

An argument broke out in our car over whether they gassed people at Buchenwald or not. Each passenger had absorbed different pieces of information about the place; no one knew exactly what to expect.

Naphtali used to tell me that the first image he saw from the train window was that of prisoners in striped uniforms shoveling snow. When the terrified passengers asked them where they had arrived, those prisoners brave enough to answer sliced their hands across their necks, signaling slaughter.

CHAPTER 4

BUCHENWALD—THE DARK TUNNEL AND SPARKS OF LIGHT

All Jews are responsible for one another.
TALMUD, SHEVUOT 39A

THEY RUSHED US OFF THE TRAIN CAR at the camp's iron gate, which bore the German words *Jedem das Seine*. To the Germans, this meant "Each man to his fate." This made a deep impression on me, and I continue to carry it with me to this day. Sometimes I think about it, and about the cruelty and cynicism contained within those three words. What a horrible destiny awaited people in that accursed place, where others tried, however they could, to rob the victims of their humanity. So much isolation lay in that sentence, and so much irony, for not one person who entered the gate of Buchenwald held his life in his own hands. The Nazis, the camp commandants, and their soldiers had unlimited control over us.

That sentence, which was soldered into the iron gate, came to mind on many later occasions. In May 2004, the Israel Defense Forces (IDF) carried out an operation in the Zeitun area of Gaza City. During the operation, an armored personnel carrier drove over an explosive charge and blew up, sending the bodies of the soldiers flying into the air. The terrorists responsible for the explosion, who belonged to Islamic Jihad, held the remains of the bodies. The IDF contacted me to ask whether they should bargain with the terrorists in order to obtain fragments, however tiny, of the soldiers' bodies to bring them to burial. My reply was unequivocal: no soldier, alive or deceased, would fall under that rubric of "Each man to his fate."

The government of Israel and the IDF have a commitment to bring back all soldiers to their families. If, God forbid, a disaster should occur, the body must be returned with appropriate respect, to ensure that no name will ever be erased from the Land of Israel. Were this not the case, the morale of a fighter going out to battle or to perform a mission might be undermined. He would be plagued by the feeling that, should he be wounded, he might be abandoned in the field. Therefore, for the security and well-being of the living, as well as to honor the dead, we are commanded to make an effort to bring all our soldiers home.

The moral strength that guides the IDF and the State of Israel is expressed in the well-known phrase *Kol Yisrael areivim zeh la-zeh* (All Jews are responsible for one another). This is the direct opposite of "Each man to his fate," which defined the Buchenwald experience.

THE CAMP POPULATION WAS DIVERSE. After several days in Buchenwald, we discovered that the camp held prisoners from dozens of nations. Among them were Léon Blum, the socialist Jew who served as the prime minister of France in the late 1930s, and Dr. Konrad Adenauer, former mayor of Cologne, who was sent to the camp for anti-Nazi activity but in 1949 would be elected the first chancellor of West Germany. Also there, by contrast, was "the witch of Buchenwald," Ilse Koch, who was thought to have scalped Jewish heads to make lamp shades from them, using them to decorate her room.

Naphtali feared that he would not be able to save my life again in Buchenwald. The rules of the camp were ironclad, and chances were slim that they would allow a child of seven, like me, to stay with the men. But, as usual, he did not give up. With the help of two friends, Naphtali wrapped me up in the down pillow that Mother had given us and put me inside the sack he had carried with him ever since we had parted from her. Because I was already used to transitions, to entering and exiting labor camps, he had no need to warn me to keep my mouth shut until it was safe to leave the sack. Despite my young age, the procedure was clear to me. Like a rabbit, I jumped into the sack, curling up as small as possible, and that is how I entered Buchenwald with my brother.

The Germans made the newly arrived Jews stand in formation, arranging them in threes. From inside the sack, I heard the familiar commotion: the shouts of *Schnell, schnell,* the *maikeh* club beatings, and the barking of the dogs. I hunched on top of Naphtali's back, motionless as a block of ice. Then I felt Naphtali removing the sack, with me inside, from his back and putting it down at his feet. A sharp and strange smell reached my nose, a smell that I did not recognize. Later I learned that it was chlorine, which the Nazis used as a disinfectant.

The Germans put us all into a large hall, where they conducted a sorting process. Concealing his fear, Naphtali studied what was going on around us. Very quickly he deciphered the method used in categorizing the inmates. The Nazis ordered the Jews to strip off all their clothes. Medical personnel inspected them and administered various inoculations. And then, to his terror, he discovered that the Germans threw all the Jews' possessions—including the clothes they had removed—into the oven, where they were incinerated. In this manner, the Germans thought, they would prevent contamination by the bacteria that the Jews—so they thought—carried on their bodies, allowing the Buchenwald camp to remain clean and sterile. Naphtali would also have to dispose of his sack of belongings. I'll never forget his cry: "Lulek, *hutch totai!*"—come here! I peeked out in disbelief, suspecting I had not heard correctly. From the sack at my brother's feet, I raised my head carefully and looked around. Previously, I had heard the voices and smelled the odors, but now I also saw the sights from which I had been spared.

The Germans waved the *maikehs* threateningly in their raised hands, their ferocious dogs barking and biting. Veteran Jewish prisoners shaved the new arrivals and disinfected them in a filthy chlorine bath.

When I got out of the sack, one of the guards, also apparently a prisoner, noticed me. He approached Naphtali and asked him what a boy like me was doing in this place, which was meant for adult men only. Naphtali looked into his eyes and with the greatest humanity, explained to him that this child had neither father nor mother. "What was I to do?" he asked. "Leave him outside in the snow, by himself?"

That guard gave us the first authoritative proof of the methods of killing in the camp. "In this place," he explained to Naphtali, "there are no gas chambers, but there is a crematorium. From that furnace," he said, glancing toward it, "smoke billows twenty-four hours a day. All the *Muselmänner* [people resigned to death] die there. Everyone who comes to this camp becomes a *Muselmann,*" he said. "It doesn't matter if he's five or fifteen, seven or thirteen. But," added the prisoner-guard, thus saving my life once again, "you should know that if this child can get to block number eight, he will be okay." When he finished what he had to say, he turned his back on us, as if he had not seen a thing.

As he walked away, a German guard caught me in his gaze. Naphtali was terrified when he saw the German's eyes focused on me, and even more so when he asked, as the other guard had, about my presence. Accustomed by now to situations of mortal danger, Naphtali took off his shoe and folded it in half, removing Father's gold watch from the sole. It was the last remaining item from the treasures Mother had given us for emergencies. Naphtali threw the expensive watch at the guard, who bent down as if to tie his shoelace and picked up the watch. Then he continued his patrol, completely ignoring the two of us.

WE ALSO HAD ANOTHER TREASURE WITH US, one of a very different nature. It was something that Naphtali had promised himself to guard from all harm, but he lost it on that very same day. After the liberation of the camp, during one of our numerous conversations about our days in Buchenwald, he confessed to me the great anxiety he felt about preserving the manuscript of our father's book, *Sanctification of God's Name in Jewish Law and Legend*. The phrase "sanctification of God's Name," or *Kiddush Hashem* in Hebrew, refers to acts of martyrdom or the fulfillment of *mitzvot* under extreme circumstances.

Father dedicated many long years to writing this book, which raised a number of previously unexplored issues. People often had asked him why he chose to write about this particular subject. During the 1920s, rabbis from the four corners of the Jewish world sent him thousands of questions on topics of Jewish law pertaining to Shabbat, a kosher diet, laws of marital relations, and bills of divorce. They asked him about legal questions, interpersonal relations, and the holy days, but almost no one asked him about the sanctification of God's Name. When they asked him why he chose that topic for his book, he replied that he had a feeling that the time would soon come when every Jew would need to know the answers to these questions. Father did not know how accurately he had foreseen the future.

One example of the questions he discussed: a toddler is hiding inside a shelter or barracks with a group of other people. As we might expect of a child his age, he begins to cry, endangering the others. Are the others permitted to cover his mouth, with the risk of smothering him, so that he will not betray them? If so, who should perform this action—his father, his mother, or a stranger? Father delved deeply into difficult dilemmas of this nature.

Another question that concerned him was to what extent a person was required to fulfill the *mitzvot* and Jewish laws when in a situation of extreme distress. On Rosh Hashanah, for example, should one blow the shofar, the traditional ram's horn whose sound reverberates afar, and thereby take the risk that the sound might reach the ears of a guard or a persecutor who might then harm all the Jews present? How stringently should one observe the commandment to die rather than commit the three cardinal sins (murder, idolatry, and adultery)? When should one ignore those prohibitions in order to remain alive?

Naphtali guarded this manuscript with his life. He had managed to rescue it from the basement of our house in the Piotrków ghetto, and carried it with him in his knapsack during the seven weeks of our stay in Częstochowa. When the Nazis deported us to Buchenwald, Naphtali carried the precious book in his sack. After saving me from that sack, which was destined for the flames, he also tried to rescue the manuscript, hiding its pages in a different, empty knapsack. He did not know that this full copy of the book would eventually be lost forever.

Despite the loss of our copy, fragments of the book were to resurface repeatedly over time. In July 1982, I traveled for the first time in my life to far-off Australia. A letter from a Mr. Haber, someone unknown to me, awaited me at my Melbourne hotel. Because this was during Israel's war in Lebanon, I had undergone an advance security briefing and took the precaution of turning the strange envelope over to authorized personnel. Once they opened it, I saw the pages of a book: a photocopy of *Imrei Cohen Responsa* by Rabbi Yehiel Michal Ha-Cohen Hollander, printed in 1937 in Piotrków, the year and place of my birth.

A note was attached to the pages of the book. "This book belongs to my uncle. I copied a few pages for you. See section 34." I turned to the appropriate page and read: "To Rabbi Moshe Chaim Lau. I received the book from Your Honor, and am sending my comments, as you had asked. First of all, regarding the sanctification of God's Name by children. . . ." Six months later, I arrived in Brooklyn to lecture about the Holocaust. Once again, a Jew I did not know approached me and offered me a gift: the entire *Imrei Cohen Responsa*.

I visited Naphtali, who was then serving as Israel's consul general in New York, and brought the book with me. It was then that I discovered that Naphtali also had a fragment of the book—a page in Father's handwriting. One of the major rabbis to whom Father had sent his work was Rabbi Dov Berish Weidenfeld of Tchebin (Trzebinia, Poland), who was exiled during the war to Samarkand, Uzbekistan, and eventually made his way to Jerusalem. Throughout his journey, he carried an annotated page from Father's book with him. When we came to Israel, Naphtali and I went to visit him, and he gave Naphtali the surviving page as a gift. Then, in New York, Naphtali pulled out this page, which he had brought from around the world. To my amazement, I saw that the page contained Father's response to Rabbi Weidenfeld's comments on the very question of whether the precept of sanctifying God's Name applied to one who had not yet reached the legal age of maturity.

On that first day in Buchenwald, we had to remove all our clothes and shoes and throw them into the pile that towered in the center of the hall. When my turn arrived for the haircut and shave, no one bothered anymore to ask what I was doing there; no one cared that I was a child, tiny and emaciated. They all performed their work like robots; no one was interested in the person who lived inside the flesh-and-blood body.

Years later, I understood that this was a psychological defense mechanism used by the prisoners who were appointed to act as guards. To prevent themselves from emotional collapse due to the realization that the individuals they faced were going to their deaths, those who performed the disinfection work did not view the other prisoners as human beings. They created a protective barrier for themselves that blocked all feeling.

Like robots, they washed and shaved the men from head to toe, using brushes to disinfect the shaved areas. They dipped these brushes in a vat of chlorine, black with mold. Perhaps because I was small, and thus an unusual sight in the camp, I managed to escape the brushing from the stinking, repulsive vat.

I stood in a long line, where I was pushed relentlessly. Then I passed the shaving (from which I was exempt, of course) and the haircut stations, finally reaching a doctor in a white coat, who gave the vaccination shots. Like all the rest, he worked like a robot. He stuck the syringe into the men as if they were on a conveyor belt, without looking at the faces of those standing before him, without gazing into their eyes. Everything was cold, alien, and, above all, automatic.

When my turn came, the doctor had to bend down to me, and only then did he notice that standing before him was a little boy. Astonishment spread across his face. During his entire stay in Buchenwald, he had never seen such a young child.

"Wie alt bist du?" He was asking my age in German. Already experienced with such questions, I answered with full confidence, "Fünfzehn." Fifteen. The doctor looked into my eyes, incredulous. He repeated his question, and I held my ground. "I told you, I'm fifteen years old." The doctor gave up on me, and turned to Naphtali, who was standing behind me. He asked if Naphtali was my father. "No," answered Naphtali, "I'm his brother."

The doctor told us that he was a prisoner from Czechoslovakia. He was not a Jew, but he did not want to hurt me. He explained to Naphtali that if I received the amount of vaccine the syringe contained, I would die on the spot. "Tell me how old he really is, so that I'll know how much to inject him with," the doctor requested. "He's seven and a half," Naphtali informed him rapidly, for everything had to be done as quickly and efficiently as possible.

At that moment, the robotic doctor became my Czechoslovakian angel. He looked around, and the moment he discerned that the Gestapo man was not looking, he emptied half the contents of the syringe on the ground, injecting me forcibly with the remaining half. When he finished, he shoved me along so as to keep up the pace and move the line forward. With his quick thinking, stubbornness, and the human spark that survived within him, the Czechoslovakian doctor—who had apparently been sent to Buchenwald for being a communist—saved my life.

I passed the selection process and remained alive, thanks to miracles and the good people I happened to meet. Often, when I think about my childhood during the war, I find myself amazed at the chain of miracles I experienced, and I say to myself that nothing happens by chance and that the hand of Divine Providence guides everything.

When the vaccination stage was over, the Nazis rushed us into a long tunnel with an arched ceiling from which showerheads dangled. As one, we all raised our eyes upward in shock. We looked at each other, faces contorted, for by January 1945, everyone knew exactly what showers in the Nazi camps meant. We knew that it was because of those showers that they were called death camps. Those who had run away and survived told of the gas chambers that looked like showers, in which masses lost their lives. We knew about the showers with gas streaming from the heads instead of water, causing instant death by choking and horrible spasms. We were sure our worst fears had come true—on our first day in Buchenwald.

Suddenly one of our group dropped dead on the smooth floor in the shower area. His name was Shlomowitz, a tailor from a town near Piotrków. His friend recounted that ever since leaving the Piotrków ghetto, the tailor had held a capsule of poison between his teeth. When he felt the moment of truth arrive, he said, when it was time to go to the next world—he would take his own life. Here, under the showers, he removed the capsule that was hidden under a temporary filling in one of his teeth, swallowed it, and died.

Then we heard the slamming of a door—and bursting from the showerheads came a torrent of ice-cold water. The purpose of the powerful streams of freezing water pouring down on us was to wash off the bacteria and terrible diseases we had supposedly brought with us. People cried, tears of joy pouring from their eyes. Beforehand, the same exact thought had passed through all of our heads: the showers were the last stop; we would not get out of there alive, and would never see each other again. Then the ice water washed down our bodies, and we realized that this was not the fatal gas. It was absurd, but the freezing cold actually warmed our hearts.

From the showers, they took us to the next station, to receive our *Häftling* (prisoner) clothes, which included a striped, grayish-brown uniform, Dutch wooden clogs, and a camp number. From that moment on, an individual stopped being a person, a *mentsch*, once and for all. Our names were erased; we became only our numbers. I received the number 117030; Naphtali received the striped uniform and the number 117029.

The Czech doctor and a friend of his, also a prisoner, found me some clothing that fit my small size. Because it was very difficult to walk in the snow in the Dutch wooden clogs, they gave me ordinary shoes. They were old, patched, and much larger than my feet, but they tied with laces, so somehow I could walk in them. On the sleeve of the striped uniform, the Nazis sewed a number and the first letter of the prisoner's nationality: *P* for Polish, *R* for Russian. We Jews were branded *Jude*.

Because I had blond hair and fair skin, I was able to take on a new, non-Jewish identity. The doctor and his friend removed the letter *P* stamped on red cloth from the corpse of a Polish prisoner and affixed it to my sleeve with a safety pin. They also fabricated a cover story for me: I was a Polish child, the son of parents from Warsaw who had been killed in the bombing of that city. By mistake, this child wound up in the city's *Umschlagplatz* along with the Jews and took a transport to Buchenwald by way of Częstochowa. I adopted this story. The Czech doctor and his friend whispered again in Naphtali's ear that if the child went to Block 8 there was a chance he might be saved. I heard their words without really understanding their import, but I recognized the spark in my brother's eyes.

Then the guards took me, along with the entire group, to Block 52. The sight before our eyes was horrifying. Thousands of people inhabited that crowded place, most of them *Muselmänner,* suffering from hunger and disease. People relieved themselves inside the block, and the stench was insufferable. Each morning, the guards removed about forty corpses of those who did not awaken.

In the corner of the block stood a barrel full of black water, which was supposed to be our drinking water. We did not have much choice, since there was no other water available. Nor was there a mug or any other container to hold the water. The prisoners drank from their cupped hands, so as not to dehydrate.

A short time after we made room for ourselves in one of the bunks, Willi, the block manager, asked in a thundering voice, "Where is the Polish child?" Naphtali lowered himself and me from the platform, went up to Willi, and announced, "Here he is." The German informed us that for the moment I would remain in Block 52, but that possibly in the future they would transfer me to another block. In the meantime, I stuck close to Naphtali.

We ate supper, a stale loaf of bread divided among five people. We used a piece of barbed wire to saw it and we drank some kind of murky liquid with it. Then Willi asked again, "Where is the Polish child?" Naphtali and I rose, and he gave us a blanket. The two of us wrapped ourselves up in it, trying to warm each other. I even slept relatively well, since Naphtali was beside me.

When I awoke, it was still dark outside. Torrents of freezing water were pouring over my body. This was how they woke us up. The cold was terrifying; my teeth chattered, my knees shook, and the wet uniform stuck to my body. Orders resounded through the block—get up immediately. Before we could understand what was happening, they pushed us outside into the snow, which was about ten inches deep. Practiced in such situations, we immediately formed rows of five for roll call. They ordered us to take off and put on our hats, over and over again—off, on, off, on—a completely aimless activity, cruelty for the sake of cruelty.

Because they had woken us so suddenly, no one had had time to relieve himself. Should a small yellow puddle appear beside someone's place, the guards would beat him with their rubber clubs, thrashings that often caused the victim to double over and collapse into the snow, never to rise again. I remember looking at the men. The whiteness of the snow illuminated their faces in the pitch darkness. I recall how the men held their legs together as tightly as possible, so as not to urinate in the snow and share the fate of those buried in the snow nearby.

I stayed in the horrifying Block 52 for two days. Naphtali was assigned the job of carrying the bodies to the crematorium and dragged a cart made of two slanted wooden planks on which the dead were placed. The prisoners served as the "horses" to which these carts were harnessed. The Nazis would attach four prisoners to a cart, two in front and two in back, and thus would the corpses be conveyed to the crematorium. Sometimes it was difficult to tell the difference between transporters and transported. The transporters barely stood on their feet as they dragged the rattling carts.

Scenes of these carts so affected me emotionally that later, when I heard, or thought I heard, the word "cart," it conjured up these horrors. In Hebrew, the word for cart is *agala*. After my liberation, when I reached the Land of Israel, I learned to say the Kaddish (mourners' prayer). When I reached the phrase *ba'agala u-vi-zeman ḳariv*, I was sure that *agala* referred to the cart the prisoners pushed in Buchenwald. Sometime later I learned that the Kaddish is written in Aramaic, an ancient language related to Hebrew, and that the Kaddish is not about a cart or even about death but rather is a declaration of God's greatness. The phrase with the term *agala* that I misunderstood meant "swiftly and soon," referring to the speedy implementation of God's reign.

After I had spent two days in Block 52, Willi announced that I was to move to Block 8. For me, the separation from Naphtali was unimaginable. I had been at his side since we had parted from our mother, and could not fathom life without him.

After the Holocaust, separations became the most difficult challenge in my life. Whenever I left positions that I had held for some amount of time, I asked my colleagues not to organize farewell parties for me, since I had trouble coping with ceremonial partings. To me, "separation" is one of the most harsh and cutting words that exists, perhaps even worse than the word "death." "Death" may be a terrible, frightening word, but it endures for only a moment. Since I believe in the eternity of the soul, I understand death as a passageway from an antechamber into a room, from this world into the World-to-Come. Separation, by contrast, means disconnection, which to me is threatening and difficult to face.

Naphtali tried to convince me that I would be better off in Block 8, that only there could I remain alive. Whoever had a *P* on his sleeve might live, and I was one of the lucky ones who had that letter affixed to his clothes. Jews, he added, were not allowed to go there at all, and so he warned me not to say that I was a Jew, for any reason. He promised to come to visit me, and I parted from him with tears in my eyes.

A fence and a guard separated Naphtali's camp, called the Jews' camp or the small camp, from Block 8, which was in the large camp, and no passage was allowed between them. Within a few hours, Naphtali stood next to the barbed-wire fence and called my name. By then, I had calmed down a bit. I understood that I had no choice, that I had to move to the new block near the camp gate. I was the youngest of the residents, though there were several other youths there.

A Jew named Margolis went in and out, occasionally serving as an intermediary between my brother and me, informing Naphtali that I was still alive. Most of the residents, Russian prisoners who had been taken captive by the Nazis, welcomed me warmly, and I became the mascot of Block 8. Even the block commandant acted decently toward me. Ironically, his name was Wilhelm Hammann, like the evil Haman in the Scroll of Esther, who plotted against the Jews. He was perhaps the only Haman in history who deserved the title Righteous Gentile. I think he was the only one in the block besides Margolis who knew who I really was. Faithful to Naphtali's instructions, I kept my true identity a deep secret and did not tell a soul.

Years later, after reading the memoirs of camp prisoners, I learned that in the camp a legend passed from ear to ear, a legend of a seven-and-a-half-year-old Jewish child alive in Buchenwald. "As I was working," wrote Ze'ev Katz of Moshav Nir Galim in his book *Memorial Testimony*, "I was told that there was a miracle, and that miracles had not ceased from the world. They told me there was a Jewish child, the son of a rabbi, who was in Buchenwald, disguised as a Polish child." At the time, no one imagined that I was this child, alive in Block 8.

After they separated us, I did not see my brother for several long weeks. I felt isolated and lonely, while he confronted an indescribable hell.

He continued living mostly within the "small camp" of the Jews, first in Block 52, later in other blocks. While around him he saw only dysentery and corpses, I lived in relative comfort.

In my block there was a prisoner named Feodor, a Russian officer from Rostov, who acted as my guardian angel. He used to steal potatoes to make me hot soup. He unraveled strands of wool from a dark, patched sweater that he found among the workers and made me a pair of earmuffs using an improvised crochet hook. The Germans used to take us out at night for marches and roll calls, ordering us to remove our hats. Standing bareheaded in the freezing cold winter air of Buchenwald in northeast Germany, our ears regularly turned blue and froze.

Each night before we went to sleep, fourteen of us would lie on a platform like sardines in a can, so close together that if one of us wanted to roll over, we all had to roll over along with him. Feodor would pass by me and check that underneath my hat I was wearing the earmuffs, so that if they woke us up in the middle of the night for another one of those accursed roll calls, at least my ears would be warm. I clearly recall several times when I stood in formation with the wool ear protectors in place, feeling blessed. Feodor himself stood at roll calls with his ears exposed to the cold.

FORTY-FOUR YEARS LATER, in 1989, when I traveled to the then-Soviet Union, I had a chance to tell Feodor's story and pay tribute to him. This was during the period of glasnost, just before the Soviet Union was divided into fifteen republics and the iron curtain collapsed. Advisers to Mikhail Gorbachev, then head of the Soviet Union, recommended that he invest in forming relationships with the Jewish world. The Soviets had not yet fully acquiesced to the international Jewish demand to "let my people go!" and the protests continued. Realizing that the international media reports on the persecution of Jews in the Soviet Union were interfering with its relations with the West, the Soviet government invited six rabbis from different parts of the world for an official visit to Leningrad and Moscow. The authorities decided they would allow the rabbis to meet with the remaining Jewish communities in those two cities and to visit their synagogues. Because I was serving as the chief rabbi of Tel Aviv-Jaffa, the largest Jewish community represented in the delegation, I earned the right to serve as its spokesman.

In Moscow, we met with several elderly Jews in the Kol Ya'akov Synagogue on Arkhipova Street. We asked them what they needed and what they would like us to say on their behalf if the Soviets allowed us to speak in the Kremlin. We were well aware of the daily struggle for subsistence that Soviet Jews faced. Yet not one Jew in the synagogue asked for food, medicine, or exit visas. Instead, the oldest of them urgently submitted, as the most vital request of the community members, their plea to be buried in a separate Jewish cemetery. When I asked him why this was the most important issue, he replied, "I'm an old man, with one foot in the World-to-Come. But I have a daughter and two grandchildren who are Jews. If I am buried with all the party members, my grandchildren will never ask questions—and they will assimilate. But if I am buried in a separate cemetery, they might ask why, and my daughter can tell them that I was a Jew. Then there will be a chance they will remain Jews."

I asked whether there was a precedent for separate cemeteries in the Soviet Union, and the Jews of the Moscow synagogue told me that the Armenian community had received its own cemetery. I kept the old man's request in mind.

We arrived in the Soviet Union on May 1, International Workers' Day, and on May 3, we were invited to the Kremlin. According to the Hebrew calendar, that day was 28 Nisan, the day following Israel's Holocaust Martyrs' and Heroes' Remembrance Day. As the spokesman of the delegation, I was given the podium. After thanking the Soviets for their hospitality, I suddenly recalled the date. I addressed our host, Tengiz Menteshashvili, secretary of the Presidium of the Supreme Soviet. "Comrade Menteshashvili, today is my forty-fourth birthday," I announced. He stared at me, face frozen. He was really not interested in how old I was, but nevertheless, I forged on. I explained that in fact I was fifty-two, but still I was celebrating this day as my forty-fourth birthday. At that point, I imagine, he must have thought that I was somewhat deranged, but still I continued my personal story.

"According to the Hebrew calendar, today is the twenty-eighth of Nisan. Yesterday was our Holocaust Remembrance Day. When the

American army liberated the Buchenwald concentration camp in Germany, where I was an inmate, I would most certainly have been killed in the hailstorm of American and German bullets if not for a certain man who held me close to him, protecting me with his body. All I know about him was that he was a non-Jewish Russian prisoner whose name was Feodor, and he was from the city of Rostov.

"Comrade Menteshashvili, I wish to tell you that in those horrendous days in Buchenwald, the Russian people and the Jewish people were joined shoulder to shoulder in the struggle against the Nazis, against Satan, against evil, against the murder of innocent people. Ever since the liberation, I celebrate my birthday on this date, for my life would have been worthless had it not been for Feodor the Russian. On this day forty-four years ago, I was reborn at eight years old, largely because of Feodor. If we managed to cooperate in those difficult days, why can't we do so today? The goal of our visit here is to combine forces with you in the war against evil, in the war against hatred."

Menteshashvili took a pencil from the center of the table. One of his assistants handed him a yellow pad, and in Cyrillic letters the leader wrote "Feodor of Rostov." The next day, the Soviet government newspaper *Izvestia* published an article about the delegation of rabbis that had come on an official visit to the Soviet Union. On another page they published an announcement: anyone who knew a man named Feodor originally from Rostov, who was liberated from Buchenwald on April 11, 1945, should please call the Kremlin at the number indicated.

Ultimately, efforts to locate Feodor proved unsuccessful, but telling the story broke the ice around the mahogany table in the Kremlin, and a friendly conversation with Menteshashvili's staff ensued. That was when I shared with the Russian leader the Jews' request for a separate burial plot. Through Kiril, the translator, Menteshashvili asked whether I knew about a precedent for this in the Soviet Union. He assumed I had done my research before making such a request.

In a confident voice, I told him that the Armenians had separate cemeteries. He listened attentively, and with the same sharp pencil with which he had written the name of Feodor of Rostov, he tapped on the table and declared in his thunderous voice: "If so, we will not discriminate! If the

Armenians have, the Jews will also have." In the same breath, he added, "Today is May third, correct? On September first, 1989, our minister of education, Alexander Yagudin, will announce that the Jews, like every other minority, have the right to send their children to any school they want. Honorable rabbi, you have spoken to me about the cemeteries, and here I am promising you Jewish schools as well."

This was a complete surprise. I did not expect such a generous gesture, and I was overjoyed. I pictured the elderly man from the synagogue whose dream of a cemetery had just come alive.

The story of Feodor, the Russian officer from Buchenwald, broke down the walls between our rabbinic delegation and the Russian leader. Years after we parted in Buchenwald, Feodor was indirectly responsible for this understanding, and, thanks to him, Soviet Jewry received its own education system and burial areas. I doubt very much that he is aware of his involvement in this achievement. During those terrible times in Buchenwald, however, he certainly knew that I remained alive in Block 8 largely due to him.

ALTHOUGH I WAS A "POLISH CHILD" and owed my life to the saving power of the letter *P*, daily life was still difficult. Yet within the darkness, there were several points of light that I insisted on keeping before my eyes. One image that constantly shines in my memory is that of Naphtali repeatedly coming to the barbed-wire fence that surrounded my block. Each time, he looked worse than he did in the previous visit—more gaunt, more emaciated. I, Lulek, his younger brother, would give him a slice of bread spread with margarine, which I guarded vigilantly only for him. I recall watching with great satisfaction as he gnawed on the thin slice. I was proud of my success—I had obtained a slice of bread for my older brother, I was permitting him to eat, and perhaps, due to me, he lost a little less weight. I even tried to obtain shoes for him, but without success.

Despite my "identity" as a non-Jewish Polish child, Naphtali's continual updates kept me informed of what was happening among the Jews in the camp. Since I was very young, I had not had time to learn about Judaism, and my knowledge of customs and holidays was very limited.

As Passover approached, Naphtali and his friends were determined to do anything to avoid eating leavened foods during the holiday. Although the only food available to them was the daily ration of three and a half ounces of bread, still it was important to them to observe the laws of Passover. Months in advance, at the beginning of January, they began to prepare by collecting potatoes. They told me about their arrangements and tried to explain their significance. Before January, the prisoners had organized a trade in potatoes: three potatoes were worth the daily bread ration. But as the holiday approached, the rules of commerce changed.

I did not keep Passover then, mainly because I did not know anything about it. One day, a feeble Naphtali dragged his feet toward Block 8 and stood next to the barbed-wire fence. Hearing his weak voice calling my name, I rushed out to him. He pulled a few potatoes from his pockets, and explained that he could not carry them because they hindered him while working with the bodies in the crematorium, so he was bringing to me the goods he had set aside for Passover. He asked me to guard them carefully. Then he explained to me, for the first time, why potatoes were so important, adding a few words about the prohibition against eating leavened foods. I guarded those potatoes with my life.

Meanwhile, Purim arrived. As with Passover, the Jews in Buchenwald decided to celebrate Purim as best they could. They could not fulfill the *mitzvot* of sending portions of food to friends, giving gifts to the poor, or holding a festive meal, but they could attempt to read the *Megillat Esther* (Scroll of Esther). No one had a *Megillah*, yet they did not concede defeat. Several days before the date, some of the older Jews in the camp held a meeting. They resolved to shake off their despair and try to reconstruct the *Megillah* from memory. Each man would write whatever verses he remembered by heart, and a committee of the elders of the block would try to reconstruct the proper order of the text.

Everyone remembered the most important verses, such as "In the days of Ahasuerus"; "For the Jews there was light and happiness, joy and glory'"; "There was a Jewish man in Shushan the capital, whose name was Mordechai"; and "Mordechai would not kneel or bow." They wrote out the verses with charcoal on yellow paper torn from discarded sacks of millet. On Purim Eve, the Jews of Buchenwald read the improvised scroll. They could not recite the blessing, since the scroll was incomplete and not written on parchment, and thus did not fulfill the conditions of the law. Still, with whatever they had dredged up from the depths of their memories, they managed to create a traditional Purim atmosphere, albeit modest, due to the circumstances.

At the end of the evening, the Jews sang the symbolic lines, charged with meaning: "The rose of Jacob rejoiced and exulted . . . / You have always been their salvation, their hope in every generation / . . . all who place hope in You shall not be put to shame / nor shall all those who trust in You be disgraced forever." When they sang "Cursed is Haman, who sought to destroy me," no one had any doubt to whom the verse referred, and the phrase "Blessed is Mordechai the Jew" inspired everyone with great hope.

The morning after the restrained holiday celebration, the Jews went out at dawn to forced labor. Some had trouble walking. Those who stumbled were buried in the snow, or else the Ukrainian guards beat them on the head with the butts of their rifles so that they would never get up again.

The same Jews who told me about the Purim celebration in Buchenwald also spoke of a Chassid of Gur named Avraham (Avrum) Eliyahu. He became another one of the heroes of my childhood, one of the figures I recall fondly. He was a tall man with broad shoulders, the type we used to call "a real Goliath," powerful and with an unusual personality to boot. Unlike most of the Jews, he had no problem walking to his work, upright and with confidence. Instead of leading the line from the barracks, he insisted on bringing up the rear, and the whole way, he would support the backs of those who had trouble walking. *Avrum deh pusher* (Avrum the pusher), *Avrum deh shtipper* (Avrum the booster), they used to call him in Yiddish. With his right hand, he picked up the weak, with his left he straightened the bent, and with his chest he pushed them forward. If he saw one of his fellow Jews sway and fall, he would grab him quickly and give him a push so that the man could continue walking on his own. Everyone thought of him as a remarkable figure; even the Ukrainians admired him.

The day after Purim Eve, after the reading of the improvised scroll, Avrum pushed and saved Jews who faltered, as usual. The Ukrainian guard, who had great respect for the tough Jew, could not restrain himself, and whispered two words in Avrum's ear: "Hitler kaput"—Hitler is done for. Within a minute, the announcement spread like wildfire from Avraham Eliyahu, at the end of the line, all the way up to the front. At once, the weakest *Muselmänner* straightened their backs and began to walk unassisted. Someone in the middle of the procession began to mumble, and the others joined in: "Cursed is Haman who sought to destroy me / The rose of Jacob rejoiced and exulted." The song of that night returned the next morning, about a month before the liberation. This was the only time the Jews ever sang on their way to forced labor in Buchenwald.

The Jews also celebrated the Passover Seder in Buchenwald. Over and over they sang the holiday song *Karev Yom* from memory: "The day is approaching that will be neither day nor night / He has placed guards over your city all day and all night / The darkness of the night will be lit like the light of day." They had no Haggadah and no matzah. Still, among them there was no leavened food to be seen—only potatoes. In the impossible conditions of the camp, the Jews tried, as best they could, to preserve their Judaism.

IN THE FIRST FEW DAYS OF APRIL, we heard the sound of cannon fire approaching and fading. Rumors flew that the war was nearly over, that the Nazis were defeated, that there was hope—perhaps a chance—we might remain alive. The residents of Block 8 were able to entertain this hope with even greater certainty, for they enjoyed relatively comfortable conditions compared to the others. We received a mug of soup once a day, we suffered fewer blows, and we did not have to work at forced labor, as the rest of the camp residents did. I know that had I not been transferred to Block 8, I would not have survived.

The Germans planned to evacuate the camp before the end of the war, which was approaching, and to transfer the prisoners elsewhere by train. Naphtali was among the residents designated for boarding these trains. He came to say good-bye to me before he left; it was important to him that I know they were taking him. He endangered himself, leaving the group and dragging himself toward my block. This was the first time he had seen SS officers standing at the entrance gate to our block, and this raised a red flag in his mind. He thought that the Germans were about to liquidate the inhabitants of Block 8, or at least the few children among them, along with the rest of the camp residents.

Despite the presence of the officers, Naphtali did not give up on our good-bye. Searching for a safer meeting place, he went to the rear of the block, where there were no SS guards. With the last remnants of his strength, he called my name. He spoke to me for just a minute, but every word that came from his mouth remained engraved in my mind, as if it were his last.

"Lulek," he said, "they're taking me. I hope, but I can't be sure, that we will see each other again sometime. There is no way back from where they're taking us. You're a big boy now, you'll be eight in a few months. I can't and won't hide the truth from you. I see no chance of being saved from this hell. It's the end of the world. We have no father, they took Milek as well, and I don't know what happened to Mother. She probably thinks and talks about us all the time, but I'm not sure she's alive. Now they're taking me, too, and you'll be alone. I see that you have friends here. Hammann, the block commander, is a good man. Feodor likes you, and Margolis also takes care of you a bit. Maybe there'll be a miracle and you'll stay alive, and all this will end sometime. I've come to tell you that there is a place in the world called Eretz Israel. Say 'Eretz Israel'—the Land of Israel. Again. Repeat after me."

I knew not one word of Hebrew, but I repeated these two words— Eretz Israel—without understanding their meaning. Naphtali explained: "Eretz Israel is the home of the Jews. The foreign nations exiled us from there long ago, and to there we must return. This is the only place in the world where they do not kill Jews. If you stay alive, you will surely meet people who will want to take you with them to other places, because you're a nice kid. But you aren't going anywhere else. Remember what I say, only Eretz Israel. We have an uncle there."

Naphtali was referring to Rabbi Mordechai Vogelman, who had been the rabbi of Katowice. He had escaped in 1940 to Palestine and became the rabbi of Kiryat Motzkin. But Naphtali did not burden me with these details. He only mentioned the existence of the uncle, and continued, "Our uncle in Eretz Israel will want to know what has happened to us. When you are saved and get to Eretz Israel, give your name, and say that you're the son of Rabbi Lau of Piotrków. That much you know. They should look for your uncle according to your name. That way he'll be able to find you. Good-bye, Lulek. Remember. Eretz Israel."

That was all. He walked toward the camp gate. I saw his back retreating until he completely disappeared from view. Naphtali recalls that, even as he moved farther and farther away, he still heard my heart-rending sobs.

The Germans took everyone out of the blocks and moved them to the gate. They would leave no prisoner alive to be a witness to the atrocities they had committed. Then they loaded the prisoners onto trains waiting at the station. Indeed, not one of those who boarded those trains ever got off. Two weeks after the liberation, the Americans found the abandoned train with hundreds of bodies in the cars, the bodies of the Buchenwald prisoners.

Naphtali was among those who remained on the platform because there was not enough room inside the train for all the prisoners. The Germans took the remaining prisoners to a building that served as a carpentry shop. They were supposed to wait there until the next train arrived. Naphtali looked for a way to escape. He broke the window and jumped from the third floor into the camp area.

Despite this attempt, on April 5, 1945, he found himself packed inside a train with dozens of other Jews who had also tried to escape. He decided to jump from the train while it was moving. For almost a week, his strength ebbing, he pushed himself onward, fueled by the power of his mission. He heard Mother's voice echoing in his ears from November 1944: "Look out for the boy." He heard Father in October 1942 asking him to save Lulek, and this sense of obligation is what kept him on his feet. He walked for long hours, through forests and fields, until he returned to the camp gate. With his last remaining strength, he crawled to Block 8 and collapsed beside it. Two hours later, on April 11, 1945, American airplanes landed near Buchenwald.

The Americans took Naphtali to the hospital, where he was placed in isolation. Someone from my block took me to see him. I was terrified by his appearance, but I was happy he was alive. I learned he was suffering from typhus. Every day, I went to the window above his bed so that we could see each other. Slowly he recovered, and then I came down with the measles.

Naphtali is my real hero. Every day of my life, I picture him jumping from the car of the death train, not to save his own life but because he left me—Lulek—alone in Block 8 in Buchenwald. In his ears rang Mother's voice from November 1944, when she threw me into his arms amid the tumult of the train station in Piotrków: "Tulek, look after Lulek." And it was Father's order that we continue the dynasty. Naphtali had a mission, and he could not allow himself to fail. This mission helped him to stay alive. He suffered long periods of sleeplessness, cold, hunger, and disease, which caused him to lose all interest in life. But he knew he could not sink; he could not give up.

In Naphtali's own words, from the end of his 1997 book, *Balaam's Prophecy*:

> *For fifty years, I carried the responsibility passed on to me by my father before he went to his death in Treblinka. He placed in my care a weak child, who was five years old but looked like he was only three or even younger. For three years, I served as father and mother, guardian and protector, to my younger brother Israel Meir, or Lulek, as we called him. I often felt despair attacking me, flinging me helplessly to my destruction. I think it was the mission my father gave me, to bring my younger brother to safety and to ensure the continuation of our family's rabbinic dynasty, that kept me alive and gave me the will to continue fighting for our lives, rather than succumb to the horrible fate that befell the rest of our family.*
>
> *On the first day of the Hebrew month of Adar, February 21, 1993, I stood with my younger brother in front of the Western Wall in Jerusalem, the holiest site in the world for Jews, and we recited the afternoon prayer together. Forty-eight years earlier, when we first arrived in Jerusalem, we had stood in this same spot. Then, young Israel Meir had gazed at the stones of the Wall without understanding what he was seeing. This time, he was praying, just two hours before his anticipated election to the highest rabbinical post in Israel. My younger brother, who had risen from the piles of ashes in the death*

camps, was chosen that day to serve as the chief rabbi of the State of Israel. I looked at him from up close, and felt tears welling up in my eyes. As I left the Wall, I felt profound relief, as if a heavy burden had been lifted from my shoulders and my conscience. At last, my almost impossible mission had been fulfilled.

CHAPTER 5

LIBERATION

Let me go, for dawn is breaking.

GENESIS 32:27

ON APRIL 11, 1945, the day of Buchenwald's liberation, I cowered in Block 8 like a fragile leaf. My only thought was survival. I gathered potato peels, gnawing them until they were but a memory. I curled up inside my hiding place, hoping no one would discover me. I knew something was going on outside. Talk of liberation filled the air, but we had no idea who the liberators were—Americans or Russians?

In every corner, people whispered their fear that even if the Russians, or someone else, arrived, we could not be certain that we would be liberated. Because of my age, I was not privy to the details, but I absorbed the tension in the atmosphere, along with bits and pieces of information. Feodor, my protector, said he feared that before the liberators arrived, the Nazi villains would realize they had nothing to lose, and would get rid of us all. As Samson cried before pulling down the pillars of the hall where he stood with his enemies, *Let my soul die with the Philistines!*

This perverse idea stuck in my mind, and I told myself that I had only to get through these last few days until our saviors arrived. Bullets flew over our heads from every direction, both from the Americans and from the besieged Germans. As I stood between Block 8 and the gate, Feodor held me close to him, covering me with his body. Outside the gate, explosions thundered incessantly, shaking our block. These explosions were a sure sign of unusual activity, but I could not fathom their meaning. I could only sense the tension, the constant whispered exchanges, and the emotional expectations of the individuals surrounding me.

On the morning of the liberation, I stood in the courtyard of Block 8, near the camp gate. Outside the barracks, people were milling around aimlessly, an unusual sight. In defiance of the camp's strict rules, they did not go to work that morning. On "ordinary" days, this scene would have been impossible, for discipline at Buchenwald was ironclad. Then one day, everything fell apart. The mighty tower of regulations collapsed into fragments, and it was as if the rules had never existed.

Several airplanes circled the skies above the camp. With each turn, they seemed to dip lower and lower, as if the pilots were trying to see what was going on in that dark and twisted place.

In my mind, the liberation is connected with these airplanes, and with the reaction of the people around me. Each time one of the planes circled above, the people standing in the courtyard waved their hats, shouting hoarsely, "Hooray! Hooray!" I did not understand for whom they were cheering or why, but I felt the intense joy they expressed.

Then the rumor began circulating that American jeeps were breaking through the gates and entering Buchenwald, and everything became clear. In his book *Balaam's Prophecy*, Naphtali describes the six soldiers who jumped down from the jeeps: "Several of them removed their steel helmets and looked at us in shock. I glanced at the faces of the dozens of prisoners standing beside me. They were as amazed as I was. We all stared at the six soldiers, one of whom was black. We knew they were the saviors we had been awaiting for such a long time."

The six soldiers pelted the prisoners with candy and cigarettes, then returned to their jeeps and disappeared, leaving the rest of the job to the full division force, which arrived on their heels.

Our suffering was over. All at once, the arrogant words carved on the gate—"Each man to his fate"—had lost their power. There was no longer anything horrible about this phrase. Within seconds, those remaining in Block 8 went out to see with their own eyes whether the rumor was true, that the gate had been penetrated. I ran toward the gate along with many other people; we were like a river overflowing its banks. Feodor gripped my hand tightly, trying to protect me. Somehow I pulled away from him, or perhaps the crowd separated us. At any rate, I ran toward the iron gate without him.

I was just under eight years old. Many of the events of that day I do not remember directly, but rather through the words of others who described them for me decades later.

After years of locked gates, suddenly the gate to freedom opened. A new life, a completely different world, began. With it came the profound feeling of a new beginning.

DURING THE EXCITEMENT there was a burst of gunshots from the guard tower. One of the shots hit the clock above the words on the camp gate, stopping the hands at 3:15. Years later, in January 1991, I visited the camp. To my surprise, I found that the clock hands still stood at 3:15. I asked our guide why they did not fix the clock and set it to the correct time. His answer was simple, but meaningful, especially to me: "This clock stopped on April 11, 1945, on the day of the liberation of Buchenwald. Since then it has remained like this, as a reminder and a memorial. We leave it broken on purpose." Staring at the clock and its frozen hands, I was taken backward in time to my childhood in Buchenwald, and pondered the long road I had taken from those days *as a fragile leaf*, to the day of liberation, until the present.

Continuing my tour of the camp as an adult, I reached the torture chamber, which had a very thick wall and a tiny window covered with an iron grate. From a distance, I could see letters carved deep into the concrete windowsill. I approached the window, and distinguished five Hebrew letters that formed the Yiddish word *nekuma*—revenge. I could only imagine how much determination that tormented Jew must have needed to carve into the unyielding concrete with his bare hands.

Moved by this discovery, I could feel the energy, the incredible strength that that Jew had mustered within himself during his final days. I could feel his suffering, his determination to leave his fellow Jews the legacy of avenging everything the Nazis had done. Years after the horrors, standing once again on the soil of Buchenwald as the official representative of the State of Israel, I gazed at those Hebrew letters carved deep in the concrete, and a tear formed in the corner of my eye.

. . .

ONE OF THOSE WHO LATER IN MY LIFE told me about that day of liberation was a man from Netanya, the sixth-largest city in Israel. In 1978, when I was forty-one years old, leaders of this seaside Israeli town asked me to respond to the call for candidates in the election for chief rabbi of the city. I was quite young for such a heavy responsibility; still, people said, my chances of winning were good. I attended a meeting with then-mayor Reuben Kliegler, city administrators, and local Labor party leaders. I told the mayor that if I were elected, I would be following in the footsteps of the dynasty of rabbis from which I was descended.[1]

I met with the mayor and his staff for four hours. The whole time, a man with white curly hair sat with us, but he did not open his mouth. Only when I rose to shake hands and take my leave did he address me and the others:

Friends, honored rabbi, before we disperse, please allow me to say my piece. In a minute you will understand why I held my tongue this whole time. In these hours sitting before Rabbi Lau, I have been reliving the eleventh of April 1945. I was deported from my hometown of Zarka, Poland, to the infamous camp of Buchenwald. On April 11, American airplanes circled in the skies above the camp. The prisoners, myself among them, burst out of the barracks. Spontaneously, we ran toward the gate, anticipating our liberation after six years of hell. As we ran, a hail of lead shot past us. We had no idea who was shooting, from where, why, or what was happening. We only knew that our lives were in danger.

---

1. After telling the mayor about my parents and my hometown, I asked him where he was from. "Galicia, in eastern Poland," he replied. "My father was from Lvov and my mother from Kraków." "And what town in Galicia are *you* from?" I persisted. The mayor tried to avoid my question, explaining that it was a small town, and that there was no chance I would recognize its name. I pressed him—even a small town has a name and an identity, I argued. He gave in and said he was born in Provizhne. I told him that one of my ancestors, Rabbi David Halevi Segal, author of the *Turei Zahav* legal commentary, had served as the rabbi of that town (see chapter 2). "My ancestor was the rabbi of your hometown, and now his descendant might become the rabbi of your city," I said. The mayor was deeply moved, and explained that as a child, his father had taken him to Rabbi Segal's synagogue.

Among those running toward the gate was a little boy. Later, I learned that his name was Lulek, and that he was just under eight years old. I realized that any child at Buchenwald had to be Jewish. I jumped on top of him, threw him to the ground, and lay over him to protect him from the bullets. And today I see him before me, alive and well. Rabbi Lau is that very same Lulek, the boy from Buchenwald.

Now I declare this to all of you. I, David Anilevitch, was saved from that horror, fought in the Palmach [the military force of the British Mandate of Palestine], and today serve as deputy mayor of an Israeli city. If I have the merit of seeing this child, whom I protected with my body, become my spiritual leader, then I say to you[and here he pounded on the table so the water glasses shook] that there is a God.

The listeners were shocked into silence, myself included, as I had never before heard this story. David Anilevitch embraced me vigorously, and we parted wordlessly. For the next nine years, I served as chief rabbi of Netanya.

David Anilevitch had saved me from the hail of bullets, and I did not even remember. The next thing I do recall, after being separated from Feodor, and after the whistle of bullets and the thunder of cannons, was the huge pile of corpses next to the camp gate.

I also remember the American soldiers entering the camp gates. Later, I learned that they were part of the Sixth Armored Division of General George S. Patton's Third Army. I recall their expressions when they caught sight of the faces of the *Muselmänner*, gaunt as scarecrows in their striped uniforms; the bodies; and the rivers of blood from those caught in the hailstorm of bullets. With their remaining ammunition, the departing Germans had shot everyone in their path. I saw the American soldiers freeze in place, shocked into silence. I was also frozen, petrified of the new army that had entered the camp gates. I did not know whether they were for us or against us, so I hid behind the pile of bodies.

The chaplain of the U.S. Third Army was Rabbi Herschel Schacter, who later became chairman of the Conference of Presidents of Major American Jewish Organizations. In full army uniform, Rabbi Schacter got down from his jeep and stood before the pile of bodies. Many of them were still bleeding; some groaned in pain. Suddenly, he thought he saw a pair of eyes, wide open and alive. He panicked and, with a soldier's instinct, drew his pistol. Slowly, carefully, he began to circle the pile of bodies. Then—and this I recall clearly—he bumped into me, a little boy, staring at him from behind the mound of corpses, wide-eyed. His face revealed his astonishment: in the midst of the killing field, in that sea of blood—suddenly, a child appears!

I did not move. But he knew that no child in this place could be anything but Jewish. He holstered his pistol, then grabbed me with both hands and caught me in a fatherly embrace, lifting me in his arms. In Yiddish with a heavy American accent, he asked me: "Wie alt bist du, mein Kind?" (How old are you, my boy?)

I saw tears dripping from his eyes. Still, through force of habit, I answered cautiously, like someone perpetually on guard: "What difference does it make? At any rate, I'm older than you." He smiled at me from behind his tears, and asked, "Why do you think that you're older than I am?" Without hesitating, I replied, "Because you laugh and cry like a child, and I haven't laughed for a long time. I can't even cry anymore. So which one of us is older?"

Then he introduced himself to me, and the tone of our conversation eased. Rabbi Schacter asked who I was. Lulek from Piotrków, I replied.

"And who is your family?" he inquired.

"My father was the rabbi of Piotrków."

"And you're here all alone, without your father?"

"Without my father, without my mother. But I have a brother. He collapsed and is lying sick, here in the camp."

Rabbi Schacter gained my full trust when he told me he had heard of my father. He had also heard of Father's cousin Rabbi Meir Shapira, the rabbi of Lublin, who had initiated the *Daf Yomi* daily-page program of Talmud study. I was thrilled.

Then the American rabbi took me by the hand, and together we made the rounds of the barracks, announcing the liberation. We entered some of them together; others he entered alone. I remember the people lying inside, with blank stares, without even the strength to get up from their bunks. These people were not among those who could run to the camp gate and shout "Hooray!" with the rest. "Jews, you are liberated!" called out the American rabbi in Yiddish. The inmates gazed at him, incredulous, as if to ask, "Who is this crazy *meshiggener* standing here in uniform, screaming in Yiddish?"

Indeed, it was a strange, surrealistic sight. The prisoners lay emaciated and prone on wooden planks, while before them stood Rabbi Herschel Schacter, upright and strong, a messenger of redemption. These Jews were like the *dying embers plucked from the fire* that the prophet Zechariah describes.

After visiting all the bunkers, Rabbi Schacter helped me find Naphtali. We went to the Buchenwald hospital, where my brother was being treated for typhoid fever. "My name is Herschel Schacter," he said, introducing himself to Naphtali. "I am the army rabbi for the division that liberated Buchenwald." He took out several cans of orange juice from his bag. "I know who you are. I am going to help you, and everything will be all right," he reassured Naphtali, and concluded with a *mazal tov*. "Congratulations! We've gone from slavery to freedom," he said, referring to the story of the Exodus. Naphtali names Rabbi Herschel Schacter as the first person to offer him relief after liberation, and says the rabbi restored his confidence in himself and in humanity.

FOR MANY YEARS, I thought that some of the details I seemed to remember from my meeting with Rabbi Schacter were the products of my eight-year-old imagination. But these details were confirmed at the April 11, 1983, conference of a group of Holocaust survivors, the Warsaw Ghetto Resistance Organization (WAGRO), which marked the thirty-eighth anniversary of the liberation of Buchenwald. The conference's main objective was to highlight the fact that it was the American army that had liberated Buchenwald. Among those invited were Naphtali; Benjamin Netanyahu, then deputy chief of mission at the Israeli embassy in Washington; Gideon Hausner, chairman of Yad Vashem; and American president Ronald Reagan. Representing the survivors of Buchenwald, besides Naphtali and me, was author Elie Wiesel, who also had been a prisoner in the camp, and after liberation had gone to France. The organizer of the ceremony, the chairman of the American Association of Holocaust Survivors, asked me to recount the episode with Rabbi Schacter to the audience. Then he smiled, saying, "I have a surprise for you."

The U.S. Marine Corps band played a familiar song, "Zog Nit Keynmol," also known as the partisans' anthem, which was my signal to go up to the stage. The hall was dark, and a spotlight illuminated my path as I began to climb the stairs to the stage. Then the spotlight left me and moved toward the speaker's lectern, focusing on the person standing there. I recognized him at once—it was Rabbi Schacter. Projected behind him on the wall was a giant picture of me as a child, leaving Buchenwald after the liberation, holding a rifle.

"Suddenly I saw a pair of eyes peeking out from behind a mound of corpses," Rabbi Schacter said, recalling the scene of thirty-eight years ago. "I pulled him away, and broke into tears."

The crowd was deeply moved by his story of our meeting in Buchenwald. President Reagan shook my hand and, in a voice choked with emotion, said, "I wanted to shake the hand of this living legend."

AFTER THE LIBERATION OF THE CAMP, I stayed in Buchenwald for a while. Buchenwald was in the suburbs of the city of Weimar, the home of Goethe and Schiller. Ironically, the concentration camp was just a ten-minute walk from the German national theater, a bastion of German culture. After the liberation, General Patton decided to invite the residents of Weimar to the camp, insisting that they view the horrors with their own eyes.

I was wandering around the camp, free and fearless, when I saw the Weimar residents, mostly women and elderly men. Suddenly, a command car stopped next to me, and a giant American soldier lifted me. Gripping my heels in one hand and my shoulder with the other, he raised me high in the air, and shouted in German to the Weimar residents: "Do you see this little boy? This is who you have been fighting for the past six years. Because of him you started a world war. He is the enemy of National Socialism, the Nazis' archenemy. A little Polish boy! You murdered his father and mother, and you almost murdered him as well! You followed the Führer—for this? You followed him in blind faith—for this?!"

The women sobbed, but I was filled with pride. The American soldier who lifted me up made his passionate exhortation to the Germans, whom I hated with all my soul. He spoke on behalf of me, my parents, and, indeed, the entire Jewish people.

I revisited this episode, a sign of the guiding hand that directs my life, years later, when I was chief rabbi of Israel and the world-famous professional basketball player Kareem Abdul-Jabbar of the Los Angeles Lakers visited Israel. Formerly known as Ferdinand Lewis Alcindor Jr., he was born a Christian, but in 1971, after reading *The Autobiography of Malcolm X*, was inspired to convert to Islam. Before leaving the United States on a promotional tour for a sporting-goods company, he held a press conference and, to my surprise, announced that while he was in Israel he intended to meet with the chief rabbi. He explained that one of his father's close friends had been among the American soldiers who had liberated Buchenwald. "This friend [of my father's]," said the basketball player, "was a giant, like me. He lifted a little boy in his arms and showed him to the Germans, rebuking them for considering this little boy their enemy, and for fighting against him with merciless cruelty." For fifty years, Abdul-Jabbar recounted, he and his father had followed the path of this little boy, and they learned that he had become a very important rabbi in Israel. "My father," he told the American reporters, "is a very religious Christian, but he cannot visit the Holy Land due to health reasons. When he heard that on this trip I would be stopping in Israel, he asked me to go to the rabbi and ask for his blessing."

The famous basketball player remained faithful to his word, and paid me an emotionally charged visit at the office of the chief rabbinate of Israel. In an interview in *Ha'aretz* magazine, Abdul-Jabbar described our meeting at my office in Jerusalem. After expressing his enthusiasm about our conversation and the warm reception he enjoyed, the black athlete explained the significance of his meeting with a Holocaust survivor. "Blacks in America today," he clarified, "do not understand the experience of slaves who escaped on the Underground Railroad, because we have never spoken with anybody who went through it. I have just had the opportunity to speak with a survivor of a dreadful horror. It was a great honor for me, and the hospitality was wonderful."[2]

MANY OF THE AMERICAN SOLDIERS spoiled me, showering me with chewing gum, candy, and chocolate. They were moved by the very fact of my survival in the impossible world they discovered.

The adults in the camp pounced on the canned meat they gave out. But it was fatty and of doubtful quality; after years of hunger, our bodies had lost the ability to digest fat. Sixty percent of those liberated from Buchenwald died of typhoid fever, the effects of which were exacerbated by careless eating. Luckily, I was satisfied with the sweets. Feodor, along with the other Russian prisoners, went out to work in Weimar and the surrounding towns. Every day, they brought back chickens and cheese, and of course they shared their fare with me.

Feodor continued to be my hero. One day, he caught a horse, jumped on its back, and galloped around me. He cut a handsome figure, and as he rode on the horse with the horse's reins in his mouth it appeared to me as if the horse were floating through the air. I remember Feodor calling out to me, "Lulek, look!" Proceeding at a full gallop, he threw a pocketknife, and it stuck in the ground ahead of him. Then he scrambled under the horse's belly, and while it galloped, he held on upside down, between its legs, and pulled the knife from the ground. Brandishing it in the air, he showed me the blade glinting in the sun. To me, at eight years old, this amazing performance embodied my feeling of freedom and bravery.

At the end of April, the great drama of returning home began. The Russian prisoners were to be sent back to their country. Feodor, to whom I was strongly attached, took it for granted that I would return to Russia

---

2. In May 2004, Kareem Abdul-Jabbar and Anthony Walton published *Brothers in Arms: The Epic Story of the 761st Tank Battalion, WWII's Forgotten Heroes*. The book tells the story of an all-black American tank battalion. In Europe for 183 days, the battalion fought in bitter battles against the Nazis. They fought in the region of Dachau, and liberated the Mauthausen and Gunskirchen camps. A documentary film broadcast in the States in 1992 claims that Battalion 761 also liberated Buchenwald, but Abdul-Jabbar explained in his book that this was erroneous, and that it was a different black unit that liberated Buchenwald.

with him. Weak and only partially conscious, Naphtali lay in isolation in the camp hospital. I was not permitted to enter his room. Occasionally, I went with Feodor to the hospital window. I would climb on his shoulders to look in through the tiny window and wave hello to Naphtali. Margitte, a volunteer Dutch nurse with the Red Cross who was caring for Naphtali, would turn him toward me so that he could see me. By that time, the whole camp knew that Tulek had a little brother; in his delirium, he spoke to me incessantly. Thanks to the Dutch nurse's kind gesture, he could catch a glimpse of me, but he was so weak he did not even have the strength to wave hello.

But Naphtali was not one to fall victim to circumstances. Despite the chaos of our lives, he did the best he could to exert control. When he fell ill, he appointed three Jews to stand guard over me: Dov Landau, who today lives in Tel Aviv, Chaim Halberstam of Brooklyn, and Shalom Tepper.[3] Naphtali gave them a clear order: keep watch over Lulek. Naphtali also instructed them that if he should not recover, they must take me to Eretz Israel. My three guardians reported everything that happened to me to my sick brother. They told him that I stuck close to Feodor and that he continued to take care of me. Through them, Naphtali sent a clear message to Feodor that I was not going with him to Russia. Rather, they told him, I was going with my brother—to the Land of Israel.

SHALOM TEPPER HAD A KEEN SENSE OF JUSTICE. About a month after Buchenwald was liberated, its survivors organized a memorial ceremony and erected a temporary monument. On it they carved the names of each nation represented by the sixty-one thousand camp victims. The monument mentioned "Russians, Poles, French, Belgians, Dutch, Spanish,

---

3. After immigrating to the Land of Israel, Shalom Tepper was killed in the battle of Fallujah in the War of Independence. Tepper, an orphan who had no living relatives, was buried in the Nachalat Yitzchak cemetery. The only person who visits his grave each year to recite the mourner's prayer is Naphtali. At a gathering at the president's residence commemorating the jubilee year of the founding of Yad Vashem, I publicized his story. Following this, I received a phone call from a Haifa resident who said he was Shalom Tepper's cousin, and that he also visits Nachalat Yitzchak once a year to recite Kaddish.

and Italians," but the Jews were missing. The communists, who built the monument, wanted to emphasize their suffering under the fascist tyrants. From their point of view, the Jews were not part of that horror story.

A few hours after the monument was erected, Naphtali found Shalom Tepper lying in a red pool at the foot of the monument. The former prisoners were kicking him all over his body. As Naphtali learned, Tepper could not bear the insult of the monument's failure to mention the Jewish victims and, after the ceremony, found a bucket, a paintbrush, and some red paint. Above the list of nations, he added the word *Juden*, Jews. Because he did not know the exact number of the Jewish dead, he simply drew a Star of David. The fresh paint dripped down, obscuring some of the letters in the names of the other nations and inciting the anger of their representatives, who beat Tepper vigorously.

ON THE DAY THE RUSSIAN PRISONERS were set to leave to return to Russia, Naphtali—although weak—left his quarantine to say good-bye. As he approached the group of Russians, Naphtali was met with a scary and depressing sight—I was standing next to Feodor, one hand holding tightly to his, the other hand holding a small suitcase. Naphtali's entire world collapsed. Perceiving his crestfallen expression, I released Feodor's hand and walked over to Naphtali, suitcase in hand. "Tulek, I'm not leaving you," I reassured him. "I'm only helping Feodor by holding the suitcase for him. This isn't my suitcase, it's his. I'm not leaving you. You told me you would take me to a place called Eretz Israel, the Land of Israel," I reminded him. I wanted to show him that I remembered every word he had said. To me, Israel was the place where no one was killed and, as Naphtali had explained to me, it was our home. I returned to Feodor to say good-bye, but it was not an easy parting.

I remember this separation with pain. I owed him my life, and more than once he endangered himself for me.

One of the prisoners in the group was a French doctor, a communist, who was childless and wanted to adopt me. He also tried to convince Naphtali to go—he explained that he had a big warm house where we would not want for anything. He promised to pamper us with all the basic comforts that had been taken from us during the last three years. But

Naphtali and I knew without a shadow of doubt that we could not be enticed.

Before Naphtali recovered, I heard a rumor that a convoy of trucks from Bergen-Belsen was about to arrive, carrying women and children survivors from that concentration camp. When I had parted from my mother in November 1944—just six months previously—I had heard a rumor that they were taking the men to the labor camp at Częstochowa, and the women and children to Bergen-Belsen. For six terrible months, I had repeated to myself that Mother was in Bergen-Belsen. It was important to me to imagine her somewhere, to know that she had an address, but I had no idea of the significance of that address. In fact, I had no idea whether she was really there, nor could I imagine the fate of those who went to that place. But now survivors from Bergen-Belsen were to arrive in Buchenwald. And if Naphtali and I had survived, there was no reason for Mother not to have done so as well.

During the time when Naphtali was still quarantined and battling typhoid fever, I made sure to visit at his window daily, in compliance with his request. He wanted to see me in order to ascertain that I had not left for Russia with Feodor. I went to him as usual, but decided not to say anything to him about the trucks rumored to arrive from Bergen-Belsen. I remember having an argument with myself over whether I should tell Naphtali about Mother. I feared that if, God forbid, I discovered that she was not among the arrivals, the disappointment would only hinder his recovery. He was so ill, I reasoned, that such a disappointment might break him, so I decided not to say anything. I would go by myself to look for our mother. And when I found her, I would bring her directly to the hospital and make sure that she saw Naphtali from that same window I peered through each day. In my mind, the surprise of finding our mother would surely lead to his speedy recovery, and our joy would know no bounds.

I began my mission to search for my mother as if possessed. My simple logic was: if I, a little boy, had managed to make it, then she, being older and more experienced, must surely have survived.

Twenty-six trucks arrived at Buchenwald. Their benches were packed with women; there were perhaps ten children altogether. Each truck had a ladder with four steps bracketed to its side. I climbed the first ladder, heart pounding and head whirling, and peered inside. The women turned to me, greatly surprised, looking at me in wonderment, as if asking themselves what I was doing there. I scanned each face, then moved on to the next one. The truck remained silent as a graveyard. The women did not utter a word; they simply stared. Not one even asked, "Who are you, little boy? What are you looking for?"

I did not find Mother in the first truck, and, counting backward from twenty-six in Polish, I looked in each of the other twenty-five trucks. I told myself that perhaps Mother's face had changed since we had parted—after all, Naphtali's looks had changed since the typhoid fever had ravaged his body. I tried to convince myself that even if I did not recognize her, she would surely recognize me, for what mother does not recognize her own son? So I worked slowly, examining each one of the women in the truck, hoping my mother might see me and recognize her son standing right in front of her.

Young and old, the expressions of all the women in the trucks were dazed, masklike, reflecting a complete lack of interest in their surroundings. Their eyes were seemingly made of glass, and in their faded clothes, they all looked lifeless. There was no spark of curiosity, no sign of warmth at the sight of an eight-year-old boy who might have been their own child. Row after row, I paused at each pair of eyes in every one of the twenty-six trucks. Not one face did I miss, and I hoped with all my might that my mother would recognize me, her son. I could not consider any other possibility.

After checking the last truck, I climbed down with a feeling of terrible emptiness. Now it was confirmed: my mother did not go to Bergen-Belsen, or else she did not leave that place alive. At any rate, I knew for certain that she was not here. I said not a word to Naphtali about the trucks that came to Buchenwald or about my desperate search for Mother. I only told him after we left the camp. I comforted myself with the thought that perhaps the Germans had transferred her to another camp. But even this hope did not last for long. Several weeks later, we received notice that she had died in Ravensbrück, at age forty-four.

IN MAY 1945, I fell ill with the measles. I burned with fever, and the sores on my body itched unbearably. Although I was in agony, my life was not in danger. Naphtali visited me on the second floor of the hospital, where I was placed in isolation, and kept a close watch on my condition. One day, I heard a knock on the window. Turning my head heavily, I saw my brother standing on the drainpipe, signaling with his hand for me to open the window. Despite my extreme weakness, I did as he asked. He said just two words, in Polish: "Come here." I wrapped a sheet over my hospital pajamas and climbed on his back. I could feel every bone in his body—he had just recovered from typhoid and was still gaunt. I gripped him tightly as he slid down the drainpipe, all the way from the second floor to the ground.

After walking for a while, we reached a row of people standing in a line. Naphtali explained that they were waiting to receive certificates of immigration to the Land of Israel. He would do anything he could, he said, recalling his promise, in order for us to make aliya together to Eretz Israel. But the number of certificates was limited by quota and distributed on a first-come, first-served basis. So Naphtali explained that he wanted me to stand in line with him despite my illness, and thus be sure to obtain a certificate. Whoever did not stand in line right now, he added, would remain in Buchenwald and never get to Eretz Israel.

I understood that nothing could stand in the way of our return "home." I knew that Eretz Israel meant life, and Buchenwald death—despite the fact that the danger seemed to have passed.

"Do you want to stay here?" Naphtali asked. To me, his question sounded rhetorical, and its answer seemed crystal clear. "No way! Not even for one day," I replied firmly. When our turn came, Naphtali signed his name on the application form, and I signed with my thumbprint, since I did not yet know how to read or write. Then he hoisted me onto his back again and returned me to my bed in the hospital, this time by way of the stairs. When I returned to my quarantined room, I was burning with fever and tormented with measles sores, but above the delirium and the misery, I knew that I had a visa to Eretz Israel, and this eased my suffering.

ON JUNE 2, 1945, we were among the first to leave Buchenwald on the train to France. With my measles behind me, I had fully regained my health. Naphtali and I took a bag of candy and food and left Buchenwald forever.

My father, Rabbi Moshe Chaim Lau.

My mother, Chaya Lau, daughter of Rabbi Simcha and Miriam (née Halberstam) Frankel-Teomim.

The Lau family before the Shoah. From left to right: my father, Rabbi Moshe Chaim; my brother Naphtali; my mother, Chaya; and my brothers Shmuel and Yehoshua (Shiko).

Here I am at one year old; this is the first and only photo of me before the genocide.

The family before the Shoah: seated, my grandfather Rabbi Zvi Yehuda Lau and grandmother Leah Hinda (my father was their second son); standing, from left, Uncle Bruno-Berchiyahu Schounthal; his wife, Aunt Metta (my father's sister—they managed to escape to Cuba); and cousins Shmuel Yitzchak Lau and Nusia, killed in the Shoah.

A 1930s class picture of the boys in the Torat Chaim Yeshiva, founded by my father in Prešov. Father, chief rabbi of the city and head of the yeshiva, is in the upper left inset. My brother Shiko is seated in the front row on the right.

Above: American chaplain Rabbi Herschel Schacter conducts Shavuot services for Buchenwald survivors shortly after liberation. I am seated third from left in the first row facing the camera, between two U.S. soldiers. Note that some people are still in their striped prisoner uniforms.

Right: When they photographed me with Naphtali in Écouis, France, both of us holding a mug of milk in one hand and a slice of bread in the other, I was all smiles.

Above: I am hoisted on the shoulders of two Buchenwald boys en route to France.

Right: Jewish DP (displaced persons) youth, members of the Buchenwald children's transport, gather outside the children's home run by the OSE (Oeuvre de Secours aux Enfants, or Society for Rescuing Children) in Écouis in the summer of 1945. In the front row, from left to right, are: Izio Rosenman, David Perelmutter, and me, looking up. The older boy on the far left wearing the checkered cap is Shalom Tepper, killed during the Israeli War of Independence.

Left: Fellow Buchenwald survivor Eleazar Schiff holds me as we arrive in the port of Haifa, pre-State Israel, aboard the RMS *Mataroa*, July 15, 1945. I was eight years old.

Here I am waving a homemade flag upon arrival in the port of Haifa, on the way to the Atlit detention camp. On the extreme left of the photograph is my brother Naphtali, always keeping an eye on me. The flag reads YE YOUTH OF AGUDATH ISRAEL OF BUCHENWALD.

A family dinner honoring my brother Shiko (Yehoshua) upon his wedding in Tel Aviv. At the head of the table is Rabbi Mordechai Vogelman. To his right is the groom in a fedora and open collar. Shiko was a member of the religious kibbutz Kfar Etzion. I am seated to Shiko's right, in a sailor suit and white hat.

Giving my bar mitzvah speech as my uncle, Rabbi Vogelman, listens.

Left: At the Kol Torah Yeshiva, Jerusalem. I stand in the center; on the left is Benjamin Dayan, who was killed in the Six-Day War, and on the right is Eli Berlinger.

Below: With a group of fellow students at the Kol Torah Yeshiva. I am third from the right, holding the book.

Right: At the Ponevezh Yeshiva in Bnei Brak, I stand next to the seated Rabbi Avraham Shapira, brother of Rabbi Meir Shapira of Lublin, a cousin of my father and the founder of the *Daf Yomi* daily-page program of Talmud study.

Left: My teacher, rabbi, and father-in-law, Rabbi Yitzchak Yedidya Frankel, of blessed memory, the chief rabbi of Tel Aviv-Jaffa, speaking at the postnuptial Sheva Brachot (wedding blessings) meal held for my wife and me at the Weil family home, February 1960. To my left is my teacher Rabbi Shlomo Zalman Auerbach.

Above: My installation as rabbi of the Tiferet Zvi Synagogue in Tel Aviv, Hanukkah 1966. To my left is Israel's chief rabbi at the time, Rabbi Isser Yehuda Unterman, my uncle Rabbi Vogelman, and my father-in-law, Rabbi Yitzchak Yedidya Frankel.

Right: Receiving the appointment as rabbi from the head of Tiferet Zvi, Mr. Aharon Dinowitz, 1965.

My wife, Chaya-Ita, and me at my daughter Miriam's bat mitzvah in 1975, along with six of our eight children. My mother-in-law and father-in-law are seated in the front; Miriam sits between them.

With President Ronald Reagan during a ceremony at the American Gathering of Jewish Holocaust Survivors and Their Descendants in Maryland, April 11, 1983. Elie Wiesel is standing behind Nancy Reagan, on the left.

Before we left, an American soldier gave me a small old suitcase from the army's supply. This suitcase has accompanied me always. It went with me to Eretz Israel, and to various educational institutions. By the time I got married, the suitcase was worn out and my wife wanted to throw it away, but I resolutely refused. "This is my home," I explained to her as I squirreled it away in the ceiling storage space. "God willing," I added, "my children will lack for nothing. But if, someday, one of them should complain that he lacks for something, I will have that child climb the ladder, reach a hand up into the storage space, find this suitcase, and take it down. Then I will say, 'This was your father's home for many years and in many places. You must not complain, because I never did.'" My wife understood my thoughts, and like me, she guarded that tattered suitcase like a precious jewel.

Although the suitcase exists no longer—Tel Aviv's heat and humidity caused it to disintegrate—a photograph of it occupies a place of honor in my living room. I obtained the photo in 1994, when I was guest of honor at an Israel Bonds fund-raising dinner at the Waldorf-Astoria Hotel in New York City. The main speaker was Elie Wiesel, who had been liberated from Buchenwald almost fifty years earlier, along with us. "I will divide my speech into two parts," began Wiesel. "Before I present this Torah award to our rabbi and teacher, the chief rabbi of the State of Israel, who represents the crown of Torah, I must make a personal tribute to Lulek." Aside from Naphtali, my wife, and me, who were sitting on the stage, no one in the audience knew who Lulek was. Wiesel continued, "I met Lulek before I met anyone else here, including my wife, Marion. He was one of the youngest survivors of Buchenwald, and even though we all recited the mourner's Kaddish, his was the most emotional, and it moved us to tears.

"When I was asked to speak at the opening of the Holocaust Education Center in Vancouver, Canada, I saw an exhibit of photographs donated by one of the American soldiers who had liberated Buchenwald. He had photographed the camp during and after the liberation. Suddenly, I saw a familiar face. 'That's Lulek!' I shouted. I told my surprised escorts that I had been there, and that I knew the boy in the photo, who was now a rabbi in Israel. I had the photo enlarged and framed, and today I would like to present it to its owner. Lulek, please stand up and come here."

Startled, I accepted the photograph. When I took it home, my children burst out spontaneously, "There's the suitcase!" In the photograph, there I am, holding the suitcase, a satisfied grin revealing my rotting baby teeth. Since I had nothing to wear, someone had broken into the camp storeroom and found a uniform of the Hitlerjugend (Hitler Youth). It was too big for me, but I had no other choice, so I wore it. A label on the sleeve bore the word "Buchenwald" and a red triangle with the number 117030 on it.

That is how I arrived in Eretz Israel—a Jewish boy of eight, wearing the uniform of the Hitler Youth. In the picture, I am also carrying a rifle. American soldiers had escorted us as we left the camp. When I boarded the train, one gave me an unloaded rifle, then said something unforgettable: "With this you can take revenge against the Nazis for your parents." I also heard another version of this story. The American soldier asked me what I wanted to do with my life, and I answered, "I want to take revenge." Hearing this, he gave me the rifle, and I kept it with me on my trip through Germany to Paris, then on to Lyon, Marseille, Genoa, and all the way to the port of Haifa, where the British took it away from me.

Since then, every time I leave the house, I look at the picture hanging in the entryway to the right of the door: a boy wearing a Hitler Youth uniform with the terrifying word "Buchenwald" on the sleeve, carrying a suitcase and holding a rifle. Affixed to the left side of the door frame is a mezuzah. Together, these symbols surround me, forming my entire world. Every time I look at the photograph, it tells me: Israel Meir, you have a mission—to justify your survival and your existence; to serve as the messenger of your murdered father, mother, and brother; and to continue the dynasty.

The Sages said, *Know from where you have come*. I work to fulfill this mission every minute, every hour, and every day of my life. The mezuzah, the symbol of acceptance of God's sovereignty, is the concrete realization of this mission. As the saying continues, *Know where you are heading, and before Whom you will give justification and accounting*.

CHAPTER 6

THE VISION OF THE DRY BONES

They say:
'Our bones are dried, and our hope is lost,
we are doomed.'. . . . And I shall put my spirit in you,
and you shall come to life.

EZEKIEL 37: 11, 14

AS WE LEFT THE GATES OF BUCHENWALD, I was carrying my suitcase, wearing the Hitler Youth uniform, and holding a fistful of candy. Naphtali carried a small bag containing our few remaining possessions. We were forging a new path in a new world, aware that out of our entire family we two were the only survivors.

I sat on the train that was transporting us toward our new lives, and thoughts whirled through my head—disturbing memories, the loss of my parents and brother, and Block 8, as well as my wonderful bond with Naphtali. I was filled with a sense of happiness such as I had never known. I had complete confidence in Naphtali's decision to take me to Eretz Israel, as promised.

We crossed the entire width of Germany from east to west on our way to France. At one of the stations, a large sign was affixed to our train. In English and French, it declared for all the world to see: THE CHILDREN OF BUCHENWALD RETURN HOME. Because of the difficulty in finding clothing, I and the other boys were clad in Hitler Youth uniforms. This created a problem, for when the train crossed into France, the populace that greeted it assumed the train was carrying Nazi youth. This sign was meant to avoid confusion.

Crowds awaited us at each station and greeted us warmly. American soldiers hugged me, moved at the sight of a small boy among the Holocaust survivors. They lifted me in their arms, threw me into the air, and tried to amuse me, expressing their love and their joy at my rescue. I sensed that they wanted to share in my fate, even though they clearly hadn't the faintest clue about my experiences over the last six years. At each station, I received a profusion of pinches on the cheek and a cornucopia of candy.

After a two-day journey, we reached Écouis, a lovely, green town in northwestern France, about fifty miles from Paris. A convalescent home stood at the edge of this town in an isolated spot, deep in a wooded area. A few cabins were scattered around a large main building, and a grassy lawn stretched between them. Previously, this property had been the estate of a wealthy local man. The OSE (Oeuvre de Secours aux Enfants, or Society for Rescuing Children), a French Jewish charity organization, had rented the property, and additional philanthropies supported it.

A group of five hundred youths came to Écouis from Buchenwald and Bergen-Belsen. The center's directors and staff tried to revive their human spirit, both physically and mentally. I was one of the youngest boys; the oldest was about twenty-five. Most of the staff there—teachers, counselors, psychologists, and nurses—spoke French, which not one of us understood, but their friendliness and caring overcame the language barrier. We felt we were loved, even without words. They spoke with their eyes and communicated with smiles. The atmosphere was pleasant, vastly different from all I had known in the past six years in the ghettos and camps.

Our house mother, Rachel Mintz, was from Łódź. In her final days, she made aliya to Israel, to Kibbutz Tzora, not far from Jerusalem, where her son was a member. At her funeral on the kibbutz, I delivered a eulogy on behalf of the youth she had cared for at Écouis, and the survivors who had lived there paid her a final tribute.

Throughout our stay at the convalescent home, Naphtali kept busy writing letters to anyone who came to mind, in the hopes of finding out what had happened to Mother. We had parted from her about seven months previously, and were encouraged by the fact that the two of us had been through so much during that time but still had managed to survive. We both thought there was no reason to assume the opposite about her. We were desperate to know where she was and what she was going through. Naphtali wrote to the Polish government, the Jewish Agency in Jerusalem, the United Nations Relief and Rehabilitation Administration (UNRRA), and any other organization that he or Rachel Mintz could think of. Rachel, our eyes and ears in Écouis, spoke Yiddish, Polish, and French, and helped Naphtali translate his letters.

One afternoon at Écouis, I found myself alone on the lawn. Naphtali was working on an article for one of Rachel Mintz's initiatives, a journal to be posted on the wall. The title of his article, as I later learned, was "Between Death and Life," and it was about us, the survivors, but his point of view was overwhelmingly influenced by his attempts to locate our mother. Meanwhile, I did not yet know how to read or write, and was completely absorbed in physical pleasures. That day, I sat on a swing in the woods while one of the French nurses pushed me. In one hand I held a tin mug containing fresh milk from the cows that grazed around the center; in the other I held a bar of chocolate. Suddenly, this pastoral scene was interrupted when one of our group came up to me and handed me an envelope. "Lulek, give this to Tulek," he said, then ran off. Because I was busy swinging and could not read, I did not pay much attention to the person who gave it to me. I sat on the envelope so as not to lose it.

When Naphtali returned from his pursuits, I gave him the envelope. He opened it, and his face turned as white as a sheet. He sat down beside me, put his hand on my shoulder, and said, "Lulek, from now on—we don't have a mother, either." I cried "as if my heart were breaking," as Naphtali later recounted. The writer of the letter was anonymous. Inside was a small slip of paper with the Hebrew words: "You must recite the Kaddish. You have lost your mother. She died in Ravensbrück." The name meant nothing to me, but Naphtali explained that it was a concentration camp for women, like Buchenwald was for men, and that it also was located in eastern Germany.

Naphtali tried to ascertain who had handed me the envelope, but I had been more interested in the swing than in the letter bearer, and had no idea who it was. "Lulek," he said, "even though you do not know how to read or write, you also have to say Kaddish. You're a big boy now." Naphtali's friends organized a quorum of ten youths so that he could recite the mourner's prayer. I took up his challenge, diligently rehearsing the strange new words.

The first Hebrew letters I ever learned were those in the Kaddish. I did not understand a word of what I was saying, but the forms of the consonants and vowels were impressed on my visual memory. I remember that I invented mnemonics for them: *yod* is the smallest of the group; *tav* is square, like a house receiving guests. *Gimel* reminded me of an animal pacing, bent forward as if bearing a burden, like a giraffe or a camel (the Hebrew words for both animals begin with *gimel*). But of all the letters, the one I liked best was *lamed*. Its long vertical neck gave it an upright stature. In my imagination, the *lamed*, which corresponds to the English *L*, stood head and shoulders above all the others—tall and straight. It was the most beautiful of the letters in the first word of the Kaddish: *yitgadal* (glorified). Later, I learned that my first name, Israel, and my last name, Lau, both contain a *lamed*, and my affection for this letter only grew.

Yod, the first letter of the first word in the Kaddish, also inspired my curiosity. How, I wondered, could this diminutive letter join the sizable ones that followed it but still lead the group, in the sense that the *yod* is the first letter of the very first word in the first sentence? It was so small, yet it sustained the entire Kaddish.

IRONICALLY, IT WAS AT TWO DIFFERENT WEDDINGS that we later discovered Mother's fate, bit by terrible bit.

One day in the 1970s, when I was rabbi of a neighborhood in north Tel Aviv, the phone rang in my home. A woman from Rishon Lezion was calling to ask me to perform her daughter's wedding. She explained that for many years, she had hoped that I would be the one to officiate at the marriage of her only daughter. I opened my diary and discovered that on the specified date, I had already promised to perform another wedding in Tel Aviv. I explained that unfortunately I could not fulfill her request due to a previous commitment. I could not, I said, be in two places at once.

The woman from Rishon Lezion insisted, saying that her daughter's wedding would be taking place in central Tel Aviv, near the location of the other wedding. She begged me to try to find a solution. I wanted to recommend another rabbi, but she would not take no for an answer. She asked what time I thought I could come to her daughter's wedding. I answered that I could not be there until around 9:30 or 10:00 at night. "I'll be waiting for you, even at midnight," she declared. Still, I hesitated to commit. I explained that I did not want to perform the first wedding under pressure. I wondered about the reason for her stubbornness. "I'll tell you at the wedding, after the ceremony," she answered mysteriously. Her words had the desired effect of piquing my curiosity.

Arriving at the wedding, I had no idea which one of the two mothers was the mother of the bride, the one who had begged me to perform her daughter's wedding, but I was easily recognizable, and as soon as I walked in, one of the mothers immediately strode toward me.

She did not make me wait until after the wedding, as she had previously said she would, but immediately took me aside. She was a relatively short woman, and had to raise her head in order to look at me. She was quiet for a moment, and then said something I will never forget: "Your mother died in my arms."

I was able to utter only two words: "When? How?"

"I will tell you after the ceremony," she answered. I had never performed a ceremony in such a state. I saw neither bride nor groom, may they forgive me; my eyeglasses were constantly moist. I had to make a great effort to stand under the wedding canopy with the happy couple. I said a few words of congratulations, impatient to continue the conversation with the bride's mother. After the ceremony, we retreated to a quiet corner and she told her story.

"I am from Piotrków. Each fall, I hear you speak at the memorial service for the residents of our city on the Hebrew date of the last Nazi *Aktion* there—the eleventh of Cheshvan. The day my daughter was born, I made up my mind that when the time came for her to stand under the *chuppah* [wedding canopy], you would be the one to perform her wedding ceremony. The son of Rabbi Moshe Chaim Lau, the rabbi who had married my parents, would conduct the wedding for my daughter. The rabbi whose mother died at Ravensbrück would officiate at the wedding of a Ravensbrück survivor's daughter. To me, the next generation is a kind of compensation for the horrors we experienced," she recounted. She, like myself, was barely able to control her emotions.

Then she described how my mother had died, of hunger and weakness, not long before the liberation. My mother had managed to survive for two and a half years of hell until her strength gave out. At Ravensbrück, the bride's mother recalled, the other women of the camp were so fond of her that they did everything they could in order to save her. Every morning, they had to leave their bunks and march through the camp gate to go to work in the munitions factory. It was the sixth year of the war, and the women were starving, clothed in worn rags, barely dragging themselves through the winter snows. Whoever was unable to march to work was shot at the exit—the Nazis would not waste the one-hundred-gram daily bread ration on an inefficient worker.

My mother was no longer able to walk, and her friends realized that her fate was sealed. But they refused to give up, and instead found a creative solution. Every morning at dawn, sixteen women, all of whom were just slightly less weak than Mother, clustered into a knot, standing her in the center and supporting her with their arms and shoulders. In this manner they walked her through the camp gate. The Germans counted heads, but they did not check the legs. Mother's head reached the height of the women encircling her, and so they did not notice her weakness. The bride's mother was one of the women in that cluster who supported my mother's body until her last moments.

Before that wedding, I had not known the date of Mother's death. Naphtali and I had decided to commemorate it on the day that we received the notice of her death. After hearing the bride's mother's story, I realized that our mother actually died a few months before liberation, close to the tenth of the Hebrew month of Tevet (December 26, 1944). As this is a fast day on which we mourn a disastrous event in Jewish history (the beginning of the siege of Jerusalem by King Nebuchadnezzar, which ultimately ended with the breaching of the First Temple walls on the seventeenth of Tammuz; three weeks later, on the ninth of Av, Nebuchadnezzar burned the Temple), this date seemed quite appropriate to me and I observed it as Mother's *yahrzeit* (anniversary of death, or memorial day). After the establishment of the State of Israel, the country's chief rabbis chose this day as the national memorial day for those Holocaust victims whose actual date of death is unknown. This was the day I commemorated.

We know the date of death for my father and brother Shmuel, as reported by survivors of Treblinka: 11 Cheshvan 5703 (October 22, 1942), the same day they were deported from Piotrków, and also the date on which thousands of Jews observe the *yahrzeit* of the biblical matriarch Rachel, whose spirit is said to be waiting for Jews to return to the Land of Israel. If I had been asked to establish a date to commemorate the memory of the *kedoshim*—the martyrs—murdered during the Holocaust, I would have chosen the original date selected by the chief rabbinate (the tenth of Tevet), which is closer to January 20, 1942, the day that the Wannsee Conference took place. It was on that "auspicious" day that the Nazis decided to implement the "Final Solution," their plot to eliminate the Jewish nation.

NAPHTALI REMAINED UNSETTLED by the mystery of who had handed me the envelope and written the tragic message. All his efforts to track down the messenger were fruitless. In 1982, my daughter Miriam was married in Tel Aviv, and Naphtali flew in from New York especially for the occasion. During the wedding ceremony, he stood next to Moshe Pszigorski, a Gur Chassid. Moshe had accompanied us on the journey from Piotrków to Częstochowa and Buchenwald, then to Écouis, and finally to Eretz Israel, where he became a school principal and director of the Aderet Bnei Akiva Yeshiva of Bat Yam. "The time has come to close the loop," he whispered in Naphtali's ear during my daughter's wedding. "It was I who delivered the letter to Lulek on the swing in Écouis, forty years ago. Today, as Lulek leads his daughter to the wedding canopy, I feel the need to unburden myself of this secret, which I have been carrying for so many years. In Écouis, I could not look either of you in the eye, and that is why I concealed my identity." An astonished Naphtali asked him how he found out about our mother's death. "You were with us all the time, in Piotrków, Częstochowa, and Buchenwald. How did you know something about my mother that I didn't know?" he asked.

"I didn't write the note," Moshe answered.

"So who did?" Naphtali inquired.

"Leibel Eisner," replied Moshe.

Leibel Aryeh Eisner was one of the most gracious people I ever knew. A Gur Chassid, he was older than we were, and joined us on the boat to Eretz Israel. While we were in Écouis, Leibel was scouring Europe searching for his wife, who was from Piotrków. Finally, he went to the camp at Ravensbrück. His wife had been deported there from Piotrków, together with our mother. He discovered that both had died in the camp. When he learned that Naphtali and I were in Écouis, he sent us the letter through a representative of one of the aid organizations. He himself felt unable to give Naphtali the terrible news. Over the years we had seen him many times in Tel Aviv, but he never breathed a word about that envelope.

THE MOMENT OUR FEET HAD TOUCHED THE GROUND of the French convalescent home, we were pelted with temptations and promises. The Jewish community and the general public did their best to convince us to stay in France. Everywhere we went, people recognized us as "the orphans of Buchenwald." They embraced us, showered us with every imaginable luxury, and promised to take care of our every need, including free housing and education. But after receiving the bitter news of our mother's death, Naphtali decided conclusively that we were headed to Eretz Israel.

One morning, Rachel Mintz requested that all the boys gather at four in the afternoon on the lawn to meet some important visitors. She read the list of the expected honored guests, which included the mayor, the local chief of police, and a representative of the army. As she spoke, she quietly slipped in the fact that the leaders of the organizations that supported the Écouis orphanage would also be participating.

When she left, the older members of our group spontaneously said that they were not going to attend the meeting. "Where were these people when the Germans murdered our parents?" they asked. "Now these honored guests remember to come visit us? Aren't they really visiting so that they can have their pictures taken with the orphans of Buchenwald and published in the newspapers?" We didn't need to hear the answers to these questions. We had gained some experience during our stay in Écouis, and witnessed the phenomenon of people wanting to ride the publicity wave generated by the Holocaust. Respected individuals searched out "the orphans of Buchenwald" and exploited our condition for the benefit of their own public relations. For these people, we were nothing more than a vehicle.

The older members of our group, who had begun to regain their sense of personal pride, politely informed Mrs. Mintz that they had decided to boycott the visit. Stunned by this independent initiative, she replied that the guests intended to present a personal gift to each one of us, and that we must not insult them, certainly not at the last minute. But her words did not sway our spokesmen. One of them stood and declared with confidence, "Don't do us any favors. We don't need their gifts, their visits, or their acquaintance. We're going to Eretz Israel. Écouis is just a stop on the way, and our home is not here. The French were not on our side when we needed them, so we won't be on their side now."

Rachel Mintz never expected such a decisive reaction, but she realized she had no chance of swaying them from their decision. She drew her last weapon: "Do it for me." To be fair, she knew that without these organizations and their benefactors, her village would have no means of existence, and she was expecting additional groups of children and adults to arrive. When the youth leaders heard her personal appeal, they decided on a compromise: we'll attend the meeting for the sake of Mrs. Mintz, but we won't cooperate. We won't applaud, and we won't look them in the eye. A photograph taken during this meeting shows no faces, only shaved heads turned down toward the grass. Five hundred youths sat silently as the honored guests spoke to their bald pates.

Rachel Mintz moderated the event in French, translating into Polish and Yiddish for the children. Each guest said a few words, then sat down on the bench in the center of the stage. Rachel Mintz introduced the last guest as a Jew who had survived Auschwitz, where he had lost his wife and children. He had owned a business in France before the war, and so managed to survive and escape to his home country. Since the liberation, he had dedicated all his time, energy, and resources to war orphans. "These are the only children he has left," Rachel explained.

At that moment, without any advance planning, five hundred pairs of eyes lifted in a look of solidarity toward the Jew standing on the stage.

He was one of us. We looked at him, and he saw hundreds of pairs of eyes fixed on him in a powerful gesture of empathy. Tears choked his throat. He gripped the microphone, and for several long seconds, the microphone broadcast only the sounds of his hands shaking. He tried to control himself, but managed to say only three words in Yiddish: "Kinder, taiyereh kinder . . ." (Children, dear children)—then he burst into tears.

It was painful to hear this adult man weeping into the microphone, but he achieved a miracle—along with him, our own cheeks also dampened with tears. We all considered it unmanly to cry, since, after all, we had survived the concentration camps. Yet each boy sitting on the grassy plaza stealthily wiped his eyes with his sleeve. We each stole a glance right and left, and discovered that our comrades were breaking down as well. Then the dam broke. All at once, the lawn of Écouis was transformed into a literal vale of tears. The Jewish guest took his seat on the platform, and we all cried—healthy, liberating tears.

Even fifty-eight years after the event, as I tell this story, my eyes fill with tears. Those tears were for ourselves, for our parents, for our families, for the simple world that was no longer—but they were also tears of hope. They were the tears of individuals who knew their mission in the world, and knew they had the power to decide for themselves, to be independent. They were no longer helpless, no longer dependent on the mercy of others.

Then, in the midst of this catharsis, a young man named Aaron Feldberg stood up. He was twenty-five, which was old for our group, but he had managed to slip in since his gaunt looks were deceiving. When we arrived at Écouis, two months after the liberation, he weighed a mere eighty-six pounds. Aaron rose from the group on the lawn and addressed the honorable guests in polished Polish.

"If you will allow me, I would like to say a few words on behalf of my friends. We would like to thank you. Not to thank you for coming, because we did not want this visit. Not to thank you for the gifts, because we do not want them. We want to thank you for the greatest gift of all, which we received from you just a few minutes ago, and that is the ability to cry. When they took my father and mother, my eyes were dry. When they beat me mercilessly with their clubs, I bit my lips, but I didn't cry. I haven't cried for years, nor have I laughed. We starved, froze, and bled, but we didn't cry. For the past few months, before and since the liberation, I have had the feeling that I am not a normal person, nor will I ever be. That I have no heart. That if I can't cry when I am supposed to, I must have a stone in my chest instead of a human heart. But not any more. Just now I cried freely. And I say to you, that whoever can cry today, can laugh tomorrow, and he is a *mentsch*, a human being. For this I thank you.

"In my hometown of Będzin in Poland, I studied the Bible and Talmud until the war broke out. My parents were religious Zionists, and made sure I learned certain chapters of the Bible by heart. For six years, I have seen neither family nor Bible, and I have forgotten almost everything. But one section sticks in my mind."

Then Aaron proceeded to recite from memory, in Hebrew, the prophet Ezekiel's vision of the dry bones at the beginning of chapter 37:

> *The hand of the Lord was upon me . . . and set me down in the midst of the valley which was full of bones. . . . And, behold, there were very many in the open valley; and, lo, they were very dry. And He said unto me, Son of man, can these bones come to life? . . . And as I prophesied, there was a noise, and behold a shaking, and the bones came together, each bone to its matching bone. . . . And the spirit came into them, and they came to life, and stood up upon their feet, an exceedingly great army. Then He said unto me, Son of man, these bones are the whole house of Israel: behold, they say, Our bones are dried, and our hope is lost: we are doomed. . . . Behold, O My people, I will open your graves, and cause you to come up out of your graves, and bring you into the land of Israel. And you shall know that I am the Lord. . . . And I shall put My spirit in you, and you shall come to life.*

When Aaron finished his declamation, he struck his breast and declared confidently: "Until now, we were just dry bones. Here in Écouis, these bones have connected together and the body is beginning to take shape. But we had no spirit, until just a few moments ago, when we began to cry. Europe was my cemetery. God told the prophet Ezekiel that He would open the graves, take us out of this cemetery, and take us to the Land of Israel. That is where we are going, and we will get there."

• • •

REPRESENTATIVES OF JEWISH ORGANIZATIONS in the United States also pressured us to go to with them. Some warned us against Eretz Israel. There's a war going on there, they said, and the Jews are fighting underground, they don't have independence. The British Mandate rules with a heavy hand, and the Jews and Arabs are embroiled in bitter conflict. "You have suffered enough in war, seen enough blood spilled. Palestine is not for you." We heard this pronouncement repeatedly from various well-wishers. These attempts at persuasion influenced the minds of many in the Écouis group.

Many of our friends wondered where to go next. Naphtali listened to all the speakers and their arguments, but continued to uphold Father's legacy. He had no doubts about Eretz Israel. His resolve inspired him to travel to Paris to try to establish a connection with a representative from the Land of Israel. Once in the big city, he found the offices of the Jewish Agency. He walked in and told the aliya representatives that fifty miles from Paris were five hundred Jewish children, orphans of the Holocaust, and that about 150 of them wanted to make aliya. This was the first time that the Jewish Agency representative, Ruth Aliav Kluger, had heard of the children of Écouis. She equipped him with candy and train fare home, and promised to visit Écouis as soon as she could. A few days later, she arrived along with several other agency representatives and leaders of the Zionist Organization of France. The OSE representatives in charge of Écouis were not pleased at their visit.

Until we received the message about Mother's death, Rachel Mintz had pressured Naphtali intensely. She spoke to him in Polish and in Yiddish, trying to convince him to stay in France. She told him that only in Europe could he discover exactly what had happened to Mother. Perhaps he might even find her alive, despite everything. She described the events taking place in Eretz Israel, painting a picture that was far from encouraging. But the envelope with the note put an end to any hesitation he might have had. We were going to Eretz Israel, and that was final. We would not stay in the Diaspora—all its comforts were not enough to tempt us. Naphtali was concerned that in America or France, he could not be sure of finding a *minyan* (daily prayer quorum) in order to recite Kaddish.

Of the five hundred youths at Écouis, 185 decided that they wanted to make aliya. The others, all our dear friends, decided to either emigrate abroad or remain in Europe. One of the latter was Elie Wiesel, who brought Jewish life behind the iron curtain to the forefront of the international agenda, giving expression to their silent cry of "Let my people go!" He remained in France for many years before moving to New York.

Some of the group chose to flee from any connection with Judaism, turning their backs on their heritage. Encounters in the dining hall of our convalescent home turned into stormy arguments with those who argued that they had suffered enough for being Jews. They opined that they had paid a stiff enough price. They wanted the Jews to be like any other nation, devoid of any religious identity. Most, however, argued to the contrary.

As a small boy, I had nothing to contribute to these arguments among the older youths. I was a passive listener, not always understanding exactly what the discussion was all about, or why it caused the speakers and their audience to raise their voices in excitement. Sometimes I heard the word "America." In my mind, it recalled the American soldiers who had liberated Buchenwald and showered me with candy and chewing gum. I had no concept of the country that lay behind that word. But one thing was clear to me beyond any doubt: whatever Naphtali said, I would do.

Only after I made aliya and began to form an independent opinion did I realize that Israel was my true home, and that I wanted to raise my family there. When I became a rabbi, I routinely rejected all offers to serve in other parts of the world, however challenging and tempting they were. In answer to an offer for the position of chief rabbi of Antwerp, I gave this explanation, which I repeated in my answers to proposals from other communities: "I came to Eretz Israel with nothing. I will never be able to repay this country for what it has done for me, most certainly not in a foreign country. I left Europe, never to return."

WE STAYED IN ÉCOUIS ABOUT A MONTH, healing the wounds to body and soul, and trying to regain our humanity. Then on Tuesday, July 3, 1945, early in the morning, we left—152 youths. Accompanied by Jewish Agency representatives, we made our way on buses to Paris, and then by train to Lyon and Marseille. Local Jews waited for us at the stations, embracing us lovingly and giving us the heartwarming feeling that the Jewish people—despite all that had happened in those six terrible years— were one giant family.

In Marseille, our last stop, we stayed for a few days in a training camp that would prepare us for aliya. We waited while the aliya representatives looked for a boat that would be willing to take us to Genoa. On July 7, they found what they were waiting for, a former French navy boat that had transported soldiers during the war. We all crammed into it, and the crowding was beyond belief. But I was secure in the thought that we were on our way to Eretz Israel, that I was with Naphtali, and doing everything he thought right. I had no misgivings—the future my brother described seemed much more promising than my experiences of the past six years.

We docked in Genoa for two hours, then boarded the RMS *Mataroa*, an Australian boat that would take us to Eretz Israel. On the boat we met counselors from the Jewish Agency and Youth Aliya, various emissaries, and a few brigade fighters who had served in Europe during the war and were hitching a ride to the Land of Israel on this rickety contraption.

I spent many hours on the voyage performing at impromptu parties on the deck, singing Yiddish songs I learned in the concentration camp and at Écouis. I had a decent voice, and since I was practically the youngest child on the boat, it became an attraction. One day, in the midst of my performance, I felt someone yank my arm from behind. I was shocked, because it hurt and recalled unpleasant memories from another time, and because I could not see who had done it. But quickly I realized it was Naphtali.

He wanted to take me down to the hoses in the ship's hold, to rinse off the hordes of lice that wandered freely all over my body. I had become so used to them that they felt like an integral part of my body, and did not bother me. But Naphtali could not stand the thought that his little brother was crawling with lice as he performed before hundreds of people. He forced my head under a powerful stream from a faucet and, dripping with water, I went back up on deck to sing my favorite song, "A Yiddishe Mama." Many in the audience had tears in their eyes, as if I were their mouthpiece.

On the boat I had my first experience in studying Jewish rituals. Two brothers, Eleazar and Hanina Schiff, helped my brother begin my Jewish education, teaching me the laws of the ritual washing of hands. When we wake up, I learned, we pour water over each hand alternately three times, first the right hand, then the left, then twice more. I did not know Hebrew, but I studied the laws assiduously. Eleazar Schiff also showed me the proper halachic way to cut my fingernails.

On the morning of Sunday, July 15, 1945, after several days of tossing about on the seas, the *Mataroa* reached the Haifa port. We were so excited, we stayed up all night. We all felt that finally we had arrived at our true home, the home destined for the Jewish people. All night we crowded on the deck so that we could see with our own eyes the object of our dreams, Eretz Israel. From a distance, we saw the Carmel mountain range, wrapped in the darkness of night, with a few lights twinkling here and there.

The platform at port was packed with people awaiting the arrival of the first Holocaust survivors from "over there." WELCOME TO THE LAND, proclaimed the placards they held. Everyone in Eretz Israel knew that this boat was carrying boys and youths whose parents had been murdered by the Nazis. Here as well, they all wanted to inundate the poor orphans with love. Many hoped to meet relatives, and others thought that through us they might obtain some scrap of information about communities and relatives with whom communication had ceased. Both groups, those waiting on the platform and the boys on deck, were intensely excited as well as curious. My eyes wandered restlessly, trying to absorb as many details as possible about the place we had reached, as yet unknown. I realized that the moment we anchored in the harbor, a new chapter in my life would begin.

CHAPTER 7

LANDING IN THE "PROMISED" LAND

Who are these who are driven like a cloud?
ISAIAH 60:8A

As WE APPROACHED THE PORT OF HAIFA, individual faces emerged from the blur of the crowd awaiting us. The throng was full of reporters and photographers, Jewish Agency representatives, and British soldiers in uniform, carrying rifles. As the boat came closer to the shore, we could feel the special atmosphere that pervaded the port in anticipation of our arrival: the tense excitement, the curiosity, the impatience of those awaiting the new arrivals, the hope of finding a relative or friend.

In my mind's eye, I can see the images of my departure from Buchenwald, the arrival at the Écouis convalescent home, aliya to Eretz Israel, and my first steps in the country. But along with these mental images, professional photographers and photojournalists documented each one of these stages, and these photographs helped me, in retrospect, to remember.

When they photographed me leaving Buchenwald, carrying the tiny suitcase with all my possessions, I smiled. When they photographed me with Naphtali in Écouis, both of us holding a mug of milk in one hand and a slice of bread in the other, I was all smiles. There is only one photograph in which I am not smiling. Three *Ha'aretz* photographers— Yehoshua Gilboa and Aryeh Nesher from the Haifa office and Haviv Canaan from Tel Aviv—documented the arrival of the first immigrants who had survived the Holocaust. The day after we arrived, their newspaper published a photo of a thin boy of eight in the arms of a young man; I have included it in this book (along with some of the other photographs discussed in these pages). The boy is glum, with no trace of a smile, his expression anxious, like that of an adult.

My first fear was of the Arab dockworkers, who wore very wide trousers. I had never seen such clothing, and it aroused my curiosity. "What are those strange pants?" I asked someone standing next to me. He answered, "Those are not Jews—they're Arabs. They kidnap little children and hide them inside those trousers. Then they take them to the market and sell them as slaves."

As soon as I heard this "sophisticated" explanation, I grabbed Naphtali's hand and declared that I had no intention of disembarking. I also attacked him verbally: "What did you bring me here for? This isn't my country! I don't want to be here at all. I don't want to be hidden inside those men's pants and sold to someone. I'm going back," I decided. The Schiff brothers rushed to Naphtali's aid and tried to calm me, but I was so frightened by the sight—and the accompanying explanation—that I refused to cooperate or listen to their reasoning. I curled up inside myself like a hedgehog, completely sure that I was right, that I should not enter a land in which children are kidnapped and hidden inside strange trousers.

When the moment came for us to descend from the boat onto the platform, I dug in my heels. Eleazar Schiff took action—he lifted me in his arms and carried me off the boat. The photographer captured that moment, which is why the photograph shows a very worried boy, who had heard a tall tale of what awaited him in the Promised Land. This was my first, traumatic encounter with Eretz Israel—it was as far removed as possible from the dreams and stories that had danced in my mind throughout the journey there.

Despite my protests, then, I was removed from the boat. The crowds that welcomed us on the platform shouted warmly, "*Shalom aleichem*! Welcome! *Shalom, shalom*!" They repeated that word endlessly. But the British soldiers did not allow us to approach the people who were waving. Aiming the butts of their rifles at us, they led us to a large hangar.

Naphtali and I searched for the two sacks of belongings that we had brought with us in order to begin our new lives. We found one sack easily, but the other had disappeared. Naphtali placed the first sack on the floor and ordered, "Lulek, stand here. You have a rifle, so guard this package while I go to look for the other one." To me, Naphtali's word was sacred. I stood stiffly at attention. On my right shoulder was the small rifle that I had received from an American soldier; at my feet was the sack, which I guarded with all my might from potential thieves. I was frightened by the Arabs with the wide trousers who were working around me, and by the British soldiers in their uniforms, with their rifles and clubs, but I tried to overcome my fears and concentrate on my mission.

I did not understand the place where we had arrived. If, as Naphtali had promised, they didn't kill Jews in Eretz Israel, then why were we surrounded by armed soldiers? Why did they need those rifles? I was well aware of what those were for; I needed no explanation.

As I was occupied with those distressing thoughts, the *Ha'aretz* photographers snapped another photo: I am standing next to the sack of belongings, the rifle on my shoulder, my expression profoundly serious. This photo is displayed at Yad Vashem. Underneath it appears the caption, "When they asked this boy, a new immigrant, why he needed the rifle on his shoulder, he said, 'To take revenge for my parents against the Germans.'"

Naphtali arrived with our second sack of belongings, but I continued to be hounded by questions. Clueless, I was transferred, along with the other youths, from the port to the British detention camp on the coast off Atlit, south of Haifa. Although we were official immigrants with certificates from the Youth Aliya organization, the British soldiers loaded us onto transport trains, counting us repeatedly—like guards counting their prisoners—and watching our every move until we left the port area.

Everything seemed to be repeating itself: again we were loaded into transport trains exactly like the cattle cars in which the Nazis had transported us to the concentration camps in Poland; again soldiers surrounded us, although their uniforms were different this time. They were not Germans or Ukrainians, but they were stern, and that was more than enough for me.

I did not even understand their language, and, as in Europe, I did not understand where we were going or for how long. We had neither food nor water in the train, and from all this I understood that we had in fact not yet escaped the camps. Or perhaps there had been a terrible mistake and our boat had taken a wrong turn, and we had gone back "over there." It was clear to me that something unforeseen had happened. Not for a moment did I suspect that the facts Naphtali had given me about Eretz Israel were inexact; in my mind, every word that left his mouth was the incontrovertible truth. He had said we were going to Eretz Israel, our home, and that at home, they did not kill Jews.

No one said hello to me, nor were there any smiles or hugs. The only conclusion I could reach, based on the data I gathered, was that the captain had made a mistake and we had reached an unknown location. What most frightened me was the repeated counting. I was afraid I would return to being prisoner number 117030. After a half-hour journey, as if to reinforce my fears, we got off the train, and British soldiers again surrounded us and took us to the detention camp in Atlit, which was fenced with barbed wire. We marched in the suffocating mid-July heat into huts that had no fans or other cooling devices. We had come from the frost of Buchenwald through the cool spring of France, straight to the choking summer heat of the coast of Eretz Israel.

We all marched into the camp in a column—my brother, his friends, and I. As the smallest one, I had the honor of leading the group, holding a large paper flag that bore a blue Star of David and a slogan written in archaic grammar—that's the Hebrew they knew: YE YOUTH OF AGUDATH ISRAEL OF BUCHENWALD, as if we represented the camp's branch of the ultra-Orthodox movement Agudath Israel.

While we were still on the boat, the Youth Aliya counselors and Jewish Agency representatives began to hold discussions with the immigrant youths about absorption into the country. Our close friends—the Schiff brothers, Pachigourski, Eizner, and others—had come from ultra-Orthodox families of the Chassidic sects of Gur and Belz, and we knew that they had hoped to remain connected to their rebbes. It was clear that they would allow no one but themselves to determine their future. Naphtali was almost nineteen, an orphan with not a penny to his name and lacking the language of the land. He did not know where he would go himself, but before anything else, he took care of me. He knew we had an uncle in Eretz Israel and planned for me to join that family.

Head high, I carried that flag with pride as Naphtali and his troop marched behind me. This image was also documented for posterity by photographer Nachum Tim Gidal of the *Palestine Post* (later the *Jerusalem Post*).

In 1993, when I was elected chief rabbi, the directors of the Zionist Archives presented me with a collection of photographs developed from Gidal's film after his death. There were photographs of the children of Buchenwald who came to Haifa and Atlit in the summer of 1945, including that photograph of me as a child of eight, holding a flag and marching at the head of a group of youths and adults. I was thrilled to meet myself, through the photos, at the beginning of my life in the Land of Israel.

We stayed in Atlit for two weeks, during which time I could barely close my eyes at night. Like jackals howling in the wilderness, people stood for long hours outside the barbed wire fences surrounding the camp, issuing heartrending cries that still echo inside me. At night, when all was silent, those cries had particular impact. We would hear a shout— "Greenberg, Drohovitz!"—that meant someone was looking for a person named Greenberg from the town of Drohovitz. Or "Goldberg, Łódź!" The noise continued for many long days and nights. People left their work, walking or hitching rides if they lived far away, in order to search for surviving relatives or to glean any scrap of information about their dear ones. We, the prisoners in the camp, were a bridge that connected "here" to "there."

Someone was also looking for Naphtali and me.

As soon as we entered the cabin at Atlit, a local representative approached Naphtali and introduced himself as Mr. Kisman, a member of Kfar Etzion, a religious kibbutz located in Gush Etzion (the Etzion bloc), between Jerusalem and Hebron. He was one of many representatives of agricultural settlements at Atlit. Mr. Kisman gave Naphtali greetings from "your brother Shiko." At first Naphtali did not understand whom he was talking about. He tried to explain to the man that there must be some mistake, and that the message must be meant for someone else. But Mr. Kisman insisted, and added that Shiko was on his way to Atlit.

Finally Naphtali realized that he was referring to our half brother, Yehoshua (Joshua) Yosef Lau-Hager, nicknamed Shiko. Naphtali had last seen him twelve years previously, when Shiko went to celebrate his bar mitzvah at the Polish home of his grandfather, Yisrael Hager, rebbe of the Vizhnitz Chassidic sect.

Our mother, Chaya, daughter of Rabbi Simcha Frankel-Teomim of Kraków, was our father's second wife. His first wife, Dvora, was the daughter of Rabbi Yisrael Hager. Rabbi Yisrael of Vizhnitz, who was also referred to by the title of his most famous work, *Ahavat Yisrael,* was the father of a dynasty of four other rebbes, one of whom was Rabbi Eliezer of Vizhnitz. Three survived the Holocaust and immigrated to Eretz Israel.

Rabbi Eliezer of Vizhnitz   called the *Damesek Eliezer*, after the title of his famous work—was childless. When he came to the Land of Israel in 1944, at the height of the war, he took with him his nephew, the young Yehoshua (Shiko) Lau, our half brother.

My father, his first wife, Dvora, and Shiko lived in Suceava, also called Schatz, in Bukovina,[1] where Father was the city rabbi. Dvora died at a young age of a serious illness and Father was left alone with the small boy. The Hager family, led by the grandfather, Rabbi Yisrael, offered to take care of Shiko while my father traveled and rebuilt his life. But my father preferred that his son live with him, even after he married his second wife, our mother. Shiko lived with them while Father served in the rabbinate of Prešov, Slovakia. When Shiko reached bar mitzvah age, he went to Vizhnitz to study in the yeshiva of his maternal grandfather and uncles. He made aliya with his uncle one year before us, and joined Kibbutz Kfar Etzion. Shiko is seven years older than Naphtali, and eighteen years older than I am.

While Naphtali and I were in Marseille with the other orphans of Buchenwald, waiting for the boat that would transport us to our homeland, Dr. Hillel Seidman, a journalist from Warsaw, came to visit us. Dr. Seidman became the first person to publish the story of the Warsaw

---

1. Parts of Bukovina are today in Romania and Ukraine.

Ghetto, which he based on his diary. He had been a close friend of our father's. When Dr. Seidman discovered the group of child survivors from Buchenwald destined for Eretz Israel, including the two children of Rabbi Lau of Piotrków, he sent a telegram to the Jewish Agency in Jerusalem, giving the details of the group and mentioning us specifically. This information reached Shiko as he was hoeing and clearing rocks from the ground in the Judean Hills near his kibbutz, preparing to plant a vineyard. A fellow kibbutz member ran toward him, waving the *Hatzofeh* newspaper in his hand, and shouted, "Shiko, you have two brothers! Your brothers are alive!" Astounded, Shiko dropped the tool that he was holding. Until that moment, he had known nothing about the fate of the members of his family who had remained in Poland.

Shiko went to tell Mr. Kisman, an acquaintance who worked with the Jewish Agency, that if he saw the Lau brothers he should inform the elder one, Naphtali, that Shiko was on his way. Shiko rushed to Atlit, hitching rides from Kfar Etzion. When Naphtali heard the news from the Jewish Agency representative, he was elated at the discovery of a lost brother, but at the same time distressed that he would have to tell Shiko about the death of our father, mother, and brother.

For me, it was a very exciting event: I had gained a new brother. Until that encounter in Atlit with Mr. Kisman, I had no idea that I had another older brother. When the war broke out, I was two years old, and Shiko was at the Vizhnitz Yeshiva in Grosswardein (Oradea), Romania, cut off from us. No one had ever mentioned to me the fact of his existence. When Naphtali left me in Buchenwald, he said we had an uncle in Eretz Israel, Rabbi Vogelman, but I had never in my life heard the name Shiko. Naphtali did not know whether Shiko was still alive, and he did not want to tell me about yet another family member who might not have survived.

Among the crowds pounding on the gates of the barbed wire fence in their desperate attempts to glean information, I heard Naphtali and another man shouting to each other: "Tulek—Shiko!" "Shiko—Tulek!" I heard the other man's voice among the hoarse cacophony of shouts coming from the throngs of strangers. Then I saw the man behind the voice: he wore khaki pants, a short-sleeved khaki shirt, and open-toed sandals without socks. At twenty-six, his mane of hair had already begun to turn white, and his forelock peeked out from under his cap.

As I was studying him, Naphtali turned to me and said, "Lulek, meet your brother." I did not know how to react. Shiko had seen me at our home in Piotrków during the first two years of my life, when he came to visit for the holidays. But to me, he was a complete stranger. He stretched his hand over the fence, trying to shake my hand but reaching only my fingertips.

I was angry, and refused to shake his hand. I protested the fact that no one had ever told me about him. I was also furious that my meeting with this secret brother was taking place while I was standing behind a barbed wire fence. The story spread like wildfire among the hundreds of people in the camp, until everyone was talking about the meeting between the two older brothers whose younger brother refused to cooperate.

When the tale reached the British soldiers, one officer was touched, and he decided to allow Shiko and me to meet for several minutes without being separated by a fence. Naphtali brought me to the camp gate. A few minutes before, the officer had opened it for Shiko, and he was waiting there for us. This time I cooperated, and we embraced each other tightly, crying and promising that nothing would separate us ever again. After the few minutes allotted for the meeting, each of us returned to his own side of the fence. Then Naphtali told Shiko about the fate of Father, Mother, and Shmuel. After taking in the bitter news, Shiko told us about his life on the kibbutz.

Three years later, during the War of Independence, Shiko's life was miraculously saved. His wife, Zipporah, née Mintzer, went to Misgav Ladach Hospital in Jerusalem to give birth to their eldest child, whom they named Dvora after her grandmother, Dvora Lau. Shiko accompanied Zipporah to the hospital, but then Gush Etzion was cut off in battle, and he had no way to return home, not even in an armored vehicle. All the residents of Kfar Etzion were butchered, except for a lucky few. Members of the other kibbutzim in the area were taken prisoner by the Jordanians. Little Dvora saved the lives of her parents from the massacre at Kfar Etzion.

For many years, Shiko taught Talmud in a municipal high school in Tel Aviv. He later served as principal of a municipal evening high school until he retired, and he now lives near Naphtali in the Katamon neighborhood of Jerusalem and continues to work in education. Shiko has written three books about the issues of halacha (Jewish law) as it pertains to the army, military ethics, and peace treaties in Jewish history and thought, from the biblical story of Abraham and Elimelech to modern times.

After his wife, Zipporah, died, Shiko married Tovah Einfeld, who was widowed of her husband, Ya'akov Yuval, and left with three little girls. I performed their wedding ceremony in my home in Tel Aviv. Shiko's son, Colonel Rabbi Moshe Haim Lau-Hager, bears our father's name. After years of service with the paratroops and tank corps, he founded a yearlong post–high school Torah study program in Yatir, which prepares youths for the army. Today, he serves as its principal, and his two daughters, Dvora and Idit, are teachers there.

When Naphtali and I were in yeshiva and working, the Mintzers' apartment in Tel Aviv served as a home base for us. They hosted both of us for many Sabbaths and holidays. When I got engaged, they also hosted my *ufruf* (the occasion when a groom is called up to read the Torah on the Shabbat before his wedding).

ALTHOUGH IN ATLIT I WAS HAPPY ABOUT GAINING A BROTHER, the rest of my experience there was filled with mixed emotions. The counselors were kind to the Holocaust orphans, but we were given to understand that things in the "Land" were not so simple. The dream of a homeland and the patriotic songs we had learned on our way there did not resonate with the reality of daily life. The transport trains that brought us to the detention camp in Atlit and the barbed wire fences that surrounded us stood in stark contrast to the words of such songs as "We'll build our land, our homeland" and "Here in the land of our forefathers' delight," songs I still remember word for word. The yawning disparity was disheartening.

After two weeks, we left Atlit, the youths who had arrived together on the boat scattering into numerous trucks. Each of us bore a white cardboard sign with the name of a particular movement, ranging from the secular-socialist United Kibbutz Movement and Hashomer Hatzair to the Religious-Zionist Kibbutz Movement and the ultra-Orthodox Agudath Israel. Apparently, the Jewish Agency had a set of criteria by which they had apportioned the immigrants.

Years later, when I was a neighborhood rabbi in Tel Aviv, I spoke about this arbitrary allocation to a group of soldiers. Major General Avigdor Ben-Gal, nicknamed Yanush, was one of the "Tehran Children," a group of Polish Jewish children who came to Eretz Israel via Iran in 1943. When he became commander of Brigade 7, Yanush invited me to speak to the officers on "Jewish identity." In his introduction, he said to me, "Today, you might have been a major general in the IDF, while I might have been a *frummie* [observant Jew]. I don't know if I would have become a rabbi, but I most certainly would have been observant." After all, both of us were but orphaned children when we arrived in Eretz Israel. The Jewish Agency clerks in charge at Atlit could have sent us wherever they liked; we had no idea what we wanted. That was the accepted norm at the time.

But my case was managed differently. God made sure that I did not arrive in the Land alone, but with my brother, who was significantly older. Naphtali announced decisively to all those who tried to take us under their wing that he would decide where he and his little brother would go. Naphtali recalled accompanying our father on trips to Warsaw for meetings of the Council of Torah Sages of Agudath Israel, which represented *haredi* (ultra-Orthodox) communities. Sometimes he joined Father at the national conferences of Agudath Israel, or at the world meeting in Marienbad (Mariánské Lázn), Czechoslovakia. At those meetings, Naphtali met members of the Agudath council. It was for this reason that he and his friends had made the flag that said "YE YOUTH OF AGUDATH ISRAEL OF BUCHENWALD" while we were on the boat—a clear declaration of where we belonged. In addition, Rabbi Hillel Bruckenthal—one of the founders of the religious Kibbutz Hafetz Hayim, which was affiliated with the Po'alei Agudath Israel, the workers' arm of Agudath—was with us on the boat and told us about the options we would have upon arrival.

According to a document I received from New York during the 1990s, which recorded the system by which Israeli officials assigned the Buchenwald boys, a Jewish Agency clerk had asked me how I knew that the rabbi of Piotrków was my father. The report notes, "The child became very angry and answered, 'How do you know that what they call you is your real name?' Laughter from all present." They doubted my credibility as well as my intelligence, but I considered myself a graduate of the university of Buchenwald. At a tender age, I had already managed to gain an intimate knowledge of many aspects of life and had overcome many dangers and trials. Yet here before me sat a complete stranger, who did not know me at all and probably did not know my father, and he was insulting me in front of other people by asking how I knew that I was myself!

Many years later, when I recall that humiliating experience, I feel a flush of anger. I thought at that time that the officials could not succeed in pulling the wool over my eyes, although I know today that if I had not had Naphtali with me as my protector, my fate would have been completely different. I would have been assigned to a location based on the quota agreements between the representatives of the various movements.

After two weeks in Atlit, I was sent with a few other youths to the "Project for Jewish Children" in Kfar Saba, an institution of Agudath Israel and Po'alei Agudath Israel, directed by Rabbi Yitzhak-Meir Levin, the head of Agudath Israel. Rabbi Levin, the son-in-law of the Rebbe of Gur, Abraham Mordechai Alter, had served as a member of the Polish parliament, the Sejm, together with Rabbi Meir Shapira of Lublin; he later became the first minister of welfare of the State of Israel. The leader of Po'alei Agudath Israel was Benjamin Mintz, a Gur Chassid who was one of the leaders of the Vaad Ha-Hatzala, the American Orthodox organization that worked to rescue European Jews from the Holocaust. After the war, Mintz traveled with Israeli Chief Rabbi Herzog to search for Jewish children hidden in churches and monasteries, in order to return them to their faith.

On the Egged (Israeli transit company) bus we took to Kfar Saba, we met a young man about Naphtali's age who wore Chassidic garb and a black hat. He introduced himself as Nachman Elbaum from Warsaw. He had made aliya two years earlier with the group of Tehran Children. Elbaum said he was studying at Ponevezh Yeshiva in Bnei Brak and had come to Atlit to help the boys acclimate. He was a Gur Chassid, energetic, bright, and cheerful, and I particularly recall that throughout our trip from Atlit to Kfar Saba he carried on a long conversation with Naphtali, in which he explained the situation in Eretz Israel.

Once we arrived in Kfar Saba, the staff offered us a warm welcome. My counselor, who introduced himself as Avner Hai Shaki, became minister of religious affairs in 1992. His job at Kfar Saba was to teach us Hebrew and the geography of Eretz Israel. This was the first time I had ever met a Jew who was not of Ashkenazi, or Eastern European, background. He was Sephardic, born in the city of Safed, in northern Israel, and he spoke with an accent that was unusual to my ears, stressing the final syllables of words and pronouncing deep guttural sounds.

On the first evening, the leaders of Agudath Israel and Po'alei Agudath Israel came to welcome us, shaking our hands and embracing us, which they had not been able to do when we were behind the barbed wire of Atlit. Many leaders of both organizations had known Father, the contemporary of some of these leaders, who had been murdered in Treblinka just three years earlier, at age fifty. Many of them also knew from the media that two of the sons of the rabbi of Piotrków had arrived in Eretz Israel. Zalman Ben-Yaakov (Yankelvich), an esteemed educator who later became a Knesset member representing the Agudath Israel party, stood up to speak, but when he saw Naphtali and me, he burst into tears, a moment of honest emotion in recognition of the orphans' deliverance.

The emotional reactions of the adults contrasted with the harsh honesty of the children. Kfar Saba was where I first heard, from arrogant local *moshav*[2] children, the expression "soap bars" used as an epithet for children of the Holocaust. In contrast to the tanned skin of the local children, our skin was white as soap; what's more, this term recalled the grisly report that the Nazis manufactured soap from the ashes of Jewish bodies during the war. We often came to blows over this insult.

My uncle, Rabbi Vogelman, came to see us in Kfar Saba. Naphtali had met him when he had traveled to Katowice with our father. But for me it was a first meeting with a new uncle. I had heard of him earlier,

---

2. A *moshav* settlement is a type of Israeli cooperative agricultural community.

in Buchenwald, when Naphtali said good-bye to me. He cut a magnificent figure: a handsome man with large blue eyes and a long, gray beard squared off at the ends. He kissed my forehead and gave me a bag containing socks and chocolate. What more could I want?

THREE DAYS AFTER OUR ARRIVAL IN KFAR SABA, Nachman Elbaum told us that he was organizing a trip to Jerusalem for Naphtali and me. The word "Jerusalem" meant nothing to me, but the word "trip" was very exciting. For as long as I could remember, I had lived in closed camps and dormitories. Naphtali and I were glad to leave yet another restrictive place and travel to parts unknown.

We went to Jaffa, then took an Arab bus to Jerusalem. In 1945, the trip took half a day; today it takes an hour, on an express superhighway. The bus made sporadic progress, and every once in a while, its engine overheated and we had to get out on the side of the road and push. The narrow road wound through a hilly landscape devoid of habitation. Finally, on approaching Jerusalem, I was thrilled to see a multistory building. An unusually large sign spread all along the width of the building, sparking my curiosity. As I did not yet know how to read or write, I asked Naphtali what it said. I sensed that he avoided answering me. I tried my luck with Nachman, but, as if they had discussed it in advance, he also avoided my question and changed the subject. The building emblazoned with mysterious words remained an unsolved riddle buried inside me.

Five years later, when I went to Jerusalem to pursue my studies, I finally solved the riddle: the building was the Diskin Orphanage. I asked Naphtali why he had hidden its identity from me. He looked at me with an expression that was half apologetic and half guilty, and then answered, "I was afraid you wouldn't want to get off the bus, because you would think we were sending you to that orphanage."

Nachman Elbaum knew all the back alleys of Jerusalem, and he took us through a narrow passage to a gigantic wall of stone. A few old men in fezzes stood facing the wall. Naphtali and Nachman focused on the stones, studying the weeds in the cracks. I recall several doves flying over the stone wall. After a minute, I lost interest in the wall in front of me.

I did not understand what was going on, and had no idea that this place had sacred significance. I gazed in wonder at the people gathered there, praying in front of the wall with all their might, as if they were standing before the holy ark in a synagogue. Nothing here reminded me of the synagogue I had known in Piotrków, where the Nazis had separated my mother and me from my brother Shmuel, nor did anything here resemble the makeshift synagogue in Buchenwald, organized on our last holiday (Shavuot) in the Gestapo's quarantine hall. The stone wall in Jerusalem did not even have a Torah scroll. I did not understand why Nachman felt it was so important to bring us to this place.

As we stood there, staring silently, Nachman disappeared. He returned in a few minutes with several young men he had found in the Old City. He glanced at his watch and announced, "It's midday—we can recite the afternoon service now." At that point, three months after the liberation, I did not yet know how to pray, so I did not join them. Nachman asked everyone to be quiet, then said, "I've brought you here so that he"—and he pointed to Naphtali—"can recite the mourner's Kaddish for his mother and father, here at the Western Wall in Jerusalem." This was one prayer I already knew by heart, so Naphtali and I said it together. Only afterward did Nachman explain to me where we had been, and the significance of this stone wall for the Jewish people. He also told me how important it was that I never forget that Kaddish, and indeed, I never will.

Nachman Elbaum also took us on a guided tour of Jerusalem, including visits to some of the great rabbis who had known Father. Much later, I learned that our arrival in Eretz Israel had kindled great interest and excitement among those who had known my father in Europe. One rabbi we visited was Shlomo David Kahane—a personal friend of Father's, one of the six members of the Warsaw rabbinical council, and then rabbi of the Old City in Jerusalem. He greeted me warmly, kissing me on the head.

That same evening, Nachman also took Naphtali to visit his own rabbi, the Rebbe of Gur, Rebbe Abraham Mordechai Alter. Gur, headquartered in Góra Kalwaria, near Warsaw, had been the largest Chassidic sect in Poland, numbering almost a quarter of a million Jews, but most of its followers were killed in the Holocaust. Rabbi Alter, also known as the Imrei Emet after his magnum opus, a Chassidic commentary on the Torah, was the de facto spiritual leader of all Polish Jewry. Born in Poland, he visited Eretz Israel six times before the war, and in 1940 escaped from the Nazis with three of his sons and settled in Jerusalem. By doing so, he set an example for his followers, demonstrating that Eretz Israel was the right address for every Jew. He built homes and established several yeshivas, including the Yeshiva Chidushei HaRim in Tel Aviv (named after the classic work of Rabbi Yitzchak Meir Alter, the first Rebbe of Gur) and the Yeshiva Sefat Emet in Jerusalem (named after Yehudah Aryeh Leib Alter, the third Rebbe of Gur). Like all Jews familiar with Polish Jewry, our father had admired Rebbe Abraham Mordechai Alter greatly. As one of the rebbe's followers, Nachman felt it was imperative to take us to see him.

By this time, it was late at night, and I had fallen asleep at the home of the Werdigers, a young couple who were followers of the rebbe. Meanwhile, Naphtali went to visit the rebbe in his home, near the Sefat Emet Yeshiva. The rebbe's health was frail and he was not receiving many visitors. But thanks to Nachman's connections, and mostly because of our family pedigree, Nachman had only to whisper in the beadle's ear and doors opened. The beadle asked Naphtali to write his name and his parents' names on a slip of paper. Then the beadle gave the note to the rebbe, who brought it close to his eyes, then asked Naphtali to approach him. In his book *Balaam's Prophecy*, Naphtali describes the rebbe's room:

> *The square room was furnished with only the barest essentials. The Rebbe sat in the center on a high armchair, his white-stocking feet resting on a footstool. The beadle approached him, and I followed suit. Before me I saw a black hat tilted on the Rebbe's forehead, a white beard circling his chin, and wide sidelocks flowing around his ears, completely hiding them. His majestic appearance inspired reverence and humility. When he noticed me approaching him, he stretched out his right hand and grasped my own. He whispered a few words that I could barely make out, studying me for a full minute. When he removed his hand from mine, the beadle signaled that the visit was finished. Again following the beadle's lead, I retreated backward toward the door, my face toward the Rebbe. Outside, the Chassidim crowded around us to hear what their Rebbe had said. The beadle*

repeated the Rebbe's words, which recalled the prophecy of Zechariah: "Brands plucked from the fire, through Heaven's mercy and the merit of our holy forefathers. May God, His Name be blessed, stand beside you and keep you wherever your paths may lead."

After this first encounter with a Chassidic court, Naphtali joined me to spend the night in the home of the Werdiger family. At 5:30 the next morning, Nachman Elbaum knocked on the door and called Naphtali to join him for morning services at the rebbe's study hall, and they walked there together. At 6:15, Rabbi Yisrael entered, son of the Rebbe of Gur and his successor; he is also known as the Beit Yisrael after the title of his book. The rabbi stopped next to Naphtali and greeted him, extending his hand, "You must be Naphtali, the son of Rebbe Moshe Chaim of Piotrków. Where is your little brother?"

The rabbi signaled to the beadle to honor Naphtali by calling him up to the Torah, and pointed out the special blessing one recites after being saved from serious danger. After Naphtali said this blessing, Rabbi Yisrael Alter asked the other congregants for quiet, to allow Naphtali to say the Kaddish alone. Then he asked Naphtali to join him for breakfast at his home. Since making aliya, Rabbi Yisrael lived by himself in an apartment across from the study hall. At that time, he still did not know what had happened to his wife and children, although eventually he learned that they perished in the Holocaust. Later in the day, Rabbi Alter invited my brother to have dinner with him so that they could talk, while I remained with the Werdigers.

Naphtali was to retell the story of that night many times. The rabbi pleaded with Naphtali, the survivor, to eat heartily, while he himself ate sparingly and in silence. Afterward, the rabbi signaled to Naphtali to follow him out into the street. They strode without speaking down several Jerusalem streets. Occasionally, the rabbi would fix Naphtali with a penetrating stare, then continue his hurried pace. They kept crossing the street, back and forth. Suddenly the rabbi stopped, grabbed Naphtali by his lapels, and asked urgently, "Did you see it?" An astonished Naphtali answered, "What?" The rabbi continued, as if it should have been obvious, "The smoke rising from the chimneys." Naphtali was shocked by this question, and gave a positive reply, but the rabbi did not relent. "You saw the burning with your own eyes?" he pressed. When Naphtali once again answered yes, the rabbi turned around and strode swiftly back up the street, his body bent slightly forward. The rabbi, who had lost his wife and children to the gas chambers, was lost in thought, contemplating the fate of his family and followers.

They walked in silence to the street corner, then the rabbi again shook Naphtali by his lapels and asked in Yiddish, "Are you sure you saw the chimneys?" Again Naphtali gave his confirmation, but the rabbi would not permit any remaining sliver of doubt, and continued to probe: "And did you also see smoke rising from those chimneys? Did it burn, or was what you saw with your own eyes just a building with a chimney?" Naphtali replied to the rabbi's questions with decisive precision. "Yes, I saw smoke, and I also saw what they put into the crematoria to make the smoke come out," he said, choking back tears.

The rabbi placed his hand on Naphtali's shoulder, and asked, "And did you see the Holy One, blessed be He, beside you?" This was one question Naphtali could not answer, and they fell silent once more. The rabbi, noticing that Naphtali was exhausted by the conversation, invited him to sleep over at his house. It was a night he never forgot, and he found it difficult to fall asleep from the emotions that the evening's probings had brought to the surface.

At five a.m. the next day, after the traditional early-morning washing of hands, Rabbi Yisrael Alter came to Naphtali's room and said he would be going to the *mikveh*, or ritual bath, before morning prayers. But Naphtali did not join the rabbi. Instead, he went to the study hall and opened up the first volume he came across—tractate *Beitzah* (Egg) of the Talmud. This was the first time he had picked up a volume of Talmud since the war had begun, although he had studied it beforehand, as a yeshiva student. After his visit to the *mikveh*, Rabbi Yisrael Alter came into the study hall. Finding Naphtali with the tome, he asked him if he would like to return to his studies, and together they studied the tractate, which discusses the laws of festival observance, and begins with a question about whether or not an egg that is laid by a hen during a festival is sanctioned for consumption. So Naphtali sat with Rabbi Yisrael Alter and was once again united with the millennia-old discourse of the Talmud.

The rabbi expressed interest in Naphtali's plans for himself and for me. My brother had no idea where he was headed, but as for me, he told the rabbi that he thought I would go live with our relative Rabbi Vogelman. The rabbi listened intently. He was known for his piercing eyes, which penetrated the person before him like a laser beam. Using his keen powers of observation, the rabbi advised Naphtali to attend a yeshiva, but not a Chassidic one. He feared that Naphtali might not become acclimated to an environment demanding a very specific mode of dress, including a beard and sidelocks, and that he might leave after a short while. The rabbi advised him to go to the opposite end of the spectrum, to a Lithuanian yeshiva, where they wore modern suits and gray hats, spoke Hebrew instead of Yiddish, and followed more lenient interpretations of the law.

Naphtali accepted his recommendation, and soon after went on to choose Lomza, a Lithuanian yeshiva in Petach Tikva. One of the teachers there acted as a father toward him, and was especially inspiring—Rabbi Elazar Menachem Man Shach, who later became dean of the Ponevezh Yeshiva.

During that stay in Jerusalem, we visited three other rabbis who knew my father well, one of whom was Rabbi Dov Berish Weidenfeld, formerly the rabbi of Tchebin (Trzebinia), Galicia, a premier halachic authority, who kissed me on the head. He later gave me a copy of my father's manuscript in which my father answers Rabbi Weidenfeld's comments. The second was Rabbi Shlomo David Kahane, who had been a member of the Vaad HaRabbanim (rabbinical council) in Warsaw before the war, survived the Holocaust, and was now the rabbi of the Old City of Jerusalem—and was the rabbi who took me and Naphtali to the Western Wall. The third was the Rebbe of Gur. In addition, we made a trip to Tel Aviv to visit the Rebbe of Belz, Rabbi Aharon Rokeach, who greeted me warmly.

After this extraordinary visit to Jerusalem, we returned to Kfar Saba. I remained there only a few days, since Naphtali's plan was that I go to live with my uncle Rabbi Mordechai Vogelman, of Kiryat Motzkin. His wife, Bella Vogelman, was my father's sister. In 1940, just as the war broke out, the rabbi and his wife left their home in Katowice, fleeing Poland along with their only child, six-year-old Leah Naomi, a pair of Shabbat candlesticks, four small volumes of the Talmud, a *tallis* (prayer shawl), and pair of phylacteries, or tefillin. I still have the prayer shawl in my home, yellowed with age, but preserved with care. (Leah Naomi gave me the prayer shawl that belonged to her father when Rabbi Vogelman died on 9 Elul 5744 [September 6, 1984], saying, "Of everyone in the world, you, his nephew, who grew up in his house, are the most deserving to receive this. You continue the family dynasty.") They spent all their money on their journey, finally arriving penniless in Eretz Israel. The settlement of Kiryat Motzkin, near Haifa, needed a rabbi, and Rabbi Vogelman was sent to fill the position temporarily. As Kiryat Motzkin evolved into a suburb, our uncle remained in his post, serving for more than forty-five years.

Naphtali thought that after the years of horror I had experienced as a young child, I needed a normal household in which to grow up, and so he thought I should live with my aunt and uncle. He planned to follow Rabbi Alter's recommendation and attend yeshiva, but was reluctant to share his plans with me, fearing that I would refuse to get on the bus if I knew he was leaving me in Kiryat Motzkin.

In those days, I had a deep mistrust and fear of strangers. Naphtali prepared me gently. "Remember that nice uncle with the beard who brought you chocolate and socks? We're going to visit him. You know I promised we would go to visit him, since he visited us in Kfar Saba," he reminded me. I was familiar with the Polish custom of returning visits, and that convinced me. I even encouraged my brother, saying that we certainly owed our uncle a visit, since he had made such a positive impression on me.

The next day we went on our visit, another chance for an outing. During the trip, Naphtali described our uncle's house, made of wood and situated in verdant surroundings. His description sounded lovely, pastoral, and, most important, unthreatening.

IT WAS NIGHT WHEN WE ARRIVED IN KIRYAT MOTZKIN. We walked together to the three-room, single-story house of my aunt and uncle at 21 Nachum Sokolov Street, which was beautiful in its simplicity. My aunt, who had not seen us in six years, was very emotional. She made an effort to hide her tears so that we would not feel sad. She told us about her daughter, who was not home that day, and she hugged us. I felt the warm embrace of a loving family. The long trip, the excitement over our new family, and the late hour combined to make me drowsy.

I woke up the next day to my new life in Kiryat Motzkin.

CHAPTER 8

LEARNING TO PLAY BALL

Like doves returning to their dovecotes . . .
ISAIAH 60:8B

MY FIRST MEMORY OF THE HOME of Rabbi Vogelman in Kiryat Motzkin: my uncle sitting me on a high blue-upholstered chair, as if I were a prince. My legs dangled in the air, too short to reach the floor. My aunt and uncle piled a profusion of candy on the table before me, including a thin cylinder wrapped in yellowish paper that looked like a cigarette. My aunt presented it to me, and I, astonished at her offer, declared with great self-confidence that I did not smoke. Everyone broke out laughing, while I, somewhat embarrassed, could not understand why they were laughing, until I discovered the contents of the yellowish paper: not nicotine, but chocolate.

The laughter, the sweetness of the chocolate, and mainly the tenderness and love that my relatives in Kiryat Motzkin radiated toward Naphtali and me all combined to warm my heart. It was only the first night in their house, but I went to sleep with a feeling of happiness such as I had not known in the last six years. I had found a home and a family. Although on the first evening I was not yet aware that this was to be my home in the coming years, I was already able to feel their warmth in an almost physical sense.

Despite this, I had difficulties adjusting. In the first few days, I did not even trust my aunt, who tried so hard to be loving and maternal toward

116

me. In my quiet way, I was watching her. I remained skeptical of her true identity, scrutinized her actions, and demanded more and more proof that she was indeed my father's sister. Only after gaining the impression that she really and truly wanted only the absolute best for me was I able to relax.

ON MY FIRST DAY IN KIRYAT MOTZKIN, my aunt gave me a colorful rubber ball, the kind that bounces high in the air. She also invited one of the neighbor's children to our house—Yigal Karper, a short, slightly plump boy with short fingers who played the piano—and introduced me to him. Another friend joined him, Uri Hashman, who was taller and thinner. They both tried to persuade me to play with them, but I hung back. I had never played with children my age before and was afraid to be alone with them. They were strangers, and because my experiences with strangers were not the most positive, I trusted almost no one. I had no idea what they might do to me, nor did I know the rules of the games they played. I agreed to play ball with my two new friends only on the condition that I would not stay alone with them in the yard. I demanded the protective presence of my aunt, who cooperated in order to assuage my fears.

The two boys were friendly toward me, happy to have a new participant in their ball games. I also wanted to try the game of catch, which was foreign to me, as I had never held or thrown a ball. The three of us played in the little yard of my aunt's house while she watched, as I had requested.

Although they were my age, Yigal and Uri were taller than I. They did not know Polish, and I could not speak Hebrew, but I discovered that children have their own ways of overcoming language barriers and are able to communicate in a shared, international language of their own. After a few tosses back and forth, one of the boys smiled at me and then the other also smiled. One of them gave me a friendly slap on the shoulder, and his friend shouted with joy after I made a successful throw. All this indicated to me that Yigal and Uri were not at all threatening and that I could relax, for they meant me no harm; they were children, just like me. This discovery made me very happy, and the suspicious tension relaxed its hold on me.

After a while the game ceased to challenge me, and I began to show signs of boredom. Dropping the ball on the ground, I went up to Yigal, then to Uri, standing on the tips of my toes in order to reach them. One after the other, I pinched them on the cheek. This was my way of saying, without words, "You're a good boy. You're okay, I like you." This was the only way I knew to express my feelings. Because I was often the youngest in any group, people were always pinching my cheek as a sign of affection. I adopted this practice, thinking it was accepted everywhere in the world. As it happened, Yigal and Uri interpreted the pinch on the cheek for what it was.

Uri has since reminded me often that, at that time, when we played ball and I pinched him on the cheek, I was always looking at him with the expression of an old man, not that of a child. My gaze was not playful, but rather deeply serious, constantly examining and reflecting. Already, in early childhood, as many people who knew me noted, I acted much older than my biological age. In my encounters with other children in Eretz Israel, this difference became very obvious.

The short meeting with my contemporaries in the yard left me with a positive impression, but I did not become an enthusiastic ballplayer; I preferred to be inside the house and to spend time with Naphtali. But he had to go away to yeshiva, and I—as he informed me—would be staying with my aunt and uncle. This came as a complete surprise to me. It was not that I had anything against the rabbi and his wife—on the contrary. But I would have to part from my brother, and this caused me great uneasiness and distress, as separations were my greatest fear.

I accompanied Naphtali to the bus that would take him from Kiryat Motzkin to Haifa. This was our first separation since that vastly different parting in Buchenwald, when Naphtali had come to say good-bye to me. Since then, we had never been separated, not even for a day. Questions filled my head, and I bombarded him with them at a rapid pace: "Why? How long will I stay here? Will I see you again?" Naphtali explained that he was going to study at a yeshiva, but I did not loosen my grip, and continued to ask, "What is a yeshiva? Where is this yeshiva?"

"In Petach Tikva," he answered.

"What's Petach Tikva?" I pressed. "Where is it? Is it close to Kiryat Motzkin or far away?"

I also asked if he would visit on Shabbat, and he said no, but he promised he would come for Sukkot. I had no idea when this holiday was, how long it lasted, or why he had chosen that specific time. Naphtali explained that it fell on a date six weeks hence, that he would have a holiday from the yeshiva then, and that he would come to stay with me.

To me, six weeks seemed like an eternity. I could not conceive of such a long period of time, and I began to sob. My entire world collapsed at the thought that Naphtali would not be with me, and that I would not be going with him wherever he went. Slowly, I had built a protective world for myself that revolved around my older brother, the only soul I had in the world, but then the bus from Haifa came to take him away.

Naphtali boarded the bus, while I remained with my aunt at the bus stop. He waved good-bye to me, and I wiped my tears. My aunt took me to the kiosk next to the bus stop and tried to sweeten my grief. "Choose whatever you want, Lulek," she offered in her soft voice. But between sighs and tears, I managed to mutter that I wanted only Tulek and nothing else. A crowd gathered around us. Everyone knew the rabbi's wife, and had heard the story of the boy who came from "over there," her nephew who had survived Buchenwald. They stared at me with a mixture of curiosity and pity. Although I felt uncomfortable, I could not stop my tears. The sight of Naphtali waving to me from the bus window remained with me for many long hours, until I calmed down and my tears were replaced by a deep sadness.

SEPTEMBER 1945, when I came to my relatives' home in Kiryat Motzkin, was the start of an entirely new stage in my life, one for which I was not at all prepared. But the day after the separation from Naphtali, I had to go to school, and this accelerated my adjustment. I could not allow myself to wallow in my sorrow. The task of adjusting to a new place demanded that I focus on other things, mustering strength from within. The only religious school nearby was in Kiryat Shmuel (a neighborhood in Haifa), which was named after Shmuel Chaim Landau, founder of the Torah Va-Avodah ideological movement, which originally advocated the integration of Torah study and agricultural work (although it later meant the integration of religious observance and a modern lifestyle). Every day, summer and winter, I walked about half an hour from Rabbi Vogelman's house to school.

I did not like it at first, but learned to do so. Even though I was eight years old, I did not know how to read or write, and so the principal put me in first grade.

After my first four-hour school day, I informed my aunt that I did not intend to go back. I could not stand the slow pace of study. I did not understand why we had to repeat every word we learned dozens of times. During those four hours, we learned one word, *shalom* (hello), and various combinations thereof: *shalom*, first grade; *shalom*, Teacher; and so on. And then I told my aunt that, in my honor, the teacher had drawn a picture of a boat on the blackboard, depicting a crowd of *kippah* (yarmulke)-covered heads gathered on deck. Within this crowd a hand was waving. "What is the person on the deck with the hand saying?" the teacher asked the class. Everyone answered in unison, *"Shalom."*

I felt that this was not for me; the pace, the method of study, and the challenges the school gave the pupils were not to my taste. My aunt understood this, and that very same day she took me to the home of the school principal, Ya'akov Blaufeld. In Hebrew, which I did not understand, she explained my arguments and my distress. For one thing, I was the oldest child in a class together with six- and six-and-a-half-year-olds. "After what he went through over there, he is much more mature than the other children," she said. But the principal thought that because I did not know Hebrew, I had to start with first grade, and that if he moved me up to second grade, I would not be able to keep up with the program of study because of the language barrier.

My aunt did not give up. She said that even in first grade, I did not understand the language, and so it did not matter whether I sat in first or in second, but that at least in second grade I would be with slightly older children. The principal could not refute this argument, but he posed one condition: that I learn all the Hebrew terms necessary to perform the basic mathematical functions, up to the number twenty. My aunt accepted this condition, and I—challenged and determined to succeed—began to study with her, even as we walked home from this meeting.

The whole way back to her house, my aunt taught me the numbers in Hebrew, as well as the terms "plus" and "minus." Twenty-two words, equaling the number of letters in the Hebrew alphabet, paved my way to second grade the very next day. I stayed there exactly one month before moving up to third grade, where I finally met children my own age. In the spring, between Purim and Passover, I moved up again, to fourth grade.

EVERY SHABBAT, MY UNCLE TAUGHT TALMUD to interested children and youths. They came to our home at 3:00 in the afternoon each week. One regular at this class was Zevik Lichtenstein, who befriended me. He later became well known as Major General Ze'ev Almog, hero of the assault on Green Island in the Suez Canal during the 1969–70 War of Attrition, commander of the Israel Defense Forces (IDF) navy commando unit, and eventually navy commander in chief. After my uncle's class, Zevik would take my hand in his and walk with me to the Bnei Akiva youth group meeting in Kiryat Shmuel.

There were others from that class with whom I met up in the ensuing years. Forty years later, when I served as Israel's chief rabbi, I received a phone call from the office of Knesset speaker Dan Tichon. He wanted to come to my office and receive my blessing upon taking up his new position.

When Dan Tichon entered the office, he stopped in front of a photo of Rabbi Vogelman, my uncle, and stood stock-still. Curious, I asked, "Did you know him?"

"Did I know Rabbi Vogelman?" he replied. "If there is one person who acquainted me with the world of Judaism, it is he. And if I have respect and appreciation for Jewish tradition and for rabbis—and I do—it is thanks to him."

"How did you know him?" I asked. To my surprise, he answered, "Maybe you don't remember me, but I certainly remember you, and have been following your progress ever since. My name was Danny Beitner, and I lived in the secular neighborhood Kiryat Chaim, but I would come to your uncle's house in Kiryat Motzkin every Sabbath, and sit at the table next to you for the rabbi's Talmud lesson." I was amazed.

. . .

AFTER I FINISHED MY SCHOOLING in Kiryat Shmuel and went on to Kol Torah Yeshiva in Jerusalem, my studies with my uncle of the tractate *Chullin* enabled me to skip yet another grade.

Meanwhile, my aunt and uncle realized that Kiryat Motzkin lacked a religious educational system, and they did not rest until they established one themselves. They understood that no religious family or young couple would come to Kiryat Motzkin, since there was no religious preschool. My aunt, who was a practical person filled with indefatigable energy, decided that first, they must establish a preschool that would teach religious customs, such as candle lighting on Friday evenings. In that post-Holocaust period, this was a true breakthrough, since many people were sharply disconnected from religion. There was a great schism between the "God-fearing" and the "freethinking" ("religious" and "secular," respectively, in today's parlance).

My aunt knew that if children began their religious education at the preschool level, the desire for continuity would necessitate a framework for the continuation of their studies in an elementary school, and then a religious high school, or separate boys' and girls' yeshiva-style high schools.

Once she made up her mind to start a preschool, she traveled to Jerusalem to meet the president of the Mizrachi Women's Organization, with which she identified ideologically. The president, Sarah Herzog, wife of the then–chief Ashkenazi rabbi of Eretz Israel, sanctioned the establishment of my aunt's dream by authorizing her to receive a payment of five lirot per month so that she could rent a room with a yard for twenty-five children. Mrs. Herzog also promised that when my aunt had registered enough children, she would receive a preschool teacher's salary.

Pleased, my aunt returned to Kiryat Motzkin, but then she faced the challenge of meeting the minimum requirement: how would she recruit children for a religious preschool without a list of religious families that had children of the appropriate ages? She improvised a creative solution. "Srulik," she said to me, calling me by an affectionate nickname, "God gave you the gift of an excellent memory. For the next few Shabbat Eves, you'll come with me on the way to synagogue. Each time we'll take a different path, even if we sometimes follow a roundabout route that takes longer. We'll pass by the single-story homes, and you'll make a mental note of the homes where we see Shabbat candles lit. After Shabbat is over, you'll remind me at which addresses we saw the candles, and I'll write them down in my notebook."

On Shabbat evenings for several weeks, instead of taking the regular path with my uncle to the main synagogue, I walked with my aunt, each time taking a different route. All the houses in our neighborhood, except for one on Ha-Shoftim Avenue, were single-story, so we could see the lighted candles through the windows. We checked each home, and wherever we saw lit candles, I made a mental note of the address.

After Shabbat ended and my uncle performed the *Havdalah* ceremony to mark its conclusion, my aunt took up pencil and paper and I reminded her at which addresses we had seen the burning candles. During the week, she would organize home visits according to this list. Sometimes I went with her, and I heard her saying to the families at the doors that she knocked on: "I'm Rebbetzin Vogelman. Excuse me, but through the window I saw candles lit in your home on Friday night. We passed by on the street and saw the light. Perhaps you have a boy or girl for me?" Some laughed and said that their children were grown already. But my aunt did not give up. She asked, "Then maybe you have a grandson or granddaughter for me?" At this point, people began to raise their eyebrows, perplexed at her use of the expression "for me."

My aunt explained with the serenity of someone on a mission to perform a mitzvah: "I want to open a preschool where children will play and learn, just like an ordinary preschool. The children will have all the usual amenities, but in addition, they'll learn the morning prayer *Modeh Ani*, sing songs from the services, like *Adon Olam*, say the *Shema* prayer, and light Shabbat candles. Maybe they'll even learn to say the kiddush, the blessing over the wine." Everyone promised to help by bringing the project to the attention of families with children of preschool age. In one year, my aunt recruited twenty-five children and opened the first religious preschool in Kiryat Motzkin. Later, a religious school opened in the neighborhood for grades one through eight, and then the Segulah yeshiva girls' high school opened, which attracted hundreds of students. And it all started with our "spy" mission to hunt for Shabbat candles.

. . .

I REMAINED SHORT AND THIN, still suffering the effects of malnutrition during the Holocaust years. Dr. Duarman-Doron of Kiryat Motzkin said I had to swallow a tablespoonful of cod-liver oil every day. Leah Naomi, the cousin with whom I grew up and who was like a sister to me, was supposed to take the same dose, but she refused. My aunt promised that for each spoonful of cod-liver oil we swallowed, she would give us a mil, one-thousandth of a lira. The bottle stood on the kitchen counter, and beside it lay two spoons, waiting. Each morning, Leah Naomi and I would go off to school, she to Kiryat Motzkin and I to Kiryat Shmuel. But I would go with two spoonfuls of cod-liver oil in my stomach and two mil in my pocket, having swallowed Leah Naomi's dose as well as my own. Perhaps that is why I reached a height of five feet ten inches (178 centimeters), and when I was inducted into the army, my physical evaluation showed I was in fighting condition.

SCHOOLWORK FILLED MY ENTIRE WORLD until November 1947, a little more than two years after my arrival in Kiryat Motzkin, when the United Nations voted to establish the State of Israel and the War of Independence broke out. Weapons convoys from Iraq and Syria drove through Syria and Lebanon to reinforce the Arabs of Eretz Israel, including those of Haifa.

Located between Haifa and Akko (Acre), Kiryat Motzkin was the scene of many battles. When the war ended after a year and a half of fighting, twelve heroes of the War of Independence received medals for their bravery, two of them for operations in the eastern section of Kiryat Motzkin.

Those operations involved an Israeli unit that was posted at the main junction for entry into the neighborhood, opposite Kiryat Bialik. The unit received intelligence updates on an Arab weapons convoy about to arrive from the north. Ostensibly, the convoy was bringing cargo destined for the Haifa port, but this was nothing more than a cover story. The vehicles did hold cargo, covered with canvas and tightly tied, but the cargo served to hide the enormous quantity of weaponry packed underneath.

I was at home when suddenly I heard shots that brought back memories of my days in Buchenwald. Scenes raced through my mind of the attic in which I hid with Mother, the honey cookies she gave me so that I would not reveal our hiding place, and the frightening search the German soldiers carried out in the building. They turned over everything in order to find Jews, slamming doors and smashing windows. I realized that here as well, in Eretz Israel, the place of our dreams, I was hearing the exact same sounds. I was scared to death, and then I heard a series of powerful explosions. In all of the Kirya neighborhoods and the entire Haifa bay area, not one window remained intact. A hole more than twenty yards (about twenty meters) deep gaped at the site of the explosion. As a result of our fighters' attack, the ammunition had exploded at the main junction. This operation took place three weeks before David Ben-Gurion declared the establishment of the State of Israel.

I remember a horrifying incident that took place in the refineries, in which Arabs attacked Jewish workers, stabbing them with knives and slitting their throats. Forty-one people were killed in this attack, including three from Kiryat Motzkin. It was hard for me to understand that, once again, I had come to a place where they killed Jews; two and a half years after Buchenwald, Jews were again being murdered, this time in their own land. All those years, I had kept in mind what Naphtali had said to me in Buchenwald, that in Eretz Israel, they did not kill Jews. But now, reality came like a slap in the face, undermining every word of his promise. I did not understand the source of my older brother's optimism, or how I could have harbored the illusion that in the Promised Land, things would be completely different.

IN THE FIRST DAYS OF THE STATE OF ISRAEL, the government lacked the wherewithal to cope with issues of state and religion. It established an ad hoc committee on the subject whose members included David Ben-Gurion, the first prime minister. The committee decided to maintain the religious-secular status quo. For example, public transportation had previously operated in Haifa and the bay area around it on Shabbat, so this arrangement would continue. In Givatayim, before the establishment of the state, the Hadar cinema showed films on Shabbat, and so it would continue to do so. But in neighboring Ramat Gan, the screens would remain dark. The result was absurd.

Kiryat Motzkin was an independent municipal entity. It was not a religious settlement, but its leaders ensured that Shabbat was respected in public. On that day, public transportation did not operate, and all the stores and movie theaters were closed.

But unfortunately, our neighborhood was geographically close to Haifa. Because public transportation operated on Shabbat in Haifa, a mixed city of Jews, Arab Muslims, and members of other religions, the Ha-Shahar bus company (which later merged with Egged) decided that its buses would drive through Kiryat Motzkin en route to the Galia beach. The bus route originated in Haifa, passed through the entire length of our neighborhood, crossed the religious neighborhood of Kiryat Shmuel, passed through Kiryat Yam—with its tent camp, Gav Yam—and then arrived at the Galia beach.

Rabbi Vogelman, who was a reasonable man, naively believed that after the establishment of the State of Israel, the fulfillment of the dream of countless generations, Shabbat would be observed throughout the state and that on Shabbat public transportation would no longer run. Disillusioned at the reality, however, the rabbi and neighborhood residents decided to take matters into their own hands. The bus route was to begin operation on the first Shabbat after the opening of the swimming season. On that day, following the Torah reading in the main synagogue of Kiryat Motzkin, Rabbi Vogelman led the congregants into the streets. The rabbi announced that they would pray the *Mussaf* (additional) service for Shabbat outside, and that he was certain that no bus would dare to break through the line of congregants.

I was about twelve years old, and I stood in prayer along with the crowd that gathered from synagogues all around. Ashkenazic and Sephardic, new immigrants and old-timers, elderly and youth, we all gathered in the neighborhood streets. Bus number 52 approached from Kiryat Bialik going west. My sensitive uncle did not dare stand in its path, but in a spontaneous gesture, he removed his prayer shawl from his shoulders and spread it on the road. I remember his lovely prayer shawl with the silver border, spread in all its glory on the black asphalt. Then the rest of the crowd followed his lead, carpeting Ha-Shoftim Avenue with prayer shawls until not an inch of asphalt was visible. With a screech of brakes, the bus stopped beside the rabbi, just in front of the prayer shawls. The driver got off, shaking all over, and pleaded to the rabbi: "Why is Your Honor, the rabbi, doing this to me? Am I not a Jew? How can I run over a prayer shawl?!"

The rabbi answered, "My son, just as it is forbidden to trample a prayer shawl, so is it forbidden to trample the holiness of the Shabbat! We are all Jews standing here around you. We have come to live as Jews here in this neighborhood, in which Shabbat has never been desecrated in public. Please, do not break the tradition of Shabbat in Kiryat Motzkin, and do not break the chain of generations."

The driver listened politely and silently. Then he got back onto his bus, put it into reverse, and drove backward until he found a spot that was wide enough to make a U-turn. Then he went back the way he came. I do not know what the situation is in Kiryat Motzkin today, but as long as I lived there, public transportation never again ran on Shabbat or Jewish holidays.

One day, we received word at our home that, following the termination of the British Mandate train system, Israel Railways was opening its first line, the Haifa-Nahariya route. On opening day, passengers gathered at the Kiryat Motzkin station. Acre, north of us, had absorbed a large number of immigrants after the War of Independence, and was also an important stop on this line. Great rejoicing accompanied the opening— Israeli flags waved at all the train stations, and a sense of accomplishment buoyed us all. For most of the residents of our neighborhood, who did not own private cars, the train was a vital mode of transportation, one that improved their quality of life.

All this was fine, well, and good—until Israel Railways distributed its Haifa-Nahariya train schedule to every mailbox. My uncle, his face alight, leafed through the schedule with great excitement. Suddenly, he let out a deep sigh: "*Oy vey*—on Shabbat!" Someone at the railroad company had decided that because the line passed through towns where public transportation had operated on Shabbat since the Mandate period, and because Ben-Gurion had elected to preserve the status quo, the railroad should operate on Shabbat. This discovery allowed Rabbi Vogelman no rest, and he did not sleep a wink that night.

Early the next morning, my uncle boarded the bus to Tel Aviv. He went to the area then known as Sharona, where many government offices were headquartered, and without having arranged a meeting in advance walked straight into the Ministry of Transportation. (Today, this complex houses only the Kirya, or Defense Ministry, because all the other governmental ministries are housed in Jerusalem.) There he found the office of David Remez, the first minister of transportation of the fledgling state. Although Minister Remez and Rabbi Vogelman had never met, my uncle's impressive stature, the fact that he came especially from faraway Kiryat Motzkin, and his insistence that he had a very urgent matter that would take no more than five minutes to discuss all opened doors for him.

The minister came out, saw my uncle standing in the hallway, and welcomed him inside. "What would you like to drink, sir, something hot or cold?" Remez asked. "Perhaps a cup of tea?" Rabbi Vogelman looked straight at him, and paraphrased Eliezer's declaration to Laban in the book of Genesis as he tried to find a wife for Isaac: *"I will not drink until I have told my errand."*

The minister's interest was piqued. Then the rabbi pulled out the train schedule from the inside pocket of his suit and—again speaking in biblical allusions, this time referring to a situation described in Deuteronomy—said: "My situation is like that of city elders responsible for a *slain corpse*. When a slain corpse is found and the killer is unidentified, the elders of the city nearest to the site of the corpse must testify that they were not responsible for the death. Since I am the rabbi of Kiryat Motzkin," he continued, "I am closest to the scene of the crime, and therefore I hereby testify that I am not responsible for what I see here on the train schedule, that the train is scheduled to run on Shabbat.

"Honored minister," he continued, "I am the rabbi of Kiryat Motzkin, which appears here on the train schedule. This is the new Israel Railways. But," he added, recalling the prayer of Hannah in the book of Samuel, *"is this the child I prayed for?* The train bears the name Israel, and with its wheels it tramples on the sanctity of the Shabbat, for which we sacrificed our souls for many generations. Is this why we came to honor the soil of our Holy Land? Is this what we longed for?" Rabbi Vogelman explained to the minister the meaning of Shabbat but its importance to the Jewish people in a twenty-minute monologue full of poetic phrases and biblical allusions that also expressed his deep pain and distress.

The whole time, David Remez remained silent. Not for one moment did he stop the rabbi's flow of words, nor did he react. Instead, he allowed the rabbi to continue his oration, while he listened in fascination. As soon as the rabbi finished speaking, Remez picked up the black telephone on his desk and asked to speak with the general secretary of the Ministry of Transportation. As my uncle listened, he asked the secretary, "Have we already printed the schedule for the first train line?" The secretary confirmed this, and reminded the minister that he was supposed to attend the opening ceremony in Palmer Square, along with the mayor of Haifa. "I ask that you change the passenger train schedule. We won't discuss the freight trains right now, but the passenger trains on the Haifa-Nahariya line will not run on Shabbat or Jewish holidays. Also, future passenger lines will not desecrate the Shabbat, and they will follow the rule of public transportation not to run on Shabbat," Remez said.

The secretary asked several times whether he understood the minister correctly, that the train should not run on Shabbat, and the minister replied firmly that this indeed was what he meant. In those days, the minister was the sole authority for such decisions.

When Remez hung up the phone, Rabbi Vogelman shed tears of emotion. He could not believe that his dream had come true. He had expected that the minister would respond with routine patronizing phrases, such as, "I hear what you are saying, and I'll think about it. I'll consult with others, I'll bring it up with Ben-Gurion"—at the time, Ben-Gurion was involved in everything. My uncle never imagined that while he was sitting there, the minister would call the general secretary and instruct him to change the schedule at once, to remedy the injustice. After he calmed down, he thanked the minister and began to walk to the door.

Remez stood up, circled his desk, and escorted the rabbi to the corridor, as his entire staff witnessed the respectful treatment the rabbi merited. David Remez, who was slightly shorter than Rabbi Vogelman, straightened himself up to his full height and gave the rabbi a friendly slap on the shoulder. In his Russian accent, he summarized their meeting: "Honored rabbi, the day will come when the Jewish people will miss heretics like me. Never again will there be a generation of heretics like my own." With this message from Minister Remez, my uncle returned to Kiryat Motzkin. All night long, he replayed their conversation in his mind, word for word. He could not fall asleep that night, either, but this time it was out of sheer excitement. Over the years, whenever issues of religion and state arose, I called to mind that meeting between the rabbi and the minister.

This incident involving my uncle taught me the importance of dialogue. Someone other than Rabbi Vogelman who discovered that the train was operating on Shabbat and holidays might have shouted to high Heaven, *Gevalt*! (Woe!), or organized a noisy protest demonstration in the Kiryat Motzkin synagogue. But Rabbi Vogelman chose a different path: he decided to meet with the leader of the system that he identified as responsible for trampling the Shabbat, and found a willing partner in dialogue who shared his concerns.

NEXT TO THE TRAIN TRACKS between Kiryat Motzkin and Kiryat Shmuel stood a series of British army camps that the British abandoned when they left Eretz Israel in May 1948. Within just a few days, they were filled again, this time with new immigrants. The cabins with the rounded tin roofs swarmed with speakers of Yiddish, Polish, Hungarian, and Romanian, almost all Holocaust survivors. Some had suffered through all six years of the war, while others had experienced the horrors only in the last two years. But what they had in common was grief. Their families were all broken, shattered, wounded. There was not one family without victims. Penniless, they arrived at Sh'ar Ha-Aliya, near Haifa—a *ma'abera* (tent camp), or absorption center—and from there were sent to temporary lodgings, including the empty British camps. In Kiryat Shmuel, a cluster of temporary single-story houses was built, known to this day as the "neighborhood of immigrants from Mauritius." When European immigrants had previously tried to make aliya to Eretz Israel, the British stopped them at the shore, deporting some of them to the island of Mauritius, off southern Africa. When these people were finally allowed to immigrate, they settled in this neighborhood.

One day, my aunt asked me to do an errand for her. I was to take the stuffed fish she had prepared to my cousin and her husband, who had just arrived in Eretz Israel and were living in the tent-and-cabin enclave near the eucalyptus grove in Kiryat Shmuel. As my aunt informed me, Mimi Hertzig was the daughter of her cousin Rochele, sister of Rabbi Meir Shapira of Lublin and granddaughter of Rabbi Shmuel Yitzchak Schor, author of *Minchat Shai*. I was very excited about this discovery of more relatives, people I had not even known existed. My aunt said that she had read their names on one of the lists published in the newspapers. She added that they had arrived in Kiryat Shmuel from Cyprus, to which they had been deported when trying to make aliya from Romania. That was when I first became aware of the thousands of Jews who had come to the shores of Eretz Israel during the British Mandate, only to be deported by the British.

My aunt's stuffed fish in hand, I went to the camp in the shade of the eucalyptus grove, there to find a missing branch of my once much larger family. Mimi and Yitzchak Hertzig eventually moved to Tel Aviv and Hebraized their name to Artzi. For many years, Yitzchak Artzi was deputy mayor of Tel Aviv, and eventually became a member of Knesset.

Witnessing the acclimatization process for new immigrants formed a significant part of my childhood in the Vogelman home. These immigrants were veritable paupers, arriving with nothing. Not that the old-time residents enjoyed material wealth, but privation did not stand in the way of generosity toward the new arrivals.

Passover was approaching, and we had planned to spend seder night at the Vogelman home, as a somewhat limited gathering—my uncle and aunt; their daughter, Leah Naomi; I, and a few other guests. But on the morning of the seder, my aunt announced a change in plans: the seder would not take place at our house. She promised me that I would still be the one to sing the traditional Four Questions, just in a different location.

As usual, I walked to synagogue with my uncle, wondering why I did not see the table set for seder. My uncle promised that we would have a large table, and asked me not to worry. We went home, and then we all walked in our holiday attire to northern Kiryat Motzkin, site of a large immigrant home. There, we celebrated the seder with a thousand new immigrants.

Not all of them were overjoyed to participate, whether because of the disturbing memories each one brought from home—and there is nothing like seder night to remind everyone of his or her roots—or because of the poverty of the immigrant house. We can also assume that after the horrors they had experienced in the Holocaust, some had even turned their back on Jewish tradition. Rabbi Vogelman was sensitive to their suffering. He approached the participants and reassured them in words and in gestures, his entire being expressing fatherliness and true spiritual leadership.

It was hot and crowded in the tin structure where we held the seder. Few knew how to sing the traditional Passover songs or tell the story of the Haggadah. But at "Pour out your wrath upon the nations," their hoarse voices rose to a shout, and it was with intense sincerity and meaning that they pronounced, "In each and every generation, a person should see himself as if he personally went forth from Egypt."

The seder my uncle performed in Kiryat Motzkin for the thousand new immigrants, who sat quietly despite their lack of proficiency in reading the Haggadah, has always served as an example for me to emulate. When my children were small, I never held a seder in my own home, except for those Passovers I spent with my in-laws just after I was married. After that, I followed my uncle's personal example and took myself and my family anywhere I felt I could make a significant contribution to the seder.

One year in the late 1970s, I was asked to perform the seder at the Soldiers' Hostel in Tel Aviv for those who had lost family members in Israel's wars, from the War of Independence to the Yom Kippur War. This was the most difficult of all the Passover seders I ever conducted, and it took me back to that very night at the beginning of the state, among the new immigrant Holocaust survivors. The six hundred people who filled the hall felt that they were forbidden to smile and sing, thinking that this was inappropriate behavior for bereaved families. The atmosphere was frosty. In vain, I tried to break the ice. I told the participants that their silence was disturbing to me, but not one of those sitting with me opened his mouth, and the oppressive silence continued.

Finally, I decided to take action: all by myself, I began to sing the patriotic songs I had learned on the boat on my way to Eretz Israel. I began with "Hineh Mah Tov," from Psalms: *Behold, how good and how pleasant it is for brethren to dwell together in unity*. I continued to sing. Slowly, hesitantly, a few voices joined in, then more and more took up the refrain, until the atmosphere gradually warmed up. The ice broke, and the evening was transformed into an unforgettable experience.

On my way home that night, I noticed a very elderly couple walking behind me. The man, his back bent, addressed me with a heavy Russian accent: "We are a bereaved family from Haifa. Our only son, Amnon, fell in the War of Independence. Ever since, for the past thirty years, my wife and I have stayed at home in the evenings. We work during the day, but at night we stay inside, listening to classical music or reading. We try not to be a burden. We feel that our presence is an encumbrance to others. But this year, the Ministry of Defense sent us the notice about the seder for bereaved families that you were to perform, and we decided to deviate from our ordinary routine and participate. Maybe, we thought, the time has come that for once, on seder night, we should not sit alone, just the two of us surrounded by four walls. I thank you for that," said the bereaved father, firmly shaking my hand.

That Passover, I found my reward in the fact that by performing this seder, I had freed this couple from the isolation to which they had sentenced themselves. I felt a close bond with my uncle's act of years earlier, when he decided that we would celebrate our seder with a thousand strangers who had no family of their own with whom to celebrate the Festival of Freedom. I recalled the passage from Psalms 146, which speaks of God as One *Who executes judgment for the oppressed, who gives food to the hungry. The Lord frees the prisoners. The Lord opens the eyes of the blind, the Lord raises them that are bowed down, the Lord loves the righteous. The Lord preserves the strangers; He relieves the fatherless and the widow.*

One of my favorite Chassidic sayings asks, Why do the unfortunates of human society appear in these verses together with the righteous? Why does the psalmist place the righteous among all these wretched types, and in the very middle of the passage, at that? Because it is this kind of righteous person whom God loves: someone like Rabbi Vogelman, who puts himself in the middle, among the wretched and the miserable, the oppressed and the hungry. I adopted this saying as my motto, just as my uncle did when I was a child in his home.

I WAS ONE FIVE MEMBERS of the first graduating class of my school. I finished eighth grade a week after my bar mitzvah, in April 1950, sailing through eight years of elementary school in five years. I was glad I could bring some joy to my aunt and uncle at the graduation ceremony, when my teachers revealed the secret they had guarded so closely. They presented me with a wooden plaque shaped like a cart full of hay, with a carter goading the horses and a farmer carrying his sheaves alongside, which had the words ISRAEL LAU, OUTSTANDING STUDENT carved in the center. For many years, this plaque graced the living room of my aunt and uncle's house. They were full of pride for the boy who, upon arriving in Eretz Israel, did not know how to read a word of Hebrew, but who brought them this honor in just five years.

Now we had to decide where I would go next. One possibility was Yavne High School in Haifa, the school of choice for many students from the Kirya neighborhoods. But at around that time, Naphtali met a young rabbi named Yosef Yehuda Reiner, a young teacher at the Kol Torah Yeshiva in Jerusalem, who would ultimately point me toward the rabbinate.

This yeshiva did not have its own building, so its students met in what was formerly a girls' high school and took their meals in a run-down hotel. They lived in rented accommodations in the Sha'arei Chessed neighborhood, ten to a room, without proper washing facilities. Rabbi Reiner had been one of my father's exceptional students at the Torat Chaim Yeshiva, founded by my father in Prešov; Rabbi Reiner survived the Holocaust, and made aliya to Eretz Israel.

When he read in a newspaper about the arrival of Rabbi Lau's sons, Rabbi Reiner asked Rabbi Vogelman, through Naphtali, for permission to serve as my mentor. "The book of Genesis," he said, "recounts how Joseph commands his brothers regarding Benjamin: *'Bring him down to me, that I may set my eyes upon him.'* I owe everything I have to the father of this boy, and I want to repay Rabbi Lau by supervising the education of his son, as if he were my own child. Give him to me at Kol Torah Yeshiva, and I will see to his spiritual as well as his physical well-being."

My aunt and uncle agreed to allow me to study at his yeshiva. They were aware that there really was no religious school appropriate for me in Kiryat Motzkin or its environs and, despite their distress, understood that eventually I would have to leave their home.

I celebrated my bar mitzvah knowing that from then on, I would be a yeshiva student at Kol Torah. Naphtali arrived from Paris, where he was acting as an emissary for the Jewish Agency for Israel. During this period of economic austerity, he treated us to a suitcase full of kosher salamis and smoked meat that he had bought on his trip. He also brought a crate of apples, a precious commodity. But despite these festive provisions, there was a gaping void beside the bar mitzvah celebration table: the photograph of the event shows my uncle and brothers at my side, while across from me stood my father and mother—in pictures on the wall.

As I delivered my bar mitzvah speech to my small family and the proud Rabbi Vogelman, I realized that I was closing one chapter of my life and opening a new one. Two months later, in June 1950, at age thirteen and two months, I took my first step into the yeshiva world.

CHAPTER 9
PRACTICE WHAT YOU PREACH

We mourn the one who is lost and cannot be replaced.
TALMUD, SANHEDRIN 11A

RABBI BARUCH KUNDSTADT was the *rosh yeshiva*, or dean (as well as founder), of the Kol Torah Yeshiva. He administered my entrance examination for the yeshiva and, after I assured him that I had never studied it before, he handed me tractate *Kiddushin* of the Talmud, opened it to page 29a, and said, "Study the page for half an hour, with the medieval commentaries of Rashi and Tosafot, then come to me and we'll see if you know how to study a page of Talmud on your own." The page I was given discusses a father's responsibilities to his son: to circumcise him; if he is the oldest child, to perform the *pidyon ha-ben* (the ceremony in which the firstborn child is redeemed by a *kohen*, a member of the priestly clan); to teach him Torah; to teach him a profession; and to find him a wife.

After I studied the page, he tested me. Then he placed his hand on my shoulder and said, "Rabbi Reiner told me about you. I had the honor of knowing your blessed father through his unforgettable sermons, which he delivered in Germany as well as in Eastern Europe. As our sages say, '*We mourn the one who is lost and cannot be replaced.*' I will try to fulfill the role of a father and teach you Torah." Not by chance had he chosen this particular page of Talmud. With this gesture, he managed to convey to me that although I was an orphan in body, I had spiritual fathers who would tend to my upbringing.

I ARRIVED AT KOL TORAH with my little beige Buchenwald suitcase, which contained my entire life, and which had traveled with me from Buchenwald to Écouis, then on to Marseille, Genoa, Haifa, Atlit, Kfar Saba, and Kiryat Motzkin. The thought that this suitcase would accompany me to Jerusalem was very meaningful to me, for it symbolized continuity, connecting me to my past and reminding me of what I had undergone during those arduous years.

Kol Torah had three locations in Jerusalem: the study hall was on the corner of Keren Kayemet and Ussishkin Streets; the dining hall and a few dormitory rooms were in the Mamilla section in a building known as Beit Saba (later called the Eretz Israel Hotel); and most of the students lived ten to a room in the Sha'arei Chessed neighborhood, in an Arab-style house with a well outside. The nights were cold, and the water in the well often froze.

On my first night in Jerusalem, after the evening service, we went to Mamilla to eat supper in the yeshiva dining hall. Just as we walked out onto Keren Kayemet Street, we were stopped by two little girls carrying large loads on their backs. They asked if we knew Israel Lau, a new student at the yeshiva.

I did not know who they were, nor did they recognize me. They turned out to be Sarah and Judith, the daughters of Rabbi Mordechai Hacohen and his wife, Rivka, my father's cousin. Rivka, a native Jerusalemite, was the only daughter of Rabbi Avraham Zvi Schor, my father's uncle and the son of Rabbi Shmuel Yitzchak Schor, the Minchat Shai. He had made aliya from Galicia and was president of the presiding judges of the Chassidic community's religious court in Jerusalem. I knew his son-in-law, the girls' father, because he had come to my bar mitzvah celebration two months earlier in Kiryat Motzkin.

The girls had walked all the way from Oneg Shabbat Street in Me'ah She'arim to Keren Kayemet Street, a good forty-minute trek, carrying a down blanket and a pillow for me. They said discreetly, "Kiryat Motzkin is near the beach, so the weather is warm. But in Jerusalem, it will start to be very cold within the month." Their offering was a pleasant and useful surprise, and I used the blanket and pillow for years, until I got married.

They invited me to visit them on Shabbat. On many a Shabbat after that, I walked to Me'ah She'arim and had the noontime meal at the table of the Hacohen family on Oneg Shabbat Street, which became true to its name—a street of Sabbath Delight.

WHEN I ARRIVED AT KOL TORAH, I joined the first-level class with Rabbi Yonah Mertzbach. That first Sunday, the tractate we studied was *Chullin* (Ordinary Things). Surprisingly, this was exactly the same tractate that my uncle Rabbi Vogelman had taught every Shabbat afternoon in his home in Kiryat Motzkin. Even when I did not understand what he was saying, I always listened carefully. The Lithuanian yeshiva world does not often study this tractate. *Chullin* covers the laws of ritually forbidden foods, a topic often neglected. The other *rosh yeshiva*, Rabbi Shlomo Zalman Auerbach, made the study of halacha his particular priority. He convinced the yeshiva rabbis, who were all from Germany and known for their punctiliousness in halacha, to integrate into the study program the tractates *Shabbat* (laws of Shabbat), *Beitzah* (laws pertaining to holidays), and *Chullin*. None of the students in the first-level class at the yeshiva had ever studied *Chullin* before, so they were completely unfamiliar with it.

Rabbi Mertzbach, our teacher, was one of the three principal editors of the Hebrew Talmudic Encyclopedia. He had a mastery of the entire corpus of rabbinic knowledge. In addition, as the rabbi of Darmstadt, Germany, before the Holocaust, he was well versed in secular subjects such as mathematics and astronomy in addition to his erudition in Bible and Talmud. His class began with a didactic introduction. The beginning words of the tractate are: "Anyone can slaughter"—in other words, anyone who is careful in his religious observance and proficient in the laws of ritual slaughter is permitted to do so, even if he is not a rabbi. He taught us the basics of kosher slaughter in that very first lesson. One necessary condition is that the knife be smooth, with no defects, such as a notch or nick in the blade, to ensure that the cut will be as quick and painless as possible.

The Talmud specifies two main categories of defects, termed in Hebrew *mesachsechet* (a nick that catches is one direction but is smooth in the other direction) and *ogeret* (a nick that catches in both directions). Rabbi Mertzbach explained that a defect of either type pulls at the slaughtered animal's trachea and esophagus, thus prolonging its suffering. While he was speaking, I raised my hand. The rabbi looked at me over the spectacles resting on the end of his nose as if to say, What could you possibly have to add to such complicated matters?

The students all looked at me from their places around the long, rectangular table. As the youngest of the new arrivals to the yeshiva, I was small and thin, and the only one in the room wearing short pants and a beret that left my forelock exposed. I came to the yeshiva in the same clothes I had worn in Kiryat Motzkin—a suit consisting of a green jacket and short pants, comical and out of place in the yeshiva. They all knew that I was "the orphan from Buchenwald" and they received me warmly. But despite their understanding and kind treatment, they raised eyebrows and shot glances of astonishment at me for daring to ask a question.

I ignored their looks and focused on the issue at hand. After receiving permission to speak, I said, "Usually we check the knife with the thumbnail, which does not stick into any of the defects, but one of the sages of the Talmud used the tip of his tongue instead, because it is more sensitive." I used the exact Aramaic expression that I had learned in the class in Kiryat Motzkin. I finished my comment, and the room fell silent. In unison, the students turned their heads toward me, their gazes a mixture of surprise and quizzical admiration. Rabbi Mertzbach raised his glasses from the end of his nose and turned in my direction. "Who's asking?" he demanded in an Ashkenazi accent. I gave my name. The rabbi asked if I had ever studied tractate *Chullin* before, and I said that my uncle Rabbi Vogelman, in whose home I had lived, used to give a class every Shabbat, and one of the topics was that tractate. Satisfied with the answer, Rabbi Mertzbach went back to his teaching.

In the afternoons, the nearly one hundred yeshiva students studied in pairs, or *chavruta*, in a packed study hall to earsplitting noise. During study hall on that day, Rabbi Gedalya Eismann called me over to him. Rabbi Eismann served as the yeshiva's *mashgiach ruchani*, the teacher-cum-spiritual counselor who is responsible for the students' conduct as well as their personal and spiritual development. We stood together next to the bookcase, and he informed me that the next day I was to attend the class of Rabbi Reiner, the man responsible for bringing me to the yeshiva world in general and to Kol Torah in particular. I was surprised by this, because Rabbi Reiner taught the second-year students, whereas I was only in the first year. But the rabbi confirmed, "That's what I said. I heard from Rabbi Mertzbach that you have already studied tractate *Chullin*. Therefore you do not belong in the first-year class, but rather in the second-year class."

I was very excited and continued in Rabbi Reiner's class for the rest of that year; in September 1951, I moved up to the third-year class, led by Rabbi Elchanan Kundstadt, a graduate of the Mir Yeshiva in Lithuania. He had escaped the Holocaust, along with thousands of others, through Russia and Shanghai on one of the special visas issued by Chiune Sugihara, the Japanese consul in Kovno, Lithuania. For his lifesaving work, Sugihara was honored by Yad Vashem as one of the Righteous Gentiles.

Rabbi Elchanan's father, Rabbi Baruch Kundstadt, had been a judge on the rabbinical court of Fulda, Germany. He founded Kol Torah Yeshiva together with his colleague Rabbi Yechiel Michel Schlesinger of Frankfurt am Main.

Rabbis Kundstadt and Schlesinger both considered it their sacred duty to found a yeshiva whose official language of study would be Hebrew instead of the usual Yiddish. The Ashkenazi community of Jerusalem objected strenuously to this innovative step of the Orthodox immigrants from Germany, fearing that it carried with it echoes of the Reform movement. But the founders did not give in, because they realized that the times demanded this change.

Thanks to their perseverance, I was able to study at Kol Torah together with Sephardic friends who would otherwise have been unable to join a Yiddish-language yeshiva. Rabbi Schlesinger passed away at a young age, and in his place the yeshiva appointed Rabbi Shlomo Zalman Auerbach, a well-known prodigy and Jerusalem native. He came to the yeshiva three times a week to teach the top class, the fifth level. In addition, every Wednesday he taught the main in-depth Talmud lecture to the entire yeshiva.

Kol Torah was particularly considerate to those students who were Holocaust survivors and had come from Europe through the Youth Aliya movement. They were older than the other students and had missed six years of study due to the war. Their knowledge was appropriate for the first-level class, or, at most, the second level, but their advanced age meant that they required sensitive treatment. The yeshiva opened a special class for these older boys, giving it the honorable title of fourth level, which Rabbi Baruch Kundstadt taught. We youngsters skipped from the third level straight to the fifth level with Rabbi Auerbach. On rare occasions, a student from the fourth level moved up to the fifth.

MY DAYS AT KOL TORAH were enriching and educational, thanks to the method of teaching at the yeshiva, which I considered a true achievement in the field of education. The emphasis was not only on intellectual study but also on social and spiritual development. An example is the different treatment my study partner and I received for the exact same infraction of the rules. My *chavruta* (study partner) was from Bnei Brak, the son of immigrants from Belgium, and a year older than I. When we were together we paid close attention to our studies, but as is natural for adolescents, after six hours of study we might exchange an extraneous word or joke. From his position next to the bookcase, the supervisor, Rabbi Gedalya, observed the behavior of all students in the yeshiva, ensuring they did not waste the precious time set aside for Torah study.

In one of our moments of lightheartedness, he signaled with his finger to my *chavruta* and cautioned him against idle chatter and frivolity, recalling the Talmudic saying, "One who neglects Torah study and engages in ordinary conversation will be fed with burning coals in the World-to-Come." But my partner was not the only one who had neglected his studies—I had also engaged in the conversation. Yet the *mashgiach* did not rebuke me. I pondered the reason for this: did I merit special treatment because I was an orphan? Was it because my *chavruta* had parents, and so the supervisor felt free to reprimand him?

The next day, as I passed by the bookcase where Rabbi Gedalya stood, he said to me, "Israel Meir, you should be more careful to avoid frivolous words, especially if—God forbid—they might contain some hint of slander or gossip." He spoke to me in a soft tone of voice, as a friend offering advice, a tone much different from the one he had used with my study partner.

Many years later, Rabbi Gedalya told me about the educational policy that made it seem as though he treated each one of us in a different manner. Many years later, I heard, he told my *chavruta*, "You probably hold a grudge against me for rebuking you for your behavior in neglecting Torah study, while I never once admonished your *chavruta*. But in fact, I was acting out of consideration. If I had said to you then, 'You're satisfactory, but you need to be even more satisfactory,' then you would have said to yourself, 'My soul can rest at ease. It's enough for me to be satisfactory. Even the supervisor, Rabbi Gedalya, says so, and that's good enough for me.' You would have continued to behave in the same way. You needed to hear harsh words that would shake you from your apathy.

"But your *chavruta*—he was the exact opposite of you. Had I reprimanded him, he might have fallen into a depression; he might even have left the yeshiva. He had neither father nor mother to assure him that the yeshiva was the best place for him, and that he must go there. He had no one to account to. If I had said a harsh word to him, he might have cut himself off entirely. Most of his contemporaries in the same situation did not remain in the world of Torah. I had the responsibility of nurturing him as if in a greenhouse. His success later in life is due, I hope, partly to our early attempts to encourage him rather than to be strict with him." This was the educational policy of the person responsible for one hundred yeshiva students. He had never studied education or psychology, and had no idea who Jean Piaget—the Swiss developmental psychologist—was, but he had experience and intuition, and mainly, he had a love of other human beings and sensitivity to their needs.

DURING MY FIRST FEW MONTHS IN JERUSALEM, I felt terribly cut off from my family: from my aunt and uncle in Kiryat Motzkin; from my older brother Shiko, who after the War of Independence moved with his wife and daughter to live with his father-in-law; and from Naphtali, who returned to Europe. There, he continued the work he had begun during the so-called illegal aliya—bringing in immigrants above the British quota.

He helped find Jewish children in Europe who had been sent during the Holocaust to live in churches, monasteries, convents, and Christian homes in order to bring them to Israel. While he was in Paris, he kept in contact with me by mail.

That year, I had to have a painful operation on my tonsils because doctors found that they were swollen to three times their natural size and were full of pus. Apparently, things did not go as planned, because I was hospitalized for a week afterward and required additional time to recover at the home of the Mintzer family, the parents of my sister-in-law Zipporah.

In addition to my yeshiva friends, who kept me company throughout my recovery, my aunt Bella from Kiryat Motzkin came and sat beside my bed for hours at a time. My sole consolation was that, in contrast to my previous illness five years earlier, in Buchenwald, when Naphtali had also been ill with typhus, this time there was someone there to take care of me.

My father's sister in New York, Aunt Metta, was also concerned for my health, and sent me a money order for eighteen dollars (eighteen is an important number in Israel that is numerically equivalent to the Hebrew word *chai*, or life) so that I could buy myself extra food to supplement the modest yeshiva rations. Because I had been malnourished during the six years of the war, I definitely needed food that was healthier than yeshiva fare. The yeshiva's lack of funds was compounded by austere conditions everywhere in Israel. Bread, coconut oil, and jam were the only items on the breakfast menu. We never saw meat. We had no margarine, let alone butter. On our bread, we spread coconut oil, which was imported through the American Jewish Joint Distribution Committee. On Shabbat, we received a patty made of meat substitute. We had chicken at two meals a year—the pre-fast meal on Yom Kippur Eve and the Purim feast. On Shavuot, of course, we ate the traditional dairy foods, and on Passover and Sukkot the yeshiva was closed for vacation.

Aunt Metta intended for me to use her money order, called a scrip in those days, as a voucher to purchase imported food items, but I did not use it for that purpose. For one thing, I knew I would not be eating alone, and eighteen dollars would not go far toward feeding dozens of hungry yeshiva students; for another, my desire for books was stronger than my desire for food. So I exchanged the voucher for cash and used it to found my library, which gradually expanded. My first purchase was the *Mishnah Berurah*, the six-volume work of the great twentieth-century teacher and ethicist Rabbi Israel Meir Ha-Cohen Kagan of Radin, Poland, known as the Chafetz Chayim. This work is a commentary on *Orach Chayim*, the first section of the halachic codex, the *Shulchan Aruch*.

I also dreamed of purchasing an entire set of the Babylonian Talmud. I had not received one for my bar mitzvah; the most valuable book I had received then was three volumes of *Orach Chayim*, a gift from Avraham Yosef Mintzer, my brother Shiko's father-in-law, who owned a store for religious books on Allenby Street in Tel Aviv.

In order to fulfill the dream of owning a Talmud, I needed to earn some money, and so I began to give private lessons. The lunch break at the yeshiva was from 2:00 to 3:00 p.m., and at Rabbi Gedalya's recommendation, I began to use that time to tutor Talmud and Mishnah. My students were Yair and Yossi, sons of the Weil family, owners of an established Jerusalem shoe store on the corner of Jaffa and King George Streets. Their father wanted to give the boys, who studied at the Horev elementary school, supplementary lessons in religious subjects. Every afternoon, I taught them in their home in Rechavia, earning 75 grush per hour (100 grush equaled one lira). In those days, a sixteen-volume set of the Talmud cost 76 lira, or almost double the average monthly wage. (A respected professional, such as my brother Naphtali, who in 1952 began working as a newspaper editor, or my uncle, a rabbi, earned about 40 lira a month.)

On the fourth floor of the Weils' apartment building lived a salesman of religious books named Mr. Kaufman. I taught Yair and Yossi Weil for more than a hundred hours, until I could go up to the fourth floor and return to the yeshiva carrying on my shoulder a long carton, which contained all sixteen volumes of the Talmud in a small-size format. Bent under that burden on the way to the yeshiva, I felt I was the happiest person in the world. Today, when I travel around the country to teach classes, I don't take a large-format tractate from the set that I received from my father-in-law for my wedding—instead I use those small, brown-bound volumes.

At that time, there were three stores that sold used religious books in Me'ah She'arim. On Fridays, when we did not have classes, I used to wander around these stores, looking for bargains. I say "wander around" figuratively. The stores were packed from floor to ceiling with books, and were so small one could barely even stand in them, much less walk around. Once, one of the owners said to me, "You're beginning to remind me of Rabbi Ovadia." When I returned a blank look, he continued, "There's a young man around here by the name of Ovadia Yosef, a married Jerusalem yeshiva student who comes to the store and asks to look at the books. He does not have the money to purchase them—he's a young father already blessed with many children. So I let him stand on the ladder. He stands there for three hours at a time, one leg on one side of the ladder, the other leg on the other side, and studies a book until he finishes it. And the book is safe inside his head, stored away, as if in a box." Years later Rabbi Ovadia became chief rabbi and the unparalleled leader and scholar of Sephardic Jewry.

THREE YEARS OF STUDIES WERE BEHIND ME. On the first of the Hebrew month of Av (late July), Rabbi Gedalya summoned me. He wanted to prepare me for summer vacation, which in the yeshiva world took place between the fast of the Ninth of Av and the first of the following Hebrew month of Elul. His sensitive eye had noticed my pallid complexion, and he shared with me his concern that I needed some sunlight in order to gain strength. "You're young," he said, "just sixteen, and a little manual labor instead of studying all day and night won't hurt you." He asked if it were possible for me to go to the seashore for the twenty days of vacation.

The only place in the world I could have gone was the home of Rabbi Vogelman in Kiryat Motzkin. But, I explained to the rabbi, my uncle was visiting his brother in Florence, and my aunt was ill and was staying at a convalescent home in Zichron Ya'akov. Naphtali was still working in France. Shiko was in Tel Aviv with his wife's parents, and I knew I could not burden them. Rabbi Gedalya listened carefully to me, wrinkled his forehead, and said, "I have an idea for you. A small group of idealists has established a kibbutz called Sha'alvim. Some of the members are graduates of our yeshiva. The kibbutz rabbi, Rabbi

146 / ISRAEL MEIR LAU

Meir Schlesinger, is also a graduate. Maybe you could go there, work in the fields a bit, have a change of atmosphere. You'll enjoy the sunshine, and come back next month with renewed strength." He cited a verse from Isaiah: *But they that wait upon the Lord shall renew their strength; they shall mount up with wings as eagles.*

His offer delighted me. Once again, I took up my beige suitcase from Buchenwald and traveled, this time to Kibbutz Sha'alvim. It had thirty-seven members, a number with which I feel a special connection, as it is the numerical value of the letters in my last name. The group of founders, an army unit from the youth movement of Po'alei Agudath Israel, had established the kibbutz in 1951 about three hundred yards from the Jordanian border, opposite the police academy of the Jordanian Legion. Behind it stood the Trappist monastery of Latrun. During the 1967 Six-Day War, the Israelis penetrated the police academy, where they discovered plans and precise maps for a mission to invade the kibbutz at night and slaughter all the residents.

The day after my arrival at the kibbutz, the residents welcomed their first Torah scroll to their synagogue. Until then, they had borrowed a scroll from Kibbutz Hafetz Hayim, but now they had one of their very own, and this was a cause for great rejoicing. I was invited to be one of the four pole-bearers for the canopy held over the Torah (reminiscent of a wedding ceremony), and I was proud to be given this great honor. One of the other pole-bearers beside me was the rabbi of the Tel Aviv metropolitan area, Rabbi Yitzchak Yedidya Frankel, who seven years later became my father-in-law. I was glad to meet another pole-bearer, Ya'akov Katz, deputy to Mayor Abba Hushi of Haifa and later a Knesset member (1955–67). Katz had known my father in Piotrków, and when Naphtali and I had arrived at the port of Haifa seven years earlier, he had been there to welcome us.

My arrival at the kibbutz was festive and joyful, and the rest of my stay continued in that vein. I followed Rabbi Gedalya's orders to get plenty of sunshine, and I learned to work outside. The kibbutz had just received five hundred sheep from Australia, and I was appointed as their shepherd. The kibbutz was still too poor to own its own lands, so I had to graze the flock far from the main grounds.

Aside from my work as shepherd, the kibbutz assigned me to dig pits in the stone cliffs using a pickax and a hoe. Since the kibbutz houses faced the Jordanian Legion, the ministry of defense had ordered the kibbutz to build bomb shelters. The company that won the construction bid was associated with the Labor-Zionist party Mapam. Its workers earned five lira and twenty grush (around twenty-one dollars) per workday. That summer, we built three bomb shelters at Sha'alvim. As we dug, we carried on fierce political arguments—me, the yeshiva student, versus the other workers, who belonged to the far-left Hashomer Hatza'ir movement, which was part of Mapam.

To me, everything was fresh and new. Every day, I did eight hours of exhausting physical labor, vastly different from the way I spent my time in the yeshiva. The food on the kibbutz was meager. We ate bread with mayonnaise, and sometimes a bit of jam. On rare occasions we had a hard-boiled egg, but who cared? I loved the work, both in construction and with the livestock. I knew that when it was finished, I would return to the yeshiva tanned and strong, and I enjoyed the development of the physical side of my nature, the importance of which Rabbi Gedalya had explained to me.

That summer, the summer of 1953, created within me a deep, affectionate connection to Kibbutz Sha'alvim. From then on, I closely followed the development of the kibbutz—the high school, the *yeshivat hesder*, and the *kollel* (advanced Talmudic institute), which all evolved gloriously and magnificently. Life on the kibbutz as a religious Jew made a positive impression on me and left me with happy memories, but it also clearly revealed to me that I belonged elsewhere, in the yeshiva world. At the end of summer vacation, I returned to Kol Torah without hesitation.

AFTER THREE YEARS AT KOL TORAH, Rabbi Gedalya recommended that I attend another yeshiva for a year. He thought I should study either at the yeshiva in the town of Be'er Ya'akov, in central Israel, east of Lod, or at the one in Zichron Ya'akov, south of Haifa. The deans of both yeshivas had been outstanding students of the renowned Rabbi Baruch Ber Leibowitz, dean of the Kamenitz Yeshiva in Lithuania. Rabbi Gedalya, the most gifted educator I have ever met, added that it would be worthwhile for me to experience other methods of study before returning to Kol Torah to join the most advanced class, that of Rabbi Shlomo Zalman Auerbach. I decided to visit both places before making my decision.

I stopped at Be'er Ya'akov on my way from Jerusalem, but my impression was that it was very crowded there and that they had no room for yet another student. I continued northward to Zichron Ya'akov, arriving in the evening on a bus that left me on the old Tel Aviv–Haifa road. I climbed on foot up the hill to the yeshiva's study hall, which was located in the town's center. Its students slept and ate in rented rooms throughout the town. The yeshiva was named Knesses Chizkiyahu, after Rabbi Chizkiyahu Mishkovsky, father-in-law of the yeshiva's founder, Rabbi Noah Shimonowitz. Rabbi Mishkovsky was one of the leaders of Vaad Ha-Hatzalah, the Orthodox organization that worked to save many individuals from the Holocaust and afterward brought hundreds of children to Eretz Israel.

The night was cool when I arrived. Carrying my small beige suitcase, I opened the tall door of the synagogue. At the end of the hall, against the eastern wall, I saw a group of young men sitting close together, swaying back and forth in the dimly lit room, arguing as they studied. I particularly recall the clear, resounding voice of a sixteen-year-old boy who studied alone, chanting in a poignant melody as if talking to himself. His voice charmed me. I remember that I stood in the doorway and listened as if nailed to the floor. Eventually I got to know the boy, Yitzchak Bernstein, well, and he later became an important dean of the yeshiva. The location and the atmosphere suited me, and that very night I said to myself that I would remain there.

I went inside, and said that I had come from Kol Torah, and that Rabbi Gedalya had sent me to see the *rosh yeshiva*. They asked me to wait until he arrived. When Rabbi Noah came in, we all rushed to the evening prayer service, and after that I approached him.

RABBI NOAH SHIMONOWITZ had a refined face with a high forehead and intelligent eyes. In Europe he had been considered a Talmud *ilui*, a young genius. After surviving many close calls during the Holocaust, he arrived in Eretz Israel on one of the illegal immigration boats and at age thirty-five was sent by the British to Cyprus—a bachelor, alone, without parents or family. Eventually he married Hannah, daughter of Rabbi Chizkiyahu Mishkovsky, but they remained childless their entire lives.

After the evening prayer, I introduced myself to the *rosh yeshiva*, Rabbi Shimonowitz, who asked if I was the son of the rabbi of Piotrków. When I said yes, he embraced me, and, as I recall, might have shed a few tears. "I'll take care of you. We'll find you a place," he said. But my heritage did not earn me any favors. He would interview me and test me, just as he would any other candidate.

I appreciated this; I wanted to be accepted not for my lineage but for my knowledge and abilities. He asked me where I had studied, and I told him Kol Torah. "With Rabbi Shlomo Zalman?" he wanted to know. I explained that I had not yet reached his class, but that every Wednesday at six in the evening, Rabbi Shlomo Zalman gave an in-depth Talmud lecture to the entire student body and that I had participated in those classes. "For how long?" he asked.

"Three years," I replied.

"If you've attended three years of classes at Kol Torah, including the weekly lecture of Rabbi Shlomo Zalman, then you are an appropriate candidate," he decided. "But I won't apply double standards. Tomorrow after morning prayers and breakfast, I'll sit in the entrance hall of the synagogue and test you on what you have learned." He examined my knowledge of Talmud, but also tried to understand what was in my heart. His penetrating gaze seemed to see beyond what stood before him to what was inside me. Following the test, Rabbi Noah said, "If you really want to learn, I can help you to become a serious scholar. But you have to want it." I did, very much so.

The year I spent at that yeshiva served as a milestone in my religious development. At that time, Zichron Ya'akov was an isolated village. That year, none of the yeshiva students got married, there were no funerals, and there wasn't even a public gathering. Nothing distracted us from our studies.

In addition to the partner study sessions, in which we applied both the broad and the in-depth approach to studying the Talmud, we attended two daily classes, taught using two different study methods. The teacher of the first class was Rabbi Eliyahu Mishkovsky, Rabbi Noah's brother-in-law, the rabbi of Kfar Chassidim and a superb scholar.[1] Every day, he made the arduous journey on two buses to get from Kfar Chassidim to Zichron Ya'akov to teach us. Rabbi Noah himself taught the second class.[2] The most senior rabbi at Knesses Chizkiyahu was the saintly and brilliant Rabbi Eliyahu Lapian, who, despite his advanced age, nourished the yeshiva with the insights and teachings that he had absorbed from the Mussar movement, the ethics-based educational and cultural movement developed as part of nineteenth-century Eastern European Orthodoxy. His exceptional oratorical skill was just one facet of his charismatic personality and he had a magnetism that inspired youths at the age when their character was being formed.

Every Shabbat at dusk, Rabbi Eli (as we called Rabbi Lapian) would give a talk on Mussar, a lesson also attended by secular kibbutz members who were drawn to his inspiring rhetoric. The rabbi asked them not to desecrate the Shabbat by taking cars or buses in order to attend the classes. He promised to extend his talk so that even after Shabbat was over they would have something to hear and in this way could drive to his class without violating the prohibition on traveling. Out of nostalgia for tradition, they would arrive each week in jeeps covered with dust from the fields, don caps out of respect, and listen with devotion to his Mussar lecture.

I recall that in one of those talks, Rabbi Eli highlighted the contrast between us, the students, and himself, the elderly man: "You are sixteen, seventeen. I'm more than seventy years older than you. Take an example from me. My eyesight is not what it used to be, nor is my ability to walk.

---

1. He was also one of the outstanding students of Rabbi Shimon Shkop, dean of the Grodno Yeshiva in Lithuania, and taught according to Rabbi Shkop's method.
2. He taught according to the method of Rabbi Baruch Ber Leibowitz of Kamenitz, which was similar to that of the Brisk and Volozhin yeshivas, where everything is analyzed from two sides. For example, the teacher might comment that "next week we read *Megillat Esther*, in the evening and in the morning. Is there one mitzvah to read it twice, or two different *mitzvot*? Each time, we recite the blessing. If someone becomes a convert on Purim morning, he is obligated on that morning, because it is two separate *mitzvot*." This method, which is characteristic of Lithuanian yeshivas, involves a particularly thorough investigation of the matter at hand.

In fact, nothing in my body is what it was, especially not my memory. Now's the time for you to grow in Torah, expand your knowledge, and absorb ever more. Take advantage of the present while your senses are sharp, your powers of analysis are focused, you have the ability to plumb the depths of each debate, and your memory retains information like a sealed box. For me, at my advanced age, that box is cracked and leaking all over.

"Remember what King Solomon said in his old age, when he wrote in Ecclesiastes: *Remember now your Creator in the days of your youth, while the evil days come not, nor the years draw nigh, when you will say, I have no pleasure in them*. What he calls 'evil days' are my days right now, the days of old age. Ecclesiastes continues, *In the day when the guards of the house will tremble*—the hands that guard my body, which is like my house, do tremble. *The sound of the grinding is diminished*—the mouth, which grinds my food and also makes sounds and speaks, is diminished, for it has lost its power. *The gazers through windows are dimmed*—those are my eyes, which are losing their sight. *And the powerful men will stoop*—those are my two legs, which carry the entire house. They are already so bent . . ." In a voice shaking with conviction, he decreed, "This is your time. Later you'll be sorry. If you waste this time, squandering it in worthless pursuits, in the end you'll reach my age—and I hope you will reach my age—with the feeling that you have missed out, with bitter disappointment. That is why every morning we pray, *so that we do not struggle in vain or increase confusion in the world*."

Rabbi Eli often expressed his wish that we grow to be *well on in years*. He said this was an expression the Bible applies to two individuals: Abraham and King David. It's clear why the Bible uses this description for Abraham, who reached the age of 175, but why does it also apply it to King David, who was only seventy when he died? This teaches us that the expression applies to special individuals. When they present themselves before their Creator on Judgment Day, they bring with them their entire lives, without one day lost or wasted. They were active each and every day of their lives, expanding their knowledge, serving the public, and helping others. They made the most of each moment. "Be 'well on in years,'" Rabbi Eli exhorted us from the vantage point of his advanced age, and we devoured every word of his admonishment and moral lesson.

Rabbi Eli had already lost vision in one eye, and, in time, his other eye also deteriorated. One day, he went to get an operation on this eye at the clinic of Professor Avraham Ticho, a respected ophthalmologist. When I arrived at the clinic that night, Rabbi Eli was lying in bed, his entire head wrapped in a bandage. Although he was in terrible pain, he behaved with powerful self-discipline. "Israel Meir, is that you?"

"Yes," I answered.

"I have a prayer book in the drawer here," he said. "I haven't recited the evening service yet, but it's late already. I never say the prayers by heart—I always read from the prayer book. Say the words along with me, so that I can concentrate and pray with full intent," he requested.

I knew that he had been praying his entire life, and that he must know every letter of every word by heart. But I opened the drawer and pulled out the prayer book, and he repeated each word after me. When we reached the phrase *Forgive us, our Father, for we have erred; pardon us, our King, for we have willfully sinned*, the rabbi could not go on, and he burst into tears. The nurse in charge of him began to shout: "Rabbi Lapian, you must not cry! The tears will prevent the incision from healing. Moisture dissolves the ointments."

The rabbi bit his lip, making a great effort to control himself and follow the doctor's orders, then continued his prayers. Afterward, he called to the nurse and asked her what time it was—it was 2:20 in the morning. The rabbi then asked the nurse if she had a husband and children. "Two children," she answered.

"I understand that you're supposed to take care of me, that's your job. But Yisroel Mayer is here beside me," he said, pronouncing my first name with a Yiddish lilt. "You go home and be with your children, make sure everything's all right. You don't have to be here with me at such a late hour. I'll be fine. Yisroel Mayer will take care of me."

Charmed, the nurse smiled, but since she knew Rabbi Eli could not see her expression, she replied, "It's my duty to be here. But I am very grateful to you." Fifteen minutes later, he called to her again: "Nurse, are you still here? I understand that you're not supposed to leave. My wife, Hannah, gave me some cookies when we were on our way to Jerusalem. Inside the drawer is a brown paper package with some cookies wrapped inside. Take it," he said, his voice full of concern and gratitude. For me, that was a very special night spent with a person of rare character who, even in a time of physical torment, did not lose one iota of his keen sensitivity to others.

That year, 1953—a leap year, according to the Hebrew calendar—I left the yeshiva only on two occasions during the six months from October to April. The first was to attend the funeral of the Chazon Ish in Bnei Brak; the second was to accompany Rabbi Eli when he eulogized two major rabbis who died around the same time—the Chazon Ish and Rabbi Isser Zalman Meltzer, head of the Etz Chayim Yeshiva in Jerusalem.

Torah was my entire world; I focused on my studies wholeheartedly. When we learned *Baba Metzia*, I studied it most of the day and far into the night, poring over 120 folios, including the commentaries, and learning many of them by heart. In the daily in-depth class, during which we applied sophisticated analysis, we reached only the tenth or eleventh folio. But in the afternoons and nights, I went over the entire tractate, completing it nine times.

The yeshiva world at the beginning of the 1950s was in the depths of penury. There was no money to support the students, and no buildings in which to house them. Classes in the Be'er Ya'akov and Zichron Ya'akov yeshivas were held in local synagogues, and in disgraceful conditions. Our dining room, located in a narrow, abandoned Arab house, had no running water. Outside, the cook placed a tub of water and next to it, a mug for ritual hand washing. I recall the *rosh yeshiva* standing in the kitchen one day, his long suit jacket removed, his shirtsleeves rolled up, a kitchen towel tied around his waist.

Why? The cook had not received her salary for two months and went on strike. Rabbi Noah, preferring not to involve the yeshiva students, took her place in the kitchen. He washed vegetables, sliced bread, peeled cucumbers, cut tomatoes, and chopped onions until he had prepared a proper supper and salad for thirty-seven hungry students.

Rabbi Noah, a dedicated scholar, was also an incomparably devoted father figure to his students, a combination that made him greatly cherished. More than once, he returned dispirited from a trip to Jerusalem, where he exhausted himself in a trying day of pounding on the doors of the Ministry of Religious Affairs, hoping to enlist support. But when he entered the yeshiva hall, he threw his hat down on the chair and sat there in his pointed *kippah*, wiping sweat from his brow and delving into study—until his face brightened. He began to explain one question, then another, shedding new light on the text and glowing with delight, as did the yeshiva students when he finally clarified it with and for them. He lived for the students; they were his "sons" and close friends. Despite its pitiable physical conditions, the yeshiva was well endowed spiritually. Rabbi Noah lived and breathed teaching, education, and the Torah.

THE SUDDEN DEATH OF RABBI NOAH left a void in my heart and deep sorrow in my soul, even though it occurred after I had already left the yeshiva. He was a Holocaust refugee, diligent and industrious, who had founded the yeshiva and built it with his own two hands. After grueling years of troubles in Zichron Ya'akov, he invested additional years in establishing a permanent home for the yeshiva in Kfar Chassidim, devoting personal attention to every detail for the sake of its students, his only children. He collapsed and died on the very day for which a celebration had been planned to thank God for the completion of the building. Instead of coming to the opening of classes in the new location, the students came to his funeral.

Once, Rabbi Noah told me how everything started, and I still remember the story well. In 1951, he joined his friend Rabbi Moshe Shmuel Shapira, also a graduate of some of the top Lithuanian yeshivas, and they went to Bnei Brak to visit the Chazon Ish, the unofficial religious leader at that time. They asked for his advice and blessing for their plan to establish a yeshiva for youths ages sixteen and seventeen that would equal the level of a *yeshiva gedolah*, a postsecondary school, for advanced students. They wanted to offer the boys a framework for continuing their studies after spending the usual three years in a *yeshiva ketana*, a high school or secondary school, after their bar mitzvahs.

The Chazon Ish replied that their energy would be wasted if both rabbis worked in the same location. "Each one of you can bear this burden alone," he said, and advised each of them to found a separate yeshiva. They accepted his advice without question, not daring to argue with the Chazon Ish. One went to Be'er Ya'akov, the other to Zichron Ya'akov.

At the beginning, students unsure about the level of study and the deplorable physical conditions were apprehensive about joining the new yeshiva in Zichron. Rabbi Noah went back to the Chazon Ish, asking permission to close it and return to Jerusalem. Discouraged, he admitted, "I am not successful. The boys come, they enjoy listening to my classes, but they don't stay with me. They go back to their yeshivas in Jerusalem, Bnei Brak, or Petach Tikva."

In answer to his grievance, the Chazon Ish told him about a rabbi in Jerusalem named Rabbi Lapian, who was a senior leader of the Mussar movement; the Chazon Ish advised Rabbi Noah to visit Rabbi Eliyahu Lapian and convince him to join the yeshiva. He gave Rabbi Noah the sage's address, telling him to say that he was sent by the Chazon Ish, who requested that Rabbi Lapian join the yeshiva in Zichron as the *mashgiach ruchani*, the spiritual supervisor.

Rabbi Noah followed this directive, but Rabbi Lapian refused to accept the offer: "After the Holocaust, after leaving Lithuania," he said, "I studied in London for many years. Now, at almost ninety years old, I have fulfilled my vow to make aliya to Jerusalem and study the order of *Kodshim* of the Mishnah and Talmud, which details the laws of the Temple and the priestly service. I refuse to leave Jerusalem. I must continue my studies. Otherwise, when the Messiah comes and rebuilds the Temple, people will ask me halachic questions and I won't know the answers. That is why I took it upon myself to study this particular order," he explained.

Rabbi Noah returned to the Chazon Ish in Bnei Brak and informed him of Rabbi Lapian's answer. The Chazon Ish did not give up: he sent a letter to Rabbi Lapian, who finally agreed to come to Zichron Ya'akov. He became the magnet of the new yeshiva. Youths, particularly from Kfar Ha-Ro'eh and Midrashiyat Noam, religious-Zionist yeshiva high schools near Zichron, began to come to Knesses Chizkiyahu, where they were captivated by Rabbi Eli's personality and erudition. He was known for his comprehensive knowledge of Talmud as well as his lectures on ethics.

At Etz Chayim Yeshiva in London, he had not served as a *mashgiach* but filled the more senior position of *rosh yeshiva*.

In February 1954, when Rabbi Eliyahu Mishkovsky fell ill and could no longer make the daily trip to Zichron, Rabbi Eli took his place. Because his eyesight was very weak by then, he taught from memory a daily in-depth class on "Hamekabel" and "Hashoel," chapters dealing with financial matters in tractate *Baba Metzia,* along with commentaries of the early and later authorities. In addition, his Mussar approach stressed practical education, beyond theoretical study: *Not study but practice is the main thing.*

He required the yeshiva students to make a point of performing at least three altruistic acts of *chessed* (loving-kindness) daily, such as helping another student who was having difficulty with a complicated Tosafot commentary in the Talmud or with the daily classes. I could not fall asleep at night until I had performed my three charitable deeds for that day. If night fell and I had not yet filled my quota, I would bend down at the tub outside the dining room and fill the washing cup with water so that the person who came after me would have water to perform the ritual hand washing.

Rabbi Eli also set other guidelines for us. Each student had a small notebook in which we wrote down the rules that the rabbi outlined in his weekly lecture. One rule was that before we went to sleep, we should place a piece of paper on top of the Tosafot commentary for the page of Talmud we were studying, then carefully slide the paper downward in order to read the next problem posed by the Tosafot, which always began, "And if you say." When we would reach the words "Then you must say," signifying the beginning of the answer to the problem, we had to close the book, and before falling asleep, think it over and try to find the answer to the problem the commentators raised. This brilliant idea meant that we yeshiva boys would fall asleep mulling over the challenge of the problem, trying to find an answer. With this method, we sharpened our brains, and in addition, we developed an unofficial competition as to who could find the answer without peeking at the commentary. Every night, I fell asleep thinking about a different problem, and looked forward to going in the next day and seeing whether my solutions were correct.

Later, I also became aware of the larger educational goal of Rabbi Eli's method of study: to occupy the mind of a seventeen-year-old boy with Talmudic issues instead of various other distractions. In fact, we were aware of almost nothing else apart from our studies. If there is a way to embody the concept "his profession is Torah study," it was our way of life at the Zichron Ya'akov yeshiva. We never saw newspapers; we were almost completely removed from secular matters. We would find out what was happening in Israel and in the world while on our way to the synagogue to pray.

Another rule that Rabbi Eli established was that at least once a week, usually on Shabbat, we would abstain from talking about other people. For one day, we erased from our vocabulary such seemingly innocuous phrases such as "he said" and "he did" in order to excise from our speech all praise, slander, and gossip, even though it might not be hurtful or defaming. Performing charitable deeds, pursuing diligence in studies, analyzing texts, guarding speech—these were all part of his method for sculpting the character of the yeshiva youths.

WHEN RABBI NOAH DIED SO SUDDENLY, at only forty-five, Rabbi Eli gave an unforgettable eulogy in the yeshiva's new hall at Kfar Chassidim. Rabbi Eli addressed him as a father addresses his son:

> *Rabbi Noah, ask me to bear witness for you in the Heavenly court, and I will bear witness for you. All the sacred books, both hidden and revealed, say that the Heavenly court asks several questions. The first question is: Did you set aside time for Torah study? Call me as a witness, and I will tell the Heavenly court of your diligence throughout the day and night, and that you did not waste one moment away from study.*

In loving tones, Rabbi Eli described Rabbi Noah's assiduousness, then continued:

> *They ask a second question there: Were you honest in your business dealings? The entire yeshiva was on your shoulders—from contractors and tradesmen to kitchen workers and the janitor. But you treated each one with your usual integrity and honesty.*

Rabbi Eli then addressed us:

I want to say something to the yeshiva students, both past and present. Rabbi Noah did not have children—you were his children. Stay here until the end of the seven-day shiva *mourning period. Not one of you should leave the yeshiva. We are going to bury Rabbi Noah in the ground of Eretz Israel, which was so dear to him, and when we return, we'll sit* shiva *and study round-the-clock, as far as we are able. Every page, every folio, every section, and every verse that you study will contribute to the ascent of his soul on High, for your ability to learn has been acquired thanks to his efforts.*

That day at the yeshiva, tefillin became the item most in demand. People had come to the funeral from out of town with the intention of returning immediately to their homes, and therefore the men who had come from Jerusalem, including me, had not brought tefillin to wear during the morning prayers. But Rabbi Eli had prevailed upon us all to stay for the week-long *shiva*. Like me, many students had not come equipped for a seven-day stay, but we all obeyed his request, and took turns with whatever tefillin were available. Emotions ran high during our studies, since we knew that every word we learned was for the spiritual exaltation of Rabbi Noah's soul. In front of us, Rabbi Eli leaned on his lectern and studied with unusual fervor, an inspiration to us all.

CHAPTER 10

TORAH FOUNDATIONS

Three who eat at one table and do not speak words of Torah, it is as if they have eaten of idolatrous sacrifices.

ETHICS OF THE FATHERS 3:3

AFTER MY "YEAR ABROAD" at the Zichron Ya'akov yeshiva, I returned to Kol Torah with four years of intensive yeshiva studies under my belt. I felt that I had become stronger and more mature during my year in Zichron, and going back to Kol Torah felt like going home.

I returned to the class of the scholar Rabbi Shlomo Zalman Auerbach. At an early age, he had become known throughout Jerusalem for his superior intellect. When he was only eighteen, he authored his first book, *Me'orei Esh* (*Lights of Fire*), on halachic problems of electricity and electrical engineering, particularly on Shabbat and holidays. It was a comprehensive study, written by a young man who had never attended a secular or trade school. Rather, he went first to the *cheder* (religious elementary-middle school) for young boys that was part of Etz Chayim Yeshiva in Jerusalem, and then to Etz Chayim Yeshiva itself. He was the outstanding disciple of Rabbi Isser Zalman Meltzer, the elder statesman of the yeshiva world. To investigate the field of electronics, which he knew nothing about, young Shlomo Zalman took private lessons in physics and electricity from an electrical engineer.

At age thirty-four, Rabbi Shlomo Zalman published *Ma'adanei Eretz* (*Delights of the Land*), a commentary on the laws of the sabbatical year, particularly the intricate halacha on first fruits, tithes, and reserving certain parts of the harvest for the poor. To create this work, he needed to study botany and agriculture (including crop varieties), as well as ripening processes.

Despite his superior knowledge, he was exceptionally modest. To his dying day, Rabbi Shlomo Zalman lived in a two-room apartment, where he raised his ten children. He dedicated his entire life to Torah study and taught at Kol Torah Yeshiva for forty-five years; being a teacher was his greatest source of pride. In his will, he stated that although there were many who relied on his halachic authority, standard laudatory titles such as *gaon* (genius scholar), *posek hador* (greatest halachic authority of the generation), or *amud horaah* (the pillar of knowledge) should not appear on his tombstone. The one sentence he allowed was: "Disseminated Torah at Kol Torah Yeshiva in Jerusalem."

Rabbi Shlomo Zalman was a rare breed, the object of admiration throughout the observant Jewish world. Secular Israelis first heard of him during his funeral, when three hundred thousand men from all points on the religious spectrum joined the procession behind his casket. He loathed politics and stayed away from partisan issues.

When I first arrived at the yeshiva, I was deeply impressed by him. Then, when I returned after my year away, the yeshiva appointed me to transcribe his class, since tape recorders were not yet available. Rabbi Shlomo Zalman taught a class at six p.m. every Wednesday. He would summarize the topic we were studying that week and would include his own interpretation. After studying a particular section of Talmud and all the related commentaries, we had to define the edges of the virtual building that we had constructed, then hollow out its foundations, and fill it with light. Rabbi Shlomo Zalman's general class was intended to clarify and illuminate the issues through his eyes, according to the way he saw them, without unnecessary, long-winded debates of the type he eschewed.

He would sit at a wooden lectern with the open volume of the Talmud in front of him and would begin to discuss the problem at hand. He always spoke smoothly, without referring to notes—in that way he could make eye contact with the students. In my role as transcriber, I recorded his every word. In a neat handwriting, I wrote quickly to keep up with his pace. After supper, at night, I would transfer my transcript onto a new page in a separate notebook. After services on Thursday mornings, I would give him the notebook with the transcript of the class from the night before. A few days later, he would return the notebook to me with his comments, notes, and corrections. Then I would give the notebook to Mordechai "Miro" Wermesser, who lived on Hillel Street in Jerusalem and had a typewriter. Miro knew how to type by touch, and he would prepare twenty copies of the transcript using carbon paper, always giving the first copy to the rabbi and the second one to me.

One day, I recorded in my notebook "He questioned the Chazon Ish," meaning that Rabbi Shlomo Zalman had posed a problem regarding an interpretation given by the Chazon Ish. The rabbi erased "questioned" and changed it to an acronym in Hebrew. I was not sure why he did this, and asked him what it meant. He answered me with another question: "Can I question the Chazon Ish? I am dust under his feet. The acronym means 'needs study'; in other words, one needs to study the Chazon Ish. Who can question him? If you do not understand him, then you need to study his writings in order to do so."

After the class, I would often accompany the rabbi from the yeshiva back to his home. Sometimes we walked in silence, other times we talked. In one of those conversations, he told me that my uncle from Kiryat Motzkin, Rabbi Vogelman, had visited him. "He is a special man," said Rabbi Shlomo Zalman. "He loves you like a son, and he would like you to pass the matriculation exams [secular graduation tests] to ease your path in the future. He thinks this will help you get along later in life. He knows that in our yeshiva, we study only Jewish subjects, not secular ones. But because of your unique situation, and also in order to please him, I acceded to his request. He is a great Torah scholar, and this is his worldview. If at night, after the yeshiva classes, you can study on your own for the matriculation exams—and you are talented—then go ahead and learn."

In order to prepare for the matriculation exams, I thought I should first take the standard preliminary exams. The rabbi asked what subjects were covered. Physics, chemistry, biology, and geography, I replied, but I explained that I was not gifted in science and much preferred the humanities. His mouth gaping in astonishment, he asked how it was possible not to like physics, since this was the science that dealt with the creation of the world; this was the greatness of the Creator as well as the greatness of Creation.

He continued in excitement: "I take the number five bus along with students on their way to the university. If I'm lucky, they make room for me. In the morning, the bus is jam-packed, but they see my white hair and so they offer me a seat. I listen to them talking in the aisle, exchanging information before a class or a test. If I hear someone talking about physics, electricity, water, or climatology, I listen carefully in the hopes of picking up something new, an interesting idea. Remember what it says in Isaiah, chapter 40: *Lift up your eyes on high, and behold Who has created these things*! How can you not like physics?" he exclaimed.

One day in 1954, while I was walking with Rabbi Shlomo Zalman from the yeshiva to his house, he abruptly stopped—and lighted my way in life, giving direction to my future. He told me at length what he had heard from Rabbi Kundstadt, Rabbi Reiner, and Ze'ev Lang, administrative director of the yeshiva, about the exceptional speeches my father used to deliver. On the basis of what he had heard from others, Rabbi Shlomo Zalman praised my father's remarkable rhetorical skill. Stories began to pour from him. "I heard," he recounted, "that your father once came to Frankfurt to speak about *yiddishkeit* [Judaism]." Then Rabbi Shlomo Zalman continued:

> *Suddenly at midnight, after speaking for an hour, there was a power failure. Hundreds of Jews, mostly from Germany, were packed inside the Frankfurt synagogue. Your father worried that the crowd might try to push its way outside in the pitch darkness, provoking a riot. He switched to Yiddish, since many of the Jews present were originally from Eastern Europe, and this language allowed him to be more dramatic in his oratory. "Jews," he announced, "it is now midnight, time for the midnight prayer service, in which we recall Jeremiah's description of Rachel weeping for her children. You know of her tomb in Bethlehem. That is* Mame Ruchel, *our foremother Rachel, weeping for the Diaspora and awaiting the day when her children will return to their borders." Your father went on to describe Rachel and her tomb*

as if he were standing before it, seeing it with his own eyes. For twenty
minutes, he held the attention of the huge crowd, until the electricity
was restored and the lights went back on in the hall. Then he returned
to his lecture and spoke for another ten minutes.

At seventeen, I did not exactly understand why the rabbi was telling
me this story on an ordinary day after class, during an ordinary walk. But
because he had heard of my father and respected him, I asked the rabbi to
allow me to tell a story I had heard from Naphtali:

In 1949, my brother Naphtali went to Warsaw to arrange aliya for
youths. He carried with him a letter from Shaul Avigor, director of
the Second Aliya Organization, to the Israeli envoy in Warsaw, Israel
Barzilai [formerly called Yulek Eisenberg, and later minister of health,
representing Mapam]. Naphtali needed the support of the envoys
in order to perform his job. He came to Barzilai with the letter and
introduced himself. "You're a Lau?" asked the envoy. "I once knew
a Rabbi Lau, whom I will never forget." Naphtali said nothing, and
Barzilai continued: "He once prevented me from fulfilling a mission. It
happened in the town of Włocławek, Poland, where they were holding
elections for town rabbi. Our Hashomer Hatza'ir group objected to one
of the Agudath Israel candidates. We preferred the Mizrachi candidate
as the lesser of two evils. The day before the elections, the Agudath
representative brought in a speaker who people said was the number
one orator in all of Poland, the very best out of three and a half million
Jews. This was Rabbi Lau from Piotrków. Our Hashomer Hatza'ir
group knew that Rabbi Lau's speaking ability gave him powerful
influence over people. We decided to sabotage his speech. I was
supposed to get there early and grab a place in one of the front rows.
My companions spread themselves around the auditorium, and one
was supposed to stand next to the electricity box at the hall entrance.
The plan was that after Rabbi Lau had said three or four sentences, I
would raise my hand in a signal to my friends around the hall, and we
would begin to heckle and disturb the crowd, interrupting the rabbi's
speech. The guy next to the electricity box was supposed to pull down
the switch and cause an electricity outage, inciting the crowd to panic
and flee the hall." The rabbi began to speak, and he was fascinating. I
was so charmed by his rhetoric that I completely forgot my reason for

*coming to the hall. I did not raise my hand to signal to the others, so
my friends did not interrupt the gathering. The Agudath candidate was
elected, and our candidate lost." When Barzilai finished his story, he
and Naphtali were silent for a minute, and then Naphtali revealed that
Rabbi Lau of Piotrków was his father.*

In his mellifluous voice, Rabbi Shlomo Zalman said, "Israel Meir, listen.
Whenever there is an event that mandates the recitation of Psalms—after
an Arab terrorist attack, or when someone is very sick—and we ask you
to go up to the ark in the synagogue and recite Psalms, we all recite after
you, verse by verse, and I am filled with inspiration. And I know all those
verses by heart! Something about your manner of delivery captivates your
audience. You recall the story in 1 Kings, when Elijah the Prophet rebukes
King Ahab for his involvement in murdering Naboth the Jezreelite and
stealing his vineyard? Elijah says, *Will you murder and also inherit?*"

I answered that I did recall the story, but did not understand the connection. The rabbi continued, "What happens to Elijah is clear, and what
happens to Ahab is clear, but the question is, why did all this happen to
Naboth? He has a vineyard in the Jezreel Valley that the king desires, but
he refuses to sell it, because it is the heritage of his ancestors. *Far be it from
me before the Lord that I should give you my ancestors' heritage*, Naboth protests. Why was he punished? Why was he condemned to death?"

In explanation, the rabbi told me a *midrash* about Naboth's punishment:

*God endowed Naboth with the most beautiful singing voice of his
generation. Three times a year, when the Israelites would make their
pilgrimage to Jerusalem, Naboth would sing on the Temple Mount,
and all the pilgrims enjoyed the beauty of his song. Then one day, pride
went to his head; he was swayed by the admiration of the crowds. The
next time he went to Jerusalem, he refused to sing until the people
begged and pleaded with him. He agreed only after the entreaties of
ministers and leaders, and finally he stopped singing altogether. Said
the Holy One, blessed be He, to Naboth, "You had a role in this world,
and it was to bring joy to other living creatures. I gave you that talent.
I placed this melodious bell in your throat, so that you would ring it*

*and your voice would carry afar. But you are withholding from my
creatures what they deserve to enjoy, not what you deserve to have.
Do not withhold a good thing from its proper owner. I am bringing
you back to me, because you have no more goal in life. You have not
fulfilled the mission for which I designated you."*

"Israel Meir," Rabbi Shlomo Zalman continued after a short pause,
"God gave you the power of speech. You have a mission in life—you take
after your father. We must not spurn God's gifts; we should not turn our
backs on Him. I don't know whether this is what grabbed you by the
hair and pulled you out of the piles of ashes in Europe. I won't try to
understand the reckoning of the Master of the Universe. But one thing
is clear to me: you must dedicate yourself to your studies, learning more
and more, so that when the time comes, you will ring this bell and make
it heard afar."

This was one of the most important conversations of my life. At every
moment of my life since then, it has shaped and influenced me.

EVEN AFTER I LEFT KOL TORAH and switched to Ponevezh Yeshiva in
Bnei Brak, I remained very close to Rabbi Shlomo Zalman. Before Rosh
Hashanah, I would go to Jerusalem to receive his blessing, as well as that
of the other rabbis of Kol Torah, to whom I was greatly indebted.

When I had been studying for two years at Ponevezh and was no
longer Rabbi Shlomo Zalman's student, one day I went to his home as
usual, to receive his blessing. We spoke in his tiny library, and afterward,
as I walked down the smooth stone stairway with the iron railing, I heard
him call out to me from above: "Israel Meir!" I tilted my head backward,
and saw him standing at the top of the stairway, signaling for me to come
back upstairs. I complied, and when we went back into his room, he said,
"Look, you have neither father nor mother. You have the potential for a
very great future, but you have no one to support you. I want to give you
a letter. I don't know if it will be worth anything in the future, for I am
just a teacher at Kol Torah. There are lots of *rosh yeshivas* and rabbis who
are more important than I am, but it can't hurt. Allow me to write you
a letter. Not now, I don't want to detain you. Just tell me where I should

send it." I was astonished. After regaining my composure, I asked him to send it to the Ponevezh Yeshiva in Bnei Brak. Within the week, I received a letter from Rabbi Shlomo Zalman, in his handwriting, written on his personal stationery:

> *Rabbi Shlomo Zalman Auerbach*
> *The holy city of Jerusalem, may it be rebuilt and reestablished speedily and in our day, Amen.*
> *With the help of God*
> *Elul 5718 (August 1958)*
>
> *It is my great pleasure to know "in a place where he is unknown" my dear and esteemed student, who excels in Torah knowledge and fear of Heaven, Mr. Israel Meir Lau, may he live a long life. For many years Mr. Lau studied with me at Kol Torah Yeshiva in the holy city of Jerusalem, may it be rebuilt and reestablished, and to our pleasure, he was successful and excelled in his studies. In addition, God has graced him with pleasant manners and noble virtues, and the precious quality of "influencing souls." He has the special ability to inspire young students with his wisdom and spirit, to teach Torah and fear of Heaven, and to implant in them the love of learning and of God. Thus may it please the rosh yeshivas and those responsible for instruction to encourage and support him. I am certain that you will be satisfied, for he is meant for greatness, and a promising future awaits him. I pray that God will help him and increase his knowledge, so that he will continue to advance in sacred virtues, and succeed in everything he does, and may God be with him.*
>
> *Signed:*
> *Shlomo Zalman Auerbach*

There are no words to describe the intense feelings of appreciation and amazement that overcame me when I first read this letter; every time I reread it, I am once again overcome, and moved to tears.

RABBI SHLOMO ZALMAN'S FATHER, Rabbi Chaim Yehuda Leib Auerbach, was *rosh yeshiva* of the kabbalist yeshiva Sha'ar Shamayim. When his father fell ill, the family invited a few students who were close to Rabbi Shlomo Zalman to form a prayer quorum to recite Psalms at his father's bedside. I entered the room with trepidation. Although in childhood I had seen countless corpses, the sight in this Jerusalem room was completely different. This was a man I had known, the father of my beloved rabbi; the knowledge that Rabbi Shlomo Zalman was about to lose a parent permeated the atmosphere. I felt it strange to think that I had been orphaned at age five, whereas my rabbi was losing his father at age forty-eight.

Rabbi Chaim Yehuda Leib, a very handsome man with a white beard covering his chin, lay in bed as if asleep. Next to his bed sat Rabbi Shlomo Zalman, his back to me. His right hand grasped his father's hand, while his left hand held an open book of Psalms. He recited them in a whisper, swaying back and forth, tears flowing onto the pages of the book. We all cried along with him. In the back corner of the room, his brother-in-law, Rabbi Shalom Mordechai Ha-Cohen Shwadron, known as the Jerusalem *maggid*—a powerful speaker, storyteller, and ethicist—stood facing the wall, reciting Psalms.

For a whole hour, we did so too, our eyes cast downward, the room silent. Suddenly, I noticed that Rabbi Shlomo Zalman made a tiny movement. He felt that his father's hand had gone limp. Cautiously and gently, as one should behave with a dying person, he removed his hand from his father's grasp. He stood up, went to the corner of the room, and tapped lightly on his brother-in-law's shoulder. Rabbi Schwadron turned around. His eyes were red and swollen with tears, and his long white beard was soaking wet.

Rabbi Shlomo Zalman did not say a word. With his empty hand, he gestured to his father, and with his other hand, the one holding the Psalms, he pointed to the door. Rabbi Schwadron was a *kohen*, a member of the priestly family descended from the biblical Aaron, and Jewish law forbids a *kohen* to be in the same room as a dead person. Rabbi Shlomo Zalman had sensed that his father was about to depart from this world. Following the biblical precept *Do not place a stumbling block before the blind*, he was informing his brother-in-law so that the *kohen* would not transgress this prohibition. Rabbi Shlomo Zalman returned to his father's bedside while Rabbi Schwadron stood in the doorway, taking a last look at his father-in-law.

I remember Rabbi Shlomo Zalman's powerful self-control at this difficult moment, and that he did not take his father's hand again, since it was forbidden to touch it or do anything else that might hasten the man's death. The sick father made a weak movement with his hand, as if to say to his son and son-in-law that everything would be all right, that he was going to a better world and they should not worry.

I remained in contact with Rabbi Shlomo Zalman throughout his life, and still remember clearly everything he ever said to me; I also shared with him every major halachic question that I confronted. He was my teacher and rabbi in my private life as well, and he attended all our family events. He never owned a car; if he did not have access to one, he would take the bus. When my eldest son, Rabbi Moshe Chaim, got married, Rabbi Shlomo Zalman traveled especially from Jerusalem to participate in the wedding ceremony. He came to the wedding hall in Bnei Brak and stood at the *chuppah*—which was outside, as is traditional—in the pouring rain. I stood facing him, holding a lamp, and watched the emotion on his face.

On another occasion, my son Rabbi David Baruch was about to get married to Tzipi, daughter of Rabbi Yitzchak Ralbag, head of the religious council of Jerusalem. After we set the date of the wedding, to be held in the Great Synagogue of Jerusalem, Rabbi Ralbag, my son—the groom—and I went to Rabbi Shlomo Zalman's house to invite him to perform the wedding ceremony. He blessed us warmly, as usual, and agreed to perform the ceremony. But an hour later, I received a message that he was looking for me urgently. When I called him, he apologized deeply, and said he had forgotten for the moment that Jerusalem had a chief rabbi, Rabbi Yitzchak Kolitz, and that the honor should be his. "I will come to the *chuppah*," Rabbi Auerbach promised, "but the rabbi of the city must perform the ceremony." That was the man—great, yet humble.

During the Gulf War in 1991, I went to Jerusalem with my youngest son, Zvi Yehuda, to invite Rabbi Shlomo Zalman to Zvi's bar mitzvah celebration. We entered the impressive library in the rabbi's modest home and he apologized, saying that he would not be able to attend the bar mitzvah—not because of the war, but because of his deteriorating health. After making his apologies, the eighty-one-year-old rabbi turned to my son, whom he had never met before, and asked, "Zvikaleh, will you be giving a sermon at your bar mitzvah?" My son answered yes, and the rabbi continued, "You won't be angry at me if I don't come to your bar mitzvah, right? But would you be willing to let me hear your sermon, so that I won't miss a chance to hear a Torah lesson?"

The boy looked at the rabbi, and in a self-confident voice, gave his agreement. The rabbi asked if he knew his sermon by heart, and the boy confirmed that he did. He stood in that little room before one of the most esteemed rabbis of his generation, and delivered his speech from start to finish. His head on his hand, Rabbi Shlomo Zalman listened to a thirteen-year-old boy with rare concentration and warmth.

When Rabbi Shlomo Zalman died, I followed the tradition of tearing my clothing, as a son would do for his father. He was the only person for whom I have ever done so. Someone saw me and, noticing my torn suit, asked in a worried voice what had happened. I answered that I had not had the opportunity to tear my clothing for my biological father. Because Rabbi Shlomo Zalman was my spiritual father, I was tearing my clothes for him.

Hundreds of thousands of followers wept at his funeral. His brother read his will, in which he made the following request: "I do not want to be a burden on my children. I pray to the Holy One, blessed be He, that He will maintain my mental function, and that I will remain lucid until the day the command comes and He calls me to my place on High. If you see that I have trouble functioning and acting normally, do not bother yourselves for me, but put me in an old-age home, so that I will not burden my children."

Rabbi Auerbach remains an example to me. I think about him often, missing him as a scholar, educator, and, mainly, as a person. Even now, years after his death, his spirit remains close to my heart, and his absence has left a void that cannot be filled.

AFTER FINISHING MY STUDIES AT KOL TORAH, I went to Ponevezh, the yeshiva of Rabbi Yosef Kahaneman and the most well known of the Lithuanian-style yeshivas, the jewel in the crown. Its rabbi was one of the leaders of religious Jewry during the Holocaust and afterward. The yeshiva was located in a massive building, and a verse from the prophet

Obadiah was inscribed over its entrance: *But upon Mount Zion shall be deliverance, and there shall be holiness*. This obscure verse is unusual for an inscription on a Jewish building, as opposed to the more common *How goodly are your tents, O Jacob*, or *This is the gate of the Lord, the righteous will enter it*. I noticed this curious verse right away, and wondered why Rabbi Kahaneman, founder of the yeshiva, had chosen it.

Rabbi Kahaneman was a recognized figure within the outstanding community of Lithuanian Jewry, which was almost entirely wiped out during the Holocaust. He had a reputation as a genius Torah scholar, a witty speaker, and a commemorator of the Holocaust. He established Ohel Kedoshim (Pavilion of the Martyrs), a memorial to Lithuanian Jewry, in his city, Bnei Brak.

When Rabbi Kahaneman arrived in Eretz Israel in the mid-1940s, he gathered a group of leaders from Tel Aviv and delivered a personal speech. "I come from hell," he began.

> *In my mind, I carry the image of three hundred Lithuanian rabbis gathered at a convention held about seven years ago. Out of those three hundred rabbis, young and old, the only one still alive is I, standing here and speaking to you today. I established a memorial in Bnei Brak called Ohel Kedoshim. But I do not want to found any more memorials to martyrs. I want to provide a home for the children of the Youth Aliya, the Tehran Children, and all the other homeless children now arriving in Eretz Israel. I ask each of you to adopt a child and act as his or her father. I will establish a home for them, but I do not want to call it a home for orphans. Rather, I will call it a home for fathers.*

Those assembled that day joined his cause with enthusiasm. Rabbi Kahaneman founded the "home for fathers" of children of the Holocaust, considering it his life's mission.

The next project that he undertook was establishing a yeshiva, which he named after his Lithuanian town of Ponevezh, and where he served as *rosh yeshiva*. Rabbi Kahaneman did not attempt to memorialize the entire six million Jews who died in the Holocaust, but focused on Lithuanian Jewry, including his own relatives and acquaintances. He did not name the yeshiva after himself, his father, or some wealthy donor, but after the community in which he had served as rabbi, which had been destroyed. He purchased from Rabbi Ya'akov Halperin seven *dunam* (about 1¾ acres) of land on a hill in the Zichron Meir neighborhood of Bnei Brak. This neighborhood bears the name of Rabbi Meir Shapira of Lublin, my father's cousin and friend.

On this land, in addition to a yeshiva for boys and the "home for fathers," Rabbi Kahaneman built a *yeshiva gedolah*, which became a model throughout the Jewish world. He was able to watch this institution, his life's mission, flourish to a peak enrollment of one thousand students and was single-handedly responsible for feeding and supporting them all; he dedicated his life to raising funds and providing for the students' daily needs.

He explained to us once that he chose to have the verse from the book of Obadiah engraved prominently on the front of the yeshiva building in memory of the victims of the Holocaust and in honor of life in Zion.

Rabbi Kahaneman had been a student of the Chafetz Chayim, who died in September 1933. Eight months prior, Hitler had become chancellor of Germany and had started implementing his plan to annihilate the Jewish people. Everyone was wondering what would happen next. The Chafetz Chayim, then in the last days of his life, was also troubled by events in Europe.

Rabbi Kahaneman was one of those who attended him while he was dying. But because he was a *kohen*, he had to leave the room just before the Chafetz Chayim passed away. The Chafetz Chayim's last sentence, at age ninety-six, was that verse from the book of Obadiah: *But upon Mount Zion shall be deliverance, and there shall be holiness*. Even in 1933, before the inferno had even begun, the Chafetz Chayim understood that the only place Jews could be safe was in Eretz Israel.

Rabbi Kahaneman left the room with that verse echoing in his mind. "That verse was like the dying will of my rabbi, the Chafetz Chayim. The Ponevezh Yeshiva in Bnei Brak is the fulfillment of the prophet's vision. Now the delivered are on Mount Zion." This is how he explained it to us, his students. In light of this verse, Rabbi Kahaneman's vision in founding Ponevezh Yeshiva became clear.

The rabbi of Ponevezh was known for his sharp wit. In the early 1950s, a wealthy American Jewish woman of Lithuanian origin was invited to a convention at which Rabbi Kahaneman spoke. She was impressed by his rhetorical skill, but maintained a negative view of religion and tradition. She promised Rabbi Kahaneman that she would give him a sizable donation to help establish his home for Holocaust orphans, but on one condition: the rabbi had to promise that in the building to which she was contributing, he would not teach any children "with *peyos*" (sidelocks). Rabbi Kahaneman gave her his word. With her money, he built two buildings on Bnei Brak land, known as the Los Angeles buildings, for the girls of the Youth Aliya.

DURING THE 1950s, Ponevezh was considered the foremost institution in the yeshiva world, in quality as well as in quantity of students. During those years, the student body numbered about one thousand. Of these, 350 were students in the *yeshiva gedolah*, and after passing a series of exams, I joined their ranks.

Rabbi Kahaneman was a first-rate educator. He lived with his wife in a room next to the main yeshiva building, and people would often ask whether the uproar of the students' debates bothered him. The rabbi always answered with a question. "Is a miller bothered by the noise of his mill? If the mill stopped working, he would worry so much he wouldn't sleep at night. It's the same with me. Should the lights ever go out here and the students stop studying, God forbid, I wouldn't sleep a wink," he explained. Indeed, in Ponevezh, the lights never went out. When the last students went to sleep, at two or three a.m., others would awaken in order to begin their first study session well before morning services.

The study method Rabbi Kahaneman established was unique and carefully structured. At the *yeshiva gedolah*, six rabbis taught three levels of classes. The three rabbis who taught the second and third levels were Rabbi Elazar Menachem Man Shach, Rabbi Dovid Povarsky of Mir, and Rabbi Shmuel Rosovsky of Grodno. All 350 students would stand while the teacher would offer interpretations of the material they had studied. In addition, Rabbi Kahaneman taught a class each Shabbat. Even at seventy-two and with only one kidney, he insisted on coming to the yeshiva daily, and he also made frequent fund-raising trips throughout the world. On his way back to Bnei Brak from the airport in the taxi—even if it were four a.m.—he would study the page of Talmud taught that day in the yeshiva. When he arrived at the yeshiva, he would give an expert class on that page, speaking extemporaneously and with his typical wit.

To fill the position of spiritual adviser of the yeshiva, Rabbi Kahaneman hired Rabbi Eliyahu Eliezer Dessler, a well-known Jewish philosopher from London and author of the three-volume work *Michtav Me-Eliyahu* (*Letter from Eliyahu*, later published in English as *Strive for Truth*). Rabbi Kahaneman's cohesive educational approach, the unique structure of Ponevezh Yeshiva, and its great teachers made it the flagship of the yeshiva world, the aspiration of every yeshiva student. Its students later became leading rabbis and *rosh yeshivas*. In the last fifty years, many pillars of the Torah world have come out of Ponevezh.

Rabbi Dovid Povarsky administered my entrance exams at his home, and I still remember the topic of the test—tractate *Beitzah*, on the laws of holidays. I quoted a new interpretation that he himself had written in his book *Yeshuat David*. Rabbi Povarsky was impressed, and said, "You bribed me—you cited my own interpretation. I don't know if any of the other students are familiar with my book." I told him that I had studied his interpretation at Kol Torah with Rabbi Shlomo Zalman Auerbach. Rabbi Povarsky smiled with satisfaction.

After the exam, he took me to Rabbi Kahaneman's room next to the main building and introduced me to him. Predictably, the rabbi asked my name. "Israel Meir Lau," I replied. Rabbi Kahaneman focused his gaze and asked if I was any relation of Rabbi Lau of Piotrków. When I said he was my father, Rabbi Kahaneman fell silent, then clasped my head with both hands and embraced me tightly to his chest. I remember that this happened after morning services, while he was still wearing his tallis and tefillin—he kept them on after services during a class he taught—and he began to weep. Rabbi Kahaneman was known for his emotional sensitivity, and I recall his tearful words: "I remember your father, whom I admired for his speaking ability. I heard him speak at the world convention of Agudath Israel in Vienna and Marienbad in 1937. As a speaker, he was unrivaled."

Rabbi Kahaneman invited me to dine with him on Shabbat evening. I, the new yeshiva student, one of 350, was invited to a meal with the revered *rosh yeshiva*—a rare compliment! When I came to his room on Shabbat Eve, he asked me if I knew how to sing Shabbat songs. I sang something that I knew; the rabbi enjoyed it and then asked if I could also give a Torah lesson. He suggested I say something from the weekly portion. Observant Jews try to mention words of Torah at every meal, following the saying in Ethics of the Fathers: *Should three eat at one table without speaking words of Torah, it is as if they have eaten of idolatrous sacrifices.*

I expounded on a certain idea, and Rabbi Kahaneman listened with interest. When I finished, he said he could detect a trace of my father's speaking ability. I could not expect a bigger compliment than this. After that Shabbat meal in his home, each time important donors from abroad came to visit—the ones he called the pillars of the yeshiva—the rabbi invited me to sit with them and give a short sermon.

I also remember Rabbi Kahaneman's behavior at the outbreak of the Sinai Campaign on October 29, 1956, when we heard on the radio that IDF tank forces had penetrated the Gaza Strip. The rabbi left his room, entered the yeshiva, and ascended the platform with its golden ark—a seventeenth-century ark originally housed in the main synagogue of Mantua, Italy, which had been disassembled and put into storage during the war. Artisans in Bnei Brak had reassembled this ark from thousands of pieces that were imported from Mantua, reconstructing the magnificent original. Rabbi Kahaneman stood before the impressive ark, and asked the yeshiva students to stop studying and to close their books. Then he announced in his unforgettable voice: "Our sons, our brothers, have gone out to war in order to defend us all. I ask you all to recite Psalms continuously until they return from the war. In this way, we will support the IDF's victory, and do our part for the war effort." The rabbi did not have to say another word. We were all part of the Israeli reality of that time.

Just a short time earlier, we had been shocked by a murder carried out in Kfar Chabad. Arab terrorists had thrown hand grenades into the synagogue during the evening service, killing Simcha Zilbershtrom and five of his students. Young Simcha had arrived in Haifa on the boat with me, and we later studied together at Kol Torah Yeshiva. His students were immigrant boys from North Africa. The six corpses lay on the floor of the synagogue, their blood-soaked prayer books open to the section of the evening service that begins, *Lay us down in peace*. From our point of view, the Sinai Campaign was revenge for their deaths. We followed the rabbi's instruction to read Psalms, especially chapter 144, which begins, *Blessed is the Lord, my Rock, who trains my hands for battle, my fingers for war*.

Rabbi Kahaneman was not involved in politics. He was a very religious person who was completely dedicated to the Torah way of life; but at the same time, he was a nationalist. Unfortunately, I spent only a short time with him, but I carry his memory close to my heart. Rabbi Kahaneman passed away in 1969, but his contribution to rebuilding the world of Torah, after the terrible sacrifice of European Jewry and the decimation of centers of Torah learning, will be remembered forever.

CHAPTER 11

PILLARS OF MY PEOPLE

The Lord went before them . . . by night in a pillar of fire to give them light.

EXODUS 13:21

Two INDIVIDUALS DEEPLY INFLUENCED and inspired my life during my childhood, though neither came from the yeshivas where I studied, nor were they my teachers or members of my family: Rabbi Yitzhak (Isaac) Halevi Herzog, chief rabbi of Israel in the pre-State period and during its first years, and Rabbi Yisrael Alter, the fifth Rebbe of Gur, known as the Beit Yisrael (House of Israel) after his most influential publication. A third figure greatly influenced me when I was older: Rabbi Menachem Mendel Schneerson, the Lubavitcher Rebbe, whom I met after I became a rabbi.

Before the State of Israel was founded, Rabbi Herzog, in his role as chief rabbi of Eretz Israel, visited and encouraged Holocaust survivors in the displaced-persons camps in Germany and elsewhere in Europe. During the trip, he also attempted to contact and bring to Eretz Israel those Jewish children who had been sent by their parents to Catholic institutions and families for safekeeping.

A few years before this trip, in 1940, during the war, Rabbi Herzog made serious efforts to arrange a meeting with Pope Pius XII, to try to convince him to condemn the Nazi slaughter of the Jews. In 1944, as Allied victory began to seem imminent, Rabbi Herzog tried to contact the pope again through his personal friend Cardinal Angelo Roncalli, who later became Pope John XXIII. (Roncalli helped thousands of Jews escape by providing them with "temporary" baptismal certificates.) Rabbi Herzog asked Cardinal Roncalli to help him arrange a meeting with the pope to discuss measures for saving those who could still be saved—among them, the Jews of Hungary. But the pope refused to meet with him, with the excuse that the Germans might find out about the meeting, and this might encourage them to take revenge against Hungarian Jewry.

Even after the war, Rabbi Herzog did not give up. He tried again to initiate a meeting with Pope Pius, to ask him to make a public request that all Catholic organizations, churches, monasteries, and families that had rescued Jewish children to return those children to their own people. Only in 1946 did the pope agree to meet him. The meeting did not go well; not only did Rabbi Herzog feel that his efforts to save the Jews were futile, but upon leaving his audience with the pope he asked his escorts for one thing—to take him immediately to the Rome *mikveh,* the ritual purification bath.

Kol Torah Yeshiva was located across the street from Rabbi Herzog's home. When I arrived at the yeshiva as a youth, Rabbi Gedalya, the spiritual adviser, wanted morning prayers to be held at Rabbi Herzog's house, since the elder rabbi had trouble walking to the synagogue. Rabbi Gedalya asked me to organize a daily minyan, or prayer quorum, at the house every morning. The house had two stories: the first floor was used for prayer services and for receiving official visitors; the second contained the family's private quarters, with a large and impressive library. Each morning for six years, as the *gabbai* (beadle), I went to the rabbi's home to be part of that minyan, which included some important personalities. One was Rabbi Aryeh Levin, known as "the prisoners' rabbi" for his visits to Jewish underground fighters imprisoned by the British during the mandate period, prior to the War of Independence. On the eve of Shabbat, he would pray at Rabbi Herzog's home, a good hour's walk from the Knesset neighborhood where Rabbi Levin lived.

Although I was the youngest participant, I was no stranger to Rabbi Herzog. He knew quite a bit about my father, and even more about my father's cousin, Rabbi Meir Shapira. He knew of Father's book, *Kiddush Hashem,* and he constantly asked me about the location of the manuscript, since he had seen it with his own eyes. Although at the time I could not answer him, later I was privileged to receive several copies (see chapter 4). Rabbi Herzog was also a personal friend of my uncle Rabbi Vogelman; my aunt worked with Rabbi Herzog's wife, Sarah, in the Mizrachi Women's Organization.

One unforgettable experience was the weekly lesson in the Jerusalem Talmud, which took place every Friday morning. Selected individuals participated in that class, including some of the greatest Torah scholars of that generation. To stand in the corner of this room, this haven of Torah, and to absorb the atmosphere of study and argument was truly remarkable.

Rabbi Herzog's personal secretary in those days was Israel Lippel, who later became director general of the Ministry of Religious Affairs. When I was elected chief rabbi of Israel, the members of the election committee gathered in Jerusalem at the Heichal Shlomo (the former seat of the chief rabbinate) to honor me on the occasion of my election with congratulations. Among them was Lippel, who then served as acting director of the Ministry of Religious Affairs. After many comments of praise and congratulations, right before people got up from their seats to leave, Lippel asked permission to say a few words:

> *Friends, after we have toasted* le-chaim *with His Honor, the chief rabbi, I must tell you a personal story. This is a story I never told any of you before, so as not to sway your decision. When I was the secretary and close associate of Chief Rabbi Herzog, there was a young man who came to the house every morning at six o'clock, at his rabbi's request, to ensure that Rabbi Herzog would have a minyan. Rabbi Herzog loved him dearly. One day, when this youth left for the yeshiva after the prayer service, the rabbi said to me, "Israel, you see that boy? His name is also Israel."*
>
> *"Certainly," I answered, "that's Israel Lau. I know him well, he comes here every day."*
>
> *"A day will come," Rabbi Herzog continued, "when he will sit on this grand chair of the chief rabbinate. Make note of this."*

Like everyone else present, I was hearing this from Israel Lippel for the first time. I lost my breath for a moment, and after recovering from my surprise, I said, "Israel, couldn't you have saved me from these revelations and told me this story a year ago? Only now you remembered?"

I RECALL RABBI HERZOG IN HIS LAST DAYS, when he could barely walk, but his mind remained lucid, his thinking sharp. Every morning after services, his assistant brought him the daily newspapers. He would scan the headlines and make comments, making sure to keep himself informed and involved. Only once did I see him lose his composure. In 1953, the United Nations returned to its several-year-old discussion and debate over the idea of transforming Jerusalem into an international entity, outside of Israeli jurisdiction. When Israel's delegate to the UN, Ambassador Abba Eban—who was the brother-in-law of Rabbi Herzog's son Chaim—spoke against this plan at the United Nations assembly, he nearly fainted from emotion. When Rabbi Herzog found out about the UN's renewed interest in the Jerusalem plan, he responded with furious resolve. "We must renew the covenant with and promise to Jerusalem," he declared, and with that, he left his house, went into town, and began to march along Keren Kayemet Street toward King George and Jaffa Streets. He continued on, partly by car, partly on foot, and slowly a crowd gathered around him and marched all the way to Mount Herzl. There Rabbi Herzog raised his right hand. His voice weak, he cried, *If I forget you, O Jerusalem, may my right hand lose its strength!* One of the elder leaders of Jerusalem, who was among the thousands following Rabbi Herzog through the streets, said to me, "That's Rabbi Herzog. Just like in 1939—in a spontaneous demonstration, he stood on the steps of Yeshurun Synagogue and tore up the MacDonald White Paper, which limited the immigration rights of Jews to Eretz Israel."

Years later, Rabbi Herzog's son Chaim (who became president of the State of Israel in 1983) stood at the podium in the UN and tore up the resolution that compared Zionism to racism. He told me that when he did so, in his mind's eye he saw his father tearing up the White Paper. "That night, when I prepared the speech, Father's image stood before me. I knew that I would be standing alone against them all, the only one to refute the UN decision. I thought I should do something dramatic, since in any case there was little chance I would sway or convince anyone with words alone, since they were already convinced," he explained. Like his brother-in-law Abba Eban, Chaim chose to use colorful language in his speech: "If Algeria introduced a resolution declaring that the earth was flat and that Israel had flattened it, it would pass by a vote of 164 to 13 with 26 abstentions." He explained, "This is why I thought I should repeat my father's act"—and so he stood at the podium and tore up the decision.

THE SECOND FIGURE WHO MADE AN IMPRESSION ON ME was the Rebbe of Gur. When Naphtali and I made aliya in 1945, the Rebbe of Gur was Rabbi Abraham Mordechai Alter, called the Imrei Emet after the title of his most famous book. He was advanced in years, and his health was poor. The Imrei Emet had made a public pronouncement to his followers that they must leave the Diaspora and make aliya so that they could return to their homeland. He founded a small study hall on David Yellin Street in Jerusalem, as well as the large Sefat Emet Yeshiva, also in Jerusalem, both of which became central gathering points for thousands of Gur Chassidic followers in Israel and abroad.

The Imrei Emet died on Shavuot 1948, during the War of Independence. Because of the war, his family could not bury him in the ancient Jewish cemetery on the Mount of Olives, so they dug his grave in the courtyard of their home in the Zichron Moshe neighborhood, across from the Machane Yehuda market. It was an unusual funeral; during the ceremony, they consecrated the site for burial by circling it seven times and reciting special prayers.

The Imrei Emet was survived by three sons: the Beit Yisrael (Rabbi Yisrael Alter), the Lev Simcha (Rabbi Simcha Bunim Alter), and the Pnei Menachem (Rabbi Pinchas Menachem Alter), all of whom served consecutively as Rebbes of Gur. In other Chassidic courts, when a rebbe dies and leaves two sons, they often divide the leadership, which results in splitting the community, but the Gur community remained united under one rabbi. After Rabbi Abraham Mordechai died, Rabbi Yisrael became the rebbe for almost thirty years, until he died in February 1977.

During the thirty years of his leadership, Rabbi Yisrael Alter raised the Gur community—which had been decimated by the Holocaust more than any other community—from ruins, transforming it into the leading Chassidic movement. The Rebbe of Gur became the undisputed leader of Agudath Israel, and led Gur in establishing schools and yeshivas throughout the Jewish world. Rabbi Yisrael, founder of this impressive network, had lost his wife and children in the Holocaust. Aside from being a Torah scholar, he was a born leader, the right person sent at the right time by Divine Providence.

After the Holocaust, many Jewish survivors turned their backs on Judaism and lost faith. The Rebbe of Gur used to say, sometimes in Yiddish, other times in spicy Polish, "One who has touched the handle on the door to Gur will always open the door again. He'll always come home." This proved correct; I can give personal testimony to this from a close friend, Yisrael Krakovsky, today in his eighties. For years, he deserted Gur, but he always remembered Rebbe Yisrael. Once, in the prewar days, when Rabbi Yisrael was still "the rebbe's son," Krakovsky cut ahead in line to greet the father in the study hall in Góra Kalwaria. Rabbi Yisrael paid Krakovsky back for his daring with a well-deserved slap. "That slap," he would say, "reminded me all those years where my roots were planted." After long years of estrangement, my good friend has become one of the leaders of Holocaust survivors in New York. He is active in three important synagogues in Manhattan, and his granddaughters study in a Chabad school.

In August 1950, when I first arrived at Kol Torah Yeshiva in Jerusalem, my worn Buchenwald suitcase contained only my bar mitzvah suit: short pants, a jacket, and a beret. This uniform is hardly acceptable in any Chassidic community, much less in Gur. After my first Shabbat dinner at the yeshiva, my friends decided to attend the weekly *tish* (literally "table" in Yiddish) hosted by the Rebbe of Gur, and they invited me to go along with them. I had no clue what they were talking about. I had never been at a rebbe's *tish*; I came from Kiryat Motzkin, where on Shabbat I attended a Bnei Akiva youth group in Kiryat Shmuel with my friend Ze'ev Almog, and he had never mentioned that word. The yeshiva students noticed my confusion and explained: a *tish* is a traditional Chassidic Friday-night open house around the rebbe's dinner table. The rebbe's followers sing, and Rabbi Ya'akov Talmud, a Gur follower who composes Chassidic songs, conducts a choir.

Their description intrigued me, as did the presence of a choir, which they said included both children and elderly men. The yeshiva students also added that it was worthwhile for me to attend, even if it were just to catch a glimpse of the Rebbe of Gur. I knew that Naphtali had been to visit the previous rebbe, the Imrei Emet, when we had first arrived in Eretz Israel, and that the rebbe had since passed away. I decided to join the other students and go to the *tish*.

We went to the neighborhood of Zichron Moshe, to the old study hall on David Yellin Street. The room was unbearably crowded. Above the crowd, on a wooden platform with three steps, stood an impressive figure with a long, flowing white beard and a *spodik,* the high fur hat that Gur members wore on Shabbat and holidays. This man stood and called out names. I was sure that this was the rebbe himself, although I did wonder why the rebbe would take on the task of calling out the names of those present. Then I realized that this imposing figure was the *gabbai*, Rabbi Shaye Noah Bikneh, who was responsible for the list of those given the honor of sitting at the Rebbe of Gur's table.

Suddenly, the hundreds of people packed inside fell silent, and we could have heard a pin drop. Waves of people swayed left, then right. Within the horde, I felt my legs being lifted from the ground; I was pushed in all directions as though I were a raft on the ocean. The multitude raised me into the air, and I was cut off from my friends.

Then I understood the reason for the human wave flowing through the hall: the rebbe had entered, clasping his hands behind his back as a general would. As soon as he walked in, the crowd parted like the Red Sea, allowing him to pass. In a fragment of a second, as he walked by me, he looked at me, and his riveting gaze was unique and unforgettable. In all my life, I merited only two such looks—one from the Rebbe of Gur, and the other, twenty-four years later, from the Rebbe of Lubavitch. Throughout those twenty-four years, I never met another person with a look as penetrating and profound as that of the Rebbe of Gur.

And there I was, a thirteen-year-old in short pants with a beret on my head, standing out in this crowd of Chassidic men, who were all wearing black silk robes with sashes and high fur hats. The rebbe passed through the throng, his eyes surveying each individual, registering exactly who was present. In seconds, the order was transmitted to add me to the list of those who were to sit at the rebbe's table. In complete surprise, I heard my name called out along with the others: "Srul Mayer, son of the rabbi of Piotrków."

I did not respond. No one had ever called me Mayer. It had been five years since I had made aliya, and I had always been known as Yisrael or Israel Lau. Occasionally, some people called me Lulek, but "Srul Mayer"? This Yiddishism ("Srul" is the Yiddish form of "Israel," and "Mayer" the Yiddish pronunciation of "Meir") was completely foreign to my ears. I did not think they were referring to me, but the words "son of the rabbi of Piotrków" echoed in my ears, and I told myself there could be no other. Naphtali was working in Paris, and Shiko was in Tel Aviv. Still, I did not dare make my way to the rebbe's table.

A few minutes later, Yehoshua Kleinlehrer, my friend from Kol Torah, who had accompanied me to the *tish*, came up to me. His voice shaking, he said that in case I hadn't heard, they had called my name. I wondered, Why are they calling my name? I had no answer, but he insisted that, indeed, my name was the one they had called and I was the one they meant. He said I must go up to the rebbe's table. Embarrassed and confused, I asked him what I should do.

Yehoshua explained the details calmly and clearly. "You see those steps where the *gabbai* is standing? Go up those three steps and look toward the table where the rebbe is sitting. They'll give you a small cup of wine in one hand and a slice of apple in the other. You say *le-chaim*, directing yourself at the rebbe, and the rebbe will answer you, *le-chaim*. It's a very great honor. You've been chosen out of hundreds in this room."

I realized I had no choice but to respond to the call, so I went up the three steps. Someone gave me a wine cup and filled it halfway, and the expected slice of apple appeared in my other hand. Then the rebbe in all his glory directed his penetrating gaze toward me. High fur hat perched on his head, surrounded left and right by his elderly disciples, he nodded his head up and down and toasted, *"Le-chaim."*

In the hall, his followers and the choir sang Rabbi Ya'akov Talmud's new tunes for *Lecha Dodi* and the songs from the High Holidays liturgy. But I was still in shock from the encounter with the rebbe and did not hear them. I was trying to digest what had just happened to me, and I could not relate to the songs filling the room. Then Yehoshua came up to me again and added another surprise. He said that the rebbe requested that the next evening, after the Saturday night *Havdalah* ceremony, I come to visit him in his home in the building opposite the study hall. "The rebbe wants to speak with you," he said. I could not breathe.

I returned to Kol Torah in shock, astounded and not comprehending what was going on. I went to the spiritual counselor, Rabbi Gedalya, and told him what had happened. I asked his permission to skip the afternoon study session at the yeshiva, since I was invited to visit the Rebbe of Gur. Rabbi Gedalya gave me a doubtful smile and answered, "Really? One must not refuse the Rebbe of Gur. I cannot refuse him, either. Go in peace."

I do not know if he believed me or not, but he did not prevent me from going. Simcha Eidelman, a friend at the yeshiva, explained that it was unacceptable to visit the Rebbe of Gur in the clothes I was wearing. He lent me his cap, long pants, and belt. Legs shaking, I arrived at the entrance to the rebbe's home. There I met up with Hanina Schiff, whom I had not seen for five years. "Lulek, how have you been?" he asked. I answered, and then inquired as to what he had been up to. Hanina told me that he was studying at Sefat Emet Yeshiva, and that he was close to the Rebbe of Gur. (Hanina went on to serve as beadle to all of the rebbes of Gur up to today.)

I surmised that he was the clue to the riddle. I continued to probe him, asking whether he was the one who had told the Rebbe of Gur that I was at the *tish*. Hanina insisted that he knew nothing of my presence, that he had not seen me since we had parted after making aliya, and so he could not have said anything to the rebbe. "But I saw you going up to the rebbe's table and saying *le-chaim*. I wondered how you got there and how they recognized you out of the throng in the hall," he said.

"But I still don't understand who called me up to toast the rebbe," I said. Hanina did not have a chance to say another word, for the door opened and someone led me into the room. I saw the rebbe pacing back and forth like a caged lion, his gaze fixed on the ground. In his left hand he held a pinch of tobacco, which he occasionally brought to his nose and sniffed. With his right hand, he lifted his high velvet *kippah* and fanned his head, cooling himself in the late-summer heat. I stood by the door, but he did not even glance at me. I thought to myself that perhaps they had brought me in by mistake and that he had not meant to invite me.

As these thoughts raced through my head, the rebbe stopped and stared at me and my outfit with his serious, penetrating gaze. He asked in Yiddish: "Who lent you those clothes?" "Simcha Eidelman," I answered. The rebbe smiled warmly, then added, "I am used to seeing your brother Naph*tuli* [as the rebbe called him, spoken with a Yiddish accent] here more often than I see you. What is your uncle Rabbi Vogelman up to?" With one question, the Rebbe of Gur covered my entire world: Naphtali and Rabbi Vogelman. This man, to whom I had never spoken, who was responsible for tens of thousands of followers, knew exactly who the central individuals in my life were. I kept my answers concise and to the point, following the accepted conversational style of a Gur Chassid.

The rebbe continued, "You were probably surprised to be called up at the *tish*. I remember when your brother Naphtali came to visit my father, the Imrei Emet, five years ago. At the *tish*, I passed through the rows in the hall and all of a sudden I saw you. It was impossible not to notice you. You look very much like your brother Naphtali. I remember the name your father gave you at your circumcision ceremony in the Piotrków synagogue. He said he was naming you Israel after his rabbi, the rabbi of Chortkov, Rabbi Israel Friedman, and also after his father-in-law from his first marriage, Rabbi Yisrael Hager, the rabbi of Vizhnitz, called the Ahavat Yisrael. Then he said he was also naming you Meir, after his cousin Rabbi Meir Shapira of Lublin, who had no children. And, he added, he also named you after the Chafetz Chayim, Rabbi Israel Meir of Radin. As your father held you in his arms, he prayed to the Master of the Universe that a spark—I remember the exact word in Yiddish, *a finek*—from each of those souls would enter the soul of his child. I never forgot his words. When I saw you among the crowd on Shabbat Eve, I realized that you were the brother of Naphtali, and I remembered your name after all this time since your circumcision." Again he fixed me with his penetrating stare, then gave me a whole apple and said, "I hope to see you here more often." I nodded, realizing that, coming from him, such a pronouncement meant a serious obligation on my part.

Ever since the rebbe revealed to me the significance of the names my father gave me, I have called myself Israel Meir. The name Meir, which I had ignored for a long time, sometimes even takes precedence over the name Israel. In many publications, I appear as Meir alone, even though I have been known as Israel since childhood.

My family is not directly related to the Gur Chassidic group. On my father's side we are Chortkov Chassidim, while on my mother's side I am a fifth-generation descendant of the Divrei Chaim, Rabbi Chaim Halberstam, the Rebbe of Sanz. But I do have a connection to Gur through my father-in-law, Rabbi Yitzchak Yedidya Frankel, who was a Gur Chassid and very close to the rebbe.

WHEN RABBI FRANKEL WAS ABOUT SEVENTY YEARS OLD, he suffered a sudden heart attack. He was rushed to Ichilov Hospital in Tel Aviv. The doctors forbade visitors and phone calls in order to avoid exciting him. My wife, Chaya-Ita, went to stay with her mother in Tel Aviv, while her brothers remained close to their father's bed. Countless individuals phoned the Frankel home asking after the rabbi's health, since he was the rabbi of the southern neighborhoods of Tel Aviv. One caller, speaking in a quick, sharp voice, asked if the rabbi was receiving visitors. After Chaya-Ita explained that his doctors had forbidden visitors, she asked who was calling. The answer on the other end was, "Alter from Jerusalem speaking." Because Alter is a fairly common name, she hung up, never imagining that the speaker was the Rebbe of Gur himself. But her brother Rabbi Aryeh Frankel from Jerusalem, who was very close to the rebbe, found out about this phone call. Word went around that the Rebbe of Gur was the one who had called, asking if it was possible to visit Rabbi Frankel in the hospital.

The brother rushed to Tel Aviv and informed Chaya-Ita of the identity of the caller. "Do you know what a great honor it would be if the rebbe came from Jerusalem to visit Father?" he said. "The rebbe almost never leaves Jerusalem! Here he wants to travel to Tel Aviv and visit our father and give him his blessing, and you're standing in his way," he protested.

An embarrassed Chaya-Ita tried to explain why she had treated the rebbe's phone call as just another drop in the flood that inundated them from morning to night, and how she had innocently answered that the doctors had forbidden visitors. The family decided not to tell their father about the missed visit.

The next day, the Rebbe of Gur somehow found out that Rabbi Frankel's condition had improved, and he decided this time to go to the hospital without asking first for permission. On the day he arrived, it happened that Rabbi Frankel's wife was at his bedside. When he entered the room where Mrs. Frankel was sitting, his first question was, "Is your daughter here? She deserves a *yasher koach*, congratulations, for her vigilance over her father." The rebbe sensed that Rabbi Frankel's daughter might be criticized for how she had answered his phone call and for trying to prevent his visit. Instead, he complimented her on her caution. The Rebbe of Gur stood beside Rabbi Frankel's bed for a minute. In his focused manner, every word a pearl, he said, "Yitzchak Yedidya, we need you. You must be healthy and strong." Then he turned and was gone.

But the news of his presence in the hospital spread like electricity through all six floors. Parents pushed children in wheelchairs down corridors, patients asked relatives to wheel their beds out of their rooms. Those capable of walking crowded in the hallways in their hospital gowns, in the hopes of receiving a blessing from the rebbe, or at least a glance from his eyes.

When the Rebbe of Gur walked out into the corridor, one of the hospital guards tried to move the patients who were blocking his passage. The rebbe, known for his energetic pace, asked the guard to stop. Then he walked by each bed and wheelchair, and personally wished each patient a full recovery. The nurses, who did not know who he was, asked the identity of the man with the angelic face. This image moves me to this day.

After Rabbi Frankel recovered, he was elected chief rabbi of Tel Aviv-Jaffa and the head of the religious courts. As the rebbe had said, we all needed him.

THE REBBE OF GUR DIED IN MARCH 1977. At that time, I was a neighborhood rabbi in Tel Aviv, and I had maintained contact with the rebbe throughout the years. On the day of his funeral, I realized that Jerusalem would be jammed with traffic, so I decided to take a taxi instead of my own car. I arrived in a somber city, virtually draped in black Chassidic garb. More than two hundred thousand mourners walked in silence for many miles, from the Zichron Moshe neighborhood through Geula to the Mount of Olives. (The Chassidim don't deliver eulogies at the funerals of their rebbes.) It was as if their father had died, and the only way to express what they felt was with deep silence. It also seemed as if all of Jerusalem mourned his death. Each of the merchants in the Machane Yehuda market had some connection with him. One merchant recounted that when his daughter fell ill, he went to visit "the holy man," as they called him, and the rebbe had laid his hand on him for healing. Another said that the rebbe was "his eyes," and now they were darkened. Such was the way the Jewish people expressed their love for the rebbe.

After the mourners covered the grave on the Mount of Olives, I searched for a ride back to Tel Aviv. I descended the hill to the Generali Building on Jaffa Road and began to walk down the street, hoping a car would stop for me; one did so before I had even raised my hand. The driver wore a beige safari cap. "Rabbi Lau, can I help you?" he asked. I told the driver that I had just returned from the funeral of the Rebbe of Gur. He smiled slightly, and when I finished talking about the rebbe, he said he also had come from that same funeral.

His appearance aroused my curiosity, since it was unlike that of the other mourners, so I asked him about his connection to the rebbe. He said he was a colonel in the army reserves, and that he managed a large industrial factory and lived in Tzahala, a neighborhood of army personnel in northeast Tel Aviv. His father was an elder Gur Chassid. The son had dedicated his life to the army, and had distanced himself from the religious atmosphere of his parents' home. When his father reached old age, the family placed him in a nursing home in Tel Aviv. On one of the eight days of Hanukkah, the son took his father on a trip to Jerusalem—to afternoon prayers at the Western Wall, and then to the Rebbe of Gur for a Hanukkah candle-lighting ceremony. The son remained outside in the car, as he had no head covering, and also because he felt he had no reason to go see the rebbe.

Six weeks later, on Tu Bi-Shevat, the Jewish Arbor Day, he offered to take his father again to Jerusalem to visit the rebbe. But this time, his father refused. "Why?" asked the son. "You enjoyed yourself so much last time."

"It was not worth it," complained the father. "The rebbe asked who had brought me to Jerusalem. I told him, 'My son, but he's sitting in the car.' Why? Did a stranger drive me? My own son won't go in with me to see my rebbe! I can't forgive the grief you caused me."

"So," explained the son, "I promised him that I would wear a hat, and go in with him to see the rebbe. I went inside wearing the hat you now see on my head. The rebbe greeted me warmly and said, 'I heard that you are careful in your observance of the mitzvah of honoring your father. And what about your Father in Heaven?' He pointed upward. 'Don't you have to honor Him?' The whole way home, the rebbe's voice echoed in my head. When I got home, I told my wife that I would like to return to my roots a bit, and at least keep a kosher kitchen, so that my father would feel comfortable. Slowly, I returned to the *mitzvot* of Judaism. In the meantime, my father passed away. When I heard on the radio that the Rebbe of Gur died, I felt it my duty to participate in his funeral, in memory of my father, but mainly since he brought me back to myself."

YEARS AFTER I MET THE REBBE OF GUR, the Rebbe of Lubavitch also became my spiritual mentor.

A short time after the conclusion of the Yom Kippur War in October 1973, I was invited to the Jewish Agency building in Jerusalem by Abe Shenkar. Shenkar, who was originally an American, was the Mapam (left-leaning political party) representative to the Ministry of Information. I did not know him, and I wondered why he was inviting me. He told me that he listened on a regular basis to my radio series on the weekly Torah portion. He had also seen some of my television appearances, and said he wanted to recruit me for a mission of "vital importance."

In the United States, and particularly in New York, Shenkar told me, there were groups of fanatical ultra-Orthodox Jews who refused to contribute to the State of Israel and vigorously opposed Zionism. However, during the Yom Kippur War in 1973, their views began to change and they began to reevaluate their relationship to the State of Israel. "I can personally tell you," Shenkar said, "that during the intermediate days of Sukkot, ultra-Orthodox Jews wearing fur hats and long white beards voluntarily went from house to house and synagogue to synagogue, carrying tin boxes and collecting donations for the State of Israel, the IDF, and the war fund. When we asked them why, they explained that the Yom Kippur War reminded them of those black days in Europe, and that this war had awakened them to the danger of annihilation facing the Jewish community in Eretz Israel."

The ultra-Orthodox had gained this impression from the media. They were shocked by the reports that thousands of soldiers had been killed in such quick succession that there had not been time to bury them in the military cemetery in central Israel. Those killed on the southern front were given temporary burial at Kibbutz Be'eri, while the victims on the northern front were buried temporarily in Nahariya. The secrecy surrounding these reports created a wave of sinister rumors, giving the Jews of New York the impression that the situation in Israel was comparable to another destruction of the Temple. The anti-Zionist groups abandoned their former policy and began to act on Israel's behalf—even those who, until then, had not recognized its right to exist. Abe Shenkar told me all this with visible excitement.

As director of the information and organizations department of the Jewish Agency, Shenkar wanted to take advantage of this momentum and send a representative of Israel to strengthen the ties of these groups to the state. But he felt it would be inappropriate to send a politician, a diplomat, or even an IDF general, and so he had thought to send me: a rabbi, a respected figure who was a Holocaust survivor, who had suffered the horrors in Europe, and who had just experienced the war in Israel. "If you go to those communities, doors will open for you," he said with confidence. I asked him how he could be so sure. Shenkar explained that he had discussed it with the chairman of the Conference of Presidents of Major American Jewish Organizations, Rabbi Dr. Israel Miller, himself an Orthodox rabbi. Miller had heard me speak during a visit to Israel, and he had given the plan a green light. With this recommendation, Abe Shenkar asked me to go on a monthlong speaking tour to act as a bridge between Israel and the Orthodox and ultra-Orthodox communities in the United States. This included Chabad, the Bobov Chassidic community, the entire Lithuanian yeshiva world, modern Orthodox institutions such as Yeshiva University, Stern College, and Flatbush Yeshiva High School, and the ultra-Orthodox educational institutions.

I agreed, but explained that I did not speak fluent English. Abe Shenkar was not worried by this, and reassured me that with half the Jews I could speak Hebrew, and with the other half I could speak Yiddish. He also proposed that in the two months before the trip, I should prepare several speeches in English and learn them by heart. I took his welcome advice.

Although I was very excited about this mission—since I had never been in the United States and was curious to discover America—I was also quite concerned about my poor knowledge of the language. As a lecturer and teacher, language is my principal tool, and I worried that I would stutter and trip over my words. I felt the level of my language would be inadequate. So I made a monumental effort to write speeches in English during those two preparatory months. Above all, while in America I wanted to be able to give the speech I had delivered during one of the most discouraging moments of the Yom Kippur War, on the banks of the blockaded Suez Canal.

At that time, I was spending my days and nights volunteering in Ichilov Hospital. Upon returning home late one night, I learned that the commander of an antiaircraft reserve battalion had been trying to reach me all day long. In civilian life, he was principal of an ORT school, part of a worldwide network of educational and vocational institutions, in Kfar Saba. "Do me a favor," he requested when we finally managed to connect. "I hear you often on the radio and sometimes on television, and I need you here with us. We'll fly you in a Hercules to the Fayid air force base, and from there drive you in a jeep to the canal. My battalion is completely demoralized. All of a sudden, on Yom Kippur, the soldiers were mobilized. Some were about to get married, some were supposed to begin university studies at the end of October, others had just opened a business, and some have accumulated debts because of their absence. I need someone to raise their morale, and fast. Come explain to them why we need this whole business."

I took him seriously, but proposed that in order to raise the soldiers' morale, an entertainment troupe would be preferable to the likes of me. The battalion commander insisted, explaining that entertainers had come and gone: after twenty minutes of show time, they boarded a plane and returned to the center of the country while the soldiers remained in the desert. The battalion's mood had declined even more, and remained at a low point. "I need someone here who will speak not only to their emotions but to their intellect," he explained, and I agreed.

From Fayid, on the west side of the Suez Canal, I was driven to a blockaded area, arriving at an amphitheater constructed entirely of sand. I sat down with the battalion commander while the entire battalion assembled on the dune before me. I spoke about our right to Eretz Israel, why this was our homeland, and why we could have no other home. The soldiers listened attentively; I could feel their minds drinking in my words. Of the hundreds of speeches I have given in my life, this was one of the few that I recall in exact detail. It was suffused with meaning for me, especially because it was delivered in the midst of the war, in a moment of calm between battles, to dusty, discouraged soldiers whose commander had contacted me out of concern for their physical and spiritual welfare. Before leaving for the United States, I wrote down that speech from memory and asked someone to translate it into English for me. I rehearsed it throughout the flight to America in order to deliver it before the religious public in New York.

During my preparations for my trip, I received a letter from Rabbi Miller. He expressed his pleasure at my agreement to help publicize the situation of the State of Israel to the Jews of New York, and promised to organize the logistics and schedule of my stay. He warned me that it would be an exhausting trip, with five appearances each day. The people were eager to know what was going on in Israel, he said. At the end of his letter, Rabbi Miller asked what remuneration I expected for my efforts. His question surprised me, as I was certain that I was traveling to America on an altruistic mission and never considered that I might be paid for my efforts. "I have never visited the United States of America," I wrote back, "and I do not know if after this visit I will ever be invited to visit there again. There are certain Jews who live on the East Coast whose reputations precede them and from my point of view are the spiritual leaders of their generation. If you could manage to organize meetings with the following people, I will consider it a more than adequate reward." In the letter, I listed those individuals whom I hoped to meet: the Rebbe of Lubavitch; Rabbi Yosef Dov Halevi Soloveitchik; the Rebbe of Satmar, who knew my father; the Rebbe of Bobov, a relative of my mother; the Rebbe of Bluzhov, who arranged my parents' marriage and was a member of the Council of Torah Sages; the great halachic authority Rabbi Moshe Feinstein; Rabbi Ya'akov Kamenetsky, dean of Yeshiva Torah Vodaas in Brooklyn; and Rabbi Ya'akov Yitzchak Ruderman, dean of Ner Yisrael Yeshiva in Baltimore. Rabbi Miller organized these meetings, which were so vital to me, and this indeed proved to be generous remuneration for my efforts.

THE HIGHLIGHT OF THIS TRIP was the long-anticipated meeting with the Rebbe of Lubavitch, Rabbi Menachem Mendel Schneerson. I had heard of his reputation, admired his wisdom, and, above all, wanted to meet him face-to-face. Since 1965, I had often thought of him. That year, I participated in a symposium on Shabbat Eve at Ha-Medurah, a Tel Aviv association of the Ahdut HaAvoda (Labor Unity) party, on issues of religion and state. Another participant was Yitzchak Greenbaum, minister of the interior in the first Israeli cabinet. He was a powerful speaker with a charismatic personality. I recall one of his statements, made that Shabbat Eve before an audience of about two hundred. "Should the day arrive when the iron curtain is raised, and the Soviet Union opens its doors to citizens of the State of Israel—if we go there and find one person who declares that he is a Jew, it will be thanks to one man who lives in Brooklyn, the Lubavitcher Rebbe." This was a surprising comment from a leftist such as Greenbaum, but he knew what he was talking about.

During my visit to the Soviet Union in May 1989 with a delegation of rabbis (when I tried to find my Buchenwald mentor, Feodor; see chapter 4), we went to the Kol Ya'akov Synagogue in Moscow, where we met some Jews who had gathered to pray. Most were elderly, but among them were also a few youths. These emissaries of the Lubavitcher Rebbe operated in secret and at extreme personal risk to preserve Judaism among the Soviet Jews, then known as "the Jews of Silence." Should the Soviet authorities catch them, they would send them to Siberia for the rest of their lives—at best. Once again, I was amazed by the power of the rebbe, who from his New York headquarters directed the Chabad movement to spread throughout the world in the service of one single goal: to keep the spark of Judaism alive.

I had a previous, indirect connection to the rebbe, initiated through his secretary, Rabbi Chaim Mordechai Hodakov, during Passover 1970. Five weeks before that holiday, the Knesset passed an amendment to the Law of Return (also called the Who Is a Jew law). A clause in the amendment defined a Jew as "any person who is born to a Jewish mother and is not a member of another religion, or one who has converted to Judaism." The Lubavitcher Rebbe wanted to add the phrase "according to halacha," in order to recognize halachic conversion as the only valid ticket of entry to Judaism.

During the intermediate days of the holiday, the rebbe organized a publicity campaign about the integrity of the Land of Israel and of the Jewish people—the Who Is a Jew issue—with a first meeting scheduled in Rehovot for the upcoming holiday of Lag Ba'Omer. The two major speakers would be MK (Knesset member) Menachem Begin, who would talk about the integrity of Eretz Israel, and me, speaking about the integrity of the Jewish people. I agreed to Rabbi Hodakov's request that I speak at this meeting, and I also spoke on the same subject at two other rallies, in Tel Aviv and Haifa. This explains the special treatment I received from the rebbe in New York four years later as a sign of gratitude.

MY MEETING WITH THE LUBAVITCHER REBBE was arranged for a night in March 1974. The organizers told me to come at midnight and promised I would be given one of his "private audiences"—one-on-one conversations the rebbe held with selected individuals. An hour and a half after I arrived, his attendants ushered me into his room, and I left at ten to four in the morning. That conversation was one of the highlights of my life.

Having heard that I was an educator, the rebbe spoke mainly about my role in youth education. I had been teaching at the Zeitlin religious high school in Tel Aviv for nine years, and before that at the nonreligious Brener and Ahad Ha'am high schools in Petach Tikva. He explained the importance of my position as an educator and the great responsibility I had in forming the character of youth who would eventually establish homes and families for future generations.

As a case in point, he recalled the story of Cain and Abel. When Cain killed his brother, we read in the Bible, *The voice of your brother's blood cries out to me from the ground*. But in the literal Hebrew, God speaks to Cain using plural forms: *The voice of your brother's* bloods *are crying out*. Who are those "bloods" who are crying out? Cain killed only one person; but, God is saying to Cain, both his blood and the blood of his descendants are on your hands. If you had not murdered Abel, an entire world could have descended from him, just as later descended from Seth, the father of Enosh. Therefore, in murdering Abel, you have not killed just one man, but an entire world. This is the source of the expression, "A person who saves one Jewish soul is like one who saves an entire world, and one who destroys one Jewish soul is like one who destroys an entire world." If this is true for the negative act of destruction, the rebbe said, how much more so does it apply to a positive act? If you save one soul, everything that stems from that soul is also to your credit.

When he finished speaking, the Rebbe of Lubavitch looked deeply into my eyes—the Rebbe of Gur is the only other person I have ever met with such a penetrating gaze—and changed the topic of conversation. He spoke Lithuanian Yiddish with a Russian lilt, peppered with many Hebrew words and a few English ones as well:

> *I want to ask you a question on a completely different topic. I want to understand a little of the soul of the Israeli people. I understand that you know the public, since you live among them. Perhaps you can enlighten me on a point about which I am very curious.*
>
> *In the last century, the world has witnessed many revolutions. Russia, for example, usually a very dogmatic country, experienced a revolution in 1917. Then in the fifties, Khrushchev initiated a revolution that overturned the previous one of Lenin and Stalin. Each leader added his own personal touch to life in the Soviet Union. In America as well, Kennedy was completely different from his predecessor, Eisenhower. Martin Luther King started his own revolution. In England, you cannot compare Attlee to Churchill, and*

in France, Pompidou is no de Gaulle. The entire world has changed,
and often Jews have marched at the head of these revolutions. The Jews
are a revolutionary people, always in the forefront. Jews were among
the main standard-bearers of these revolutions. In Russia, France,
and Germany, a large representation of Jews backed Marxism and
socialism.

The only place where nothing has changed is the State of Israel. For
forty years, the same individuals have gripped the helm of government
in the state of the most revolutionary people in the world—the Jewish
people. Since 1930, when the Workers' Party was founded in Eretz
Israel, and up until this day, in 1974, more than forty years later—the
same people have served as leaders. During those years, we experienced
the Holocaust, the establishment of the State of Israel, the ingathering
of the exiles, and harsh wars. Now, two months after the Yom Kippur
War, elections are held again, und de zelbe zach [and the same old
thing]. Golda Meir, Pinhas Sapir, Moshe Dayan are elected, while
Begin has lost nine times already, and there is no revolution. What
has to happen so that the State of Israel will experience what is taking
place all over the world—change? Explain to me, please, this stability.
You've come from there, and I'm curious to know.

I did not know how to answer this intelligent and accurate analysis
of the situation. The Lubavitcher Rebbe's knowledge of the issues was
as deep as it was broad. No one had ever asked me such a question and I
was completely unprepared. I had come to meet the Rebbe of Lubavitch,
to get to know him personally. I had assumed we would discuss education, the dissemination of Jewish knowledge in general, and Chassidism
in particular, topics with which I was well acquainted. But the rebbe had
asked his question, and although it came to me as a complete surprise,
God supplied me with the answer.

"I want to tell the rabbi about an episode I experienced during the last
war, the Yom Kippur War," I said. "All this happened just five months ago.
Maybe this story contains the answer to the question the rebbe posed. The
war broke out on the afternoon of Yom Kippur, which fell on Shabbat. In
the synagogues, we were reciting the prayer that describes the cruel execu-
tions and martyrdom of ten great leaders. At 1:50 p.m., a siren suddenly
pierced the air, and the first victims fell. The next evening, at 9:00, the

phone rang. The caller was Mr. Veller, owner of the Sky Blue banquet hall on the corner of Shenkin and Ahad Ha'am Streets in Tel Aviv. In a strong Viennese dialect, he asked me to do him a favor, and told me his story."

A few months earlier, a young couple had planned to get married between Yom Kippur and Sukkot. Despite the war, the bride and groom insisted on having their wedding as planned, since in Judaism it is considered inauspicious to put off a wedding. The groom obtained a twelve-hour leave from the army and arrived at the hall in uniform. The bride was wearing her white wedding gown. Their relatives were waiting for the rabbi to arrive, but he did not show up. Perhaps he thought they would not hold the wedding during the blackout then in effect, or maybe he thought that everyone was in the army, fighting, and no one was in the mood for a wedding. The hall owner asked me to come save the day. I asked him to check who was supposed to perform the ceremony, but the young couple had no idea. They only knew that the rabbinate had promised to send someone.

I explained to the hall owner that I could not drive my car because I hadn't yet painted the headlights according to the blackout rules and that it would take me about forty minutes to get from my house to the hall. I asked him to check whether the couple had a *ketubah*, a Jewish wedding contract, and documents proving they had officially registered with the rabbinate. Since I did not know the couple, I worried that I might be unwittingly aiding a couple who had not in fact officially registered, perhaps creating a problem of bigamy, a union forbidden by halacha, or a mixed marriage. After Mr. Veller confirmed that the couple had the necessary documents, I told him that I would come to perform the wedding. I arrived, out of breath, to a hall with tables set for 250 guests, with white linen napkins and rolls on each table. Only fifteen guests had arrived. The bride's face was wet with tears, and the smile on her face when she saw me arrive was unforgettable. The guests were also relieved.

I performed the ceremony, said a few words of blessing, and the young couple and their relatives were pleased. When it was over, a waitress working in the hall came over to me. I recognized her face from other celebrations I had attended, but I did not know her name. She rolled up her sleeve to reveal the tattooed number on her arm that showed she was a survivor of Auschwitz. Then she said, in Hebrew with a heavy Polish accent: "Honorable Rabbi Lau, you will probably be angry with me for talking this way. I know it is forbidden to say such things, but you are the only person in the world to whom I can say it, and who will understand me. I know that you are a child of the Holocaust, so I can tell you that if my son does not return from the war, I will take my own life. I have nothing to live for. If he does not come back, I will no longer wake up in the morning." I replied that certainly this was forbidden. "With that number on your arm, after all you have been through, how can you say such things? After what we went through?"

The woman in the white apron asked me to listen to her story. She explained that she could talk while at work, since the small number of guests made her assistance unnecessary.

I was about seventeen when I was released from Auschwitz. I was there for three years, working in a sewing workshop. Although I was weak and thin, I held on. The Germans took me to Auschwitz after I saw with my own eyes how they slaughtered my father and mother. I was fourteen, and they threw me on the train. All those years, I saw Father and Mother and the pool of blood before my eyes. I was liberated at the end of January 1945, and I began to search for the way home, to the shtetl. I knew I had no parents, but I hoped to find one of my brothers or sisters. I found no one.

Someone said that refugees were gathering in Łódź and that I should try to get there; perhaps I might find someone from my family. I got to Łódź by train, in carts, on foot. Refugees from every town streamed to the city, but not one of them was from my village or my family. In Łódź I met a young man who was exactly like me—a lone survivor in the world. We started dating. We signed up together for aliya to Eretz Israel, and requested aliya certificates. We had to wait a long time to get them, and meanwhile they transferred us to a displaced persons' camp in Germany, where we got married. The British would not allow us to make aliya, but we arrived on the day of the establishment of the state, when the gates opened for everyone.

I was pregnant then. They took us to a new immigrants' camp and recruited my husband into the army, to fight in the War of Independence. He was killed at Latrun. He did not yet have an Israeli

identity card number or a military identification number—just the
number from Auschwitz on his arm. After he was killed, I gave birth
to the boy I mentioned to you. I named him after three people: my
husband, my father, and my husband's father.

I work mornings at the post office on Allenby Street and evenings
for Mr. Veller as a waitress, to give my boy everything that I never had.
I live in a two-room apartment. One room is a museum. On the walls
are some black-and-white photos of my father and mother, and a few
of my husband from Europe and from the boat. The rest of the walls
are plastered with color photos of my boy, who was born in 1949. Now,
in 1973, he is twenty-four years old. Yesterday they took him from the
synagogue straight to the war, and since then I haven't heard a word
from him. If he does not return, I will have no reason to wake up in the
morning.

I took a deep breath. It had been difficult for me to hear this story
from the waitress in the banquet hall, and just as difficult to retell it to
the Lubavitcher Rebbe. He listened intently, his blue eyes penetrating and
focused, and I continued.

"Perhaps we are a bit tired of revolutions, Rebbe. We have no more
strength for such things. How much can we fight? How long? Perhaps
this waitress is a living example of what my generation went through.
Who does the rebbe expect will go out into the streets again with flags
to start revolutions? All we want now is a little peace and quiet." Pearls
of tears formed in his eyes and dripped onto the back of his hand, which
rested on my own. The rebbe did not know that waitress from the Sky
Blue wedding hall in Tel Aviv, but her story struck the depths of his soul.
All he could murmur was an emotional and teary, "Now I understand. I
understand very well."[1]

My next trip to New York was eight years later, when my brother
Naphtali was Israel's consul general in New York and I was rabbi of
Netanya. During that trip, I again had a private visit with the Lubavitcher
Rebbe. I remember that just before I entered his room, two men left,

---

1. The waitress's son returned safely after lengthy service in a reserve unit, and his
mother honored me by inviting me to perform his wedding ceremony.

one after another: the rabbi of Jerusalem, Rabbi Betzalel Zolty, and the chairman of the Knesset finance committee, Avraham Schapira. No sooner had I opened the door and walked inside than the rebbe said to me in Yiddish, "It's been eight years since you last visited me."

In this conversation, the rebbe asked me as an aside if my children had reached marriageable age. I said that the night before I left the house, we had arranged the first date for my eldest daughter, Miriam. My son Moshe Chaim was two years her senior, but he was not yet ready for marriage offers. He wanted to study Torah, and was doing so at the Hebron Yeshiva in Jerusalem. The rebbe asked about the family of the young man proposed for my daughter. "Actually, it is a well-respected one," I answered. His grandfather was Rabbi Zalman Sorotzkin, known as the rabbi of Lutsk, who had been president of the Vaad ha-Yeshivot, the nationwide committee for yeshiva education, and head of the Council of Torah Sages of Agudath Israel.

The rebbe paused for a moment, then said, "The grandson of the rabbi of Lutsk and the granddaughter of the rabbi of Piotrków, who sat together on the Council of Torah Sages before the Holocaust, meet in the Holy Land in order to build a Jewish home together. This will bring satisfaction to their grandfathers in the world beyond, and great joy in Heaven." When I got home, I found that the couple was waiting for my return in order to ask for my blessing. This would be the first home I had the honor to establish among the first post-Holocaust generation of my family.

After that visit, I went to see the Rebbe of Lubavitch many times. Once, I attended a class of his, and there I understood the essence of this man's uniqueness and was able to express it in one phrase: "Bequeath to the next generation!" Since then, I have adopted the following phrase, from the reader's recitation of the morning service of Rosh Hashanah, as my motto: "My Creator, grant me the understanding to bequeath the heritage."

It was during one of my trips to New York, when I accompanied my father-in-law, Rabbi Yitzchak Yedidya Frankel—who was invited to lecture at a conference on *Kiddush Hashem*, the sanctification of God's Name—that I attended a class given by the Lubavitcher Rebbe about the significance of the day celebrated as the "Second Passover," the fourteenth day of Iyar in the Hebrew calendar.

I have never seen such a packed hall. People stood crammed next to each other, heads touching. On the platform stood a long table, and behind it sat a row of elder Chassidim, among them leading rabbis of the United States and Canada. As the rebbe strode quickly into the hall, a small book by Maimonides under his arm, the atmosphere was electric. The rebbe gave a class that lasted four hours, without using notes or opening the book, not even once. In his class he referred to both classic and esoteric sources, early and late authorities, from all periods. He cited entire sections by heart.

Throughout the class, he focused on the significance of the Second Passover, which the sages called Little Passover. His basic idea was: On the eve of the Exodus from Egypt, God commanded the Israelites to offer the Passover sacrifice, and after that to offer it every year, as a symbol of the migration from slavery to freedom. But those who were ritually impure due to certain illnesses, or because they had touched an impure animal or corpse, were forbidden from offering the sacrifice and from traveling to the Temple in Jerusalem.

These individuals complained to Moses that they could not participate in the national sacrifice and thus feel part of the nation. "Why should we be diminished?" they asked. We are also Jews, they argued. The Holy One, blessed be He, accepted their complaint and decreed in His Torah that anyone who was impure or far away and thus could not offer the Passover sacrifice on time, together with everyone else, would be offered a second chance one month later, so that he would not be cut off from the Jewish people.

The gist of the Rebbe of Lubavitch's lecture was that the Second Passover symbolized a powerful concept that directly spoke to all of those present in the audience: there are fellow Jews in our midst who are impure through no fault of their own or who are simply so distanced from Judaism that they have no connection to it. And they call out—or even if they do not, we must listen to their silent call: "Why should we be diminished? We are also Jews. Do not discriminate against us. We also want to participate with the Jewish people in the exodus from slavery to freedom." The entire concept of repentance stems from this: we also want to repent. I was far away, but now I want to come closer, explained the rebbe, clearly and precisely. I had heard a similar argument from him in our private conversations. He spoke extensively about bringing Jews back to the fold, and emphasized that we should not call this *kiruv rechokim*, bringing back those who have strayed afar, since who are we to determine who is far and who is near?

This class was fascinating; every so often, my father-in-law would hit my leg out of sheer excitement over the rebbe's insight. Rabbi Frankel was a gifted orator himself and a great scholar; he was also critical, difficult to impress, and rarely given to superlatives. But he had never seen ability such as that of the Lubavitcher Rebbe. After the class, as we left the hall, Rabbi Frankel said, "I witnessed the magnificence of Polish Jewry; I had the honor of visiting Rabbi Kook, who gave me a personal letter; and I have known most of the great scholars of recent generations. But I have never seen such command of the material. That is genius."

IN SEPTEMBER 1991, when I was chief rabbi of Tel Aviv, I went to visit the Lubavitcher Rebbe again. Earlier that week, a violent confrontation had broken out between blacks and Chassidim in Crown Heights. Almost two thousand New York City policemen were keeping order in the Brooklyn neighborhood. On Sundays, the rebbe received visitors from all over the world, and from the early hours of the morning, a long line wound around the sidewalk in front of his house. My wife, several of our friends, and I joined the line. When we entered, I told the secretary that the rebbe had asked me to check something about a certain *mikveh* (ritual bath) in Tel Aviv, and I wished to report that I had fulfilled his request. When I reached the rebbe, I said three words: "I did it." He looked at me with his blue eyes, and said in his usual rapid speech: "You must hurry to finish all your activities in Tel Aviv, because in less than two years, you must go up to Jerusalem as the chief rabbi of Israel."

I froze in place. At the time, elections for the rabbinate were not even an issue. They were planned for March 1993, a year and a half away, and no one was even discussing it. I was speechless, and in my confusion I asked, "What about your blessing, Rebbe?" His answer was concise: "You have my blessing, and more. In the sacred texts, it says that for one who rises to a challenge, Heaven grants special spiritual powers so that he will be able to fulfill the tasks before him. You have already been granted this. Now your agreement is all that is lacking." The only thing I managed to say was, "If I have a special blessing from Heaven, I would like to utilize these powers to confer on the rebbe a blessing that he will live a long and healthy life, because the Jewish people need him."

With that, I left the room. Standing on the sidewalk was Uri Savir, then consul general of Israel in New York, and next to him, David Dinkins, mayor of New York, who had come to talk to the rebbe about the riots. When I approached them, Uri Savir congratulated me: "*Mazal tov*, chief rabbi of Israel." I smiled, and he described how the rebbe's announcement had spread rapidly among the crowd amassed on the sidewalk. I asked Uri if he took this seriously. He looked at me as if he could not believe his ears, and replied, "If the man sitting in there can determine who will be the prime minister of Israel—Peres or Shamir—then of course he can determine who will be the chief rabbi."[2]

On 3 Tammuz 5754 (June 12, 1994), the year after my election as chief rabbi, the Lubavitcher Rebbe died. I heard about his passing from a radio journalist who asked me to speak about him. I was in shock. Although the rebbe had suffered a serious stroke and could no longer speak, his death was nevertheless difficult to process. From my car, on the way to my office in Jerusalem, I said a few words in his memory for the radio interviewer: "Although the Lubavitcher Rebbe left no mortal descendants, and never had children, today, after his death, thousands throughout the world have been orphaned."

I recalled his contribution to the preservation of Judaism, particularly in the Soviet Union, but also in other places where Jews had little influence: Morocco, Yemen, and South America, for example. "People say in jest, There are two things that are found everywhere in the world: Coca-Cola and Chabad. [Chabad is a Hebrew acronym for the three major principles of Lubavitch Chassidim—wisdom (*chochmah*), understanding

---

2. In Montefiore Cemetery in Queens, where the rebbe is buried next to his father-in-law, a video screen plays a film documenting the fifty years of the rebbe's leadership, including selections from his speeches. In it appears the encounter where the rebbe announced my future election as chief rabbi of Israel.

(*binah*), and knowledge (*deah*).] There is one man responsible for this: the Rebbe of Lubavitch, who created the movement with his own hands during a span of fifty years."

I could not miss his funeral, and did everything I could in order to get to New York on time. I left Israel on a flight organized especially for the funeral, but reached the cemetery after the burial. I stayed in the United States for only three hours before I returned to Israel. A mountain of paper covered the grave—letters and notes on which people had written their wishes and the names of their loved ones, for whom the rebbe was to be an advocate on high.

Even though the burial had concluded, thousands of people still surrounded the pile of earth, reciting psalms and then making way for others as they finished. The crowd was hushed until a terrible broken cry pierced the air. It was a Chabad Chassid with a long, white beard, who had also arrived on the plane from Israel. He looked like a former prisoner of Zion (a Soviet Jew imprisoned or exiled due to Zionist activity) who had suffered long years in Siberia. He took off his shoes, and in his stocking feet walked on the moist earth packed with stones, spread his arms to Heaven, and cried out with all his might, *"Tateh!"*—Father, in Yiddish.

Our blood froze, and tears filled my eyes. That moment, in the Brooklyn cemetery, I understood what it was to be a Chassid mourning his rebbe. In the second book of Kings, when Elisha sees Elijah the Prophet ascending to Heaven in the chariot of fire, he cries out, saying, *Father! Father! The chariots and horsemen of Israel!* For this reason, the students of prophets are called their "sons." Perhaps that Chassid had not had a real father for more than fifty years, but it was on the day the Lubavitcher Rebbe died that he was truly orphaned. And it was for this loss that he cried a terrible cry to Heaven.

CHAPTER 12

MAKE ME A MATCH

A man shall leave his father and his mother and cling to his wife . . .
GENESIS 2:24

I WAS A STUDENT AT PONEVEZH YESHIVA when I began to receive marriage offers; I had become a prospective groom. Suggestions for meeting a suitable bride proliferated when I turned twenty-one, the accepted age for marriage in the yeshiva world. Many of my friends predicted that I would be the first to marry, because of the pressing need that I felt to establish my own home. They thought of me as their contemporary in age, but older in spirit, and this led them to consider me as the one who would be the first to become a groom. They all knew that I did not have an ordinary home. During vacations, I did not go to my parents' home, as did most of my yeshiva friends, but rather to my aunt and uncle's home in Kiryat Motzkin. I visited them twice a year, on Passover and Sukkot. During the summer, they usually went to a health resort in Zichron Ya'akov, and it was not always possible for me to join them. Thus I had an intense desire for my own home.

I received very generous offers for marriage. Many came from families abroad, but I rejected out of hand all offers to live elsewhere. I did not object in principle to the daughters of families abroad, but I considered it a fundamental understanding that my intended bride would build her home in Israel.

205

The name of one young woman in particular was suggested to me several times: Chaya-Ita Frankel, daughter of Rabbi Yitzchak Yedidya Frankel. She was the first daughter in five generations of Frankels. When the excitement over her birth subsided, her parents began to search for a name for the infant girl. Her two grandmothers were Chaya on her mother's side and Yuta on her father's side. So as not to insult either family, they decided to name her after both. Many people give children a middle name, so they thought to name her Chaya Yuta, with Yuta being the middle name. But then everyone would call her by her first name, and the feelings of Grandmother Yuta's family might be hurt. To avoid that risk, Rabbi Frankel decided to name his daughter with a combination of both grandmothers' names: Chaya-Ita. ("Ita" is the Hebrew version of the Yiddish "Yuta.")

The first person to mention the name Chaya-Ita Frankel to me was Yerachmiel Boyer (later mayor of Bnei Brak), my study partner at Ponevezh Yeshiva, who knew Rabbi Frankel from Tel Aviv. One day while we were sitting in the yeshiva dining hall the topic of matchmaking came up, since many of the 350 yeshiva students were getting engaged. Yerachmiel said, "Israel, I have an idea for you. You're the son of a rabbi, you grew up in the home of a rabbi, and you have the rabbinate in mind. The best thing for you would be to marry a rabbi's daughter." Since Yerachmiel Boyer was not a professional matchmaker, I did not take his suggestion seriously. When he mentioned Chaya-Ita Frankel, his attempt at matchmaking initially came to naught.

However, I had first heard Chaya-Ita's illustrious father, Rabbi Yitzchak Yedidya Frankel, at the 1958 Jerusalem reburial of Rabbi Meir Shapira, the initiator of the daily *Daf Yomi* Talmud project, who had been buried at the entrance to the Lublin cemetery in Poland. The Polish authorities wanted to pave a new highway through the cemetery and decided to reduce its size and dig up some of the headstones. Since Rabbi Shapira's grave was in the way, it had to be moved. Through the efforts of his brother, Rabbi Avraham Shapira, the Rebbe of Tłust (present-day Tovste, Ukraine), who lived in the United States, Rabbi Meir Shapira's bones were brought from Lublin to Har Ha-Menuchot (the Mount of Rest) in Jerusalem. The burial procession left Lod Airport for the Great

Synagogue of Tel Aviv, where Rabbi Frankel, who knew Rabbi Shapira from Lublin, gave a particularly moving eulogy, saying a prayer not only for Rabbi Shapira but also for the three million Jews of Poland who were killed during the Holocaust. Although Rabbi Frankel made aliya in 1935, and so did not experience the horrors of the Holocaust himself, every day he mourned its millions of victims: in any public address he gave, he always mentioned the Holocaust. In fact, Rabbi Frankel's gravestone, in the Nahalat Yitzhak cemetery, bears the inscription "Lamenter of the Holocaust and guardian of its memory."

I returned to the grave on the day I was elected to be the Chief Rabbi of Israel. On that occasion, I felt a sense of obligation to visit three graves: first, I went to the grave of my father-in-law, Rabbi Yitzchak Yedidya Frankel, in Tel Aviv. On the way from Tel Aviv to Jerusalem, I visited the grave of Rabbi Meir Shapira, in Har Ha-Menuchot, and finally, I visited the grave of the Rebbe of Gur, in the courtyard of Yeshiva Sefat Emet.

The reburial for Rabbi Meir Shapira ended at night, and I returned to Tel Aviv in a taxi with my cousin Shmuel Yitzchak Lau, whom we call Shmil Itche. His father was my father's brother, Rabbi Yisrael Yosef Lau, the rabbi of Kolomea, Galicia (present-day Kolomyia, Poland), who had been forced by the Gestapo to shatter the tombstones in his town's cemetery. Shmil Itche reached Eretz Israel before the Holocaust and was many years my senior. In the taxi, he inquired as to my welfare, and we spent the hour-long ride talking. When he heard that I was a few months past my twenty-first birthday, he told me I should get married, build a home, and start a family. "You need to make a match, cousin," he urged. I told him about the various suggestions I had received, but, I added, I was deeply engrossed in my studies and did not feel pressured to marry.

"You belong in the rabbinate," decreed my cousin. "I heard you speak at Yankele's bar mitzvah, and I can tell that you belong there." Shmuel Yitzchak was talking about his only son, Ya'akov Lau. I recalled the speech I had given at that bar mitzvah, my second speech in Israel and the third speech of my life. (The first was to save my life when I was a six-year-old in the Częstochowa forced labor camp, and the second was at my own bar mitzvah in Kiryat Motzkin.) This third speech occurred when I was a Ponevezh student and the family asked me to congratulate the bar mitzvah boy on their behalf. Rabbi Frankel was present, as he was rabbi of the south Tel Aviv Florentine neighborhood. This was the first time Rabbi Frankel heard me speak. In later years, he often reminded me of that speech, even though he followed the Gur Chassidic tradition of not complimenting people in their presence.

I earned my first public compliment from Rabbi Frankel only when my first granddaughter was born. I was then rabbi of Netanya, and he was rabbi of Tel Aviv. Our whole family celebrated the birth of the new baby by spending Shabbat together in a hotel in Bnei Brak. On Shabbat Eve, I came down with food poisoning and threw up all night long. In the morning, everyone rose for services in the hotel, but I could hardly stand up. My face was green and I could barely open my eyes. In the dining room, I drank tea with lemon and did not touch the food. For me, the food was like Hanukkah candles—as Jewish law states, Hanukkah candles are to be looked at from a distance but it is forbidden to derive any practical benefit from them.

Because I had just become a grandfather, when it came time for the naming ceremony for the baby girl they asked me to say a few words of Torah. Rabbi Frankel spoke before me, but when my turn came, I was so weak that at first I could not open my mouth. But with my remaining strength, I managed to rise and speak for about twenty minutes. When I sat down, everyone heard Rabbi Frankel's baritone voice say in Yiddish: "Israel never needs doctors or medicines. Give him a lectern and a microphone if possible, and that is his cure: when he speaks—he forgets what's bothering him. It is also his great asset: when he speaks, all his listeners forget their troubles as well." This was surprising coming from him, as I had never heard him say anything like that before to my face, although I had heard that he often praised me behind my back.

Ya'akov Lau's bar mitzvah was Rabbi Frankel's first chance to hear me speak. Although he said nothing to me then, apparently he took note of the name of the young man from Ponevezh Yeshiva who spoke like a rabbi.

Sitting in the dark in the backseat of the taxi on the way back to Tel Aviv from Rabbi Shapira's funeral, Shmuel Lau, the father of the former bar mitzvah boy, said to me: "You should join a rabbinic family." Then all of a sudden, my cousin slapped me on the knee and announced, as if he had seen the light, "I have an idea! Rabbi Frankel's daughter, she's just the right one for you." I looked at him in surprise and listened to him praise her. He knew the rabbi's family, prayed at his synagogue, and knew the people about whom he was talking. But Shmuel Lau did not stop at theorizing—he took action. A few days later, he went to Rabbi Frankel's house and told him about his cousin at Ponevezh. Rabbi Frankel listened attentively and commented that he remembered the young man, the son of the rabbi of Piotrków, who had spoken at the bar mitzvah. Although his daughter was still young, and they had not yet considered matchmaking, that conversation planted a seed.

The Frankel family was especially esteemed in the Eretz Israel of those days, particularly in Tel Aviv. Rabbi Frankel was born in Luntschitz (Łęczyca), Poland. When he finished his studies with Rabbi Akiva Asher, the latter told his student's father, Rabbi Aharon Frankel, that he should go to the big city to find another teacher. "I have given him all I can," said Rabbi Asher to his father. Yitzchak Yedidya went to Warsaw, to the yeshiva of Rabbi Menachem Ziemba, who was considered the great sage of Poland but who made a living from commerce in iron.

Rabbi Frankel had come to the yeshiva in Warsaw as a boy of thirteen and introduced himself to the yeshiva secretary, saying that his name was Yitzchak Yedidya Frankel, he came from Luntschitz, and he wished to be accepted at the yeshiva to study Torah with Rabbi Ziemba. The secretary asked him to show his recommendations from his previous places of study, but the youth had brought no documents with him.

He spoke in the typical manner of residents of Kotsk (Kock), near Lublin, direct and to the point. The byword of Kotsk was "truth." From his point of view, he said, documents could be forged and recommendations exaggerated, so therefore they were useless. The youth even gave an example from the sources, citing the sage Akavia ben Mahalalel: "Your deeds will either bring you near or distance you." In other words, society will judge you by your present deeds, not by your past deeds or connections. He asked the yeshiva secretary to examine him without documents or recommendations. When he finished speaking, he heard the voice of another speaker, whom he did not recognize, asking him how he knew the sayings of Akavia ben Mahalalel.

"From the Mishnah," the youth replied.

"And do you know all his sayings?" continued his interrogator. The young Frankel began to cite by heart all the sage's statements throughout the six orders of the Mishnah, such as the familiar passage from Ethics of the Fathers: *Consider three things and you will not come into the grip of sin—know whence you came, whither you go, and before Whom you will give justification and reckoning.* He also explained the previous citation, which came from the time when Akavia was on his deathbed. At that point, his son said to him, "Father, order your colleagues regarding me"—in other words, instruct your colleagues, the great sages of the Mishnah, to take care of me and grant me a position. Since his father did not leave him any money or property, he thought, at least the family name and connections would be worth something. But Akavia ben Mahalalel replied, "Your deeds will either bring you near or distance you"—and these were his last words.

Yitzchak Yedidya received rabbinical ordination at a very young age and became rabbi of the town of Rypin, Poland. One day, after the birth of his eldest son, Isser, and while his wife was expecting her second child, he had to travel to the city of Danzig (Gdańsk). It was 1934, and Rabbi Frankel, only twenty-one, walked through the city streets wearing his Chassidic garb. Suddenly, two Polish men began to chase after him, shouting anti-Semitic epithets. He realized that they would not leave him alone, and began to run away, but they pursued him. As he was running, an unknown hand grabbed him and pulled him by the arm inside a building, quickly locking the shutter. A Jew of the city had noticed the disturbance and saved the young man.

On the way back to Rypin, Rabbi Frankel decided he would not remain in the Diaspora a day longer than necessary. He resolved to leave Poland and make aliya to Eretz Israel. His wife tried to dissuade him, but he insisted: "Only Eretz Israel; there is no other place for us."

His wife asked how he could make such a fateful decision without consulting with the Rebbe of Gur. So Rabbi Frankel traveled several days by train to Góra Kalwaria, near Warsaw, to Rabbi Abraham Mordechai Alter, the Imrei Emet. The Rebbe of Gur was of diminutive stature, whereas Rabbi Frankel was quite tall. When the rebbe heard his question regarding Eretz Israel, he looked up at him and said in Yiddish, "Yitzchak Yedidya, tell me the truth. Did you come to ask for my advice, or to receive my blessing?" Rabbi Frankel lowered his gaze. Ostensibly, he had come for advice, but in front of the Rebbe of Gur he could speak only the absolute truth. He answered, "I came to receive a blessing."

The rebbe asked his assistant to phone his son-in-law, Rabbi Itche Meir Levin, leader of Agudath Israel, to ask for his assistance in obtaining aliya certificates. In the meantime, the Frankels' second son was born, and they named him after the previous Gur Rebbe, the Sefat Emet— Yehuda Aryeh Leib. A while later, they received certificates in the name of Yitzchak Yedidya Frankel, Channah Leah Frankel, Isser Frankel— then a year and a half old—and the infant Aryeh Frankel. The family packed their belongings into one suitcase, and in another bag they placed the prayer shawl, tefillin, and candlesticks. Carrying the babies in their arms, they began their journey to Eretz Israel. When they reached the train station in Warsaw, Mrs. Frankel needed to find a secluded corner to nurse Aryeh. While they were busy looking around for one, their only suitcase was stolen, along with all their earthly possessions.

The rabbi and his wife searched frantically for the lost suitcase—to no avail. But then another thief at the train station noticed the distress of the mother of the babies. His sympathies were aroused and he instructed Rabbi Frankel to follow him to meet the ringleader of organized crime in Warsaw. When the chief criminal, who happened to be a Jew, heard the story of the theft, he calmed the young rabbi and promised that when he returned to the station, he would find the stolen suitcase—and that is exactly what transpired.

The Frankel family reached Eretz Israel by boat in January 1935. They settled in the Florentine neighborhood of Tel Aviv, where Rabbi Frankel taught at a local religious school. There, he became a kind of unofficial one-man ministry of absorption—helping new immigrants settle into the country—as well as a pillar of support for the family members who followed him to Eretz Israel. His own family also expanded to include three more children—all in all, he and Mrs. Frankel had four boys and a girl. He became neighborhood rabbi and then chief rabbi of Tel Aviv-Jaffa, all without politics, without public relations, without recommendations—solely on the strength of the one principle he followed his entire life: "Your deeds will either bring you near or distance you." The people loved him dearly.

Residents of the Florentine neighborhood considered Rabbi Frankel the "father" of their community, which was a crowded cross section of immigrants from Bukhara, Salonika (Thessaloniki, Greece), Morocco, Yemen, Poland, Hungary, and Romania. At one point, he succeeded in uniting them to begin a nationwide tradition. In the Diaspora, they had all celebrated the holiday of Simchat Torah, the day on which Jews finish the yearly cycle of Torah readings, on the day after the eighth day of the Sukkot holiday. In Eretz Israel, Simchat Torah falls on the same day as Shemini Atzeret, the last day of Sukkot. Typically, after the conclusion of the holiday at sundown, Jews recite the weekday evening service in the synagogues, then go home and say the concluding *Havdalah* prayer. They dismantle the special booths they had constructed for Sukkot and return to their everyday routines.

But in the Ahavat Chessed synagogue on Emek Yizrael Street in south Tel Aviv (today named Yedidya Frenkel Street), at the end of the holiday in October 1942, Rabbi Frankel asked his congregants to stay behind for a few minutes. The congregants wondered at his strange request, but they respected their rabbi's wishes. He removed a Torah scroll from the ark, and in a voice quivering with emotion, announced to the congregation, "In Poland and elsewhere throughout war-torn Europe, the telephones aren't working, the telegraph stations are closed, the mail no longer runs. Entire communities are cut off, and we do not know what has happened to their Jews. At this exact hour, in Warsaw, Kraków, and every other city in Poland, they should be beginning their Simchat Torah celebrations. But we do not know whether the synagogues are open, whether the Jews are allowed to go to them, whether they are performing the traditional processions holding the Torah scrolls. We are completely cut off from them, and despite our attempts to make contact, the communities do not answer. But all Jews are responsible for one another. Let us act in their stead and perform processions on their behalf, at least symbolically."

The congregants began to circle the platform, holding the Torah scrolls in their arms. Rabbi Frankel chanted loudly, "Please, God, save us; please,

God, make us prosper!" Singing songs, they completed the processions and replaced the Torah scroll in the ark. From that day on, every year at the end of Sukkot, residents of the Florentine neighborhood met at the end of Emek Yizrael Street to perform the Simchat Torah "processions of the communities," which were called that because of the variety of Jewish communities that participated. This was how Rabbi Frankel initiated a nationwide Israeli tradition of "second processions" (*hakafot sheniyot*), a second round of dancing with the Torah scroll held on the night after the holiday of Shemini Atzeret/Simchat Torah.

For these processions, the rabbi donned a Bukharan robe and *kippah* to honor the majority of the residents of the Florentine neighborhood, who were Bukharan Jews. He marched at the head of a parade that transformed Florentine, a poor neighborhood whose residents were mostly new immigrants, into a pilgrimage destination for many official government representatives. As long as he lived, each Israeli prime minister and IDF chief of staff participated in those processions. Later, the idea for these "second processions" spread to Jerusalem, to the main square of Tel Aviv, Kfar Chabad, and the central army training base, and from there to all the synagogues and religious councils throughout the country.

DURING MY LAST YEAR OF STUDIES AT PONEVEZH YESHIVA, I later learned, Rabbi Frankel took an interest in me, asking and checking into my background as a potential groom for his daughter. Because she was his only daughter and the apple of his eye, he intended to investigate every aspect of my personality, and he did so with characteristic thoroughness.

Although I knew nothing of it, he met with the *rosh yeshiva*, Rabbi Kahaneman. Rabbi Frankel also spoke about me to Rabbi Dovid Povarsky, the man who had examined me and accepted me into the yeshiva. Rabbi Frankel talked with youths from Tel Aviv who knew me and asked them about my personality, and went to Jerusalem to meet with Rabbi Auerbach, who had been largely responsible for building my character, and knew me in my early teens. Rabbi Auerbach was not one to mince words, and he used a phrase that means the world to rabbis and Torah scholars: "What he acquires for himself, he will grant to others." For Rabbi Frankel, this saying from the Talmudic tractate *Baba Metzia* summed me up in a nutshell. Years later, he told me that Rabbi Auerbach had applied this aphorism to me, suggesting that I was one who not only had the qualities necessary to achieve his goals but also had the ability to pass on these qualities to others—one who would not live his life for himself alone, but would influence his community. One Aramaic sentence was enough for my mentor to express all that.

My cousin Shmuel Lau also continued to push the match. We agreed that I would be his guest on the seventh day of Passover, and after the festive meal, I would accompany him to Rabbi Frankel's home and join the rabbi in his walk to the Tel Aviv seashore, where he would conduct a mass recitation of the "Song of the Sea," which Moses and the Children of Israel sang after the miraculous crossing of the Red Sea (Exodus 15). Rabbi Frankel organized this event each year on the last day of Passover. According to the agreed plan, the rabbi's daughter and I would have our first conversation on our way back from this event. Actually, we did not manage to speak at all, because she was standing near her father, and hundreds of people crowded around the rabbi to have a word with him. Obviously, they were unaware that at that very moment, a match was about to be made.

At a later date, Chaya-Ita and I finally met, and exchanged views and opinions, thoughts and plans. Chaya-Ita disagreed with her parents in her evaluation of our first meeting. Her parents said, "You seem to find him an appropriate candidate." Their daughter replied that she felt we had established an emotional foundation, but that her parents had to decide whether I was indeed suitable for her. The traditional Jewish matchmaking concept combines the children's feelings and the parents' thoughts.

After meeting with Rabbi Auerbach, Rabbi Frankel seemed to be satisfied. He asked his daughter when we planned to meet next. If she were willing, he said, she should invite me to their home so that he could speak to me in person. One night I went to their home after Shabbat was over, and although I did not think her father would give me a negative answer, I really did not know what to expect. Rabbi Frankel arranged for his wife and Chaya-Ita to be out of the house, visiting her brother, Rabbi Isser Frankel, who lived in south Tel Aviv, so we were alone.

We sat on the balcony, which offered a view of the entire city of Jaffa. The rabbi served me a post-Shabbat evening meal, and, after we had eaten it, said something that I will always remember: "I can call you Israel, right? Have you noticed the second chapter of Genesis, which describes the creation of Adam and Eve? Adam says, *This is now bone of my bones, and flesh of my flesh: she shall be called woman, because she was taken out of man.* Here the Torah diverges from the Creation story and says, as if in parentheses, *Therefore shall a man leave his father and his mother, and shall cleave unto his wife and they shall be one flesh.*

"The entire institution of marriage is contained in this verse. This is the basis for generation upon generation. This is what it will be like when you get married, like Adam and Eve. This is why we recite as one of the seven blessings under the *chuppah*, 'Let the loving couple be exceedingly joyful, just as You made Your creation joyful in the garden of Eden, so long ago.' Every couple is a continuation of Adam and Eve.

"Now I ask you," continued Rabbi Frankel, "really, why does the Torah emphasize the negative side of this—*Therefore shall a man leave his father and his mother?* We understand the importance of the positive statement, *and shall cleave unto his wife*—to establish a home and family. But why does the Torah use the verb *to leave* regarding the parents? For twenty years, the parents invest in their child. They can't sleep at night while he burns with fever, they work overtime in order to support him, they take care of his every need. And after twenty years, he leaves his father and mother. What is this—a divorce from the parents? What did they do to deserve this? Why does the Torah have to say, *to leave?*"

I listened carefully, and thought that this was indeed a fascinating question, but was this why I had come to the rabbi's house? I wanted to hear what he thought about my proposed marriage to his daughter! Was this, in fact, a parting meal? He wines and dines me, and then all of a sudden poses a question from the Torah, putting me on the spot? I had no answers.

Thinking quickly, I admitted to the rabbi that I had never thought about that verse. I told him that I had heard many homilies from my friends about engagement and the seven wedding blessings, but none of them had addressed his question. Rabbi Frankel was not surprised. When

I finished, he said in a fatherly manner, "I tell you what I think. Sometimes I stand under the *chuppah* before a bride and groom whom I don't know. Often, I ask myself whether the match will last. After all, these are two different worlds we're talking about. How can they possibly *cleave* to one another? I ask myself, 'Yitzchak Yedidya, what can you say at the wedding ceremony of these two worlds?' But on second thought, I think to myself that there, standing on either side of the couple, are the parents. Twenty or thirty years ago, they stood in the exact same position, excited brides and grooms at their own weddings. They also were not born in the same mold, but the connection between them has held. Now they're marrying off the next generation. In other words, when we look at the parents' home, when we see the father respecting the mother and vice versa, and we see that they live in a home of peace and love, this is a personal example for the chain of generations to follow."

At this point, Rabbi Frankel stopped speaking for a moment. Then he continued. "Israel, the verb *to leave* does not have to be understood literally. That same word, whose Hebrew root is *ayin-zayin-bet*, can also mean 'inheritance,' as in the word *i-za-von*, whose root is also *ayin-zayin-bet*. There is material inheritance, which parents bequeath to their children after a long life, and there is spiritual inheritance, which they grant their son or daughter the day the child leaves home and gets married. Leaving one's father and mother means one should inherit their example. The Torah presents this as a condition: only if a man *leaves* his father and mother will he have a true chance of *cleaving* to his wife. That is how they will succeed in raising a family."

He thought for a moment, giving me a chance to digest his words. Then he continued: "I have heard of you and your reputation for some time. My daughter has received marriage proposals from around the country and beyond, but your name has come up repeatedly." Rabbi Frankel named those who had suggested me for his daughter, including his friend from the yeshiva in Warsaw, Rabbi David Weissbrod-Halachmi, and my brother Shiko's brother-in-law, Israel Mintzer. "I have considered you and asked about you. I have heard of your talents and distinguished qualities, and I have no doubt about any of them. But one thing bothers me: where is your 'leaving'? You have no home, you have no parents to leave, as the verse says, and you have no spiritual inheritance."

I felt tears choking my throat. His words were like a eulogy for me and my destroyed family. Rabbi Frankel was telling me, in fact, that because of my personal history as a Holocaust survivor and orphan who had no home, because I did not grow up with a mother and father and had no example to follow, it would be difficult for me to build a Jewish home and family. He said, "I recall the speeches of your father, Rabbi Moshe Chaim Lau. But you did not grow up in his shadow and did not know what family life is like. You have spent almost your entire life in institutions, dormitories, and yeshivas. This is what bothers me about placing my daughter in your hands. Still, after checking into your background, talking with all your rabbis and friends in Jerusalem and Bnei Brak, I learned something about your brother."

At that time, Naphtali was an editor at the *She'arim* newspaper of Po'alei Agudath Israel, to which Rabbi Frankel contributed a column on halacha every Friday. Rabbi Frankel said, "I have noted the behavior of your brother, who came to the big city of Tel Aviv but remained an observant Jew. Of everything I have heard about you, I believe and hope that this one worry I have will prove unfounded. It doesn't interest me one bit," he added, "that you have no money, or that there is no father-in-law to share expenses with me. Believe me that my daughter has had offers from wealthy men, but they do not interest me. I also came to Eretz Israel with nothing, with two babies, one about a year, the other just two months old. I taught school and to this day, I live in a rented apartment. I am only interested in the groom's personality."

Rabbi Frankel lived in Tel Aviv for fifty-one years. He was chief rabbi of that city for fourteen of those years, but he never owned his own apartment or car, and the material side of life did not interest him at all. But he feared the scars I might have from lack of family. He was worried that I did not know the meaning of affection, generosity, or compromise. That was why Rabbi Frankel made sure to have private conversations with my roommates at the yeshiva. He wanted to know how I got along with others, and whether orphanhood had taken its toll on my interpersonal relationships.

At the end of that long, private conversation, Rabbi Frankel declared, "If for your part you are willing, then we are willing to accept you as part of our family. Welcome." I felt overwhelming joy, along with a piercing sadness that my father and mother could not be with me at this happy moment. Meanwhile, Mrs. Frankel and her daughter had returned home, and Rabbi Frankel told them about our conversation. That week, in early June 1959, we invited my two brothers, Yehoshua and Naphtali, and my cousin Shmuel Yitzchak Lau, who had acted as matchmaker, to a meeting with Rabbi Frankel's four sons, and we toasted *le-chaim* at the *vort*, the signing of the engagement agreement. The engagement ceremony was held a few weeks later, on my birthday, 22 Sivan 5719 (June 28, 1959). Eight months later, in February 1960, we were married in Tel Aviv.

SEVEN WEEKS AFTER OUR WEDDING, during Passover, two events occurred that changed my life.

One was related to the sad fact that Rabbi Aharon Frankel, my wife's sixty-nine-year-old grandfather, entered Tel Hashomer Hospital for a leg amputation. Professor Mark Moses performed the operation after blood clots had turned the leg completely blue.

After the Passover Eve prayer service, we went to Rabbi Frankel's house to await the beginning of the seder. Rabbi Frankel, who visited his father daily, had promised to perform a shortened version of the seder for all the patients in the ward, including his father. After the seder, he had to walk quite a few miles back from Tel Hashomer to the Florentine neighborhood, so we knew that our seder would begin late and waited in his home for him to return.

While we were still waiting for the rabbi, Ziskind Finkelstein and Yosef Eliyahu Horonchik, the two beadles of Or Torah Synagogue, entered. Or Torah was the synagogue where Rabbi Aharon Frankel normally officiated. This synagogue, also in the Florentine neighborhood, had begun to lose congregants. Many were moving to the northern end of the city. In addition, they now had no rabbi to attract the remaining residents to services. The beadles, worried about the situation, asked me to come to the synagogue the next morning, on the first day of the holiday. They wanted me to lead both the recitation of Psalms in the Hallel section of the service and the prayer for dew, as well as to give a sermon. I agreed, thinking that instead of praying at Rabbi Frankel's synagogue, I would pray at his father's. On that seder night, waiting for Rabbi Frankel to arrive from visiting his sick father at Tel Hashomer, I received my first request, albeit unofficial, to act as a pulpit rabbi.

I had received my ordination in the summer of 1959, around the time of my engagement, but it was on that first day of Passover that I began to serve as a rabbi, although unpaid, in my wife's grandfather's synagogue. When Rabbi Frankel finally came home and heard about this, he was thrilled. And when I told his sick father, he asked me to keep his seat warm for him. Unfortunately, he returned to his synagogue for only three months. After recovering from the first leg amputation, the doctors had to amputate the other leg, and he never returned to the synagogue. I served there as rabbi for five and a half years, until August 1965, when I became rabbi of the Tiferet Zvi Synagogue in the northern section of the city.

The second event I consider a turning point in my life also occurred during the intermediate days of Passover. I was with my wife in her parents' home, a three-room apartment. Two of the rooms were connected and served both as a dining room and reception room, while the third was Rabbi and Mrs. Frankel's bedroom. My wife and I slept in the dining room. At four in the morning, we heard the earsplitting sirens of ambulances and fire trucks. I opened my eyes, peeked outside, and saw the sky red as blood.

Rabbi Frankel's apartment stood opposite Volovelsky Center, which housed many artisan workshops, mainly carpentry shops constructed of wood. Fire often broke out in those shacks, as the result of electric short circuits or burning cigarettes. The sight was frightening—the flames reached the skies. It seemed that the fire would never stop spreading, and that it threatened the entire Florentine neighborhood.

I asked myself whether I should wake up the whole household so we could flee, but then I heard noises in the corridor. Carefully, I opened the door between the dining room and the hall and discovered that the narrow corridor was jam-packed. Rabbi Frankel stood there in his robe; like a policeman, he was directing the flow of people climbing the fifty steps that led up to his apartment. Those who could not enter the tiny, crowded apartment stood on the stairway. The residents of the wooden shacks in Volovelsky Center waited there in silence.

As I discovered, this was a regular ritual. Once every few months, whenever a fire broke out, the neighborhood residents would come to Rabbi Frankel's home to deposit their valuables, confident that their treasures would be safe there. The rabbi pointed to the floor, showing the river of people where to place their things. A pile grew in the center of the room: candlesticks, records, books, Hanukkah menorahs, albums, and photographs. One man left a hand-cranked gramophone. Another pushed his way through to the rabbi, gave him a bag, and said that rolled inside the rubber band were six hundred dollars, his savings for his daughter's dowry. Then a young woman came up. On the floor, nestled on a down pillow, she had placed her little baby.

When I saw that baby, whose mother brought it to the rabbi's house to save it from the flames, I broke down. I left the room, went out onto the balcony opposite the flames, and cried. I remembered myself as a little boy in an attic in Piotrków, hiding with my mother from the Gestapo soldiers. I remembered Mother pushing a honey cookie into my mouth so that I wouldn't cry. As I wept, I thought that if I were going to be a rabbi, I wanted to be one like Rabbi Frankel. A rabbi in whom the public had complete trust, a rabbi to whom a mother brings her most precious possession, her baby, in order to save its life.

On the day of my inauguration as chief rabbi of Israel, I held that image in my mind. I spoke about the events of that early morning, and when I finished, I added, "I may know the contents of one book after another, as well as endless rabbinic responsa, but the main question is: 'What kind of rabbi will I be?' " I described my father, and Rabbi Meir Shapira of Lublin, my uncle the rabbi of Kolomea, and my uncle from Kiryat Motzkin. But, I declared, seeing Rabbi Frankel in action during that Passover was the clearest demonstration of the ideal image of a rabbi.

When the fire died down, four hours later, the Florentine residents took back their belongings and left with the knowledge that there was one place that was safe—Rabbi Frankel's home. This knowledge gave them great strength and faith. The image of that night remains in my mind, and has served as a beacon for my rabbinic career to this day.

The first place my wife and I lived together on our own was at 18 Peretz Street in Tel Aviv, between the central bus station and Moshavot Square, in a two-room apartment up seventy-five stairs. Our first three children were born there. It was not easy to climb those stairs with two baby carriages, or to carry up the groceries, but we lived like that without complaining.

In the first few years of our marriage, the deputy minister of religious affairs, Dr. Zerach Warhaftig, offered me the job of rabbi of the Adath Israel community in Hendon, London. The job was for a minimum of three years. When Rabbi Frankel heard of this offer, and that we were considering a four-day preliminary visit to London, he did not sleep all night. In the morning, he asked his son Aryeh to try to convince us to cancel the trip. I discussed the matter with Rabbi Frankel and tried to understand the reason for his worry. He was decisive: "Israel, they'll never let you leave. Not after three years, and not after thirteen. I don't want children on paper. My daughter and you will write me aerograms, and send postcards every few days, and then pictures of the grandchildren. That's a family on paper. I want you with me, nearby," the rabbi insisted.

I put his mind at ease, answering, "You are my father. I cannot make a decision, even one I would like to make, if you have a significant objection. I respect you for the courage you displayed in accepting me as a husband for your daughter, as I was—an orphan, without a penny to my name. So I accept your recommendation." I refused the tempting British offer and remained in Israel, near my father-in-law.

I often heard my mother-in-law quote her husband with this sentence, short and to the point: "I was never disappointed in Israel. Despite his less-than-perfect opening hand, my intuition told me that things would work out." To me, these words were worth their weight in gold.

Years later, one of my daughters received an offer of a match with the son of a very highly respected rabbinic figure. I took it as a great compliment that my daughter had been offered an ideal young man from an excellent family. But as part of the offer, the prospective groom's family demanded various conditions that were difficult for us to accept. I was then rabbi of Netanya and asked my wife to go to Tel Aviv and ask for her father's opinion about the prospective match and the conditions.

When Rabbi Frankel came home for lunch, Chaya-Ita sat in the kitchen with her parents and recounted the details. Rabbi Frankel listened carefully but did not say a word. He finished his soup and the main course, and she kept talking, but he remained silent. Chaya-Ita thought perhaps he was not interested, or did not consider the matter important enough. She felt he was not even listening to her. When she finished, she looked at her father and protested, "Father, you haven't said a word. Have you been listening to what I've been telling you?"

He focused his gaze on her and replied, "Do you want to hear it from me? How can Israel even listen to such a humiliating offer for your wonderful daughter? Who are they next to him?" Shouting, he added, "*Yichus* [pedigree]? They want *yichus*? Is he lacking in *yichus*? Is there another family like his, with thirty-eight generations of rabbis? And after what he went through as a child, today he is rabbi of Netanya! And I tell you that Netanya is not the last stop for him—he'll continue to move up. And now he has to give in to conditions that others are setting for him? Are they doing him a favor by giving him their son? They should thank him for even agreeing to meet with them. I have never told you what I think of your husband, but you know how much I esteem him. And you, don't you dare accept this offer," he advised.

After these words, my wife returned home satisfied. As the sages say, "There is no joy like the removal of doubt." Thanks to his decisiveness, a weight fell from her shoulders. She also had had many doubts about the match. But after her father voiced his thoughts, there was no more room for doubt or hesitation. We accepted his word, and rejected the marriage proposal immediately.

The harmony within the Frankel family was especially impressive. Mrs. Frankel's greatest happiness was to stand beside her husband in everything, to back him on every issue. The admiration and support she gave him were unique.

I remember one example that sheds light on the entire Frankel family. Aryeh, one of the Frankels' sons, was considered a gifted Talmud scholar, modest and very gentle, a true genius. He lived in Jerusalem, and took the bus every day to Petach Tikva, where he was a judge on the religious court. On his fiftieth birthday, instead of returning from work to Jerusalem, he went to his parents' home in Tel Aviv and announced, "I've come to drink a toast with you and to thank you for the fifty years you have given me." His parents had planned to go to Jerusalem that evening and bring their son a birthday present, as they usually would, and especially in honor of his fiftieth year. The parents knew that their son was not the type to have a birthday party for himself; nonetheless, they thought, he would be willing to drink a *le-chaim* with them. But their son preceded them, deviating from the usual practice, and thanked his parents for the gift of life and for raising him.

Two days later Aryeh traveled from Jerusalem to Petach Tikva, as usual. When the bus approached the Lod airport, he suddenly said to the person sitting next to him that he could not breathe. The bus stopped, some passengers laid Rabbi Aryeh on the floor of the bus, and someone performed CPR. In the meantime, they called an ambulance from the airport nearby, which rushed him to Assaf Harofeh Hospital. At the entrance to the emergency room, he said to Rabbi Yosef Segal of Jerusalem, whom he had met on the bus and who had accompanied him to the hospital, "Recite *Shema Yisrael* with me. I feel like I'm going to die."

Rabbi Segal was shocked, and tried to calm him down, saying that they were only taking him to the emergency room and nothing would happen to him. But Aryeh began to recite the words of the *Shema* by himself, and then the refrain "God reigns, God has reigned, God will reign forever and ever." As he recited those words, he passed away. During the bus ride, Rabbi Segal had learned about Rabbi Aryeh's family, and he did not know how to inform the father, Rabbi Frankel, of his son's death. He knew that I was Rabbi Aryeh's brother-in-law, and he phoned me in Netanya.

I went to Assaf Harofeh at once, but there was nothing I could do except weep over the loss. The doctor on duty in the emergency room was a new immigrant from the Soviet Union. When I asked him about Rabbi Aryeh's final minutes, he answered in a shocked voice, "He must be a holy man. I have never seen a soul depart so pristinely, so peacefully."

In the meantime, Aryeh's brothers Isser and Shimon went to inform their parents. When Mrs. Frankel heard of her son's death, she collapsed on the floor, and her heart stopped. A doctor from Ichilov Hospital worked for hours to stabilize her. They took her, on a ventilator and

unconscious, to the hospital in an ambulance, while we all got organized
to go to my brother-in-law's funeral in Jerusalem. The *shiva* (mourning
week) was held in Jerusalem, but Rabbi Frankel wanted to go first to
Ichilov to visit his wife, for he feared they were hiding a double tragedy
from him.

I drove, and he sat beside me, the torn garment as the sign of mourning
for his beloved son visible on his right lapel. When we reached Carlebach
Street and I was about to turn toward the hospital, he asked in a broken
voice if I would drive by his home so that he could take another garment
to cover the torn shirt he had worn for the funeral. Only then did we
go to the hospital to visit his wife. This devoted husband, sensitive to his
wife's state, feared that when she would see the shirt he had torn for their
beloved son, she would recall his death, and the terrible knowledge would
cause her situation to deteriorate even further. The rabbi hoped that she
would still be sedated and that her mind would be free of the tragedy for
a while, and he did not want anything to remind her of it.

When we reached Ichilov, Mrs. Frankel was barely conscious, an
oxygen mask on her face. Rabbi Frankel moved close to her, and whispered, "Channah, I need you." I had no idea if she registered what he
said, but he wanted to strengthen her, to tell her how much he needed
her, so that she would fight her battle and win. I thought I saw her smile
at him. When he said those words, admitting in a very uncharacteristic
manner how much he needed her, she pointed to herself with her index
finger, then pointed to him, and nodded her head as if to say, "I need
you, too."

Even when they were surrounded by death, illness, and endless pain,
it was obvious that their relationship was so unusual and rare that it was
almost otherworldly. Mrs. Frankel recovered after several weeks, but
all her life she carried with her the intense pain of the death of her son
Aryeh.

Rabbi Frankel often borrowed an expression from the biblical Jacob:
For I will go down to the grave mourning for my son. The Rebbe of Gur,
Rabbi Simcha Bunim Alter (the Lev Simcha), came to visit him during
the seven-day mourning period, and despite the concise speech characteristic of this Chassidic group, he said, "Two months ago, during the High

Holidays, thousands filled the Gur study hall in Jerusalem. But there was no one like Aryeh there . . . "

Two years later, in September 1986, Rabbi Frankel died of cancer, at almost seventy-three. On his seventy-second birthday, he said he thought that now he had fulfilled the verse in the book of Exodus: *I will fill the number of your days*. In Hebrew numerology, the word for "I will fill" has the numerical value of seventy-two. In the intensive care unit at Ichilov, in his final hour, he asked me to remove his oxygen mask for a moment because he had to tell me something. I leaned over to hear him, and he said, "Don't let Mother carry a sack on her arm, wandering from house to house among the children. Let our home stand, and you go to her just as you used to visit us." He was a great man, and of all the great personalities I have met in my life, none has influenced me as much as he, not only throughout the twenty-five years that I lived under his wing but afterward as well. His wife died in January 1997. In the ten years of her widowhood, she did her utmost to preserve the unity of the family, and she was our crowning glory.

When I joined the Frankel family, Rabbi Yitzchak Yedidya acted as a father to me. When I was about to get married, I began to call my future mother-in-law Mother. I had last pronounced this word at age seven and a half, when my mother pushed me at the last fraction of a second into the arms of my eighteen-year-old brother Naphtali, realizing with a mother's intuition that that was the only way to save my life. My brother cried out to her, "*Mameh, Mameh*! What will I do with the boy?" while I cried bitterly and screamed in desperation, "Mother! Mother!" My mother boarded the death train, and I never saw her again. I did not utter that word for many years, until I used it for my mother-in-law, Mrs. Channah Frankel.

PART II

THE RAM'S HORN

And Abraham raised his eyes,
and saw — behold! a ram —
and afterwards it was caught in a thicket by its horns.
So Abraham went and took the ram
and offered it up as an offering instead of his son.

GENESIS 22:13

CHAPTER 13

REMEMBRANCE

And none spoke a word to him: for they saw that
his grief was very great.

JOB 2:13

IN MAY 1960, Naphtali phoned me with the news: Adolf Eichmann had
been captured. David Ben-Gurion, prime minister of Israel, was about
to announce it to the public. Agents of Mossad, the Israeli intelligence
agency then led by Isser Harel, were responsible.

This news is what led me to tell my family what the name Eichmann
meant to me. In May 1960, experiences that had been buried inside me
began to break out. The dam burst.

When I was young, I almost never talked about my memories from
the Holocaust period. I collected them inside me, keeping them to myself.
I did not share them with others because I felt they were my personal
memories, and also because of a profound silence that surrounded the
subject—the silence of the Shoah.

I never told my personal Holocaust story in its entirety, not even to my
wife or my in-laws. I recounted a few snippets here and there, when it was
relevant to the situations and people I met throughout my life, but never
in an organized or detailed manner. Even Naphtali, who knew our Holocaust story more accurately and thoroughly than I did, remained silent.

I AWAITED THE TRIAL WITH TREPIDATION. Everyone knew that this Holocaust trial would have singular historic significance. The day it began, I

saw Naphtali standing under the balcony of my apartment. He was a journalist for the *Ha'aretz* newspaper, which had sent him to cover the trial in
Jerusalem. On his way back, instead of going home, he preferred to come
directly from the central bus station to my house. "What happened?" I
asked him, concerned. He asked if he could come up to talk. Naphtali sat
with Chaya-Ita and me the whole evening. All night he reminisced about
the war years. This was the first time I ever heard him speak in a clear and
chronological way about that accursed period. For the first time in our life
together, my wife was exposed to the horrors that my brother and I had
experienced in the Holocaust.

The Eichmann trial was a turning point, and not only for us; it conjured
up the memory of the Holocaust among those who had chosen to repress
it or to keep its details a terrible secret. Many people began to talk—some
more, others less—about what they had undergone in those dark days. The
trial informed the world of the Holocaust and its horrors. In large part, this
was due to the unforgettable testimony of Ka-Zetnick, the pen name of the
writer Yehiel Feiner, who Hebraized his name to De-Nur, or "spark," the
meaning of the Yiddish word *fein*. (*Ka-Zetnik* is Yiddish slang for "concentration camper," and derives from *ka tzet*—the Yiddish pronunciation of
KZ, the acronym for the German *Konzentrationslager*.)

His testimony was short, just nine lines, and because of this, it stood
out among the hundreds of statements given at the trial. He stood on the
witness stand, gazing at Eichmann, who was inside a glass booth, and
described Auschwitz as another planet. He began to describe the victims
descending from the trains, passing Mengele for selection. He was not able
to finish his sentence, he could not utter Mengele's name. He could only
repeat, "I see. . . . I see. . . . I see." In his mind, Ka-Zetnick was viewing
his experiences in replay. Emotionally, he returned to his imprisonment
in Auschwitz. He lost control, collapsed, and fainted on the witness stand.
Because he was taken away for treatment, his testimony ended.

After the Eichmann trial, I occasionally met with Ka-Zetnick. He had
known my father, who taught in the Chachmei Lublin Yeshiva with Rabbi
Meir Shapira, my father's cousin. Yehiel De-Nur was the outstanding student of Rabbi Israel Yosef Pikarsky of that yeshiva, one of the leading
rabbis of the last century.

De-Nur/Ka-Zetnick lived near me, but he almost never left his home. I used to go visit and talk with him. Mainly I listened to him. I shared a few of my memories with him, and we developed a close relationship.

It was not just at the Eichmann trial that he saw the horrors of Auschwitz taking place before his eyes—this unique vision influenced his entire life and all of his writings.

After making aliya, Ka-Zetnick married Nina, the daughter of Dr. Yosef Asherman, one of the most respected physicians in Israel at that time. Nina's parents, he told me during our meetings, were not thrilled about their relationship. She was the only daughter of an affluent, distinguished family, and they considered her world far removed from that of this Holocaust refugee with his strange habits, odd manner of expression, and unkempt dress, whose entire being was difficult to comprehend. Ka-Zetnick was the direct opposite of the image the Asherman family worked to uphold.

Despite her parents' objections, the wedding proceeded, and was held in the courtyard of the Asherman home. Ka-Zetnick, who was afraid of crowds, requested that the guests be limited to a handful, not many more than the required quorum of ten men. In the middle of the ceremony, which took all of ten minutes, Ka-Zetnick's entire body began to shake and he murmured, "Move! Give me room! Let me breathe, I can't breathe. Everybody move."

Dr. Asherman tugged at Ka-Zetnick's sleeve, trying to hint that he should behave himself and not be disruptive, but Ka-Zetnick could not calm down. At the end of the ceremony, he said to his new wife, in a trembling voice, as if awakening from a dream: "Everyone came to my wedding. I had no room to move. My father was standing here, and my mother smiled at me, and my sister and brother and aunts and uncles, and my rabbi—everyone crowded around me." One by one, he listed the names of his family members and guests, certain beyond a doubt that they had all been present at his wedding. He had felt suffocated by the crowd.

That was what he was like. He lived the events of the Holocaust as if they were taking place before his very eyes, instead of being relegated to the past. He wrote some of his books, such as *House of Dolls* (1955), while isolated in a hut in a field, disconnected from the present, his entire being given over to the reality "over there." As he confided to me during my visits, he wrote using "the blood of my heart."

"One sentence in your short testimony angered me," I said to him in our first meeting. "You coined the phrase 'Auschwitz as another planet'— but it is not accurate. If Auschwitz were indeed another planet, it would be easier to accept the Holocaust. But in truth, the disaster of Auschwitz is that it happened on the very same planet where we had lived before, where we live now, and where we will continue to live. Those who carried out the cruel murders of the innocent were ordinary people, who returned home from their murderous acts to water the flowers in their manicured gardens. They tended the flowers lovingly and carefully so they would blossom, just after they had torn infants to pieces and shattered the skulls of men and women. Just after shoving thousands of people into the gas chambers to their deaths, they came home to play with dolls together with their little girls, and listen to classical music, eyes closed, engrossed in the uplifting spirituality of Bach and Beethoven. They knew exactly what was going on in the camps, but were able to continue enjoying life as if unaffected. Is that another planet? Absolutely not. Those were people just like you and me, and that's the whole problem. When you transfer all those horrors to another planet, you minimize the issue. You are saying that something like the Holocaust can never happen to us again. In my humble opinion, you are wrong."

Ka-Zetnick fell silent. He did not argue; he merely withdrew into himself. To me, it was abundantly clear that we must not use the term "another planet," because the Holocaust was no such thing; the term is a gross falsification of history. Unfortunately, we have no guarantee that this twisted atrocity will never happen again. Experience has taught me that we have to believe the threats of the evil and insane, and not underestimate their power. I cannot afford to give credence to statements like, "He's a *meshiggener*; he doesn't mean it; it's impossible, the world would never let that happen." Every time I hear such phrases, I am petrified. I have no doubt that we must take every fanatic seriously, even the most powerless.

Who took that diminutive Austrian private seriously, the one who articulated his criminal racial theory in the basements of Munich? No one. At the beginning of the 1940s in Europe, people insisted that the world would not permit such theories to be acted upon. Still, not long ago we heard wild hyperbole from such leaders as Yasser Arafat, who called for one million martyrs to march on Jerusalem, and Mahmoud Ahmadinejad, with his genocidal threats against Israel and his denial of the Holocaust.

After the Holocaust, we cannot allow ourselves to ignore or belittle the significance of those who make such violent proclamations. Every "fanatic" has genuine intentions, and these intentions have the potential to become reality if we do not take them seriously and do not do everything in our power to stop them. If it happened there, in the center of civilization, it can happen again, anywhere.

Buchenwald was located just eight minutes away from Weimar, the cradle of German and European culture. While enjoying drama, dance, and music productions in the elegant theaters, audiences of the 1940s could view the smoke rising from the nearby crematoria. It was impossible to miss, but they chose to close their eyes. No German could hide behind the false assertions—we did not know, we did not hear.

WHEN THE TWENTIETH ANNIVERSARY of the Warsaw ghetto uprising came, two years after the beginning of the Eichmann trial, the communist Polish authorities planned an impressive commemoration ceremony in Warsaw. They invited a delegation from Israel, which included Rabbi Yitzchak Yedidya Frankel and Gideon Hausner, who had achieved world renown as the chief prosecutor in the Eichmann trial.

The event was broadcast all over Europe. Participants included the president of Poland, the prime minister, and ministers of the Polish government. But the ceremony gave the false impression that the ghetto fighters were Poles, not Jews. Not a word in Hebrew or Yiddish was heard, nor did the organizers ask the Israeli representatives to speak. From the point of view of the communist Poles, the rebellion symbolized the heroic struggle of the socialists against German fascism. The organizers did not ask Hausner to speak at the ceremony, even though he was an international figure thanks to his brilliant prosecution of Adolf Eichmann, chief architect of the mass deportation of Jews to death camps.

But the patriarchal, impressive figure of Rabbi Frankel stood out. To the audience, his physical appearance was a stark reminder of those whom the speakers were eulogizing. For twenty years, since the destruction of the ghetto, the likes of such a man, wearing the garb of a traditional Jew, had not been seen in Warsaw. To the Poles, Rabbi Frankel resurrected the image of the authentic Jew. For centuries, such Jews had been an integral part of their world, but after the Second World War, they became a relic of the past, a museum display. No one viewing the ceremony could ignore him.

The ceremony took place beside the monumental Warsaw Ghetto Uprising memorial, designed by Jewish Polish sculptor Nathan Rapoport. The Polish speakers described the Second World War as an epic struggle of fascists versus communists, the latter having taught the world a lesson in heroism—but made no mention of Jews or Judaism.

Then, during a pause between speeches, in a moment of complete silence, Rabbi Frankel decided to take action. Interrupting the ceremony's detailed schedule, he rose to speak, unaided by a microphone, since he was not one of the formal speakers. Rabbi Frankel broke into a spontaneous cry from the depths of his soul, reciting Kaddish for the millions of Jews murdered on European soil: "*Yitgadal ve-yitkadash shemei rabba*—Magnified and sanctified be His great Name."

For years, whenever he would describe that moment, his eyes filled with tears and he recounted the story as if he were again saying Kaddish on Polish soil: "When I said Kaddish, I did not see the people around me. I saw only the Jews of Luntschitz, Rypin, Warsaw, and the other Polish towns, and I said Kaddish for them. Around the monument, I saw people who had climbed trees before the ceremony began that night—they had not been invited, but did not want to miss it. They staked out posts in the treetops, and when I finished saying Kaddish, I saw them responding, 'Amen.' I could not hear them, but I saw their faces. They were my choir, my congregation."

Another image he recalled from that trip was the delegation's visit to Treblinka. Next to the spot where the train tracks ended was a field full of human bones, lying exposed for all to see. When Rabbi Frankel saw them, he froze. He described that bloodcurdling sight to me: "I was like the prophet Ezekiel. I stood *in the middle of the valley which was full of bones . . . and lo, they were very dry.*" He was carrying a copy of a Polish newspaper that had reported the previous day's ceremony, and he began to gather the bones from the field into that newspaper. A Polish photographer documented the rabbi from Tel Aviv, with his wide-brimmed black velvet hat and his long beard, bending down to the ground in tears, gathering the dry bones of the butchered Jews of Treblinka into a Polish newspaper.[1]

When Rabbi Frankel asked the Polish guide who accompanied the delegation why they did not bury, or at least cover, the human bones, the answer was chilling: "Rabbi Frankel, you have no idea how many times we have covered them, with earth and even with asphalt pressed by a steamroller. But a year later, it all bursts from the ground, as if we had done nothing." Jews from Antwerp and New York who visited Treblinka regularly confirmed his words: sometimes the bones were exposed, sometimes covered. It was as if Polish soil had heard and obeyed the *Yizkor* (literally "remembrance"), a memorial prayer for Holocaust victims—*O Earth! Do not conceal their blood and let there be no resting place for their cry.*

Rabbi Frankel returned to Israel with the bones he had gathered wrapped inside the Polish newspaper. He contacted several stone factories and asked for donations of stone. Out of the large stones he received, he built a monument in the Nahalat Yitzhak cemetery in Tel Aviv, and there he buried those bones from the valley of death in Treblinka. The monument bears the single word TREBLINKA. Each year, on Holocaust Memorial Day, Rabbi Frankel conducted a memorial service at the monument for Treblinka survivors. His son, Rabbi Isser Frankel, went on to continue his father's tradition.

ON SHABBAT DURING THE DELEGATION'S VISIT TO POLAND, they attended services at the Nożyk Synagogue, the sole remaining synagogue in Warsaw. During the Holocaust, the Germans had used the building as a horse stable. In the spring of 1963, eighteen years after the end of the war, our

---

1. The next day, many European newspapers carried this photograph, and it won first prize in a journalistic photography competition that year.

delegation, along with the remaining Jews of Warsaw, gathered there for Shabbat morning services. The weekly Torah portion was from Leviticus 10:6, focusing on the deaths of Nadav and Avihu, sons of the high priest Aaron. Rabbi Frankel emphasized the verse *But let your brothers, the whole house of Israel, mourn the burning which the Lord has kindled*. There was no more fitting passage for that time and place, or for that group of Jews from all corners of the earth, who had not set foot in Poland since the Holocaust. That verse from the Torah was speaking to them, and indeed, they did "mourn the burning . . . "

Rabbi Eliyahu Katz, rabbi of Bratislava, then part of communist Czechoslovakia, was present at the memorial ceremony and at the synagogue. The Czechoslovakian authorities had approved his trip to Poland out of transparent propagandist intentions, to show the world that they did not oppress minorities and that Jewish life continued under the communist regime. However, in reality there was someone following him and watching his every move. Observers noticed that throughout the delegation's stay in Poland, he did not utter a single word. But that Shabbat, in the synagogue, the Jews honored the rabbi from Bratislava and asked him to speak.

Rabbi Katz, his body completely stooped, mounted the platform, kissed the ark curtain, turned to face the congregation, and, as if expressing the feelings and tears of the Jews of Eastern Europe, he delivered a sermon on the weekly portion with just two words in Hebrew, which translate as: *And Aaron was silent*.[2]

Not only during that visit to Poland but in every speech Rabbi Frankel gave thereafter he mentioned the Holocaust. He also took upon himself a daily custom of reading at least one chapter of the *Yizkor* books (memorial albums compiled after the Holocaust to remember former Jewish communities), which grew in number over the years as more information about lost communities became available. The *Yizkor* books contain descriptions of the vibrant Jewish life during pre-Holocaust centuries as well as details about the war period. Rabbi Frankel collected piles of these books on top

---

2. In the Bible, Aaron was silent after the death of his two sons—he could conceive of no response. So, too, were the Jews after the Holocaust. Rabbi Katz later became rabbi of the city of Be'er Sheva, in the Negev Desert.

of the armoire in his bedroom, and read selections from them every night before reciting the bedtime *Shema* prayer.

ONE DAY IN TEL AVIV, I HAILED A TAXI. After I got in, the taxi driver looked at me through his rearview mirror and began a conversation. "You're Rabbi Lau, aren't you?" he asked, and continued: "You're a Holocaust survivor, right? I've heard you talk about it on one of the radio programs. I've got to tell you a personal story. I also experienced the Holocaust as a youth. Today I have three children. I make a point of going home every day to eat lunch with my wife and sons. At work, they know I'm a stickler about this. It's important for me to be with my kids at lunchtime when they come home from school, to sit together, eat, and talk with them. That's the only time of the day that I see my children. At night, when I go home from work, they're already asleep.

"This week," he said, "in the middle of the meal, my eight-year-old son asked me, 'Daddy, tell me, is it true that you're a bastard?' I felt the blood drain from my face. The food stuck in my throat, and I felt like I was choking. I scolded him: 'How dare you talk to your father like that! What do you mean, a bastard? We don't say such things!'

"The boy was taken aback. He tried to defend himself," the driver recalled, "saying that some kids in his class had used that word. The kids asked the teacher what it meant, and she tactfully explained that a bastard was someone who did not know who his parents were. 'We have a grandmother and grandfather on Mommy's side,' my son explained. 'Mommy knows her father and mother. But you? On your side we don't have a grandmother or a grandfather. That means you don't have parents, and you don't know who they are. So doesn't that mean you're a bastard?' "

As the driver told me his story, I detected signs of his rising anger. "I jumped up from the chair, tears choking my throat. I ran into the bathroom and cried as I have never done before," he told me, and added, "You're the first person to whom I've told this terrible story." I felt for him, but I replied that his son's thought process was correct. "Your behavior was out of line. Your father and mother are not around. They can't give your son coins for Hanukkah *gelt* [money], and your son can't hide the *afikoman matzah* from them at the Passover seder. So how can he know of their

existence? Why don't you tell your children what happened to them—
how they lived, how they died, and who they were? Of course you can't
tell an eight-year-old boy all the details of the Holocaust, and certainly not
about your parents' bitter end. But up until that terrible ending, they had
a full and rich life, and your children must know about it, for the sake of
your family's continuity, for the personal history of each one." The taxi
driver nodded his head, and when I got out, he was able to thank me. In
my imagination, I could hear the conversation that took place in his home
at lunch the next day.

My exchange with the taxi driver was just one example of the general
atmosphere that pervaded Israel in the first years of the state. People preferred not to talk about the horrors of the Holocaust. Some of them did
not want to reopen their wounds, and others felt shame, albeit unjustified.
Still others did not want to burden their children with their pain and the
Nazis' distortion of the entire concept of humanity.

But that is only part of the truth. The survivors may have preferred
not to speak, but the Jews of Eretz Israel also took part in that silence—
they preferred not to listen. The Holocaust survivors who came to Eretz
Israel after the war found a reality there that cultivated an active spirit
of heroism. The pre-State military organizations carried out remarkable operations in order to establish the state. The Jewish population in
the mid-1940s numbered around 600,000; many people were involved in
quasi-military operations or were contributing and volunteering in other
ways. And then we arrived, the Holocaust refugees. Our war was behind
us, while the nascent state was preoccupied with the 1947–48 war that was
then threatening its life.

To the fearless natives of Israel, we were just "bars of soap" who had
come from "over there."

Many years later, when I was chief rabbi, I received a call from Dov
Shilansky, then speaker of the Knesset. He was also a Holocaust survivor,
a native of Shavli, Lithuania (present-day Šiauliai), who had been interned
in the Dachau concentration camp. He asked me to help him change the
verses of a prayer memorializing the Holocaust victims. He explained
that because I was the first chief rabbi to have experienced the Holocaust,
I would be sure to understand his great distress about this prayer. He

referred to the phrase "in memory of the martyrs of the Holocaust who went like sheep to the slaughter." Shilansky was horrified at "like sheep to the slaughter," and asked me to try to eliminate it. I agreed with him, and fulfilled his request.

My father did not go like a sheep to the slaughter. He and the Jews with him stood tall until the very last moment of their lives. They were proud of being Jews, and they made every effort not only to preserve the divine spark in every individual, but also to give it practical expression.

The Israeli nation was then fighting to come into being, and it formed a negative, mistaken picture of Holocaust victims and survivors. Many survivors felt ashamed when longtime Israelis, mainly out of ignorance, identified them with helplessness and human destruction. To survive the beatings, the cold, the hunger, the disease, the humiliation, the orphanhood, and the grief, and to remain alive—is there any greater heroism than this?

On January 27, 2005, a memorial ceremony was held in Auschwitz-Birkenau to commemorate sixty years since the liberation of the camp by the Red Army. Leaders from Israel, Europe, and the United States attended the ceremony. Wearing their warmest clothes, they sat for three hours in penetrating cold under an incessant snowfall. They expressed amazement at the endurance of the camp prisoners, forced to stand in that same cold in their threadbare striped uniforms, for many long years.

Historic milestones such as the mid-1950s trial of Israeli politician Rudolf Kastner[3]—and especially the 1960s trial of Eichmann, one of Hitler's top henchmen—broke the survivors' reticence. For those who still suppressed their Holocaust memories, the dam broke with the 1993 Israeli trial of John "Ivan" Demjanjuk, accused of being "Ivan the Terrible," a notorious SS guard at Treblinka.

---

3. In 1953, an Israeli of Hungarian descent named Malchiel Gruenwald accused Kastner—also a Hungarian Jew—of being a Nazi collaborator. Gruenwald charged Kastner with, among other crimes, making a traitorous arrangement with Nazi leaders for the escape via train of relatives, friends, and other Hungarian Jews from Hungary. Kastner sued Gruenwald for libel, resulting in a dramatic two-year trial that led to Gruenwald's acquittal in 1955; Kastner was vilified by the judge as one who "sold his soul to the devil." Kastner was assassinated in March 1957. The courts later overturned the verdict in 1958.

Passing years and old age also elicited the realization that the survivors were the last living participants in and witnesses to the Holocaust, and that they had a duty to tell their life stories. Some feared they would go to their deaths with their secrets, and the world would never know. The expanding phenomenon of Holocaust denial also pressed them to share their experiences from those days. In parallel, Israeli schools began to require students to research their family roots, thereby deepening their awareness of their personal histories. Young boys and girls conducted extensive interviews with grandparents, who described their histories in detail, telling their grandchildren the stories they had spared their children from hearing. One reason why the Holocaust survivors did not share the horrors of their experiences with their children was because, more than anything, the survivors wanted to protect their children and to raise emotionally healthy Israelis. When these children grew up, and the parents saw that they had managed to raise successful, healthy children, they then felt able to pass on their personal stories to their grandchildren, native Israelis who had grown up with emotionally strong, normal parents. In addition, the film producer and director Steven Spielberg initiated an important project of recording testimonies of Holocaust survivors for the Yad Vashem archives, a significant contribution to the commemoration of the Holocaust. Youth also travel to the sites of destruction in Poland and other concentration camps through the March of the Living program, schools, the IDF, and other organizations. All these forces have combined to break the wall of silence that enveloped Holocaust memories.

In 1951, the Knesset declared 27 Nisan (shortly after Passover)—the day of the last battle for the Warsaw Ghetto—as Holocaust *and* Heroism Remembrance Day (my emphasis). But in my view, the *and* is not an *and* of connection, but rather signifies separation. It is an *and* that has the potential of affixing a negative label to the six million, as if to say: There was a Holocaust, and alongside it, there was also heroism, as if the Warsaw Ghetto uprising and resistance leader Mordechai Anielewicz represent heroism, and all the rest represent the Holocaust. There was just a handful of true heroes, and all the others, the anonymous, were victims, "sheep to the slaughter." This is a distortion of the truth, a harsh blow to the memory of the dead, and especially an affront to the survivors.

People who preserved their spark of divinity and remained human beings were no less heroic than those who threw Molotov cocktails at German tanks from house windows. The choice of name for this day can be understood to imply partiality. It ignores the saying in Ethics of the Fathers: *Do not judge your fellow until you have stood in his place.* In my opinion, it would be truer and more just to call this day Remembrance Day for the Heroism of the Holocaust or Remembrance Day for the Holocaust and Its Heroes.

THOSE WHO ENDURED the horrors of the camps are not the only "Holocaust survivors." That group includes a wide range of Jews from all over the world. At the beginning of the 1980s, Ed Koch, mayor of New York City, invited me to his office. He is a warm Jew, sensitive and emotional, a great lover of Israel and the Jewish people. At our first meeting, he introduced himself to me and declared that he was also a Holocaust survivor. Out of politeness, I refrained from asking him what exactly he survived and where he had been during the Second World War. I wanted to give him a chance to tell his story himself. He said that he had been born in the Bronx and had lived his whole life in New York, but insisted that he was a real survivor. Smiling, I dared to ask how that could be—and Ed Koch began to explain.

Years earlier, he had traveled to Germany for an educational trip. At one of the stops, the guide showed the group the globe that had sat on Hitler's desk. "It reminded me of Charlie Chaplin's movie about the great dictator. But unlike the one in Chaplin's movie," Koch recounted, "that big globe had lots of numbers written on it in black marker. When the guide spun the globe, Europe blackened with numbers. Other continents had far fewer black marks. The guide explained that when World War II broke out, Hitler recorded the Jewish population of each country. After all, they represented his life's goal. Albania, for example, bore the number 1 for the single Jew living there. Our enemy decided that he would not rest as long as that one Jew from Albania, a total stranger to him, remained alive. The territory of the United States bore the number six million.[4] That includes me," said Ed Koch with undisguised anger. "So I am also a

4. The population statistics are slightly inaccurate.

Holocaust survivor—if the Allies hadn't stopped the Nazi beast, no doubt I would have been destroyed."

I shook his hand warmly and said, "Today I have learned an important lesson from you, and I will carry it home with me to Israel. I've heard that not all Jewish communities feel a connection to Holocaust Day. From now on, I'll tell them about the Jew born in New York who lived all his life in an American city, but who feels like a Holocaust survivor, and justifiably so. For the Nazis had no limits. If Hitler had succeeded, and the world had allowed him to continue his atrocities, he would have gone on to destroy all the Jews, in every corner of the globe. This was his declared goal, his reason for living."

DURING ANOTHER VISIT TO NEW YORK, I received from my friend George Klein, one of the founders of the Museum of Jewish Heritage in New York, a photograph of Hitler's final political testament. It was written in German on April 29, 1945, and signed by Hitler and four witnesses. The most disturbing sentence there, and the most important one to study and remember, is the last: "Above all, I charge the leaders of the nation and those under them to scrupulous observance of the laws of race and merciless opposition to the universal poisoner of all peoples, international Jewry." Hitler's definition of Jews as "the universal poisoner" is a chilling reminder of the fanatic potential of the human mind, and the extent of our duty never to let the world—or ourselves—forget.

CHAPTER 14

"HE GIRDS ISRAEL WITH STRENGTH"

Blessed are You, Lord our God,
Who girds Israel with strength.

BIRCHOT HASHACHAR (MORNING BLESSINGS)

SHMUEL "GORODISH" GONEN—the native Israeli, authoritarian colonel, and commander of the Seventh Brigade—made a powerful statement to his soldiers during the Six-Day War, as quoted by Shabtai Tevet in his 1968 book *Exposed in the Turret*:

> *When you hear the order "Move," you tank soldiers will understand that "move" for us, the Israel Defense Forces, means in only one direction: forward. Always forward, and only forward. Because we, the Jewish people, have nowhere else to go.*

When I met Gorodish, I asked him how he—one who grew up in Jerusalem during World War II—could say such a thing, since he had not experienced the Holocaust in person. Gorodish evaded my question, saying, "Never mind. I myself don't know where it came from. It wasn't planned." But his hedging made me realize how deeply the memory of the Holocaust is embedded in the consciousness of every Israeli, even those without any direct connection to it. Gorodish symbolized the typical Israeli army man. He was not a spiritual person, no Ka-Zetnik or *Muselmann*, but still, the Holocaust for him was a formative national experience.

243

244 / ISRAEL MEIR LAU

Indeed, Israel's wars have made vital contributions to the memory and awareness of the Holocaust.

MOST ISRAELIS REMEMBER THE SIX-DAY WAR for the IDF's heroic triumph. But they forget that during the three weeks before the victorious ending, throughout the preparation period and the days of fighting, the war lay under the black shadow of the Holocaust. Each year, I cite Gorodish's words when I speak about the Holocaust before the director of the Israel Security Agency and senior members of the IDF general staff and use it in my speeches at IDF bases. I begin my talks with the weeks before the war, taking my listeners back to the stadium of Hebrew University in Givat Ram, where an abbreviated version of the usual IDF parade was held to celebrate Israel's nineteenth Independence Day on 5 Iyar 5727 (May 15, 1967).

According to the cease-fire agreement with Jordan, Israeli planes were forbidden to fly above Jerusalem, which was then divided between Jordan and Israel, so the air force could not perform their usual Independence Day flyover. Chief of Staff Yitzhak Rabin stood on the platform in the stadium, with President Zalman Shazar on his right, and the prime minister and minister of defense, Levi Eshkol, on his left. At one point, an intelligence officer approached the chief of staff and handed him a slip of paper, a note that was a prelude to the Six-Day War. It said that Egyptian president Gamal Abdel Nasser had transferred tanks from north Yemen to the Sinai front, and had positioned a force of Egyptian soldiers in Sinai, ready to fight.

Immediately after Independence Day, in mid-May 1967, I remind my audience, Israel declared full mobilization of the reserve forces. It then began a three-week preparation period until the outbreak of the war on June 5. Ordinary activity halted, the streets were emptied of young men, and a total blackout went into effect. People cleaned out bomb shelters and stockpiled food.

On May 30, King Hussein of Jordan flew to Cairo to sign a mutual defense treaty. The Arabs threatened Israel on all sides: Syria from the north, Jordan from the east, and Egypt from the south. The public atmosphere during the waiting period was heated. Demonstrations called for appointing Moshe Dayan as minister of defense, and penetrating questions arose regarding the IDF's readiness for war. Senior officers criticized Levi Eshkol for not giving the order to attack the Arab countries that were choking Israel on all three borders. They repeatedly emphasized that the IDF was not prepared for defense, only for offense. Eshkol addressed the nation on the radio, mixing up the pages of his prepared speech. No one could see what had happened, since this was before the days of television in Israel, and the listeners assumed that he was stuttering instead of broadcasting confidence and decisiveness.

Five days before the war began, Moshe Dayan accepted the defense portfolio, but the feeling on the Israeli street was hardly one of security. It reminded many people of the atmosphere on the streets of Europe at the end of the thirties. Most Holocaust survivors who had made aliya were still alive, and the talk of a state surrounded by Arab countries who wanted to destroy it and throw the Jews into the sea carried distinct echoes of the tortured past. In addition, the public had the strong feeling that Israel was isolated in the international arena, just as the Jews had been isolated three decades earlier. The blackout darkened the streets, while fear darkened the mind, although most of the country still trusted the strength of the IDF.

At that time, I was a synagogue rabbi and a teacher at the Zeitlin High School in Tel Aviv. In addition to my usual work as a lecturer for the chief army rabbinate in the central and southern commands, the IDF had appointed me as a reserve-duty recruitment officer because I had a car and a telephone. I helped the students at the school prepare for the possibility of war; together, we readied hospitals and old-age homes. The Holocaust hovered behind the newspaper headlines and the radio news; its memory was inescapable. Although people did not speak directly about it, everyone felt it, in an almost tangible manner. It clutched every Israeli around the neck. We felt as if we were walking through a dark tunnel and could not see the light at the end.

When I read the words Gorodish spoke to his soldiers, I realized that the legacy of the Holocaust did not belong solely to the survivors, but to all Jews, even if they did not often express it.

ANOTHER COMMENT I MENTION EACH YEAR is one that was made by Minister of Defense Moshe Dayan at the beginning of the 1970s. On May 15,

1974, three Arab terrorists took one hundred teenagers from the religious high school of Safed hostage. They were on a premilitary training trip and were camping overnight in the elementary school in Ma'alot when armed terrorists broke in. In return for releasing the hostages, the three demanded the liberation of Arab terrorists imprisoned in Israel. Three terrorists held 110 hostages—students, teachers, and training instructors.

During the interminable, exhausting hours of negotiations, the terrorists demanded that their imprisoned comrades be released and flown to Damascus. The Israeli government refused, deciding instead on a military operation to release the hostages. Moshe Dayan lay in a rifle pit behind the school fence; next to him lay his political adviser and personal assistant, my brother Naphtali Lau-Lavie ("Lavie" is the Hebraized version of "Lau"). Dayan had never spoken with Naphtali about his past or about the heavy burden he carried from the Holocaust days; Naphtali buried his memories deep inside, rarely giving them emotional expression.

Before sunrise, while still in the pit, Dayan fixed his one eye on Naphtali, gave him a long look, and said,

> *Throughout this whole long night and the day before, lying here in front of the Ma'alot school, I have learned one thing: to understand the Holocaust better. I have been thinking constantly of 110 individuals, most of them native Israelis, youths in the premilitary program. Many of them know how to handle weapons, especially the teachers and instructors who have been in the army. How is it that these klutzes left their rifles in the truck cabins instead of taking them with them into the school? The "It won't happen to me" syndrome strikes again. I ask myself, how is it that out of the 110 people confronting three terrorists, not one of them stands up, not one of them takes action? I understand that psychology functions differently in the face of the barrel of a Kalashnikov. Human behavior in such a situation is completely irrational. Every imaginable act—distracting the terrorists, attacking them, jumping out of the building—flies out of the mind.*
>
> *Tonight I understand the Holocaust. You were starved, freezing. I saw the photographs. I saw the situations in which people were caught. I saw people who descended to the lowest depths, physically and psychologically. And you also knew that even if you killed the Gestapo officer with your fingernails, you had nowhere to go afterward. Even*

if you managed to get over the electrified barbed-wire fence, where would you run to in your striped uniform, with your Jewish face? And without identity papers? Tonight, here in Ma'alot, I now understand all that.

People always talk about "sheep to the slaughter." Here, terrorists are holding hostage 110 young Israelis. These youngsters know that the entire State of Israel is with them. They are not within enemy territory, nor are they in a threatening or alien location. They're in their home. They know that underneath the school windows, our people are waiting with outstretched tarpaulins so that they can jump—but still, hardly any of them makes a move. Here in Ma'alot, I realize that under such conditions, human psychology works in an entirely unpredictable way.

In his book *Balaam's Prophecy*, Naphtali recounts that after the battle over the building, he and Dayan rushed inside. Dozens of boys and girls and several adults lay dead and wounded on the floor. Others sat crying for help. "The terrible sight took me back thirty years, to the sights of horror that have gripped me ever since Auschwitz and Buchenwald," Naphtali wrote. "I stood there helpless, and felt my legs collapsing under me. I rushed outside and sat on a stone next to the playground. A soldier passing by gave me his canteen, and I took several sips until I felt able to stand."

Gorodish's pronouncement to his tank soldiers on the eve of the Six-Day War and Dayan's revelation at Ma'alot are a thread that visibly connects then and now, there and here, those who came to Israel from the hell of Europe and native Israelis. At times when Israel finds herself at war, people often ask me how I feel from the perspective of a Holocaust survivor. I usually answer, "Does one have to be a Holocaust survivor in order to understand the situation?" We are besieged, our lives are threatened, and the danger of our destruction has not yet passed. We Jews are still struggling for survival. All Jews are, in a certain sense, Holocaust survivors. But for the survivors of that original Holocaust, when the siege is tightened, the issue moves to the forefront, taking on added significance.

IN 1973, I SERVED AS RABBI OF THE TIFERET ZVI SYNAGOGUE in north Tel Aviv. This synagogue had 930 seats, and each year on Yom Kippur, they were completely filled. But that year on the morning of Yom Kippur, which fell on Shabbat, I noticed a few empty seats. Although this aroused my curiosity, I did not spend too much time wondering about it. The next ominous sign, however, was the sound of car engines, unusual on that late morning. Usually, the streets of Tel Aviv are silent and empty of vehicles on Yom Kippur, except for the occasional ambulance or police car.

Finally, in the afternoon, the usual quiet of the holiest day of the year was broken by the sound of streams of men in army uniforms entering the synagogue, carrying lists. They approached the congregants one by one, clapped them on their shoulders, and whispered something in their ears. The words "emergency call-up order" began to float through the room, intermingling with the words of the liturgy. It was obvious that something unusual was going on. That afternoon, the synagogue was almost completely emptied of young men.

The smell of war was in the air, and it came as a total surprise. In contrast to the Six–Day War, the headlines in 1973 had not reported that war was on the way, and the radio news did not mention the tense situation. Discussions took place in army headquarters, but did not filter through to the citizens. For this reason, the mobilization of the reserve soldiers from the synagogues hit us like a bolt from the blue; no one had prepared for such a possibility.

At exactly ten to two that afternoon, the wail of a siren shattered the silence, shocking the congregants. Someone announced that the radio was broadcasting call-up codes to the various reserve units. In a split second, the entire atmosphere was transformed. First, the army called up its logistics personnel: drivers, cooks, communications experts, and medics. Many members of combat units remained in their seats in the synagogue and continued their prayers. The night after Yom Kippur, though, a complete blackout went into effect, wrapping Tel Aviv, like the rest of Israel, in darkness.

For my IDF reserve duty, I usually served as a speaker for the army rabbinate and as a call-up administrator for the southern command, but I did not receive a call-up order that Yom Kippur. No one needed speakers in the first stage of that terrible war, but at such a time I could hardly stay at home doing nothing, without contributing to the war effort. I found out that Ichilov Hospital in Tel Aviv had been transformed into an army hospital, and I thought I might be of assistance there. They were sending all civilian patients who were in reasonable condition back to their homes and transferring the others to different hospitals so that they would have room to receive soldiers who had been wounded in battle.

I called Pinchas Scheinman, director of the Tel Aviv religious council, who was responsible for the administration of the neighborhood rabbis in the city. Scheinman welcomed my offer, and informed the hospital that on behalf of the Tel Aviv city rabbinate, Rabbi Lau would be officially in charge of all the religious and spiritual matters there. I worked there, day and night, for three months while also continuing my classes at Tiferet Zvi synagogue, since even in times of war, life must go on, and we must stick to our routines.

During the Yom Kippur War, 475 severely wounded patients came to Ichilov from the southern front. The army had sent the slightly and moderately wounded cases to other hospitals, while helicopters flew the more serious cases to Ichilov. Most of them had severe burns, while some had injuries to the head, spine, or eyes. The surgery staff worked around the clock with incomparable dedication. I spent countless hours at the hospital, mainly in Dr. Theodore Wiznitzer's surgery ward, with the severely burned tank-crew members. There I learned just how ridiculous and false was the common saying about war that "The wounded do not cry out." They cried out and then some, as they were suffering intense pain. I have never heard such screams as those emitted by the burn victims when they took showers for the first time after Dr. Yohanan Plashkes performed their skin grafts.

In one of the rooms of the surgical ward lay four tank soldiers who had been almost totally burned while inside their tanks. One of the soldiers emitted such powerful screams that I could not comprehend how he had the strength to do so, even with the large quantities of morphine injected into his body. We begged him to try to be quiet, so as not to disturb his three roommates, but to no avail. Our explanations that agitation would prevent his recovery also failed. All at once, the youth's shrieks ceased; he did not even sob. The sudden silence in the room surprised me, and I feared that the worst had happened. I was afraid to look at his bed lest it would confirm my fear.

But no—the wounded man had fallen into a peaceful sleep. A strange calm came over his scorched face, leaving no trace of the powerful screams that had borne witness to his extreme suffering. As it turned out, his mother, who had not left her son's bedside, had found a tiny piece of skin near his knee, just a few square centimeters in size, which was entirely without burns or grafts. The mother began to stroke that piece of intact skin, repeating his name over and over. "Mother's here. Calm down, my son, calm down," she kept saying, continuously stroking that unscathed piece of skin and making a concentrated effort to stifle her tears.

Her words and their motherly cadence, loving and familiar, were the only things that brought respite to his tortured spirit. Finally he could close his eyes and rest. After returning home in the early hours of the morning, I told my wife that on that night at Ichilov, next to the bed of the burned soldier, I finally understood the meaning of the verse from the last chapter of the book of Isaiah. He begins his prophecy in anger, with God saying, *Children I have raised and exalted, yet they have rebelled against Me*. In chapter 40, the prophet makes a transition to *Console, console My people*, and in the last chapter, he uses a meaningful metaphor for that concept of consolation: *Like a man whose mother consoles him, so will I console you, and in Jerusalem, you shall be consoled*. Of all the images he could have chosen, he decided on the image of a mother consoling her son. "Tonight," I said to my wife, "I arrived at a deeper understanding of that verse. Nothing helped that wounded man, nothing calmed him—not the morphine, not the explanations, not even the rebukes. Only when his mother came to him lovingly, stroking him and whispering in her maternal way, was he able to calm down and sleep peacefully."

Thirty years after the war, I met another of those burned tank soldiers at a Tel Aviv reunion of wounded who were hospitalized in Ichilov. He came up to me with anticipation and introduced himself as Moshe Shemesh from Ramat HaSharon. I did not recognize him, but he said that he spoke of me frequently. "I was burned on practically every inch of my body. Only a tiny part of my nose was unharmed. No one stood by my bed except for you, and of course the devoted medical staff. Everyone was sure that I was alone in Israel without family, but you stood there, and you looked up my name on the medical chart and kept talking to me." He continued:

> *I remember exactly what you said to me. "Moshe," you asked, "can we call your parents? Can we inform someone from your family so that they can come stay with you? I can't be here with you all the time. There are hundreds of other wounded in the hospital and the nurses are overwhelmed. You need someone to be with you all the time."*
> *But I would not give you my parents' phone number or address. I saw the three other wounded men with me in the room. My eyes worked fine. I could barely speak, and I could not move a limb, but my eyes functioned. I knew I must look exactly like them, and they were a horrible sight. I know my parents. I knew that my mother would have had a heart attack if she had seen me in that condition.*

Geula Rabinowitz, wife of Tel Aviv mayor Yehoshua Rabinowitz, was standing beside me at the side of his bed, and she urged me to convince the boy to call his family. I succeeded by virtue of a fabrication. "You have a mother and father, right?"

"Yes," he answered.

"Did you know that ever since the war began, they have been running from one hospital to another, pressuring the army to demand the names of the dead from the enemy, because you have not been in touch and they don't know whether you're alive or where you are? Don't you worry about your parents' well being? They can't sleep at night!"

"Okay, you convinced me," he admitted. "But I can't get up to call."

I brought a portable public phone to his bed, slipped in a phone token, and dialed the number he gave me. Slowly, gently, I prepared his mother, saying that he was alive and next to me. I won't describe the meeting between this soldier and his family. Thirty years later, they thanked me.

On the fifth floor of the hospital, in Dr. Moshe Lazar's eye department, I noticed a young man sitting cross-legged on his bed, singing Hebrew songs to himself. I went in to see him, and found out he was from Ma'alot. He had lost both eyes during the fighting. To pass the time and ease his pain, he kept singing a popular song in a broken voice: "I promise you, my little girl, that this will be the very last war." Coming from that suffering blind soldier, those words were powerful; powerful as well was the hope that their promise would indeed be fulfilled. I stood beside his bed to talk to him, so that at least he could share what he had to say, if not what he saw. He said that it was complicated for his family to travel to Tel Aviv from Ma'alot, but that despite the difficulty, he did have some visitors, albeit fewer than the other patients. I was impressed by the optimism of this blind soldier, who despite his severe injuries, sang songs and enjoyed the few visitors who took the trouble to visit him.

As I was talking to him, an older woman approached me and asked if I was a rabbi. I replied in the affirmative and asked whether I could help her. "Me personally, not at all," said the woman, "but my son needs you. Can you go to him?" I excused myself from the blind soldier and followed the mother. She led me to a room in the neurosurgery ward, and said, "This is Yehuda, my son."

On the bed lay a young man, his head wrapped completely in bandages. His nose, mouth, and a small section of his eyes barely stuck out between them. He looked like he had just come out of brain surgery. A sheet covered his body from the chin down, so I had no idea about the condition of the rest of his body. He was still anesthetized, in the recovery stage after his operation. After a few minutes, when he could focus on what was happening around him, he noticed me standing next to his mother, and asked whether I was a rabbi. Again I answered yes. "Then what time is it?" he asked. I was sure he must not be completely recovered yet, but I looked at my watch in a serious manner and replied that it was twelve o'clock. Still he was not satisfied, and asked whether I meant twelve noon or twelve midnight. I replied that it was twelve noon. "If so," he asked, "could someone who has not yet put on tefillin today put them on now?"

I noticed that the way he phrased his question was a bit awkward. Instead of saying, "to *lay* tefillin" as we usually do, he used the phrase "*put on*." The blessing over the tefillin that religious Jewish men recite over this daily mitzvah is "Who has sanctified us with His commandments and commanded us to lay tefillin." His questions about the time of day were unusual; I replied that one was permitted to lay tefillin throughout the day. But the man was still not satisfied and continued to probe. "Tell me, if I can't put on the head tefillin because of the bandages, is it okay to just put on the one on my arm?" That was a question worthy of a Talmudic discussion: are both the head and the arm tefillin required for proper performance of the mitzvah?

This question reminded me of Buchenwald. One Jew in the camp had hidden an arm tefillin under the wooden floor of the bunker, and he used to lay that one only. Recalling this image, I replied to the wounded man on the bed that one could lay arm tefillin without laying head tefillin. When he heard my answer, he pulled his left hand out from under the sheet and asked, "If so, then put it on for me." I did so willingly. I recited *Shema Yisrael* together with him, and as we were reading the verses, he fell asleep. Gently I removed the tefillin from his arm and left the room. Later, we became friendly, and when his condition improved, I heard his story, which I had wondered about since our first meeting. It had taken place during the Sukkot holiday following Yom Kippur.

On the eve of Simchat Torah, the last day of the holiday of Sukkot, Second Lieutenant Yehuda sat with five other officers, all older and more senior than he, in a command car beside the Suez Canal, waiting for orders. As they sat, a truck stopped next to them. On it stood a *sukkah*, a traditional booth constructed for the holiday. Two Chabad representatives invited the young officers into the *sukkah* to toast *le-chaim*, eat some cake, and recite *birkat netilav lulav*, the traditional blessing over the four species: *etrog*—or citron, a citrus fruit similar to a lemon—and palm, myrtle, and willow, whose branches are gathered to form the *lulav* bouquet.

The officers tried to avoid the request, explaining that even in civilian life they did not observe the laws of Sukkot—and were even less inclined to do so now, in the middle of such a war. But the Chabadnik on the truck did not give up, and tried to convince them, arguing, "What do you care? At any rate you're just sitting here doing nothing. Come up, the whole thing will take you no more than ten minutes," he said, pressuring them. The officers looked at each other and decided to accept his offer. They went into the truck, partook of pieces of cake and small cups of sweet wine, and prepared to recite the blessing over the *lulav*. Suddenly they heard a deafening explosion. They all threw themselves onto the floor of the truck, feeling their bodies to make sure all their limbs were intact.

When they glanced outside, they discovered that the command car, where they had been sitting a minute ago, had taken a direct hit. Not a fragment of it remained.

When quiet reigned once more, Second Lieutenant Yehuda said to one of the Chabad men, "You would probably call what happened here a miracle." The Chabad man answered him with a question: "What would you call it?" Yehuda felt that his life had been saved thanks to the *sukkah* and the *lulav*. He gave the man a long stare, then pointed upward and said, "I feel I owe Him something in exchange for my life. My life was saved because you insisted we get into your truck and recite the blessings." The Chabad man proposed that he take upon himself the daily mitzvah of laying tefillin.

Yehuda agreed, and wanted to fulfill his vow right away. He asked the Chabadnik to lay the tefillin on him then and there. But that would not have been appropriate, as it was the end of Sukkot, a holiday on which we do not lay tefillin; it would only be possible to begin laying tefillin after the holiday ended. "But I don't know where I'll be then," Yehuda explained, and added that he did not own a pair of tefillin. "I did receive a pair for my bar mitzvah, but since then they've been stored in the closet at my parents' house." The Chabadnik asked for his name and unit number, and promised that in a few days, after the holiday was over, he would have his own tefillin.

Second Lieutenant Yehuda crossed the Suez Canal to Fayid, Egypt—once part of the biblical Land of Goshen—and the tefillin, their IDF stamp clearly visible, managed to reach him there. He took upon himself the mitzvah of laying them every day. But in Fayid, Yehuda was wounded in the spine and transferred by helicopter to the neurosurgery unit at Ichilov for cranial surgery. When he opened his eyes in the hospital, the first thing that concerned him was that he had not fulfilled his vow since his injury, and he asked his mother to find a rabbi to answer two urgent questions. Was it permissible to "put on" tefillin at such a late hour, and was it permissible to "put on" the arm tefillin without the head tefillin?

DURING THE YOM KIPPUR WAR, I had a painful personal connection to death when one of my students, Ya'ari Stern of Zeitlin High School in

Tel Aviv, was killed the day before his wedding. He had already bought a wedding ring during the one-day leave the army had allowed him just before the special event. For a long time, his fiancée, Ora Frankel, wore that ring on a chain around her neck.

AT MY OWN INITIATIVE and as the result of a television program, I became acquainted with another painful story of death in that war. Before the first-year anniversary of the war, I received a phone call from Chaim Hausman, a producer in the department of religious programming for Israel Television. He proposed that I host a half-hour program the night after Yom Kippur, in October 1974, on the topics of Yom Kippur, fasting, and prayer. He also asked me to work in the one-year anniversary of the war. I did not know how I would connect these two weighty issues, but the producer reassured me, saying that his staff had gathered material from combat soldiers and their families, including letters and postcards sent from the front. All I had to do was come to the studio a few hours before the show was to be recorded and rummage through the crates, and I could cull ideas for the opening of my program.

The idea sounded challenging, and I followed his suggestion. I sifted through a large pile of postcards, but what attracted my attention was a piece of thick, rough brown paper, like that used as packaging for the large sacks of flour and rice sold in local grocery stores. I saw that someone had written a note on this rough paper. I pulled it out of the pile, and when I read what was written on it, I told the television staff in a shaking voice that I had to meet the writer—or, God forbid, the addressee. That note touched me so that I still remember it by heart.

As I learned, the writer was the son of Holocaust survivors who were in their sixties during the Yom Kippur War. The writer's father had lost his first wife and children in the Holocaust, and his mother had lost her first husband. The widow and widower met each other, and were subsequently on the same ship destined for Eretz Israel. The British sent them to Cyprus, where they got married during the months of waiting. When the gates of aliya finally opened, they went to live in Bnei Brak.

Their only son attended the national religious elementary school there, then a yeshiva high school, and was active in Bnei Akiva (a global Zionist youth organization) in his area. When he joined a Nahal army pioneering group, the army sent him to a training course for paratroop officers. On his base, he met a young woman soldier from a Hashomer Hatzair kibbutz in western Galilee. The disparity between the young man wearing a knitted *kippah* under his red beret and the woman from the fervently secular kibbutz created tension. They argued endlessly, on everything from the Holocaust and Divine Providence to religion and nationality, religion and state, and Jewish values and socialism.

One day, the woman soldier entered the paratrooper's office carrying a kit bag on her back. She said she had come to say good-bye, since she was about to be released from the army and was returning to her parents on the kibbutz. After the officer said a few polite words of parting, she turned toward the door and made as if to leave. But then she turned back. She admitted that although she had no idea about his feelings for her, her feelings for him went far beyond their arguments over religion. "I have just one request," she said. "If I write to you, please answer me. In the meantime, stay healthy and well."

She said good-bye and began to walk away again, but this time he was the one who called her back. He explained that he thought it would be better if they ended their relationship right then and there, because in truth, he felt deeply for her, more than he could express. The young officer was afraid that if they wrote to each other regularly, their relationship would intensify. He explained that they could not create a life together because their backgrounds were so different. "We eat different foods, and your Shabbat experience is totally unlike mine. A chasm we can never bridge separates your parents on the kibbutz and my parents, elderly Holocaust survivors from Bnei Brak. They would be gravely hurt if we pursued a serious relationship. I am an only son, and I can't do that to them. If we have children, we'll argue about which kindergarten they should attend, then which school. Let's say our good-byes now," he insisted. They parted.

Three weeks later, the woman, now a civilian, knocked on the paratrooper's door at the base. In civilian dress, knapsack on her back, she said, "I've begun to follow the ways of our forefather Abraham. The Bible says that God said to Abraham, *Go forth from your land and from your birthplace and from your father's house*. I left my father's house when I went into the army, but ever since my return to the kibbutz, I have not been the same. My parents and friends also noticed that I did not seem at home. I told my parents about you. During those weeks, they got to know you without ever meeting you. I got some money from the kibbutz in addition to my release grant from the army. I want you to find me a room in Bnei Brak, and if possible, some kind of job. I don't care what: waitressing, dishwashing, cleaning. But the most important thing is that you find someone to teach me the prayers, the laws of Shabbat, and how to keep kosher. If I decide it's for me, and you decide I'm for you, perhaps we can build a future together. If not—no big deal, I'll learn about Judaism and then go home."

The paratroop officer did as she requested. His mother helped him find a room in the apartment of an elderly woman Holocaust survivor, who was living alone in a three-room apartment and wanted a young woman companion to stay with her. The young woman received room and board in return for being in the apartment each evening at a certain time and doing the old woman's shopping. She found someone who volunteered to give her classes in Judaism. Her relationship with the paratroop officer deepened, and after a year, they married. They lived in Bnei Brak near his parents, and had two sons.

When the younger son was two weeks old, the Yom Kippur War began. That Shabbat, the officer was praying with a group of his Bnei Akiva friends in Bnei Brak. During the services, many of his friends were called up to reserve duty, but he did not receive an order. After the fast, he went home, recited the *Havdalah* concluding prayer, and phoned his unit. The clerk asked him to wait at home until they called him. But he was impatient and tense, so he donned his uniform and pulled on his army boots.

His wife prepared him a bundle of provisions, including a brown paper bag of cookies. After midnight, a jeep stopped in front of the house. His unit had come to pick him up. He kissed his two sons, got into the jeep, and never came back. Among the personal possessions sent to his wife after he died was the brown paper package, on which he had hastily written, "My dear, it's either me or this note—only one of us will reach you. If I come home, which is not my present feeling, you'll never see this note. But if the note gets to you, it means I'll never come back. You will be free to begin a new chapter in your life. This is the time to thank you for the long journey you made for me. I know what your considerations were, and I know how difficult that journey was. I never expressed the appreciation you so deserve. As I said, you don't owe me anything, but I have one request to make of you: educate the two sons God gave us in the same way my parents educated me. Yours, . . . "

The widow of the paratroop officer continued to be religiously observant. When she heard about the television program and the request to send letters from combat soldiers, she sent in the note from her deceased husband. When I spoke with her about the circumstances surrounding that brown paper note, she asked me, "Tell me, honored rabbi, isn't this a lesson in ethics?" Indeed, it is, in the full sense of the word. It is a personal example of an ordinary man who throughout his life followed his spiritual compass and conscience. The uniqueness of this note is that it shows what occupied the mind of a combat soldier in the last moments of his life: the religious education of his children, continuing the chain of generations. He thought of himself as a bridge between generations. At first, he acted out of consideration for his parents; at the end of his life, he thought of his children's future. No impressive monument in a town square ever memorialized that paratroop officer; no city side street bears his name; no stamp bears his portrait. He was just one of the 2,659 victims of the Yom Kippur War.

THE GULF WAR OF 1991 bore a marked resemblance to the horrors of the Holocaust. The threat of a chemical or biological attack from Iraq loomed. We sat with arms folded, doing nothing, helpless, in rooms sealed with plastic and rags dipped in baking soda, equipped with gas masks manufactured in Germany. All this was a blatant reminder of the gas chambers. In those days I was chief rabbi of Tel Aviv and I remained in the city, although many of the residents feared for their lives and left, rendering it a ghost town.

In contrast to my good friend Mayor Shlomo "Cheech" Lahat, who called those citizens who chose to leave deserters, I refrained from passing judgment on them. I have always followed an iron rule taken from Ethics of the Fathers, and it applied to this issue as well: *Do not judge your fellow until you have stood in his place.* Everyone has his own spiritual complexity and pressures from his parents, children, or spouse. For this reason, I felt I could not attempt to fathom the souls of those who preferred Jerusalem or Eilat to Tel Aviv, which was threatened by Iraqi missiles. I did not judge the elderly who had experienced the Holocaust and whose endurance had been stretched to the limit.

My mother-in-law, Mrs. Frankel, stayed with us at the beginning of the Gulf War. Three days into the war, we were pleased to accept my sister-in-law's offer for Mrs. Frankel to stay with her in Jerusalem until the threat had passed. The danger was all too real and I, too, was afraid. But I felt strongly that as chief rabbi of the city, I could not leave. My departure would be a harsh blow to the morale of those residents who had chosen to remain in their city, or who did not have the opportunity to leave. When I saw the mass exodus, I was not overly impressed with the Tel Avivians' spiritual strength. Those were not their finest hours. I worried about the mistaken interpretation our enemies might give this phenomenon, since it might encourage them to initiate additional attacks. But certainly the biblical principle of *You should carefully guard your souls* mandates that the civilian population take every possible precautionary measure.

The Gulf War also brought several visible miracles. One Friday night, a synagogue in the Ramat HaTayasim neighborhood of Tel Aviv suffered a direct missile hit and collapsed into ruins. The missile fell just six minutes after the last congregant had left the synagogue following evening services. The name of that synagogue was Heichal Ha-Ness, "Hall of Miracles."

Everything is in God's hands. That war was a test for Israel, but we were not condemned to death. Iraq fired thirty-nine Scud missiles at our tiny country. Houses were destroyed, but the fact that almost none of our citizens was hurt is not coincidental. The Gulf War also had a positive influence on the Israeli attitude toward the Holocaust survivors, deepening the public's understanding of their behavior and identification with their experiences during those dark years.

CHAPTER 15

WORKING AT GOOD WORKS

Who by fire . . . who by the sword . . .
who will suffer . . . who will be elevated.
YOM KIPPUR LITURGY

AT EIGHT IN THE MORNING one Sunday in February 1996, a peak traffic hour in Israel's capital, a suicide bomber blew himself up on the number eighteen bus in Jerusalem, killing twenty-six passengers. My office manager at the chief rabbinate knew that as soon as she heard about a terrorist attack, she had to gather as much information as possible about the dead as quickly as she could, so that I would be able to attend the funerals or at least pay a *shiva* call during the weeklong mourning period.

Several hours after the attack, I found a neat list on my desk with the names of twenty-four victims and their addresses in Jerusalem. But on the radio, I had heard reports of twenty-six killed. Two names were missing. My secretary explained that she had obtained the list from Jerusalem's welfare department, which was responsible for gathering information on each of the victims. I insisted that she call again and ask for the names of the other two who had been killed. She did so, and the municipality was able to confirm the two others, a new immigrant couple from the Ukraine, the Kushnirovs. They were survived by their two sons, a boy of eight and a half and a baby of five months. The family probably was not sitting *shiva*, the office informed me, so there was no need to provide the address. I persevered, and

260

found out that they lived in the Katamon neighborhood. I will never forget that visit.

I arrived at the apartment in the afternoon to find three adults in shock: a relatively young woman and two older neighbors from the building. Vladik, the older boy, sat on the floor, while Tomer, the baby, lay in his playpen. When I entered, Vladik stared at me in astonishment; a stranger was entering his home, wearing a long black coat and a hat, surely for him a strange and unforgettable sight.

I wanted to talk with him, mainly to distract him from the tragedy. I sat on one of the two simple, narrow beds in the room, and the adults sat opposite. They stared at me—and I at them. After a minute or two of uncomfortable silence, the young woman introduced herself in Hebrew with a heavy Russian accent. Her name was Larissa, and she was the sister of the dead mother. She said she had just gotten married three weeks before the attack. Before I could introduce myself, she addressed the boy: "Vladik, do you know who has come to visit us? *Glavnyi ravvin*, the chief rabbi of Israel, Rabbi Lau." The boy raised his eyes and looked at me as if asking, What is this rabbi doing here? His aunt continued, "You know, Vladik, that when Rabbi Lau was eight years old, he also did not have his mother or father. He came to Israel without parents, and just look— today he is the *glavnyi ravvin* of Israel. Take a lesson from him, Vladik. Everything is in your hands." When Larissa finished speaking, the boy stood up from the floor, came over to sit next to me on the thin mattress, and lay his head on my chest. He sat like that for a whole hour, without saying a word.

After a while, I said one thing to him: "It's true that our fates are sim- ilar, but there is one big difference between us. I came to Israel with an older brother who took care of me. When I was your age, I had no respon- sibilities other than worrying about my own future. But you, on the other hand, have a double responsibility, despite your young age: besides your- self, you must also take care of Tomer, the baby sleeping in the playpen who doesn't know what's going on. That is the big difference between us, and it means you have a responsibility."

When I said good-bye to the grieving family, I said that if they were willing to, they should come visit me in my office in Jerusalem after the mourning period. Some time later, Vladik and Larissa came to my office. I was happy to learn that after the *shiva*, Larissa and her new husband had legally adopted her deceased sister's two children. I thought about what a challenge this was for the husband in particular, who received two young children as part of the dowry.

Four and a half years after the terror attack on the number eighteen bus, I met Vladik again. Each year on the day before Passover, Chabad organizes a bar and bat mitzvah celebration at the Western Wall for one thousand immigrants from the former Soviet Union. Regularly honored guests include government ministers, the mayor of Jerusalem, and the chief rabbis of Israel. Throughout my ten years as chief rabbi, I never missed this ceremony. I gave my speech, then passed out tefillin to each boy and candlesticks to each girl. One by one, the boys and girls mounted the platform to receive their gifts.

Suddenly, someone hugged me from behind and grabbed the bag of tefillin from my hands. I turned around. Behind me stood a tall, muscular youth whom I did not recognize. Noticing my embarrassment, he introduced himself: "I'm Vladik. Today is my bar mitzvah. You came to visit us in Katamon when my parents were killed in the attack on bus eighteen. Remember? I was with my brother, Tomer. Remember Aunt Larissa told me that you were also without parents at eight years old?" I replied that I remembered quite well, but more important, he should remember what Aunt Larissa had told him. "Everything is in your hands," I said, repeating her assertion word for word. "She said that if you desire it and try, you can succeed. I share her blessing, and hope that the Master of the Universe will light up your path in life." We parted with a strong handshake.

Unfortunately, during the ten years in which I served as chief rabbi of the State of Israel, I had many meetings similar to the one I had with Vladik.

WHEN THE ELECTIONS FOR CHIEF RABBI WERE HELD IN 1993, the Labor Party, to which twenty-six of the 150 electors belonged, appointed a seven-member committee. Its mission was to judge the characters of the three candidates for chief Ashkenazi rabbi and the three candidates for chief

Sephardi rabbi. They were to write a recommendation indicating which candidate to support, and present it at the meeting at the Labor Party offices. I was then chief rabbi of Tel Aviv-Jaffa, and I was a candidate for chief Ashkenazi rabbi, along with the chief rabbis of Haifa and Rehovot. The mayor of Haifa, Aryeh Gur'el, spoke in favor of the rabbi of Haifa, while the mayor of Rehovot, Michael Lapidot, spoke on behalf of the rabbi of his city. I did not have a mayor to speak on my behalf, since the mayor of my city, Shlomo Lahat, belonged to Likud (the right-wing party). But three others spoke in support of me: Brigadier General Ephraim Hiram spoke about my meetings at army camps in the Golan Heights, and how I raised the morale of the soldiers in my discussions with them. "I am completely secular, an army man. I don't know anything about rabbis," said Hiram. "But," he continued, citing the Shunammite woman's response to the prophet Elisha in the book of Kings, "because *I dwell among mine own people* I know that he is the man." Next came the mayor of Yehud, Mordechai Linik. He said that he was a Holocaust survivor, and that he had worked in the forced labor camps in Russia. He began his life in Israel in a tent camp, and succeeded in reaching the position of mayor. "I know all the candidates, but among them is one who rose from the ashes. He is a symbol of our revival as a people, and so is worthy of our support. That is Rabbi Lau." The third one to request the floor was Yuval Frankel, a Labor Party member in Yitzhak Rabin's camp, who began by saying, "I speak for the younger generation. If there is a rabbi who speaks to us, understands us, and feels with us, that rabbi is Rabbi Lau."

I HAD NEVER IDENTIFIED WITH ANY SPECIFIC PARTY, although I constantly received phone calls from people who proposed that I take on a political role. I always thanked the callers for their support, but explained that I had to think not about election day, but about the day after. I said that I preferred to avoid the label of one party or another. I learned this motto from my father-in-law, Rabbi Frankel, who was a rabbi in Tel Aviv for fifty years, and chief rabbi of that city for fourteen of those years. He reached his position without any political support; he was a rabbi for the entire Jewish people, and knew that only with this attitude could he succeed in his position. I told myself that if I were not chosen for whatever position I was running for, it wouldn't be so terrible, but if I were, I had to be sure I had the trust of the public, and not of some party. I stood in seven elections for various positions, and I never lost.

In 1993, after five years of serving as chief rabbi of Tel Aviv, I was elected—with God's help—as chief rabbi of Israel. Support for my election crossed the lines of communities, parties, and worldviews.

BY DEFINITION, a chief rabbi must fulfill two roles. For the first five years of his term, he serves as presiding judge of the supreme rabbinical court and president of the chief rabbinical council. In the latter position, he is responsible for the religious matters in the state: *kashrut*, Shabbat, religious councils, burials, and examinations for rabbinical ordination. In the second five years, he acts as president of the supreme rabbinic court and head of the religious judiciary system. But the law does not define what the chief rabbi does with the rest of his time—i.e., the events at which he appears or the audiences to whom he speaks. Every person who holds the job can use his time as he sees fit, after first implementing his role as a teacher of Torah and halachic arbiter.

I decided to focus on an area that I considered of top importance, a mitzvah as well as a mission: social welfare activities related to illness and grief, especially visiting the sick and comforting mourners. My sensitivity to this matter and the special place it held in my world, both personally and as chief rabbi, stemmed, I think, from the influence of the Holocaust on my life and how it remains with me in all that I do. I often recalled the image of myself as a small child, sick with the measles and lying alone in isolation. At the time, Naphtali had typhus and was also in isolation in the Buchenwald hospital, so not a living soul came to visit me to ask how I was feeling or hold my hand. This childhood memory is deeply embedded in my consciousness. This is what compels me to visit hospitals all over Israel, offering words of encouragement to those suffering in pain. This is what leads me to houses of mourning, to comfort the grieving with the few words one can say in trying times.

I saw it as my responsibility to be present at the hospitals for every dedication of a wing or department, to say a few words to encourage and strengthen those doing the work. Another issue I took upon myself, as a rabbinical judge, was to visit the homes of battered women and the families of women murdered by their husbands, attempting to understand how a couple could descend to such an abyss in their relationship, and trying to learn from these tragedies how to help couples in distress.

As do observant Jews everywhere, I begin my day with the morning blessings, which include a list of *mitzvot* whose rewards a person *enjoys in this world, but whose principal remains intact for the World-to-Come.* These are: honoring your father and mother—which, to my deep sorrow, I did not have the opportunity to fulfill—acts of loving-kindness, attendance at the house of study morning and evening, hospitality to guests, visiting the sick, providing for a bride, escorting the dead, absorption in prayer, and bringing about peace between men. The list of *mitzvot* concludes with these words: *But the study of Torah is equivalent to them all.* When a person repeats these precepts every day for sixty years, he develops a deep sense of obligation to them. Therefore, in my opinion, observant Jews should ideally have a deep commitment to charitable acts in general, and to visiting the sick in particular.

During my term as chief rabbi, the First Intifada (the Palestinian uprising of 1987–93) broke out, bringing with it terror attacks that destroyed many precious lives. Thousands of wounded were hospitalized and permanently scarred; I got to know most of them. For some, I performed wedding ceremonies or attended bar mitzvah celebrations. While most were hospitalized in Jerusalem and in the center of the country, my visits to see them took me to all the hospitals in Israel.

Among the countless stories of lives cut off during the intifada, I was especially touched by a family with whom I developed a meaningful relationship. The roots of our connection lay in my term as chief rabbi of Netanya, when I became acquainted with Yosef Friedman, an immigrant from Hungary, a Torah scholar, and an intellectual, who had singlehandedly established a vinegar factory in Netanya's old industrial zone. Both he and his wife were Holocaust survivors, and they raised a small family. Yosef Friedman attended the Talmud classes that I gave at the Beit Meir synagogue, and contributed to the cultural life of the city's religious community.

After I was elected chief rabbi of Netanya, he called me and said that his eldest daughter, Tzira, was getting married. Although we had known each other only a short time, he asked me to perform the ceremony. I asked about the groom's family, and he said that his future son-in-law, Mordechai Schijveschuurder, came from a family who lived in Holland, and that he had made aliya on his own. I remembered that tongue twister of a name.

One day about twenty years later, my secretary in the chief rabbi's office in Jerusalem informed me that a man with a name difficult to pronounce had called, asking to meet with me to discuss an educational matter. She transferred the call, and on the line was the very same Mordechai (Moti) Schijveschuurder whose wedding I had performed so many years previously. I invited him to my office and asked about his family. He said that he and his wife were blessed with many children, and that they lived in Neria (Talmon), in the Shomron region (Samaria), in the ancient territory of the biblical tribe of Benjamin.

He had a business importing chemicals from Holland, and his wife commuted every day to Jerusalem to teach in an ultra-Orthodox school for children with hearing disabilities, called Shema Koleinu (Hear Our Voice). Dissatisfied with the religious education his children were receiving, Moti had decided to abandon his import business and establish a regional Talmud Torah, an ultra-Orthodox elementary school for boys, in his settlement. He named the school after his father, Yosef Schijveschuurder, a leader of Agudath Israel in Holland, borrowing a phrase from Psalms: *Nohag ka-tzon Yosef—He Who leads Joseph like flocks*. He asked if I would come speak at this school, to give support to the children as well as their parents, and to encourage others to enroll their children. "If the chief rabbi would come all the way to Neria just to address the pupils," he said, "maybe other parents will be convinced to send their children to our school." He added that he needed support, because he was having trouble paying the teachers' salaries. I agreed to make the trip.

In July 2001, almost one year after the Second Intifada began, at two in the afternoon, a suicide bomber blew himself up in a crowded pizza restaurant, Sbarro, in the heart of Jerusalem. Fifteen people were killed, and about one hundred injured.

At nine that evening, the phone rang in my home in Tel Aviv, and the voice of a young woman, choked with tears, spoke on the other end of the line: "I'm calling from Bikur Cholim Hospital in Jerusalem. Do you remember Tzira Schijveschuurder? This is her sister speaking. Tzira was killed today at the Sbarro restaurant. Her husband, Moti, was also killed. It's summer vacation, so they took a day off and went to Jerusalem with the kids. They went into Sbarro to have pizza for lunch. Three of the five children with them in the restaurant were killed: Ra'aya, Avraham Yitzhak, and Hemda. The youngest was two years old, the oldest fourteen. The three older boys were saved. Two were in the army, and the third was not with the family. The two little girls that survived, Leah-le and Chaya-le, are wounded and hospitalized."

After the shock subsided, I asked whether Tzira's parents knew about the terrible disaster, and if so, how they were responding to the dreadful news. She said that the parents were in Netanya, and that they had needed medical treatment for the shock. The parents had recalled that I had performed Moti and Tzira's wedding, and asked if I would eulogize them at the funeral that was to take place the next morning at ten, on Har Ha-Menuchot in Jerusalem. Of course I agreed to their request.

How can one describe the funeral of a father, mother, and their three young children? How can one comprehend the five stretchers side by side, two covered with a tallis and three draped in the Israeli flag? How is it possible to look into the eyes of Leah, a girl of ten, as she observes the stretchers of her family members, while she herself lies on a hospital bed, bandages covering her entire body, a doctor on one side and a nurse on the other?

Leah had insisted on attending the funeral of her parents and siblings. The hospital personnel had agreed to this exceptional outing, bearing in mind that if she did not go, she might never forgive herself. Apprehensive and heavy-hearted, the staff allowed the wounded girl to go to the funeral—along with her hospital bed, her intravenous drip, and her indescribable pain, both physical and emotional.

I stood before her. My eyes met hers, and I could not utter a word. I could only cry out: *How long shall the wicked, O Lord, how long shall the wicked triumph?* After a minute of silence, I recalled a Midrash of the sages.

*We stood on the banks of the Sea of Reeds, surrounded by enemies,
after four generations of slavery, forced labor, and evil decrees. Said
Uzza, ministering angel of Egypt in the heavenly host: "Master of the
Universe, Israel doesn't deserve a miracle. My children, the Egyptian
people, do not deserve to drown in the sea. What difference is there
between the two? One is a nation of idol-worshippers, and so is the
other." At that moment, Michael, ministering angel of Israel, Israel's
advocate on High, gave a sign to Gabriel. Gabriel swooped down to
Egypt and removed bricks of mortar and clay from the wall of Pithom
and Raamses, finding a Jewish infant stuck inside. When the Hebrew
slaves did not manage to finish the work quota on time, the Egyptian
taskmasters would grab the Jewish babies from their homes and push
them into the walls, just to fulfill the quota of bricklaying. Gabriel
placed the tiny body in Michael's arms. When Michael put the baby
on the arm of the balance, the body of the cruelly murdered infant
outweighed the entire nation.*

"What is happening right now in the heavenly host?" I asked in my
eulogy. "When Avraham, Hemda, and Ra'aya go up to Heaven? Five
members of one family—five cruelly murdered young ones. How old was
Moti? How old was Tzira? They were at the beginning of their lives. He
was an educator, she taught the disabled, and together they raised a family
of eight children of their own. Now more than half of this family has been
destroyed."

Two days after the funeral I went to visit the wounded from the
Sbarro attack who were in Shaare Zedek Hospital. I tried to speak to a girl
of sixteen who was severely wounded. "I was sitting in Sbarro with two
friends," she finally said, "and we were eating pizza. Beside us were two
tables joined together. A big family sat there, the father, the mother, and
the kids. All of a sudden, we heard a terrible boom, and saw frightening
flames. In a second, I felt that I was burning. I heard the man sitting with
his family at the table next to me say, 'Children, say *Shema Yisrael* out loud
with me.' They said it, and then there was a heavy silence . . . and I woke
up in the hospital."

That horrifying image stuck in my mind. Moti Schijveschuurder knew
that his family was going to die, and he made sure that the last words that

came from the mouths of his young children were *Shema Yisrael*. I recalled my father as he entered the gas chambers in Treblinka along with the Jewish communities of Piotrków and Prešov, the words of *Shema Yisrael* on his lips.

The day after my visit to Shaare Zedek, I went to visit the surviving members of the Schijveschuurder family. The children had decided to sit *shiva* in Neria, in the home their parents had built. In the middle of the afternoon prayer, an ambulance stopped at the door to the house, and Leah, supported by attendants on both sides, came inside. She had insisted on being released from the hospital in order to sit *shiva* for a few days with her siblings.

Hours later, I rose to leave, but could not bring myself to say my good-byes. I stopped beside her. I asked about her sister, who was also in the hospital, and Leah told me that before leaving, she had gone down to the intensive care unit to tell Chaya that she was going home. "She knows that you spoke at Mom and Dad's funeral," Leah said to me. "She also knows that you conducted their wedding ceremony. We've seen your picture often in the wedding albums, and Grandpa Friedman has also spoken of you many times. Chaya asked me to send regards to all the visitors, and added that Rabbi Lau would also certainly come to visit. She asked you to visit her in the hospital. 'Remind him that it's just as much of a mitzvah to visit the sick as it is to comfort mourners. Ask him to come visit me, too.' "

The first thing I did the next morning was to visit Chaya in her hospital room. Her face was burned, her arms and legs broken, and despite the quantities of morphine she had received, she was obviously suffering intense pain. Feeling helpless, I wondered what I could say to her. Spontaneously, I found myself telling her a story without naming the protagonist.

"I know a boy of eight who lost his father and mother. But unlike you, who are lucky to have a grandfather and two grandmothers, he had only one brother, until he came to Eretz Israel and discovered that he had another brother here. You, however, have three brothers and a sister.

"This eight-year-old boy came to Israel without knowing Hebrew and without knowing anyone except for his older brother. But you, everyone in Israel knows and loves. Everyone has heard about the terrible thing that happened to your family, and they are sending you lots of love from all ends of the country. Everyone is waiting for you to stand on your feet and leave the hospital healthy. I heard that the prime minister visited you here, and that minister of education, Limor Livnat, brought you a book of Psalms and a teddy bear. During my visit yesterday at your home, I met Mr. Moshe Katzav, president of the state. Those are expressions of love. Unlike your situation, almost no one waited for that eight-year-old boy I told you about. Almost no one knew of his existence. The authorities of the emerging state did not know about him, and they certainly did not love him. But still, he managed. He didn't give up, he didn't cry over his bitter fate, and he didn't feel sorry for himself. He tried to rebuild his life in the new country as best he could."

At that moment, to my total surprise, the girl said, "I know—that boy was you."

"And so," I replied, "take an example from my personal story." It was a short conversation. With the staff of doctors escorting me, I felt uncomfortable continuing, and it was difficult for her as well, as talking was a superhuman effort. At that moment, not an eye in the room was dry.

A few months later, the family asked me to perform the wedding of Chaya's older brother. It was a very emotional ceremony. The groom walked up to the wedding canopy without father or mother. Instead, the Friedman grandparents and Grandmother Schijveschuurder from Holland led him to the *chuppah*, along with his aunts and uncles. Everyone was crying, and they were tears of pain as well as happiness. Little Chaya and her sister, Leah, came up to me. If not for their tears, I could hardly believe that these were the same two girls who had recently been orphaned, had mourned their three siblings, and had suffered terrible physical injuries. These charming girls knew how to rejoice. I knew they would be all right, like the boy in the story I told Chaya when she was in the hospital.

IT WAS NOT ONLY JEWS WHOM I AIDED in coping with illness and distress.

My close relationship with King Hussein of Jordan began when I visited the families of the seven girls from Beit Shemesh who were killed by a Jordanian sniper during a school trip to Naharayim on the Israel-Jordan border. King Hussein paid a special visit to Israel in order to visit the grieving families. Before the parents of each victim, he went down on his knees to beg forgiveness for the evil deeds of his country's soldier, the murderer of the innocent girls. Coming from the king, this rare gesture was impressive. Along with the grieving families, the entire nation admired his personal initiative and was deeply touched.

The next day, when I arrived in Beit Shemesh to visit the mourners, as was my habit in such disasters, King Hussein's visit was the topic of the day; everyone was talking about it. His gesture, devoid of political calculations, impressed me as well, for the king had displayed sensitivity to the pain of others. I had heard much about him, and, like every Israeli citizen, I kept an eye on his activities on behalf of peace. But we had never had a real conversation.

When the king became ill with cancer, he was hospitalized at the Mayo Clinic in Rochester, Minnesota. At the time, I was supposed to be in Chicago for just one day. I thought to visit the king at his bedside. In reciprocation of his gesture in Beit Shemesh, I wanted to express to him the best wishes of the Israeli nation, which prayed for his full recovery. I informed the ministry of foreign affairs of my desire to visit, and Efraim Halevy, our ambassador in Jordan, sent my request to the king's family. The family appreciated the idea, but they informed me, through Halevy, that on that particular date the king was supposed to begin a new round of chemotherapy treatment. Because he had lost all his hair, he preferred to see no one except for his close family. I respected their decision.

I was already in Chicago when my cell phone rang. On the line was Iman al-Majali, director of King Hussein's office. Al-Majali was the king's confidant, the one who organized his schedule and was present at all his meetings. He addressed me with the title *hakham akhbar*, or great sage. He said the king knew I was in the United States and that I had wanted to take the time to visit him in the hospital. "The king is a religious man and greatly values your prayers and blessings. He is annoyed with those who said he can't receive visitors. It is true that he does not receive everyone, and he certainly does not want to be photographed. He wants to be remembered among his people in his full glory, not in his present condition. But he is not at all willing to give up your visit and your prayers," said al-Majali.

He asked when I would be able to visit. I replied that I could visit the hospital the very next day. Al-Majali concluded the call by emphasizing that he and the king would be waiting for me. I can't explain why, but before leaving for Israel, I had had a feeling that perhaps I would be able to visit King Hussein after all. I had taken with me from Israel a large Hebrew-English Bible in a white leather binding to offer as a personal gift to the king.

The next day, August 23, 1998, I went to the Mayo Clinic, Bible in hand. I was escorted into the room adjoining the king's hospital room and waited. Then the king came in, his hand connected to an intravenous drip. He wore his suit jacket on top of hospital pajamas and shook my hand warmly, and with a tiny smile, apologized for not wearing a tie. He explained that it was hard for him to fasten the tie on top of the hospital clothing, but because he felt that this was no way to receive a chief rabbi, he was wearing his jacket in my honor. We both smiled, then sat and talked for forty minutes.

Toward the end of the meeting, I presented him with the Bible. On its inside cover, I had inscribed a verse from the book of Jeremiah: *Heal me, O Lord, and I shall be healed; save me, and I shall be saved, for You are my praise.* To this inscription, I added: "On behalf of the entire Israeli nation, which admires your character and your efforts on behalf of peace, I pray for your well-being, and wish you a full and speedy recovery."

King Hussein took the Bible, and after reading my dedication, he brought the upper edge of the book to his lips and kissed it. He closed his eyes in pain, lifted the Bible, and placed it on his forehead. I noticed the tears flowing from his closed eyes. Then he lowered the Bible, kissed it again, and said, "*Hakham akhbar*, great sage, do you have children?" I answered yes. "And grandchildren?" he inquired, and again I answered yes. "And they are all in Israel?" he asked. "They are all in Israel," I replied. "I promise you before Allah," said King Hussein, his voice weak but confident, "that if He grants me life, I will dedicate all my strength, the rest of my days, to the ultimate goal: for your grandchildren and mine to live in friendship, as good neighbors. I promised this to someone I deeply loved and admired, a great fighter and hero, Yitzhak Rabin."

I thanked him, and noted that I had sat across from him when he had eulogized Rabin at the funeral on Mount Herzl. "I felt that you, King Hussein, were speaking about Yitzhak Rabin from the depths of your heart," I emphasized. King Hussein nodded. "I loved his honesty and his courage." Then the king changed the subject, surprising me with his knowledge. "I know about your past and about your childhood experiences. I know that for you, the sanctity of life is of supreme value. Perhaps that value is what brings you here to the Mayo Clinic to visit me. I promise you that I will return to Jordan, and I'll do everything I can on behalf of peace between my people and yours."

I tried to encourage him, expressing the idea that the Mayo Clinic was now his battlefield. "You were always very brave, very determined, and a great hero. Do everything, gather all your strength and your talents, in order to win this battle," I demanded of him, meaning every word. The king wept.

Forty minutes later, when we had finished our conversation, King Hussein insisted on accompanying me to the elevator, walking slowly and with effort past the rooms of the doctors, the nurses, and his guards. "You are a *hakham akhbar*. I must honor you; I am a believing man," he explained as he shuffled heavily toward the elevator, IV tubes stuck in his hand, elegant jacket on top of the hospital pajamas. Even in his most difficult moments, King Hussein made the effort to preserve his royal image by paying attention to his personal appearance and his majestic manner of speech. He had absolutely no self-pity, despite the terrible illness attacking his body.

Six months after my visit, he passed away. I received the news from Iman al-Majali. Through the Israeli ambassador to Jordan, al-Majali asked me to join the Israeli delegation attending the funeral. He explained that my visit at the Mayo Clinic had been an unforgettable experience for the king, and that he had mentioned it frequently. "The leather-bound Bible you gave him," al-Majali added, "was with him until the last moments of his life."

At the funeral, after the burial, the king's son, Abdullah, stood to receive the dignitaries who congratulated him on his ascension to the throne. I happened to be the third to congratulate him, after Syrian president Hafez al-Assad and French president Jacques Chirac. I said that I hoped he would continue breaking new ground as his father did, walking in the path of peace. He confirmed the words of al-Majali, who stood beside him, that his father had not stopped talking about my visit, and that he would follow in his father's footsteps to establish true peace with us.

ONE AFTERNOON IN THE FALL OF 1997, as I was making my way from the offices of the rabbinate in Jerusalem to my home in Tel Aviv, the radio announced the hospitalization of the Egyptian ambassador, Mohammed Bassiouni, in Ichilov Hospital. According to the news report, the ambassador had suffered from heart trouble and had been rushed to the hospital, where he underwent bypass surgery. I asked Rubi, my faithful driver, to drive by Ichilov on the way home so that I could check on Bassiouni, whom I knew from many government functions.

When I reached his room, I learned that he had just left the recovery room after surgery and was still sleeping. I asked the staff to give him my good wishes when he woke up, and to say that I would visit him the next day. On my way out, I heard a woman call out behind me, "Chief Rabbi, Chief Rabbi!" It was Mrs. Bassiouni, who had recognized me from behind the wall of bodyguards surrounding her husband's room, and asked them to allow me in. She was agitated, and had pushed through her husband's bodyguards in order to reach me. I explained that since the ambassador was sleeping, I should leave, but she insisted. Her husband had a deep belief in Allah, she said, and since he was a believing man, he needed my prayers. She repeated her request that I come into the room and stand by his bed. I could not refuse, but then the thought entered my head that this would not be the best plan.

When the patient opened his eyes, the first thing he would see through the haze of his sensory disorientation, over the tubes to which he was connected, would be the figure of a tall man wearing a black hat and suit. The shock was likely to give him a heart attack, which was the last thing on earth I wanted. But while I was standing on one side of the bed, his wife and bodyguard on the other, Bassiouni opened his eyes and looked at me. A big smile spread across his face, as if to say, "*Hakham akhbar*, bless me." I did so, wishing him a speedy recovery.

A month later, the phone rang in my office in Jerusalem. Mohammed Bassiouni was on the line. He asked if he could come meet me right away. Within the hour, he arrived at the office of the chief rabbinate in Jerusalem, carrying a personal letter from the president of Egypt, Hosni Mubarak. The president invited me to visit him at the presidential palace the next day, December 17, 1997. Surprised, I asked how this had come about, since I was neither a political representative nor a statesman. "I would like to know why His Honor, the president, wants to see me," I asked.

Bassiouni smiled and said, "You know that many people in Egypt think I have been in Israel too long. During the eighteen years I have been here, various foreign ministers have tried to replace me many times, and the present foreign minister is threatening to do so also. But I have an important supporter in the president's circle, my friend Osama El-Baz. While I was recovering from the heart operation, I told him that you were the first person I saw after I returned to consciousness. When the issue of my replacement came up, Osama El-Baz told this story to Mubarak. In order to prove to Mubarak how well accepted I am in Israel, El-Baz said that the chief rabbi had especially traveled from Jerusalem to Tel Aviv and was the first person to visit me, shake my hand, and pray for my speedy recovery. Mubarak's jaw dropped in astonishment, and he said, 'I would like to meet this man.' "

Before I left for Egypt, the Israeli foreign minister, Ariel Sharon, called me at home. "I heard that you're about to meet with President Mubarak. I have a request for you," he said. "We have an Israeli citizen named Azzam Azzam who is sitting in jail in Cairo, despite his innocence. Please ask the president to release him. Perhaps a religious leader will have some influence on him."

I traveled to Cairo the next day. Unfortunately, due to his medical condition, Ambassador Bassiouni was unable to accompany me. Cairo had obviously prepared for my visit: traffic was blocked on all the streets that I traveled through, and people stood on the sidewalks and stared curiously at my motorcade. At our meeting, Mubarak told me that ten thousand policemen were securing the streets of the capital during my trip. I was surprised at this enormous number. "If not, all my opponents and the opponents of peace with Israel would step outside and operate freely,"

Mubarak explained. "God forbid, if something happened to a visitor like you, what would I do? I can't permit even the slightest thing to happen to you during your stay with us."

About twenty people, including three Israelis, attended our meeting. Mubarak began by recalling that Israel had a new prime minister, Benjamin Netanyahu. I explained, setting aside the political opinions of the prime minister, that Israel had had enough of war, and above all wanted peace with its neighbors. As evidence, I mentioned the fact that it was Netanyahu, the right-wing Likud leader, who had returned Hebron to the Palestinians. The room was quiet for a moment. I did not know if I had angered the president, and wondered how he would react, but I was very clear about expressing our desire to end the wars. "You are right," Mubarak thundered, breaking the silence.

I told him about the special arrangements that Rabbi Eliyahu Bakshi-Doron and I, chief rabbis under Rabin's government, had made after the massacre at the Cave of Machpelah, in Hebron, in order to allow both Jews and Muslims to pray there. Ten days per year were set aside so that only Muslims could enter and pray, and ten days per year were reserved exclusively for Jews. On the other 345 days, separate entrances and rooms served the faithful of each religion. The massacre had taken place in March 1994, during the Jewish holiday of Purim. From then until my meeting with Mubarak in December 1997, the agreement worked, and not a hand had been raised in aggression there, and certainly no blood had been shed. In my opinion, this was decisive proof that if we wanted to live in understanding and calm, it was certainly possible.

I also raised the topic of Azzam Azzam to Mubarak, and he proposed a plan of action that I will not describe here. Upon my return, I outlined the plan to Foreign Minister Sharon and to Azzam's family.

Toward the end of our discussion, Mubarak made a request. He introduced it by saying that he himself was a secular person, but that in Cairo there lived the Grand Mufti of Egypt, Dr. Mohammed Tantawi, the most senior religious representative in the country and president of Cairo's Al-Azhar University. Mubarak voiced his sincere request that I meet with Dr. Tantawi. I was not surprised, since I had expressed to Bassiouni my desire to meet with this cleric.

We went to see Dr. Tantawi, known as Sheikh Al-Azhar. The meeting took place in the office of the president of Al-Azhar University, in an old, dark building on campus. Al-Azhar is the educational institution for the imams, muftis, and *kadis* (religious court judges) of the Sunni followers of Islam. Our conversation lasted about an hour and a half.

When I saw through the window that dusk was falling, I remembered that I had promised to attend the afternoon and evening services at the Shaarei Shamayim synagogue in Cairo, the only synagogue in Egypt that sometimes has a minyan. I knew that the Jews were anticipating my arrival. I explained this to Sheikh Al-Azhar, thanked him for the warm conversation, and apologized that I had to leave. Then I asked, out of politeness, if he would be willing to pay me a visit in Jerusalem. I promised to receive him with the same degree of respect that he had shown us.

His answer was abrupt: "Only if my passport is stamped with the seal of a Palestinian state. I will not have my passport stamped with the seal of the State of Israel." I was unwilling to let this extremist view pass, and pressed him. "Here we have been talking about friendship and good neighborliness, so why does the stamp bother you? My passport has the Egyptian stamp, and I am proud to have visited President Hosni Mubarak. Every attempt to advance peace and understanding between us is welcome."

But Sheikh Al-Azhar did not change his position. In his eyes, the Israelis had stolen Jerusalem from the Muslims. I could not allow such a statement to go unchallenged. "I have done a little 'homework' on you," I admitted. "I know you have a doctorate, and I was curious about the topic of your dissertation. I found out that you wrote about Jews and Judaism in the Koran. So I conclude that not only do you know Islam, but you know about Judaism as well. I also know something about Judaism, but I don't know anything about Islam. So please permit me to ask, how many times is Jerusalem mentioned in the Koran? After all, we're talking about the holy city, Jerusalem. Islam's fundamental text must surely make mention of such a holy city," I said.

The sheikh gave me a long, silent look. I continued to press my point: "In our Bible, the word 'Jerusalem,' and its synonym 'Zion,' appear not just once or twice, but 821 times. This proves the centrality of Jerusalem in

Jewish faith and consciousness. Jerusalem appears everywhere in the Bible and in relation to almost every topic. The Bible repeatedly mentions that we must preserve access to the holy sites for believers from all religions and nations. As Isaiah the Prophet says in chapter fifty-six: *Even them I will bring to my holy mountain, and make them joyful in my house of prayer: their burnt offerings and their sacrifices shall be accepted upon mine altar; for mine house shall be called an house of prayer for all people.* But as for sovereignty and historical connection, the number 821 teaches us something. So tell me," I asked again. "How many times is Jerusalem mentioned in the Koran?"

Again the sheikh held his tongue. "I can make a guess," I said, and he looked at me in silence. "Is the answer zero?" I asked. Fawzi Zafzaf, his deputy, nodded his head. With that unforgettable affirmation, I left for the synagogue to recite the afternoon and evening services with the tiny Jewish community of Cairo. I had the feeling that despite Israel's official peace with Egypt, we had a long way to go to achieve a stable and lasting peace, because some people, parties, and movements still refused to accept the existence of the State of Israel as a fact.

THE SHORT VISIT TO EGYPT and the two key meetings there showed me, once again, that we must never lose the hope of achieving peace among peoples and nations, religions, and races. We achieve this peace not through the highest echelons of authority, but rather through personal contact between individuals and with humanitarian gestures. This is the true power of influence—when relationships between people encourage leaders to meet together and reach mutual understanding, friendship, and eventually, real and lasting peace

CHAPTER 16

YITZHAK RABIN—THE BRIDGE THAT COLLAPSED

Restrain your voice from weeping . . .
JEREMIAH 31:15

ON SATURDAY NIGHT, November 4, 1995, Yitzhak Rabin was assassinated. The Hebrew date, 11 Cheshvan 5756, coincided with the memorial date for commemorating the death of the biblical Rachel. On this date as well, the Jewish community of Piotrków was massacred in Treblinka: 28,000 residents of the city and its environs, including my father and my brother Shmuel Yitzchak. As was my custom on the Piotrków *yahrzeit*, I went to Beit HaSofrim (the Writer's House), a museum in Tel Aviv, for the annual memorial ceremony for the Piotrków community, attended by the second and third generations. I returned home after ten o'clock at night.

When I returned home, Rabbi Yitzchak Ralbag of Jerusalem, father-in-law of one of my children, phoned to ask if I had heard the news. He said that Yitzhak Rabin had been shot and rushed to Ichilov Hospital. I was horrified. Without knowing Rabin's condition, the identity of the gunman, or the motive behind the crime, I hurried to the hospital. Thoughts raced though my mind: I was convinced that the assassin must be a terrorist.

It took seven long minutes to get from my house to the underground-level trauma room where the doctors were fighting to resuscitate the prime minister. Leah Rabin and the Rabins' daughter, Dalia, were holed up inside the nurses' office, and I joined those waiting outside. They included Shimon Peres; IDF chief of staff Amnon Lipkin-Shahak; U.S. ambassador Martin Indyk; and Rabin's close friends Eitan Haber, Shimon Sheves, and Haim Ramon. We all waited anxiously for news of the prime minister's condition. At one point, we had reason to hope for the best: the hospital director came out and announced that the monitor had jumped, hinting at signs of life. But a few minutes later, three doctors in white gowns exited the treatment room. They did not speak, but, as if by advance agreement, they shook their heads in unison from left to right, as if to say, "That's it— there's nothing more to be done. Yitzhak Rabin is dead."

Who had been the killer? We had heard it was a young Israeli but hoped it was not a Jew. But we soon learned that a radical right-wing Jewish law student from Tel Aviv's Bar-Ilan University, Yigal Amir, had shot Rabin three times. I expressed to the person next to me my fear that not only had Amir murdered a friend and leader but he also had destroyed the remains of the bridge connecting the disparate sections of Israeli society. Rabin was one of those working to heal the rifts between right and left, religious and secular, and his murder set these efforts back considerably.

As a personal favor, Shimon Peres asked me to accompany him into the room where Leah Rabin was sitting, and explain this to her. Leah was sobbing uncontrollably. Peres said, "His Honor the rabbi says we can hold Yitzhak's funeral on Monday, to allow world leaders to arrive . . ." But she did not wait for him to finish his sentence, and said that she did not care what they did. "Do whatever you want. It doesn't matter to me at all. Yitzhak is gone—my entire world is destroyed."

Peres grasped my hand and we left the room. We approached Martin Indyk, the American ambassador, who was in the middle of a phone call. After we updated him about the date of the funeral, he continued his conversation, and then informed us that President Clinton would attend. The dissemination of this news led many world leaders, including Egypt's President Mubarak and Jordan's King Hussein, to announce their attendance as well.

Before I left the hospital, reporters asked for my thoughts on the assassination. I replied that it was still too early to eulogize Rabin, but not too early to warn against the danger of civil war, which I had sensed was a possibility given the tension in the atmosphere during the previous few hours. I added that I hoped I would be proven wrong.

BEFORE THE FUNERAL PROCESSION BEGAN, Israeli news personality Ilana Dayan asked me to give a TV interview about my encounters with Yitzhak Rabin. This was one of the rare occasions in which I had great difficulty speaking, as my throat choked with emotion. My early acquaintance with Rabin was like that of every citizen; I knew he was an army man who had ascended through the ranks and had reached the highest rung of the ladder. A photograph of him taken in 1967 had won me over. In it, he stood next to the Lion's Gate in the Old City of Jerusalem during the Six-Day War. Beside him was Moshe Dayan; generals Uzi Narkiss and Rehavam Ze'evi stood in back. With his stance, Rabin seemed to be apologizing for the space he occupied. This officer with the shy manner fascinated me. After the war, upon receiving an honorary doctorate from Hebrew University, Yitzhak Rabin delivered an address at the campus on Mount Scopus in Jerusalem. To me, his speech seemed to embody the essence of the midrashic saying *The book and the sword descended from Heaven tied together*. Rabin began by stating that he was not receiving the degree on his own, but as the representative of all the IDF commanders. I appreciated this deeply, and it reminded me of the cantor's chant on Yom Kippur: *Here I am, impoverished of deeds. . . . I have come to stand before You and implore You on behalf of Your people Israel who have sent me.*

The first time I met Yitzhak Rabin was when we appeared together at a benefit evening in Tel Aviv for the *hesder* program in the Golan Heights, which combines army service with study in yeshiva. I spoke on behalf of the book, while he spoke as the representative of the sword-bearers. His speech was impressive, and I found him contemplative but somewhat aloof. Our next meeting was at the beginning of the nineties in Netanya, at the funeral of David Anilevitch, the deputy mayor of Netanya, Labor Party activist, former Palmach fighter, and Buchenwald survivor who saved me from a hail of bullets on the day of liberation (see chapter 5). I was then chief rabbi of Tel Aviv, but because of our shared past in Buchenwald and my years as rabbi of Netanya, the family asked me to deliver a eulogy.

I eulogized Anilevitch, emphasizing his boundless altruism. "Your soul," I said, "is now ascending to Heaven. But it will not arrive unescorted; thousands of notes with your signature that helped people to obtain apartments, fund their studies, and receive needed medical care are now falling down from Heaven like snowflakes, receiving your soul as it rises on high." Rabin, then a candidate for prime minister, appreciated these words. I saw him exchanging whispers with Yuval Frankel, secretary of his election headquarters. Later, Yuval told me that Rabin had suggested I should serve as chief rabbi of Israel.

Rabin and I walked together at Anilevitch's funeral, and agreed that we should meet to talk. We held our meeting in June 1992, ten days before he was elected prime minister. I invited Yitzhak Rabin and his wife; the Tel Aviv mayor, Shlomo Lahat, and his wife; and my neighbor Moshe Bornstein to my house. To Yitzhak's surprise, our meeting went on for more than four hours. "Four hours have passed and I haven't smoked even one cigarette?" he pondered, incredulous.

That evening, we spoke of the differences between him and previous prime ministers, and he expressed his deep respect for Levi Eshkol, Menachem Begin, and David Ben-Gurion. When I cited sections of Begin's speeches, imitating his dramatic voice, Rabin smiled—but said that such dramatics were not his style. Above all, I remember Yitzhak's question about my personal history: "I know about your past in the Second World War from stories and also from your brother Naphtali, when he was spokesman for the Ministry of Defense. I know he saved your life by hiding you inside a sack. I know you two came to Israel as orphans. But herein lies the great mystery that I am unable to solve: how is it that an orphan boy, without any source of emotional support, grows up to be the chief rabbi of Tel Aviv? And this is certainly not your last stop. Who educated you? Who brought you up?" I told Yitzhak Rabin about Rabbi Vogelman, and about the yeshiva world that nurtured within me the goal of continuing the chain of rabbis that was the tradition of my family so that I could snatch victory from the Germans. Rabin listened attentively.

On February 22, 1993, nine months after Rabin was elected prime minister, I was elected Ashkenazi chief rabbi of Israel, while Rabbi Eliyahu Bakshi-Doron was chosen chief Sephardi rabbi of Israel. On the first day of our terms, we met with Yitzhak Rabin. In addition to the office of prime minister, Rabin also held the positions of minister of defense and minister of religions. The first thing he asked in our meeting was how he could help us in his role as minister of religions. Rabin had a precise understanding of the status of the chief rabbinate, and I explained one of its most serious problems—that it was a department within the ministry of religions. I urged the prime minister, who was also minister of defense and of religions, to make the chief rabbinate independent rather than part of the ministry of religions so that it would be free of governmental bureaucracy and politics. This effort ultimately proved successful.

When our official meeting was over, Rabin asked to speak to me privately. "Honorable rabbi, every Shabbat, I try to be in my home in Neve Avivim [a neighborhood in Tel Aviv]," he said, giving me his personal telephone number and telling me to make a note of it. "During the week, I might say and do certain things—or, conversely, refrain from doing or saying certain things—that you might have an opinion about. If you have comments or want to consult with me about anything, the best time to call is one hour before Shabbat or half an hour after Shabbat. I'm usually at home then. I would appreciate it very much if you would use that telephone number. Keep in touch." To this day, that number is listed in my home telephone directory.

I initiated a discussion with Rabin following the Oslo agreements, which determined that Israel would evacuate its forces from Gaza and Jericho and transfer control over those areas to the Palestinians. Some individuals contacted me regarding the ancient synagogue in Jericho—which has a mosaic floor bearing the words *Shalom al Yisrael* (peace on Israel)— because a yeshiva inside the synagogue was functioning there, although without a dormitory. Knowing of my close relationship with Rabin, they worried about what would become of the synagogue and yeshiva when the agreements were implemented. At their request, I called the prime minister and asked for his opinion, while informing him that I wanted to give him a box of Cuban cigars, a gift from Fidel Castro.

"Honorable rabbi," he said, "Leah is abroad and I am on my own. If you have an hour for me, I'll wait for you tonight at nine in my home in Tel Aviv. I'm not interested in the cigars, since I only smoke cigarettes, but

perhaps we can sit and talk. I also have something that I want to show you."
I went to his house, my driver, Rubi, bearing the box of cigars. Rabin opened
the door wearing flip-flops on his feet. He apologized for not serving me
anything to eat, for reasons of *kashrut*, and offered me a glass of water. Then
he went to the corner of the room, removed a document from his briefcase,
and—referring to Peres, then foreign minister in Rabin's government—
said, "Shimon just returned from Cairo this evening. At a meeting with
Arafat, organized by Mubarak, they added the qualification [to the Oslo
agreements] that you requested: 'Religious affairs in the "Shalom al Yisrael"
synagogue in Jericho shall be under the auspices of the Israeli authorities.' "
The document also specified that the synagogue would be used during
the day for Torah study by Israelis, and that Palestinian policemen would
secure the road accessing the synagogue. Official matters out of the way, we
enjoyed the rest of our hour in relaxed conversation.

AFTER ADDRESSING THE MATTER OF JERICHO, I focused on the handing over
of Bethlehem to the Palestinians. Again, individuals contacted me and
reported that every evening at midnight, Jewish groups came to Rachel's
Tomb at the entrance to Bethlehem in order to recite the special prayer
service *Tikkun Chatzot* (a mystical prayer recited at midnight, when the
Gates of Heaven are believed to be open to our prayers). If Bethlehem
were to follow the same procedure as the synagogue in Jericho, Palestinian
policemen would secure the access road—which was much more heavily
traveled by Jews than the road to the Jericho synagogue—and Jews would
be afraid to use it, especially at night.

That week, the government held a special meeting on this issue, at
which Shimon Peres reported that he thought he could still negotiate this
point with Arafat. Concerned individuals measured the distance between
the Jerusalem neighborhood of Gilo and Rachel's Tomb; it was only about
five hundred yards, and no Arab houses stood in the area. Thus many
requested that IDF soldiers take responsibility for securing this stretch
of road. The foreign minister supported this proposal, but Rabin refused,
arguing that we had signed an agreement and promised to return the area
south of Gilo to the Palestinians. He did not intend to give up Rachel's
Tomb, but the road was the Palestinians' responsibility. Either we trusted

them and armed them with rifles, he said, or we didn't. In the special meeting held on Wednesday, the government decided to refer the issue to the regular session on Sunday.

Between Wednesday and Sunday, dozens of callers asked me to try to influence Rabin to change his mind. The pressure mounted. That Friday was the first time I took advantage of his offer to phone him before Shabbat. I called Yitzhak's home in Neve Avivim and asked him to join those who wanted to assert our rights to Rachel's Tomb, the very Rachel who expresses the foundations of Zionism in the book of Jeremiah: *"Restrain your voice from weeping and your eyes from tears, for your work will be rewarded," declares the Lord. "They will return from the land of the enemy."*

Rabin listened, then queried, "What's so special about this tomb?" I explained that believing Jews from the Diaspora went to pray at three main holy sites when they were looking for a spouse, suffering from fertility difficulties, or before an operation. These sites were the Western Wall, the Cave of Machpelah, near Hebron, and Rachel's Tomb; we could not take the right to pray at Rachel's Tomb away from them. Rabin insisted that he was not denying them that right, but that the matter should be handled in the same way as that of the synagogue in Jericho. Rachel's Tomb would remain under Israeli sovereignty, but the Palestinians would secure the road. "What's the difference?" he asked in all sincerity. "Jericho," I answered, "is a historic synagogue, but this is the tomb of our mother Rachel, and we cannot abandon our mother." With this statement, so fundamental to my belief, our conversation ended. Yitzhak asked me to allow him to sleep on it.

On Sunday, just after the government session, Rabin called the chief rabbinate, and announced in his unmistakable baritone, "Rabbi, when you said, 'We cannot abandon our mother,' you moved me. In the government session that recently ended, I went over to Shimon's side and we made a unanimous decision. We'll insist that Rachel's Tomb and access to it will remain under the full control of the Israeli government and the IDF." The tears choked my throat so that I was unable to even express my thanks to him.

In 1994, I again worked with Rabin on behalf of an issue central to the Jewish people. I wanted his help to block a successful petition to the

Supreme Court to allow the import of nonkosher meat, which had been forbidden since the establishment of the state.

I contacted the prime minister in his role as minister of religions, explaining that this decision was potentially damaging to the image of the Jewish state. In addition, I noted, as minister of religions he would now need to pass countless laws to protect the system of *kashrut* in all public institutions, the IDF, banquet halls, and similar venues. The system of *kashrut* supervision that had operated until now would collapse, and in its stead, we would need an inflated system that was beyond the capacity of the present ministry of religions. Rabin listened to me intently, and commented that the situation as I described it sounded unacceptable. He asked me to allow him to take care of it. Because the issue fell under Israel's Basic Law, the Knesset needed a supermajority to defeat the amendment that would allow nonkosher meat to be imported.

Rabin proposed that I meet with the chairman of the Knesset economics committee and explain the importance of the issue. In this manner, he said, I would be helping him to recruit a majority in the Knesset to pass the new law. The chairman, a member of the political opposition, advised me to drop the matter; he saw no chance of recruiting a supermajority to prohibit the import of nonkosher meat. He compared the situation to Menachem Begin's observation that almost all votes of no confidence in the government ended as votes of confidence. "Honored rabbi," said the committee chairman, "if you bring this to a vote, this will be the first time ever that the Israeli Knesset votes by majority *in favor* of importing nonkosher meat to Israel. Personally, as one who keeps kosher in my home, I would be sorry to see that happen," he concluded.

I thanked him, then called Yitzhak Rabin and told him about the conversation. Rabin summarized it with a sentence that was short and to the point: "Nonsense. Let me take care of it." On December 29, 1994, as part of the vote on the government budget, the Knesset voted on the proposed law. Seventy-four Knesset members supported the law prohibiting the import of frozen nonkosher meat, fourteen opposed, and one MK abstained.

Only after the vote was held did we realize that, because of the hasty formulation of the proposed law, it addressed only frozen meat. Thus in 1995, the Knesset raised the issue for a second vote. They deleted the word "frozen" from the proposal, inserting "meat and its by-products" instead. The results of the vote were decisive: sixty-six in favor, eleven opposed. Yitzhak Rabin did superlative lobbying work. He spoke with each member of Knesset personally. After the vote, I phoned to thank him for his efforts to pass this law. "You have no coalition obligations, and only one person around your government table wears a *kippah* on his head. So why did you make this big effort?" I asked. If we had not had a close relationship, I would never have dared to ask such a question. "I did it for two reasons," he answered. "First of all, we already have so much home-grown *treif* meat that we don't need to import nonkosher meat from outside." We both laughed, and then he added, "But seriously, this is the Jewish state, isn't it? How else can this be manifested?" That was all he said, as he was not given to flowery statements, but I will never forget it. His words echoed in my mind on the day of his murder, when I stood in the intensive care unit at Ichilov Hospital and said that he represented the remains of the bridge between religious and secular Israelis, and that after the murder, this bridge might very well collapse. To this day, I have not recovered from that Saturday night. And I think the tears in the fabric of our nation are in some part the result of that murder in the square.

Thirty days after Rabin's killing, I flew to New York in order to speak at an enormous rally in Madison Square Garden, along with Vice President Al Gore, Shimon Peres, and Leah Rabin. Tens of thousands wept as my friend, singer Dudu Fisher, chanted the *El Maleh Rachamim* mourning prayer, concluding the thirtieth-day memorial ceremony.

Every year on the anniversary of his murder, I speak to the students of the Rechavia high school in Jerusalem about Yitzhak Rabin's assassination, civil war, and groundless hatred. Then I visit the monument at Mount Herzl cemetery, where I participate in a meeting of religious and secular Jews organized by the national students' organization. These activities are the least I can do to honor the memory of Yitzhak Rabin, a personal friend and unforgettable national leader.

CHAPTER 17

PAPAL PARLEY

They shall not hurt nor destroy in all my holy mountain.
for the earth shall be full of the knowledge of the Lord,
as the waters cover the sea.

ISAIAH 11:9

ON SEPTEMBER 21, 1993, a few days before Yom Kippur, the pope glanced at the ceiling, and then he said something I will never forget. The words that he uttered in English still echo in my ears: "Wherever I go, with whomever I speak, we are obligated and committed to the continuity and the future of our elder brother, the Jewish people."

After hearing these words, so honest and full of conviction, I felt I could speak to him about the future of the Jewish people.

MY MEETING WITH THE POPE at his summer residence in the Italian town of Castel Gandolfo was preceded by sincere efforts on the part of the Community of Sant'Egidio, and by prolonged deliberations on my own part.

I developed special ties with this Rome-based Catholic lay association, which considers itself a close friend of Israel and organizes a yearly interfaith conference to promote international peace. The Community of Sant'Egidio first invited me to participate in this conference during my tenure as chief rabbi of Tel Aviv, but I could not accept, since the conference is regularly held in October, during the Jewish High Holidays. But in 1993, they moved the conference to September and so I was at last able to participate. This was during my first year as chief rabbi of Israel.

288

On the afternoon of the conference, the participants gathered at La Scala theater in Milan. On the stage stood four speakers, each presenting the concept of peace from his own particular perspective. The cardinal of Milan, Carlo Maria Martini, represented Christianity. At that time he was being considered as a possible successor to Pope John Paul II. Prince Hassan of Jordan was supposed to have represented Islam, but he was replaced at the last minute by a professor of Islamic theology from Oran, Algeria. I represented Judaism. The fourth participant was Mikhail Gorbachev, the former president of the recently dissolved Soviet Union, who represented the atheist and secular point of view.

Before the conference, I received word that Pope John Paul II wanted to meet with me. I was well aware of the strained history of relations between the Vatican and the chief rabbinate. I recalled that Rabbi Isaac Herzog, who served as Ashkenazi chief rabbi before the establishment of Israel and during its first decade (1936–59), had requested at least three times to meet with Pope Pius XII, trying to enlist the Church's assistance to help save the Jews of Europe from decimation by the Nazis. He was flatly refused. Only after the Holocaust, in 1946, in response to Rabbi Herzog's third request, did the pope agree to meet with him (see chapter 11).

I also knew of the willingness of Rabbi Yitzhak Nissim, Sephardi chief rabbi of Israel (1955–72), to meet with Pope Paul VI during his visit to Israel in 1964. Rabbi Nissim offered to meet the pope in Jerusalem, next to the entrance of the Chamber of the Holocaust museum on Mount Zion, after the pope's visit to the nearby Dormition Abbey. But the pope informed the rabbi that he did not have room in his schedule for this meeting, no matter how short. In response, Rabbi Nissim refused to join the other state dignitaries who welcomed the pope upon his arrival from Jordan at an official reception at Megiddo. According to Moshe Nissim (Rabbi Nissim's son and deputy prime minister, 1990–92), his father said, "If he wouldn't come to Jerusalem to see me, either to my home on Balfour Street or to the office of the chief rabbinate on King George Street, and refused to meet me even at the entrance to the Chamber of the Holocaust on Mount Zion, then I won't wait for him on the road to Megiddo."

In contrast to his predecessors, the attitude of Pope John Paul II to the Jews, and to the Holocaust in particular, was vastly different. This pope was born in Poland, and knew quite a bit about the history of the Holocaust. I realized that his request to meet me had a personal flavor, but still I hesitated to accept. After much deliberation, I gave the Sant'Egidio representatives a negative answer. I explained that I could not enter the Vatican due to the Christian statues and crosses that were there. For me, visiting the Vatican was not a matter of saving lives, as it was for Rabbi Herzog, who thus had to overlook most other considerations; it was merely a courtesy visit. There was no justification, I decided, for the chief rabbi of the Jewish state to enter the Vatican, with its Christian statues and crosses, which directly opposed our worldview. Furthermore, because this was a generation of intermarriage and assimilation, I worried that such a meeting between rabbi and pope, publicized as a friendly dialogue, might send the wrong message to young Jews whose identity had not yet been formed.

I asked myself if I should be the one to break down the walls that had divided us for so many years, and my answer was—no. Added to the equation was the constant badgering by the representatives of Sant'Egidio for me to attend the meeting. Their intense efforts set off an alarm in my head. I tried to understand what they were trying to achieve with this meeting, and what the Church's interest was. As I had been appointed chief rabbi only six months earlier, I wondered whether they had an ulterior motive. How would the media portray the meeting? Whom would it affect? Was I unwittingly serving as a tool for a goal unclear to me?

After I declined, I assumed that the Vatican would drop the subject. But a few months later, the Sant'Egidio representatives once again contacted me by letter and telephone with a new proposal. The pope had a summer residence in Castel Gandolfo, about a forty-minute drive from Rome, where he resided during the months of July and August. Since the Sant'Egidio conference was planned for Milan in mid-September, the pope was willing to extend his stay at Castel Gandolfo in order to meet me. I studied the proposal and decided there was no problem with meeting the pope in a private house. But in order to justify my visit and prepare appropriately for the meeting, I wanted to raise several points and to know the pope's stance on them in advance.

The first topic was four IDF soldiers who were missing in action: Yehuda Katz, Zachary Baumel, Tzvi Feldman, and Ron Arad. The pope had connections in countries with which the State of Israel had no diplomatic ties, and I wanted to know if he would discuss with me the possibility of helping locate the soldiers. My second question concerned whether he was willing to work on a manifesto of world religious leaders opposing terror in the name of religion. A third topic that was very disturbing to me was Christian missionary activity in Israel. It was unacceptable, I felt, for missionaries to take advantage of people in economic and social distress in order to try to convert them. Would the pope be willing to discuss with me ways of stopping this activity and allowing religion to be a free choice, instead of one purchased with material means?

Another relatively minor point that I raised for discussion was whether the pope would authorize public access to the Jewish books and manuscripts in the Vatican library. A few weeks later, I received a positive reply from the Vatican, affirming that the pope was willing to discuss all the issues I suggested. This time I was able to confirm the meeting wholeheartedly. I felt I was walking on firm ground, that this meeting was justified from the viewpoint of Jewish law and statecraft, and could have educational value for both Jews and non-Jews.

Before leaving for Italy, I deliberated regarding an appropriate gift to offer the pope. My wife thought that since I would be speaking with him about Ron Arad and the other Israeli MIAs, and because I would be meeting with him during the days preceding Rosh Hashanah, it would be fitting to bring him a shofar, the ram's horn traditionally blown on that holiday. On it would be engraved a phrase from the daily prayer service, *Sound the great shofar for our freedom*. I thought this was an excellent idea.

Before the meeting with the pope, which was planned for Tuesday, September 19, I attended the annual conference of the Community of Sant'Egidio in Milan. I borrowed the main point in my speech there from the vision of the prophet Isaiah about the end of days: *The wolf also shall dwell with the lamb, and the leopard shall lie down with the kid.* "To our ears, this prophecy sounds exaggerated, like an impossible dream," I said to my listeners in Milan. I spoke extemporaneously, with no written notes, because I wanted to see their eyes and read the expressions on their faces. "But I want to tell you what a relative of mine said about this verse. Rabbi Meir Shapira was a rabbi in the city of Lublin, Poland, and I bear his name. 'Why,' he asked, 'do we consider such a situation untenable? Indeed, such a thing has happened, and the vision of Isaiah the prophet already came true once—in Noah's ark. Two by two, the animals entered the ark. Inside it was a huge assortment of animals, yet they behaved themselves. Not one of them bit, or stung, or devoured a weaker one. When the flood ended, the animals left the ark. Each one went to its own habitat, and there they remain until this very day.' If so, what is so special about Isaiah's prophecy?" I felt four thousand pairs of eyes riveted on me as I asked Rabbi Shapira's question.

After a short pause, I continued. "The answer Rabbi Shapira of Lublin gave was brilliant in its simplicity. In Noah's ark, wolf and lamb, leopard and kid lived together because they had no choice. Outside raged a common enemy—the flood. They knew that any inappropriate or unpleasant behavior on their part meant they would find themselves outside the ark, sentenced to destruction. With no other option, they controlled their instincts and cooperated against their common enemy. Isaiah the prophet is not talking about a situation of no choice. Rather, he is speaking of free will: *They shall not hurt nor destroy in all my holy mountain; for the earth shall be full of the knowledge of the Lord, as the waters cover the sea*. In other words, even when the animals have the option to devour, crush, trample, and bite, they will not hurt or destroy each other. One day—and this is the ideal dream of the peace we long for—human beings will understand and recognize that we must live and let live, and that we must do so with maximum mutual respect.

"Ladies and gentlemen, after hearing this question and answer, let us take a look at our own times. We have yet to reach the days of Isaiah. Yet we have the responsibility to adopt the basic concept of Noah's ark. Let us live together as in Noah's ark, at least because we have no choice. The animals faced the common enemy of the flood. Today as well, humanity has many common enemies. I, as a Holocaust survivor, experienced the *blood, fire, and pillars of smoke* that we recall at the Passover seder. I suffered in the flesh the true meaning of a common enemy to all of humanity.

I experienced the evil, the hatred, the bestiality, the descent to levels where no preying animal ever stood. In nature, a lion does not devour a cub; a tigress does not prey upon the cub of another tigress. Yet with my own eyes, I saw what were known as human beings destroying their own kind. I saw them attack and dismember other human beings who were weaker than they. We all have common enemies: the atom bomb, the AIDS virus, cancer, heart disease, poverty, ignorance, crime, violence, and terror. We must unite to conquer these common enemies. As religious leaders, can't we understand that we are living inside a Noah's ark?"

The next day, at the press conference in Milan, the reporters pelted me with countless questions on such topics as the right of the Jewish people to Jerusalem. I put Jerusalem on the center of the map for the Italian media. Later, the Israeli ambassador in Rome, Avi Pazner, accompanied me to the meeting with the pope at Castel Gandolfo, along with my brother Naphtali. The ambassador's car was full of Italian newspapers whose headlines quoted my speech: "Jerusalem is the eternal capital and holy city of the Jewish people, according to God's will." The subtitles read, "This was the chief rabbi's first shot in anticipation of his meeting with the pope."

WHEN I ARRIVED AT THE TWO-STORY BUILDING where the meeting with the pope was to take place, I discovered that the escorts would remain on the first floor, while the meeting would be held on the second floor, in private. Avi Pazner accompanied me on the stairs leading to the second floor. At several points on the stairway stood soldiers of the Swiss Guard, who saluted me as I passed. Suddenly, Pazner clapped his hands to his head and exclaimed, "I can't believe it! Last week I was among the diplomatic staff invited here for Gorbachev's meeting with the pope. A statue stood at every corner of this stairway. But now I see not even one. The pope had all the statues removed in your honor. Good for him."

Indeed, I saw not one statue on my way to the meeting room. In my letters, I had not raised this issue, since I knew the meeting had been moved from the Vatican to the pope's summer home, and did not consider the possibility that there would be statues in his private residence as well. But the pope was obviously very sensitive to my concerns and read my letters with full attention, for he made sure the statues were removed before our meeting.

At a certain point on the stairway, the pope's chief secretary asked Pazner to leave me. The ambassador knew about this in advance, and he left me with the secretary, who, like the pope, was Polish. "Is the brother who saved you here?" whispered the secretary. I replied that he was waiting on the first floor. The secretary asked me to have him come up, as the pope wanted him to be present at our meeting. I was impressed by the effort they had made to learn about my background and their knowledge of my brother.

Naphtali accepted the pope's invitation, of course, and together we went up to the meeting floor. We passed many rooms, large and small. Suddenly the pope came out of one of them and greeted us in Hebrew: "Shalom." We followed him into the room, in which three chairs stood. The pope insisted that I sit in the middle, with him on one side and Naphtali on the other. Before we sat down, he pointed out the lake, which we could see through the window. Then the pope pointed in the direction of the Vatican. He explained that the air at Castel Gandolfo was cleaner and purer than in Rome, and thanked me for agreeing to meet him there instead of at the Vatican.

When we sat down, the pope asked politely whether I had been well received in Italy. I replied that I had been received with great warmth. "Still, if you will permit me, there is one thing bothering me," I noted. The pope tensed and tried to soften the harsh impact of my words. He said he had seen on television how the audience at La Scala had received me with resounding applause, and how they had responded with enthusiasm to my speech. I replied that I had no complaints in that direction, and that truly everyone had welcomed me very cordially. "There is just one word," I said, "that has been grating on my ears. In Israel they call me *harav harashi*. In English-speaking countries, I am 'the chief rabbi.' In Russia I am *glavnyi ravvin*, in France *grand rabbin*. In Switzerland they call me *Oberrabbiner*, and in South America I am *gran rabino*. But here, in Italy, starting with my landing at Fiumicino Airport, everyone calls me *rabbino capo. Rabbino capo di Israele.* And I wonder, *capo*? Am I a *capo*? Of course, I realize that the word *capo* in Italian means 'chief,' but to me the word *kapo* has one and only one meaning. It is short for *Kameradenpolizei*, camp guards, and implies the dark days of the Holocaust." I did not have to expand on this explanation. The pope understood exactly what was bothering me. He smiled and replied, "To me, you will always be *naczelny rabin*"—"the chief rabbi" in Polish.

After this friendly introduction, we moved to the body of this historic conversation. I asked the pope's permission to tell him a story I had read in *The Holocaust: A History of the Jews of Europe during the Second World War*, by Sir Martin Gilbert, who is known as Winston Churchill's official biographer. I was interested in hearing the pope's reaction to the story. The pope nodded his head in acquiescence.

A young Jewish couple in Kraków, David and Helen Hiller, had a two-year-old son named Shachne. When the Nazis arrived in Kraków in 1942 and transferred some of the Jews to the slave labor camp of Płaszów and some to Auschwitz, the Hillers left their baby with Catholic neighbors, the Jachowicz family, until they could come back for him. Unfortunately, the parents never returned.

The child grew up. By age four, he had memorized the Sunday prayers that he heard in the Catholic Church. When he turned five, Mrs. Jachowicz contacted the local priest and requested to have the child baptized as a Christian. The young parish priest asked her if she could imagine the reaction of the child's biological parents to such an act. Mrs. Jachowicz answered that she had to be honest with him. "I remember the scene exactly," she said. "As I held the child in my arms, my good neighbor Helen stood by the door and waved good-bye to her son. She requested of me, 'Mrs. Jachowicz, if I do not come back, please try to return the child to the Jewish people.' "

"If that is what she wanted," the young priest replied, "I am not willing to baptize him, not under any circumstances."

I addressed the pope with great emotion: "This priest, sir, was named Karol Wojtyła. It was you." Then I asked if he remembered this specific incident. For a moment, silence filled the room. Then, with a broad and warm smile, the pope said, "That boy, Shachne Hiller, is today a religious Jew in Brooklyn. By the way, this is not the only incident of this type. I did the same thing in all similar cases." His reply surprised me. I made a quick calculation and discovered that forty-eight years had passed from 1945 until our meeting in 1993. For all these years, the pope had followed the path of that Jewish boy from Kraków whom he had refused to baptize.

IMMEDIATELY AFTER THE MEETING, I returned to Israel, to Netanya, where I had served for nine years as chief rabbi. The local Bnei Akiva yeshiva was dedicating a new study hall that day, and I was supposed to speak at the ceremony. Everyone, including the media, knew where I had been. When I arrived, I announced that I would tell only one short story. I told the story of the rescue of the Jewish child, Shachne Hiller. This child was rescued twice, I explained: once by a Polish Catholic family who saved him from the Nazis' clutches, and again by a Catholic priest who saved him from the Catholic Church. "Today this priest is the pope, the leader of the Church."

Upon hearing this story, a Netanya resident named Zonnenschein, whose grandson was a student at the Bnei Akiva yeshiva, collapsed in a faint. It turned out that this Jew, who worked as a guard in the local branch of Bank Mizrachi, had been a childhood friend of David and Helen Hiller of Kraków. Thirty-eight years later, hearing me report that their little boy, Shachne, was alive and well in Brooklyn, Zonnenschein was overcome with emotion.

For years afterward, I continued to receive updates about Shachne Hiller, who prayed in a small Belz Chassidic synagogue in Brooklyn until he moved to New Jersey.

AFTER MY EMOTIONAL CONVERSATION with the pope about Shachne Hiller, the walls separating us as Catholic and Jew fell, and we continued our meeting as two human beings. Following my plan, I raised the issue of the Israeli soldiers missing since the battle of Sultan Yakoub in Lebanon in 1982. I began with the story of Yosef Katz, father of missing soldier Yehuda. Yosef was an Auschwitz survivor who lived in Ramat Gan. "This Auschwitz survivor had a son who studied in the combined yeshiva-army program," I explained, adding that I had taught Yehuda's sister Pirchiya in high school. The pope listened attentively. "The son entered the army, went into the tank corps, and fought in the war in Lebanon at Sultan Yakoub. Since then, we know nothing of his whereabouts. His parents, Yosef and Sarah, like other parents of MIAs, jump at every ring of the phone and chime of the doorbell, hoping for news of their son's fate." John Paul II attended carefully to the details, asking how many years the soldiers were missing. When I replied, he asked, "Tell me, *naczelny rabin*, do you believe that they are still alive?" I replied honestly that I often asked myself that question, but I did not have a clear answer.

"When our upcoming meeting was publicized in Israel," I continued, "some of the parents visited my office in Jerusalem to encourage me to speak with you about their children's fate. I told them that I was going to meet with you because of them, that they were the reason for this meeting. At the end of our conversation, one of the parents asked to speak with me privately for a few minutes. He said, 'I am not sure that my son is alive. I want to believe it, but I am not convinced. Yet I made a vow that as long as I live, I will do everything possible to keep the memory of my son in the public consciousness, so that his name will not be erased from the Jewish people. At the very least, I would like to be able to place a monument engraved with my son's name in the cemetery, so that at least his name will remain in the world. If I can achieve this, all my efforts will have been worthwhile.'

"I have come to you with the words of this father," I told the pope, who was deeply moved. "All that this father wants is to be able to visit the cemetery once a year and recite the 'memorial service,' " I said, using the English term. John Paul II corrected me, recalling the Hebrew word from his days in Kraków and saying in an Ashkenazi accent, "Kaddish, Kaddish. He wanted to say Kaddish for his son," the pope said, repeating the word three times. We were silent for a moment while the pope withdrew into himself. Then he promised to do everything he could. "It's not a lot, but now that I know more or less whom we are talking about, I will do everything I can to act on their behalf." His gesture pleased me, and I encouraged him. "You were witness to the tragedy of the Jewish people. Here again, we are speaking about parents, some of whom are Holocaust survivors. How much more must they suffer after what they endured during the Holocaust period?" I wondered together with him.

He was quiet for another moment, then changed the subject. To my complete surprise, he said, "I remember your grandfather, Rabbi Simcha Frankel-Teomim, from Kraków." Ostensibly, my meeting with the pope was an encounter between two religious leaders. But the pope's personal tone, his interest in events of almost fifty years earlier, astonished me. "I remember him walking on the Sabbath to the synagogue, surrounded by many children. How many grandchildren did your grandfather have?" I was forced to admit that I did not know. I knew that we had an extensive family, but I had no idea of the exact number of family members living before the outbreak of the war, when I was only two years old. I glanced at Naphtali, who was sitting next to me. He knew the answer—he replied that we were forty-seven grandchildren, and that was only on our mother's side. John Paul II asked how many survived the Holocaust. I knew the answer to that—only five, and two of those were my brother and myself.

I told the pope about yet another terror attack in Israel that had taken place the evening before my departure for Milan. Crying "*Allah hu Akhbar*" (God is great), an Arab terrorist had stabbed a bus driver in the neck on a bus traveling from Tel Aviv to Ashdod. To me, the use of God's name to justify the murder of innocent victims was adding insult to injury, I explained to the pope. I asked his opinion on how to stop this despicable phenomenon. His reply was unequivocal: "I object to violence and terror, and I speak out against them at every opportunity. I am also willing to sign a manifesto stating this, but we need the agreement of the other side."

From violence and terror, we moved to the topic of anti-Semitism. The pope spoke with determination. "I have visited one hundred and twenty countries, and in every one I have spoken about anti-Semitism. Tell me, honorable chief rabbi," he asked, "do you believe that anti-Semitism based on religion still exists today, as in the first days of Christianity?" I requested his permission to begin answering this incomparably serious issue with a joke. He smiled in surprise, and I quickly explained that this joke held a kernel of truth, serious and solid. When he indicated, with anticipation and curiosity, that I should proceed, I described Johnny, a tall, tanned American standing in the center of a town somewhere in the American Midwest on a Sunday afternoon. He rolls up the sleeves of his jacket and shouts, "A Jew! Give me a Jew! I need a Jew here!" His friend tries to placate him, asking why he could possibly need a Jew. After all, there aren't any Jews in their town. But Johnny insists that he must kill a Jew. "I'll destroy him! I'll rip him apart with my own two hands!" roars Johnny. The astounded friend tries to understand what insanity has come over Johnny. "What's wrong with you? Are you drunk or something? Why do want to kill a Jew all of a sudden? What has a Jew ever done to you?"

Johnny has his answer prepared. "To me? Why, he crucified our Lord! He hanged him, so I'm going to kill him." The friend reminds Johnny that this "event" took place two thousand years ago, but Johnny refuses to accept historical fact, shouting, "What do you mean?! I heard it from the priest in the church, just half an hour ago!" The pope smiled. He did not laugh wholeheartedly, but rather looked into my eyes and said, "I think a picture of the two of us, publicized around the world, will pull the rug out from under the feet of those primitive-minded individuals who still blame your people for something you did not do." Again, I was struck by his determination.

I went on to the other issues I had planned to raise. I described to the pope the activities of the missionaries in Israel, the way they took advantage of those most economically vulnerable and of new immigrants with tenuous Jewish roots. I emphasized that the missionaries were not engaging these individuals in a theological-ideological debate but were rather making a cheap attempt to purchase their faith, to convince them to abandon their ancestral tradition because of temporary economic difficulties. This was untenable, both logically and religiously. To my view, it was commercialization of people and faith, and we had to stop it. The pope begged me to understand that these were fringe groups whose methods ran counter to the mainstream view of his Church, and that he was very dissatisfied with their activities; he spoke of this phenomenon almost with disgust. He led me to understand that it existed mainly in very underdeveloped countries, and that he had had enough of it.

The final issue I had placed on our agenda was public access to the Jewish sacred manuscripts stored in the Vatican library. The pope replied that he was granting permission to anyone interested in viewing these spiritual treasures, according to the accepted procedures. In addition, he would also order that these texts to be copied onto microfilm. The original works would remain in the library, where they would be preserved from the ravages of time. Our conversation lasted about forty minutes. When it ended, the pope asked that my escorts, who were waiting on the first floor, come upstairs so that he could shake their hands. My wife was among the guests. The pope went to meet her, stretching his hand out toward her. She was flustered, for in accordance with Jewish laws of modesty, women do not shake hands with men. I was filled with apprehension at the thought that this momentary awkwardness might destroy the friendly atmosphere we had worked so hard to create. All eyes in the hallway turned toward the pope to see how he would handle the situation. The pope's Polish secretary whispered something into John Paul's ear. The pope at once raised his outstretched hand in the air, lifted the other hand in parallel, and waved both hands up and down, greeting her in Hebrew, "Shalom, shalom, shalom." John Paul II quickly found a diplomatic solution for a situation that had the potential to be extremely embarrassing.

MY MEETING WITH THE POPE AT HIS SUMMER RESIDENCE at Castel Gandolfo developed into a positive and meaningful relationship. As far as I know, there was no precedent for a relationship so personal, thoughtful, and sensitive between a chief rabbi of Israel and a pope.

In January 1994, the Vatican decided for the first time to establish diplomatic relations with the State of Israel. I do not consider my visit directly responsible for this historic decision, but clearly my meeting with the pope helped contribute to the initiative.

Four months later, on Israel's Independence Day, the president of Israel invited the diplomatic staff to a reception at his residence. Shimon Peres, who then served as foreign minister, asked me if I had seen the *Washington Post*. I replied that I had not, and Peres told me that the pope had visited the United States and given an interview to that newspaper. When the journalists asked him his opinion on the status of Jerusalem, he recalled that several months ago, the chief rabbi of the State of Israel had visited him, and that my conversation with him gave him food for thought on that very issue.

I had not been a party to the discussions preceding the establishment of diplomatic relations with the Vatican, but the juxtaposition of my visit and the *Post* interview caught my attention. Furthermore, I learned that that year, John Paul II had appointed a committee, headed by Cardinal Edward Cassidy of the Vatican, to craft an apology to the Jewish people on behalf of the Church. They planned to present this apology to me. I could not believe my ears. Cardinal Cassidy visited me twice in Jerusalem with various drafts, once by himself, and the second time with Cardinal William Keeler of Baltimore and Archbishop Henryk Muszyński of Gniezno, Poland. The drafts spoke in a general manner about crimes committed during the Second World War by members of the Church against the Jewish people and other nations. But the truth was that at best, some individuals of stature in the Church had stood by passively. At worst, they participated in provocations against the Jews, distributed racist publications, and gave speeches in favor of Hitler's "Final Solution." The drafts that the honored cardinals presented to me contained not one word of condemnation against these individuals. They also did not include any criticism of the behavior of Pope Pius XII, who could have prevented the killing of vast numbers of Jews but instead did nothing.

I commented that the drafts were excellent as the beginnings of an apology, but that they must include additional statements. When the cardinals asked exactly what I meant, I explained to them that Pope Pius, unlike his successor, Pope John XXIII, was a witness to the Holocaust and its horrors yet did nothing to prevent it.

I proposed that the three cardinals go with me to visit Yad Vashem, Israel's Holocaust Museum, located just ten minutes from my office. There they could see with their own eyes the boulevard of trees, each one named for one of the righteous gentiles who worked to save Jews during the Holocaust. I told them that if, during the 1930s and '40s, the pope had uttered the one sentence that should have been said, that avenue would stretch from Yad Vashem in Jerusalem all the way to the Vatican in Rome. Countless Catholics would have joined the few righteous individuals who helped Jews and saved their lives. After I said these words, which I believe wholeheartedly, the Catholic cardinals left my office. They made a few corrections in the document, added several phrases, and finally published a text about which they did not seek my opinion.

But my meeting with the pope had many other repercussions. One was that in 1999, the nine hundredth anniversary of the Crusaders' conquest of Jerusalem, a delegation of five hundred religious leaders of various Christian denominations visited Israel in order to ask forgiveness for the murder of innocent Jews during the Crusades. I was invited to address the visitors in the grand hall of the Great Synagogue in Jerusalem. Their delegates wished to present to me, as the representative of the Jewish people, a scroll with a request for forgiveness signed by the leaders of the delegation. They asked me to accept it in the name of the Jewish people throughout history.

I replied that I had neither the mandate to grant pardon nor the power to forgive. I did express my honest appreciation for the fact that they had come to Jerusalem, and said that the formulation and expression of their apology had educational and historical importance. I prayed, and wished to believe, I said, that similar incidents would be avoided in the future. But, I clarified, in no way did the presentation of the missive to me erase the past or forgive its despicable sins.

WE MUST NOT FORGET THE PAST or erase even one iota of what happened during the Holocaust. I see myself as a messenger of memory, and do all I can to perpetuate memory and prevent the blotting out of what has happened.

One of the most unforgettable memorial assemblies at which I spoke took place on Holocaust Memorial Day in 1995, on the fiftieth anniversary of the end of the Second World War. The participants who gathered in Madison Square Garden in New York included President Bill Clinton, who spoke vehemently against anti-Semitism. I spoke about the obligation to remember, and about the lessons of the Holocaust. One of the lessons we should learn from it, I said, was that the State of Israel was the Noah's ark of the Jewish people. I proposed an alternative scenario. What would have happened if the 1947 United Nations decision that gave birth to Israel had taken place in 1937? Or if a similar decision had been made at the League of Nations meeting in Geneva in 1937, or at the post–World

With Elie Wiesel at Auschwitz-Birkenau in 1988 during the March of the Living, an annual educational program that brings students from around the world to Poland.

My teacher and mentor Rabbi Shlomo Zalman Auerbach at the completion of a Torah scroll, during the dedication of Chaye Moshe Yeshiva in Jerusalem in memory of my father, Rabbi Moshe Chaim Lau.

With the Lubavitcher Rebbe, Rabbi Menachem Mendel Schneerson, during one of several conversations I had with him.

From left to right: Sephardi Rabbi Eliyahu Bakshi-Doron; President of the State of Israel Ezer Weizman, Prime Minister Yitzhak Rabin, and me, during the February 1993 ceremony at which Rabbi Bakshi-Doron and I were installed as chief rabbis of Israel.

Presenting my teacher and mentor Rabbi Elazar Menachem Man Shach with my book *V'yachel Yisrael*, on Jewish law, in 1993. To my right is Yitzchak Ralbag, father-in-law to my son David and the head of the Religious Council of Jerusalem.

During my tenure as chief rabbi of Tel Aviv, I had occasion to converse with two of the greatest and most influential halachic authorities in recent times, Rabbi Ovadia Yosef (left) and Rabbi Yosef Shalom Elyashiv (right).

With Fidel Castro in Havana, 1994.

Above: Speaking in Jerusalem at an event for Rabbi Menashe Klein's Kiryat Ungvar, 1987. From right are state comptroller Yitzchak Tunik, Chief Rabbi Mordechai Eliyahu, me, and fellow Buchenwald prisoner Elie Wiesel.

Left: Posing with the prayer stand from a destroyed Moscow synagogue, at a ceremony celebrating the laying of a new cornerstone, 1989. From right: Rabbi Yosef Aharonov, me, Rabbi Levin, and my dear friend Shalom Dov Berka Wolf.

Right: The Grand Synagogue in Piotrków, 1994, which serves as a public library today. In one of the cupboards we found this image of the tablets of the Ten Commandments, which had been on the eastern wall. It was riddled with bullet holes (probably from the episode when we were imprisoned there with our mother and other Jews of the town in 1942). On the right is Cantor Benjamin Muller, from Antwerp.

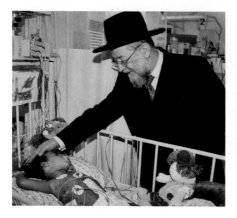

Visiting a child who was gravely injured in a terrorist attack in Hadera, 2002.

With Prime Minister Yitzhak Shamir (center) and Naphtali at a party in my home commemorating the publication of Naphtali's book *Balaam's Prophecy*, 1993.

With Yitzhak Rabin at the wedding of my daughter Shira, 1994.

With Nelson Mandela, president of South Africa, in Pretoria, 1993.

At the Ministry of Defense in Tel Aviv, with Prime Minister Ariel Sharon and President of the State of Israel Shimon Peres.

With Pope John Paul II
during an interfaith
meeting at the Notre
Dame of Jerusalem
Center, March 23, 2000.

With President Bill Clinton in Jerusalem,
1996.

The Dalai Lama offers me a prayer shawl
on June 14, 1999, in Jerusalem.

At an exhibit at Yad Vashem
in 1995, the chairman of the
directorate of Yad Vashem,
Avner Shalev, points out
to Vice President Al Gore
and his wife, Tipper, a
photograph of me taken
by Paul Goldman. The
photograph shows me
posing with my rifle in a
Hitler Youth uniform (the
only clothes available at the
time that fit me) after my
arrival in Haifa during the
summer of 1945.

With my brothers
Yehoshua Yosef "Shiko"
Lau-Hager (left) and
Naphtali Lau-Lavie
(center).

At the Forum 2000 Foundation conference
in Prague with Sheikh Zafzaf, deputy
director of Al-Azhar University in Cairo,
in 1998.

With Mikhail Gorbachev at a meeting of
the S. Daniel Abraham Center for Strategic
Dialogue at Netanya Academic College,
June 2003.

With Prime Minister
Ariel Sharon and the
mayor of Jerusalem,
Ehud Olmert, in 2002,
at the dedication of the
plaza on the crest of
the Mount of Olives in
memory of Rehavam
Ze'evi, the minister
of tourism, who was
assassinated in 2001.

Right: Walking under the notorious gate with the inscription Arbeit Macht Frei (Work Sets You Free) at Auschwitz-Birkenau during the annual March of the Living on April 25, 2006. Walking beside me, from right to left: President Shimon Peres, Knesset member Avraham Hirschson, and Poland's deputy parliament speaker (and future president) Bronisław Komorowski.

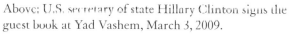

Above: U.S. secretary of state Hillary Clinton signs the guest book at Yad Vashem, March 3, 2009.

Right: Yulia Selutina and Yelena Belayaeva receive a Righteous Among the Nations medal and certificate on behalf of their late father, Feodor Mikhailichenko (above right), in the synagogue at Yad Vashem, August 4, 2009.

With President Barack Obama during the Righteous Among the Nations award ceremony at the Israeli Embassy, January 27, 2016, in Washington, DC.

Yad Vashem chairman Avner Shalev (left), Israeli prime minister Benjamin Netanyahu (right), and I inspect Auschwitz-Birkenau blueprints during the opening of the exhibition Architecture of Murder, at Yad Vashem, January 25, 2010.

Speaking at the World Holocaust Forum at Yad Vashem, January 23, 2020, marking seventy-five years since the liberation of Auschwitz-Birkenau.

War I San Remo conference of 1920, or in the controversial Balfour Declaration of 1917, in which Great Britain first recognized the Zionist aims of the Jewish people? How would history look then, and how many millions of Jews would still be alive today? I knew that these questions had no answers, but it was meant to be an intellectual exercise—something to ponder.

WE MUST NOT SPEAK of the six million who were butchered, or of the million and a half children who were murdered. The human mind cannot process—either emotionally or experientially—the concept of millions of people. Rather, we must speak of little Shloimy and Moishy, young Leah-le and Sarah-le. The story of Anne Frank is a perfect example of the impact of the individual story. At each assembly I attend, I address the audience and ask them not only to speak of how the martyrs of the Holocaust died, but to learn how they lived and who they were. Most important, those gathered should consider the State of Israel the national home of the Jewish people and think about their obligation to deepen the roots of basic Jewish education in order to ensure historical continuity.

I believe that the number of Jewish victims in the Holocaust is more than six million. Physically, the Nazis did kill six million Jews in acts of indescribable cruelty. But in terms of emotion, faith, and consciousness, they killed far more than that. Most of those who survived are also victims in some way. Some walk among us as the living dead. Their bodies function and they manage to work, but they have no living spirit. My grandfather Rabbi Frankel-Teomim brought this point home when he recalled a phrase from the prayer service on Yom Kippur: *Our Father, our King, act for the sake of those who went into fire and water for the sanctification of Your Name.* Rabbi Frankel-Teomim said that those who go into fire are completely incinerated, with not one limb remaining, only ashes. In the Holocaust, those who *went into fire* are those who choked in the gas chambers, starved to death, and died all kinds of horrible and cruel deaths. They are the ones who number six million. But those who go into water remain whole in body. Not a hair from their heads falls off, not a fingernail is missing. Their bodies are complete, yet they have no living spirit. Those who *went into water* are those who seemed to have survived the Holocaust; whole in body, but devoid of joie de vivre and faith, which would have given them the strength to persevere.

Surprisingly, another memorial assembly that made a distinct impression on me took place in Berlin, in commemoration of the sixtieth anniversary of Kristallnacht. On this "Night of Broken Glass," which took place from November 9–10, 1938, the terrors of the Holocaust began when mobs in Germany and Austria burned more than one thousand synagogues, smashed stores, and killed ninety-one Jews. Another 30,000 Jews were arrested and sent to concentration camps. In November 1998, Ignatz Bubis, president of the Central Council of Jews in Germany, invited me to speak at Berlin's Great Synagogue. I agreed on one condition: I refused to sleep on German soil, and so I asked to leave Berlin on the same day as my arrival. Bubis agreed.

Beside me sat Gerhard Schroeder, who had been elected Germany's chancellor the week before. He was wearing a large white *kippah* on his head. On my other side sat Roman Herzog, president of Germany.

When it was my turn to speak, I spoke in English about anti-Semitism. I said that the only lesson we have learned from the Holocaust is that we have learned nothing at all—since at this very moment, genocide was taking place in Kosovo, just a two-hour flight from Berlin. If we allowed one million people—mostly children—to starve to death in Biafra from 1967 to 1970, we have learned nothing at all. Further, I addressed those Jews who, when the iron curtain was lifted from East Germany, had passed from East to West, merely exchanging one diaspora for another.

I studied the occupants of the first row, Herzog and Schroeder, finding not a trace of bitterness in their expressions. At the end of my speech, in the presence of the president and chancellor of Germany, I called for the Jews to abandon the killing fields of Europe and come home to the Land of Israel.

After my speech at the Berlin assembly, a young yeshiva student mounted the platform. He was wearing a black hat in the style of the Gur Chassidim. A fringe of a beard encircled his face, which was very Jewish-looking and becoming to a young scholar. He wore a long black suit coat and black socks over his pants. This yeshiva student was Yitzchak Meir (Itche Meir) Helfgot, a graduate of the cantorial school in Tel Aviv, then serving as a cantor in Frankfurt. He stood in front of the microphone, and with no musical accompaniment, sang the Gur Chassidic tune for *Ani Ma'amin* (I believe), a composition written by the great Gur composer Ya'akov Talmud: "I believe with complete faith in the coming of the Messiah, and even though he may tarry, still I await his arrival any day."

When Schroeder heard this song, I saw that his face, which usually looked very stern, seemed quite moved. He crossed and uncrossed his legs, too excited to find a comfortable position. He grabbed my arm and said in German, "It's so pure! He sings from the bottom of his heart." I told Schroeder that the cantor was from Israel, adding that he was a Chassid who faithfully represented those in whose memory we were gathered. At this assembly commemorating the sixty years since Kristallnacht, Bubis understood that the prayer for the dead with an organ accompaniment was not enough, that it would not express the true spirit of the event. So he brought the young cantor from Frankfurt to Berlin to sing his deeply moving version of the song of faith in his exceptional voice.

Three months later, I went to Amman to march in the burial procession of King Hussein of Jordan. I walked in the same row with four U.S. presidents: Bill Clinton, Jimmy Carter, Gerald Ford, and George H. W. Bush. As we strode, I felt two hands gripping my shoulders. I was startled by the unexpected embrace and turned around to discover that it was Gerhard Schroeder. "Chief Rabbi, ever since our meeting at the assembly in Berlin, I recall the song of that wonderful Jewish cantor with awe. Could you remind me of the tune he sang?" he asked, to my astonishment. A moment later, after regaining my composure, I hummed the tune into his ear. That tune had burst from the heart of a Gur Chassid and touched the heart of the chancellor of Germany, so much so that he left his row in the funeral procession, bypassed the phalanx of guards, and approached me to express his admiration and to hear it one more time.

From my point of view, this was another small brick laid at the virtual memorial monument to the Holocaust and its dead. Sometimes I am surprised to discover how, where, and to what extent the Holocaust is engraved in people's minds and hearts. That is why I find a purpose in commemorating the Holocaust everywhere. I try to prevent memory from sinking into oblivion. Sometimes, the Holocaust arises from seem-ingly unrelated topics, even when it is not the main topic of discussion.

In May 2003, the Community of Sant'Egidio invited me to address a conference held in Aachen, Germany, on the topic of peace. At this con-ference I experienced an unplanned confrontation that involved an inter-pretation of the Holocaust from a completely unexpected point of view. I spoke of my view on peace between states and peoples, as well as Judaism's stance on this issue. When I finished my speech, a Palestinian religious leader stood up. Directing his remarks to me and the other conference participants, he made harsh accusations: "I would like to express to you the feeling of the Palestinian people, that in fact we can be considered victims of your Holocaust. We are now standing on German soil, and I do not wish to deny the Holocaust at all. But I have one question. Why do we have to be its victims? Until the end of the Second World War, you lived with us in peace. We and the Jews of the Land of Israel maintained close and peaceful relations. After the events of the Holocaust, you looked for a homeland, and invaded our home. Because Europe destroyed your homes, you took advantage of our weakness and disorganization, and uprooted us from our homes. Due to this, we have been in exile for more than fifty years. Why do we have to pay the price for your Holocaust?"

When he finished, I rose to reply. First I corrected him, explaining that we had not invaded, nor had we come to a strange land. We ourselves had been exiled from the Land of Israel in 586 BCE by the Babylonians, and again in 70 CE by the Romans. I expressed my approval of the fact that he did not deny the Holocaust, but I could not allow his mistake to stand uncorrected. Islam was born in 622 CE, 550 years after our Second Temple in Jerusalem had been destroyed.

I recalled that the Bible speaks of the wolf dwelling with the lamb, and promises that *nation shall not lift up sword against nation*. In that same holy book, the prophet Jeremiah promises the Jewish people that they will return home: *thy children shall come again to their own border*. The prophet Isaiah, describing his vision of the end of days, speaks of the ingathering of the scattered Jewish people who will return to their land. And as for the friendship between Jewish and Muslim peoples during the period before the Holocaust, I pointed out that here on German soil it is appropriate to recall the only religious leader in the world who flew to Berlin in order to shake Hitler's hand and encourage him to pursue his "Final Solution": the spiritual leader of the Palestinians, the Mufti of Jerusalem, Haj Amin al-Husseini. Other leaders remained silent, unjustly, but at least they did not encourage the Jews' adversary. At that time, the Palestinian refugee problem did not exist, nor were the Holocaust refugees looking for a national home. At that time, I told him, I was in my home, in my hometown in Poland, and I did not intend to throw anyone out of his home.

I reminded the Palestinian religious leader of another historical fact. In 1929, ten years before the Second World War began, Palestinians murdered sixty-nine Jews in Hebron, tearing babies from their mothers' arms, with no provocation from the Jews. "As partners in dialogue, we must understand things correctly," I proposed to the Palestinian, "and deal with the problem. But to present yourselves as victims of our Holocaust is a complete distortion of history." When I had finished speaking, the chairman of the conference, Cardinal Roger Etchegaray, the pope's right-hand man, told the audience that I was one of the youngest survivors of Buchenwald. The Palestinian said not a word. At the end of a difficult and tense day of discussions, I crossed the border from Germany into Holland in order to spend the night in a Dutch town.

CHAPTER 18

FOR THE SAKE OF PEACE

You shall choose life . . .
DEUTERONOMY 30:19

AT EACH STAGE OF MY RABBINIC CAREER, in the many positions I held—district rabbi of north Tel Aviv, rabbi of Netanya, rabbi of Tel Aviv-Jaffa, and of course chief rabbi of Israel—I met with kings and queens, presidents, and religious and government leaders. Many of these meetings were held in private—long discussions in an honest and curious attempt to get to know and understand one another. The topic of the Holocaust arose in most of these discussions, and to my surprise, almost all the leaders I met with revealed impressive knowledge of my personal story. Each leader, in his own way, remarked on a particular aspect of those terrible six years of the Second World War that had determined the fate of the Jewish people as well as my personal destiny. I list some of those personages below to indicate the variety of people I have been privileged to meet. Several of these meetings are worthy of describing in detail because they shed light on some of the ways in which Jews are perceived by others.

At the top of the list are U.S. presidents Jimmy Carter, Ronald Reagan, and Bill Clinton, as well as Soviet president Mikhail Gorbachev. I met in Grenada, Spain, with King Juan Carlos, accompanied by Israeli ambassador Herzl Inbar and the leader of the Jewish community, Yitzchak Kirov. We had an extended conversation about Jewish-Arab relations during the

Golden Age of Jewish culture between the eighth and eleventh centuries, when Jews and Muslims got along well in Spain. I was always looking for a way to encourage a modus vivendi between Israel and our Arab neighbors. During this heart-to-heart talk with the Spanish king, I asked him to contribute to our efforts to achieve peaceful coexistence between Jews and Muslims—the kind that had existed in Spain centuries earlier.

Václav Havel, president of the Czech Republic, invited me in the fall of 1998 to the Forum 2000 conference to speak about the promotion of peace in the ancient stronghold of Prague. I contacted the president of Lithuania, Valdas Adamkus, regarding the three hundred or more Torah scrolls stored in the national library in Vilnius (Vilna), including those belonging to the great scholar the Vilna Gaon, after they were hidden in basements for dozens of years. A number of these scrolls had originally been confiscated by the Nazis from Lithuania's Jewish community. (When Soviet authorities wanted to burn many of the scrolls in the immediate postwar years, they were saved by Antanas Ulpis, a non-Jewish Lithuanian librarian.) I asked the president to intervene and return the scrolls to the Jewish people so that we could send them to Jerusalem, and they were returned to Israel in 1992.

Following the terrorist attacks on the Israeli embassy (1992) and Jewish community center (1994) in Buenos Aires, Argentina, in which more than one hundred Jews were killed, I met Carlos Menem, president of Argentina. My purpose was to ask why the Argentineans were not attempting to catch the perpetrators of this horrible attack. Accompanied by the leaders of the Argentinean Jewish community, I also met with Menem's successor as president, then-attorney Fernando de la Rua, an amiable man and a great lover of Israel.

ONE OF MY MOST EXOTIC MEETINGS took place with members of the Makuya, a vociferously pro-Israel Japanese Christian sect, whom I met when I was chief rabbi of Netanya. I was invited by the Makuya to attend a conference of religious leaders in Kyoto. Located on top of Mount Hiei, the conference center was a series of bamboo halls within a lovely, spacious Japanese garden. I felt that this breathtaking scenery embodied the essence of the wonders of Creation.

After my speech, the conference organizers asked me to meet the Most Venerable Etai Yamada, 253rd head of the Tendai sect of Mahayana Buddhism and de facto leader of Japan's sixty million Buddhists. He was then a gaunt ninety-four-year-old who bore a strong resemblance to Indian spiritual leader Mahatma Gandhi. Yamada-san received me while sitting cross-legged on the floor of his bamboo home. His entire being expressed asceticism; he looked as if he did not draw nourishment from this world. Yamada-san addressed me in a quavering voice, in Japanese: "Now that you are between the walls of my home and under my roof, and I am shaking your hand—now I can return my soul to my Creator. I have awaited this visit for many years, and after this, I can depart this world for a better place.

"When I was young," he recounted, "I did not know any Jews, nor did I know anything about Judaism. In the nineteen thirties and forties, we learned about the Jews through the *Protocols of the Elders of Zion*, which was translated into Japanese and distributed in a pocket-size edition. Every Japanese child had a copy in his schoolbag. Our leaders, as you know, had made a pact with Nazi Germany in their war against the free world, and especially against the Jews. Although my nation did not kill Jews or build concentration camps, and had no connection with the 'Final Solution,' still they fought the Americans, thus forcing the United States to focus the majority of its forces on the fight against us instead of on the effort to save you from destruction in Europe. In fighting against the U.S., we helped the Germans to murder Jews. I know your history, and I have been following your career for years. As a member of the nation that aided the killers, I am guilty of the murder of your parents. Although I almost never leave the walls of my house, much less the city of Kyoto or my native Japan, I traveled to Poland and placed a wreath on the monument in the Warsaw Ghetto. Now, finally, in the name of my entire people, I have the opportunity to ask you for forgiveness and atonement—you who suffered through the Holocaust as a child, whose parents were murdered by the Nazis. If you grant me this request, I can return my soul to the Creator."

I listened attentively, surprised by his determination and well-articulated point of view. But I could not grant his request for forgiveness.

I explained to Yamada-san that according to the Jewish tradition, an observer who stands on the sidelines is as guilty as the perpetrator himself. The argument that he did not contribute directly to the crime did not absolve him of guilt. Therefore, I explained to the Japanese leader, I did not know if I had the mandate to forgive him in the name of the victims. As for myself, I had one mission to fulfill: to remember, and not permit the world to forget. Still, I emphasized my great appreciation for his honest statement, his humane approach, and his sincere gesture: his trip to Poland to place the wreath on the monument. "Your words deserve to be remembered forever. Not only I, but all members of your nation and your hundreds of millions of believers, should hear them," I added.

I gave several examples from our biblical and rabbinic texts regarding the legal status of one who witnesses a crime but does nothing to stop it. I recalled the lamentation of King David for Abner ben Ner, captain of Saul's army, who was killed by Joab ben Zeruiah: *Your hands were not bound, and your feet were not placed in chains. As one who falls before villains have you fallen!* The Talmud, in tractate *Sanhedrin*, explains: *David chastises Abner at the latter's funeral.* David reprimands the dead Abner for not preventing King Saul from spilling innocent blood, despite Abner's position of influence with the king. When Saul heard that Achimelech ben Achituv of the priestly city of Nob aided David in his flight by providing him with food and the sword of Goliath, Saul slaughtered Achimelech along with his entire household. "Yet you were silent, and permitted the slaughter," David rebukes Abner. He then observes that no one had bound Abner's hands and feet, and David asks rhetorically, *Where were you? Why did you not protest?* With the story of this biblical precedent, I explained the source of my position to the Japanese Buddhist.

I gave Yamada-san another example from tractate *Sanhedrin*. In the first chapter of Exodus, Pharaoh, king of Egypt, says, *Let us deal wisely with them, lest they multiply.* He asks his advisers to propose methods of embittering the lives of the Israelites, to enslave them and ensure they will not multiply. In fact, this is history's first "Final Solution," the first Wannsee Conference.

According to the sages, Pharaoh's three advisers were the seer Balaam ben Beor, Jethro before he becomes priest of Midian, and the prophet Job.

Balaam is the one to suggest the "Final Solution." As he informs the king, he has foreseen in the stars that a Jewish child will be born who will cause Pharaoh great trouble. He proposes turning the Hebrew midwives into collaborators, like the Nazi *kapo*. They will perform the first "selections," Mengele-style. Pharaoh adopts Balaam's proposal, ordering the midwives: *When you deliver the Hebrew women at the birth stool, if it is a son, you shall put him to death, but if it is a daughter, she may live.* Midwives Shiphrah and Puah, whom the sages identify as Jochebed (Moses's mother) and Miriam, refuse to cooperate. As the Bible recounts, *But the midwives feared God, and did not as the king of Egypt commanded them, but saved the men children alive. . . . And Pharaoh charged all his people, saying, Every son that is born ye shall cast into the river, and every daughter ye shall save alive.*

When Balaam offers his suggestion, Jethro the humanist pounds on the table and protests the murder of innocent babies. After this incident, Jethro no longer feels comfortable in Egypt and flees to Midian, where he becomes a priest. Jethro is the very one to open his home to the other refugee who escapes Egyptian tyranny. After Moses kills an Egyptian who strikes a Hebrew man, he, too, flees to Midian, where he encounters Jethro's daughters, who tell their father: *An Egyptian delivered us out of the hand of the shepherds, and also drew water enough for us, and watered the flock. And he said unto his daughters, And where is he? why is it that ye have left the man? call him, that he may eat bread.*

Job also disagrees with Balaam, but he has nothing of Jethro's courage and resolve. He remains silent, especially because he sees that Pharaoh likes Balaam's idea and adopts it. According to the Talmud, this is one of the reasons for the afflictions Job later suffers. To understand this, we have to digress to a Midrash of the sages. When Job hears of the death of Nadab and Abihu, the two sons of Aaron, he says, *This is what I most fear.* This is a surprising comment. Why should Job be concerned about the death of Nadab and Abihu? Why should their death inspire his fear? The Talmud offers a reason for the deaths of Aaron's sons. *Moses and Aaron were leading, and Nadab and Abihu*—the second generation of leadership—*were following them. . . . Nadab said to Abihu, 'When will these two elders die, and you and I become the next leaders?' Said the Holy One, blessed be He, to the brothers: 'We'll see who buries whom.'* Then the Talmud cites a popular

Aramaic saying: *I've seen many old camels coming to market, laden with the hides of younger camels.*

As the story continues, Job is troubled by Nadab's provocative question. But Abihu says nothing in reply. Why, then, is he punished together with Nadab? The answer is that he is punished because he remains silent. In other words, one who remains silent instead of preventing sin when necessary becomes a partner in crime. Says Job, *If this is how the Creator operates, this is what I most fear. For I also remained silent when I sat in conference with Pharaoh, when Balaam made his proposal. Who knows what awaits me?*

I left our meeting with the feeling that Yamada-san sincerely believed in what he was saying, and that he truly wanted to ask for my forgiveness. As a believing man, he harbored a genuine fear of the World-to-Come, and he wanted to reach it free of sin. Although I could not grant his request, I appreciated it deeply.

ONE OF MY MOST EXCEPTIONAL MEETINGS was with the leader of Cuba, Fidel Castro. Over the years. I had developed a very personal desire, never fulfilled, to discover what had become of the Jewish refugees from Europe, especially those from Poland, who had gone to Cuba. Before the war and during its early years, the entire world closed its gates to the Jews. Following the MacDonald White Paper of May 1939, the British followed a strict quota for aliya certificates to Eretz Israel. Cuba was one of the only countries to throw out a tiny life preserver.

In 1939, a group of prosperous German Jews, all learned professionals, crowded onto the ship *St. Louis*. They had applied for entry visas to the United States and had not received them yet. But they did have landing certificates for Cuba, which was meant to be a stop along the way. They packed their suitcases with precious possessions and jewels, and set forth from Hamburg for the shores of Havana. Unbeknownst to them, political conditions in Cuba were changing, and after the ship landed in Cuba, the Cuban government decided not to honor the landing certificates unless large sums of money were paid. After failed negotiations on behalf of the Jews, the ship was forced to try to seek harbor in the United States, but President Roosevelt, swayed by pre–New Deal immigration restrictions and popular isolationist opinion, declined to grant the refugees entry and so they had no choice but to sail back to Europe. Although Jewish organizations negotiated with European governments to allow the passengers entry to Great Britain, the Netherlands, Belgium, and France, many eventually fell under Nazi rule and met their deaths in the concentration camps.

When other Jews in Europe heard of the fate of the *St. Louis*, they looked for another place to which they could flee. Meanwhile, the situation in Cuba changed again, and the country welcomed these Jews and opened its doors to them.

My aunt Metta, my father's sister; her husband, Bruno-Berchiyahu Schounthal; and their two young children saved themselves by fleeing to Cuba from Brno, Czechoslovakia. After the war, they immigrated to the United States, and in their old age, after the State of Israel was established, they made aliya. This family connection aroused my curiosity to learn more about the life of the Cuban Jews.

The Cuban Revolution (1953–59), led by Fidel Castro, plunged Cuba into turmoil, ultimately leading to the overthrow of dictator Fulgencio Batista and the establishment of a communist government. The upheaval forced Rabbi Meir Rosenbaum of the Nadvorna Chassidic dynasty to leave his adopted country in the late 1950s. Since then, Havana had been without a rabbi. I was well aware that the governments of Cuba and North Korea, the only two countries in the world that remained fanatically communist through the 1990s, forbade all religious education and communal life, including Judaism.

Every once in a while, I heard fragments of information from individuals who made brief visits to Cuba, including representatives of various intelligence agencies. But these bits and pieces were not enough to form a complete picture. I learned that despite the restrictions, some individuals still identified themselves as Jews. I realized that I had no chance of meeting them, since Israel had no diplomatic relations with Cuba and since bearers of Israeli passports, especially chief rabbis, were not permitted to enter. Further, Castro was known for his close relationship with both Saddam Hussein, ruler of Iraq, and Hafez al-Assad, leader of Syria. I relegated my idea of visiting Cuba to the back burner, but the flame of curiosity continued to burn within me. I guarded a small spark of hope that one day I would reach the country and discover the fate of the Jews who had found refuge there. Thankfully, the right time finally arrived.

Toward the end of 1993, a delegation from Bar-Ilan University in Ramat-Gan, near Tel Aviv, came to see me—David Altman, vice president of the university, and my friend Professor Yitzhak Yochai, a native South American. They asked me to deliver a speech in Caracas, Venezuela. Bar-Ilan University had a very active group of supporters in that country, they said, and its chief rabbi, Rabbi Pinchas Brenner, was a member of the university's board of governors. To thank the Venezuelan Jews for their support, once every two years Bar-Ilan sent a lecturer to their capital. I agreed to make the trip, which was arranged for February 1994. During the week of my stay, I had several speaking engagements per day in such venues as schools, kindergartens, and B'nai B'rith lodges. When the trip organizers asked if I desired some sort of compensation for my efforts, I shared my secret wish with them: "I have a dream, and perhaps you can help me fulfill it. For many years, I have dreamed of visiting the Jews in Cuba. I don't know if there is a synagogue there, or if there is any sort of Jewish life there. I know that there are Jews living in Cuba, but I don't know how many there are or what their situation is. Because Cuba and Venezuela have diplomatic relations, perhaps you can arrange a visit to Havana for me. That is all I ask. If you can help me make this possible, it will be an unforgettable reward."

David Altman and Yitzhak Yochai promised to check into the matter. A few days later they replied, saying that the Cuban ambassador to Venezuela happened to be a personal friend of Rabbi Brenner. A preliminary conversation between them had led the rabbi to believe that the Cuban authorities would not object to a visit from the "*gran rabino de Israel*" and the possibility that I might meet the Jews of Cuba. However, Rabbi Brenner warned me in advance that I should not get my hopes up.

I was overjoyed, and made one more small request: if the visit did indeed take place, I asked that Rabbi Brenner, who spoke Spanish, accompany me. They asked if my wife would come with me, and when I said yes, they said that Rabbi Brenner would bring his wife also. I flew to Venezuela with a small but still smoldering hope.

During my stay in Caracas, I met a group of very warm Jews of European origin. Most were children of Holocaust survivors, and some I had encountered previously in the Venezuelan delegation to the March of the Living at Auschwitz. I also spoke to the Sephardi community in a synagogue jam-packed with congregants thirsty for Torah teachings.

One day, Rabbi Brenner received a formal invitation from the Cuban authorities asking our delegation to come to Havana for two days. My excitement was irrepressible. When we heard the news, Yaakov Chalfin, a wealthy Venezuelan Jew, loaned us a private eight-seater plane to fly us to Cuba. At the same time, a group of young Venezuelans organized another plane that would contain male passengers only. As they were worried we might not find a minyan in Havana, they preferred to be on the safe side and so they put together a ready-made prayer quorum for our two-day stay. In Caracas, we also packed kosher food for our trip.

As the two small passenger planes landed at the airport in Havana, I prepared myself spiritually for the moment I had so anticipated, of finding some weakly glowing ember of Judaism still burning. I hoped to be able to fan it back to life and transform it into a healthy flame. When I disembarked from the aircraft, I was introduced to a man known only as Armando, a bearded young man, neat and polished, whose appearance recalled Fidel Castro and Che Guevara and who was to be my personal escort during our visit. He spoke fluent English, Spanish, Portuguese, Russian, and even used the Yiddish pronunciation for Tisha b'Av: *Tish'buv*.

Armando was Castro's right-hand man, and apparently also head of the secret service. He stayed by my side from the moment I landed on Cuban soil until the moment I left. After introducing himself, he introduced the minister of religions, Señora Caridad Diego, who also escorted us. Castro placed his black automobile at our disposal for the two days of the visit.

In February 1994, the streets of Havana were practically empty of cars, as the U.S. embargo against Cuba had caused a severe shortage of gasoline. Precious fuel was reserved only for the tractorlike vehicles that transported loads of laborers to their jobs. Private cars were nowhere to be seen. Castro's black car, with bodyguards alongside and a fleet of motorcycles in front and in back, created a tumult in the streets of the capital. People stared, and within minutes, all of Havana was busy trying to determine the identity of the honored guest who had arrived in their country.

THE CAR LEFT THE AIRPORT AREA and drove straight to the Jewish community center in Havana. In the afternoons, I learned, a few children and elderly persons visited the center. Once a month, "Rabino Simon" from Guadalajara, Mexico—originally from Buenos Aires—came to the center; his last name, Steinhandler, proved a tongue twister for my escorts. The Cuban government allowed him to visit Havana once a month in order to teach the Jewish children Hebrew songs. In 1993, Rabbi Shimon Steinhandler had performed the first bar mitzvah ceremony in Cuba after a thirty-five-year hiatus. In order to prove the existence of a full Jewish life in Cuba, my hosts arranged for Rabbi Steinhandler to be present during my visit; he had arrived from Mexico especially for the occasion. Among the guests invited to the center was the president of the Jewish community center, Dr. Jose Miller, a surgeon born in Eastern Europe.

We drove through the main street of Havana, which was named Fifth Avenue to suggest its elite Manhattan counterpart, but they couldn't have been more different from each other. Fifth Avenue in Havana was narrow and run-down. Visitors could still distinguish the remnants of architectural beauty in the buildings lining the street, but there were many signs of neglect in the faded paint and cracked walls. This street was home to foreign embassies and luxurious private residences that had obviously seen better days. People stuck their heads out from windows and balconies, wanting to witness with their own eyes the marvel of the Comandante's black car cruising the streets. As if that attraction were not enough for them, a surrealistic vision appeared: from the car descended a man wearing a high black hat and a long black suit coat, the likes of which had not been seen in the streets of Cuba for ages. The Jewish children awaited me on the small balcony of the Jewish community center.

When I left the car, tense with the accumulated excitement and stress of the journey, I saw a man on the sidewalk across the street, and I was willing to bet he was a Jew. His face, his skeletal thinness, and, above all, the fear I could read in his eyes left me with no doubt that this was a Jew from Europe. I could not tell from which country or city he hailed, but I was certain that he was Jewish. He stood about three yards from me, and I decided to act—I would approach him and attempt to engage him in conversation. Armando and Señora Diego got out of the car on the other side and walked toward me slowly, but still I dared to greet the man with "*Shalom aleichem*" (Peace be with you), careful to pronounce it in a clear Ashkenazi accent. Without hesitation, he gave the appropriate response: "*Aleichem shalom.*"

At that moment, I understood that I was at home. My discerning eye had not failed me. "And what is this Jew's name?" I asked.

"Getzel. Elyakim Getzel Kreplach," he answered.

"And where is this Jew from, what is his origin?" I continued to probe. He said he was born in Shedlov (Szydłów), Poland.

"What is a Jew from Shedlov doing here?" I asked, and he laughed, as if I understood nothing.

"Did I have a choice?" he asked. And then he began to speak about himself in the third person, as though he were the narrator of a story by the great Yiddish writer Sholem Aleichem.

"Getzel smelled catastrophe approaching," he recounted. "Getzel was a young man, and he understood that Poland was no longer the place for him. If Getzel wanted to survive, he had to leave—not just Poland, but Europe itself. It started in Germany, then spread to Austria and took the Sudetenland, Czechoslovakia, and then all of Europe went up in flames. A giant bonfire." That was how he described it, in simple, precise language. Meanwhile, more people gathered around us, and he spoke excitedly—at last someone was listening to him, and in Yiddish! He continued: "America was barred, Eretz Israel remained a dream, and then someone in Poland mentioned that Cuba was still open. I was a young man. I took out all my savings. I won't describe what I went through until I finally got here, because you don't have time to hear it, but here all the doors were open to me. I've been here ever since, more than fifty years now."

When I asked if he had a family, he continued his Sholem Aleichem–esque narrative, quoting a biblical verse: "*If he comes in alone, he shall go out alone.* I'm alone here." Hearing Getzel's words, I felt he looked even thinner and more miserable than he had previously. By then Armando and Señora Diego had caught up to me, and gestured toward the Jewish community center, where the invited guests were waiting. I had to cut our conversation short—as far as my hosts were concerned, it had gone on too long. As I walked away with the escorts, I turned halfway toward Getzel and said quietly, "I hope I'll see you during the two days I'll be spending here, and that we'll be able to talk. Think about whether there's anything I can do for you." His eyes clouded over with a thin film of tears, and his concise reply was honest and firm: "Nam mich a heim mit dir kein Eretz Yisroel." Take me home with you to Eretz Israel.

Getzel's words touched my soul. I could not reply, as my escorts were directing me toward the entrance of the community center. To this day, his plea remains with me and allows me no rest. For a long time, I harbored the feeling that my meeting with Getzel was worth the entire trip. I had searched for this Jew for many years, and found him in my first moments in Cuba.

Throughout my visit, Getzel trailed me faithfully. Everywhere I went, I glimpsed him in the background, although he hung back and did not approach me again. He was in the audience on the second day; after I delivered my speech at the Jewish center I saw him sitting in the fifth row, but he did not dare to draw near. They had seen him and photographed him, and he sensed that it was risky for him to seem too interested in me. But when he had the chance to hide behind someone else's shoulders, he would signal briefly with his hand so that I would notice and remember him.

While at the Jewish center, I asked the visitors about Jewish life in Havana. They said that there were three synagogues in the city, one active, the other two closed. When I asked if they had a minyan, they replied, "A Cuban minyan," by which they meant eight old-timers from Poland and two Torah scrolls, which made up the necessary quorum of ten. Nowhere else in the Jewish world did I ever hear of such a thing.

The central synagogue was a magnificent building—tall, broad, and airy, with chairs still upholstered in red velvet, mostly rat-eaten. On the only chair still intact, the upholstery was very luxurious. I could tell that in the past, the community here had been wealthy and had invested in their main synagogue. But by the time of my visit, everything had changed. The spaces for the holy ark, the cantor's lectern, and the choir room looked as if they had not been touched for many years: they were covered with layers of dirt, dust, and human excrement. Apparently, the city's homeless had taken shelter in the building and used it as a bathroom.

As I scanned the building, among the excrement I suddenly noticed a piece of white glossy paper with Hebrew letters printed on it. Despite the repulsive filth, I could not restrain myself—I grabbed the clean edge of the paper and lifted it from the ground. It was a folded booklet of the holiday prayers, and included a special prayer of thanksgiving for the third Independence Day of the State of Israel. This prayer was composed by Rabbi Meir Rosenbaum, the community's rabbi: "We, the Jews of Cuba and the Jews of the entire world, offer this special prayer for the peace, safety, and well-being of our brothers and sisters, the citizens of the State of Israel, now suffering the afflictions of its redemption."

Rabbi Rosenbaum had composed this prayer after the War of Independence, when great waves of aliya engulfed the young state, forcing the government to impose rationing. The Jews of Cuba, whose economic situation was obviously very comfortable at the time, as evidenced by the once-luxurious synagogue, had recited this special prayer that they had composed for us, expressing their sincere concern for the situation in the State of Israel. I brought those pages back with me to Israel as unequivocal proof of the glory days of the Jewish community of Cuba of the past, and its neglect at the time of my visit.

The entire Cuban Jewish community numbered about two thousand individuals, most of whom were only partly Jewish. Due to intermarriage and the communist ideology, they had had no genuine Jewish education or Jewish communal life. Their government also did not allow them contact with the flourishing Jewish community of Miami, just a half-hour flight away.

OVER THE YEARS, I have learned that if I want to get to know a Jewish community and its roots, I must visit its Jewish cemetery. So I asked to visit the cemetery in Havana. Armando and Señora Diego escorted me there. Among the tombstones, I discovered one belonging to a Jewish soldier from Havana. The inscription included these words in Hebrew: "Here lies the holy youth Yitzchak Isaac ben Arye Leib ben Dov, who fell in battle in the just war in Korea on 5 Sivan 5712–1952." The epitaph ended with the traditional phrase, "May his soul be bound up in the bond of eternal life." Apparently, this Jewish soldier was one of the Cuban communist volunteers who had enlisted to aid North Korea in the war against South Korea and its Western allies.

While the American army lost Jewish soldiers in this war, Jews were also killed on the communist side. Another Cuban Jew had brought this soldier's body from North Korea back to Havana. His tombstone was engraved in three languages: Hebrew, Spanish, and Russian—killed "in the just war in Korea." I was looking at another facet of Jewish history and the fate of the Jewish people. Quite possibly, this soldier's parents had fled Europe and the talons of the Nazi beast. They had found refuge on the other side of the world, only to have their son go off to the northern end of the farthest Far East country, there to fall in the name of the communist battle against so-called imperialism. There in the cemetery in Havana, standing with the other travelers next to the Jewish soldier's tombstone, engraved with Hebrew lettering and a Star of David, I recited an emotionally charged Kaddish, assuming that no one but myself was praying for his memory. Armando, Fidel Castro's right-hand man, joined the men of the "portable" minyan in responding *Amen*.

At the end of an eventful day, we arrived at a suite in a luxurious home belonging to Castro. This lovely building was made entirely of granite and mahogany, and was surrounded by a beautiful garden, but it was almost empty of furniture: simple iron-frame beds, two plain wicker chairs—that was all. The sight was depressing. The building was surrounded by terrible poverty.

Although we could not taste the local delicacies because they were not kosher, we enjoyed a generous helping of culture. The magnificent theaters buzzed with activity, and the streets resounded with the songs of singing groups and musicians.

While preparing for the trip to Cuba, I had not considered the idea of meeting Castro himself because I assumed that it was impossible. Still, in light of my visit to the pope five months previously, my wife and I agreed that we would prepare a gift, just in case. Again, we chose a shofar, and had a phrase from the daily liturgy engraved on the frame into which it was set: *Sound the great shofar for our freedom.*

We hoped that we would have the opportunity to present our gift to Castro and thus to hint at our request for freedom of emigration, and for allowing all Cuban Jews who so desired to make aliya to Israel. On the second day of my visit, my hosts informed me that the Comandante had requested a meeting with me. Armando added that Castro had heard a great deal about me, was following my visit in Cuba, and had now invited me for a personal conversation. When I asked that my travel companions also be allowed to attend, the answer was that only the men would be allowed to go inside with me.

We arranged to wait at the residence, and in the evening Castro's staff would escort us to his palace. At five minutes before 10:00 p.m., we arrived at Castro's offices. He received me with outstretched arms, a translator standing on his right. Although I was certain that Castro knew English well, as he was an educated attorney who lived just a stone's throw from the United States, apparently his national pride motivated him to speak only Spanish.

Our conversation lasted more than three hours and was one of the most fascinating discussions in which I have ever engaged. The personal side of the Cuban leader intrigued me. I had expected to meet an anti-Israel communist, stubborn and strict. At one point, Castro did mention that our enemies were his friends, referring to Saddam Hussein and Hafez al-Assad. "They give me arms and oil," he explained. "Gorbachev destroyed communism, such a beautiful and just concept," he continued. "He is dismantling the Soviet Union and turning it into a Western capitalist country. Nothing will be left to stop American imperialism, and for that Gorbachev will go down in history as an eternal disgrace."

I expressed my opinion that the entire world backed Gorbachev and his initiative in raising the iron curtain, but my views had no impact on Castro, who responded with a well-known metaphor: "So what? I'm David. There's this huge country right here next to me, and it's Goliath. I do not have to explain to you, *gran rabino*, who won the battle. Of course it was David." This exemplified the sharp and pointed nature of his discourse.

Suddenly, his finger waving in the air, Castro switched to a completely different tone. He abandoned the ideological facade and focused on the personal and humane: "There is one thing I must ask in order to understand you. I need to satisfy my curiosity. I know everything about you. I know that your brother hid you inside a sack and carried you on his back in the concentration camps during the war against German fascism. I know that during childhood you were orphaned of both parents, and that you went to Palestine at age eight, before the Jewish state was founded. But there is one thing I don't understand, and this I want to hear from your own mouth. How did you get to where you did?

"Here in Cuba, a child of eight who grows up without his parents, and especially without knowing the language, will turn into a juvenile delinquent. He'll become the terror of his neighborhood and his community, or else the victim of criminals who will abuse him. But you came to Israel barefoot and penniless, and today you are like the Jews' pope. Who raised you, *gran rabino*? Who educated you? How did a boy from the streets, who started out with nothing, get chosen to be the senior religious representative of the country?"

It took me a moment to recover from this surprising question. Then I told him that two years earlier, in June 1992, Yitzhak Rabin had sat in my house and asked me the same question. "I'll give you the same answer I gave to Rabin. I represent the thirty-eighth generation of a rabbinic family. My father left my older brother a spoken last will and testament, asking him to do everything he could to keep me alive so that I would continue the chain unbroken. My father had wisdom, good sense, and a keen awareness of the human maturation process. He realized that since I was just two years old when the war began, if I survived I would be able to put the war behind me and begin my life afresh. Of course, he had no way of knowing that the war would last six years. My older brother, by contrast, was thirteen, already in the formative years of his personality. So he lost his six best years, and began to live again when he was already nineteen.

"I grew up in the home of my Israeli uncle, who had been a respected rabbi in Poland and served as a rabbi in Israel as well. Then I went to study in yeshiva, and a young rabbi, my father's former student, took responsibility for me. I remained in the yeshiva world, in the company of spiritual giants. Then I became the protégé of my father-in-law, Rabbi Yitzchak Yedidya Frankel, for twenty-seven years. My role as a rabbi is deeply entrenched, and has never been interrupted throughout my life. I have always felt obligated to continue my family dynasty. Although I was without parents, my father and mother were with me continuously. They never left me, not even for one minute. My family—my brother, and another older brother whom I met in Israel—always encouraged me to continue in my father's footsteps. Thanks to all this, I became chief rabbi."

Castro was fascinated, and listened with intense curiosity. He asked if I thought my children would also continue our ancestral tradition. I replied that two of them were already ordained rabbis; they were the thirty-ninth generation of rabbis in the Lau family. When he asked how many children I had, I replied eight; then Castro asked if their mother was with me. I answered yes, but I reminded him that his staff had instructed us not to bring the women to the meeting, so my wife and Mrs. Brenner had remained back in the residence, although they would very much like to meet him. Then Castro switched to English for the first time. Dramatically, as if delivering a line from a movie, he announced, "Let's bring the ladies."

His messengers rushed out, and we continued to talk until the two women arrived. Throughout our conversation, Castro skipped lightly between topics. He abandoned the subject of children and the rabbinic dynasty, returning from the personal to the public. He noted that he admired Yitzhak Rabin as well as the brave step that Shimon Peres took in Washington in September 1993, following the Oslo accords. "You must understand the complete about-face that these two individuals made," I said, trying to clarify their position. "Although I am far removed from politics, I know both of them personally. They were ministers of defense who encouraged settling the Land of Israel in its length and breadth. Rabin was minister of defense during the Six-Day War and widened the borders of the state. For these two to decide to give twenty thousand rifles to the Palestinians and to return Gaza and Jericho as only the first step is a very dramatic revolution," I continued. Castro widened his eyes in admiration, and said, "Good for them! That's what it means to be a brave soldier."

In the meantime, the women had arrived. My wife presented Castro with the gift we had prepared. He studied the shofar, and I explained the significance of the liturgical phrase that we had chosen to engrave on its frame: *Sound the great shofar for our freedom*. "Unfortunately, our countries have not had diplomatic relations since 1959. I still don't understand why you cut off relations with us," I said. In one short sentence, Castro explained that the reason was because we were oppressors of another nation. But I decided to continue my tack. I mentioned a number of communist countries in Eastern Europe that had diplomatic relations with Israel at the time of our meeting. "We have no argument with Cuba. We share no borders—nothing stands between us. If we have a disagreement about something, this is why we have diplomats and embassies, so that we can send messages and discuss things through them. Why close yourselves off in a ghetto when we can learn from each other? At least we know we have something to discuss—we've been talking for two hours already. Would you ever have believed that you would sit with a Jewish rabbi from the State of Israel and enjoy a conversation with him? I thank you for the time you are granting me, because I have always been interested in the image you have projected and your personality, and I was curious to meet you."

Fidel Castro smiled broadly and replied that he was also finding our discussion enjoyable and interesting. "Why shouldn't we talk?" he asked rhetorically. I took advantage of the open and comfortable atmosphere and tried my hand at diplomacy. "Since you so admire Rabin and Peres, perhaps you could send them, through me, some sort of gesture expressing your personal esteem, without getting into politics or policy," I proposed. Castro raised his eyes to the ceiling and said quietly, "I am poor. I have no money, no fuel, no food. You, by comparison, are an empire. What can I possibly send you that you are lacking?" he inquired with complete honesty.

I tried to explain that the monetary value of the gift was not the important thing; rather, the value lay in the calling card attached to it. "Besides," I added in the spirit of friendly conversation, "you are world famous for your Havana cigars. If you send a box to Rabin or Peres with your card saying 'Presidente Fidel Castro'—" He cut me off and corrected me: "Comandante Fidel Castro." I apologized, then continued: "Whenever someone sees the cigars on the desk of the prime minister or the minister of defense, and asks what they are, the leaders will reply, 'Fidel Castro sent these to me.' When Rabin or Peres shows the questioners your calling card, it will be a clear sign of some sort of connection between you. It will be an opening for dialogue, the beginnings of hope for friendship and understanding."

Castro asked if the two leaders smoked cigars. I told him that Rabin was a heavy cigarette smoker, and that Peres had recently undergone stop-smoking treatment in Italy. But in this case, the importance of the cigars was that they would serve as tokens, sitting on the men's desks next to Castro's card (see chapter 16). Every visitor to our leaders' offices would understand from this nonverbal display that dialogue between Israel and Cuba was possible, that "we had something to talk about, and, mainly, someone to talk with," I emphasized again, so that my words would sink in. When I had finished, Castro struck his hands together with a resounding clap and asked Armando to bring him a pen so that he could note the names of the cigar recipients. "Rabin, Yitzhak"; "Peres, Shimon," he wrote, and in a personal tribute, added "Kollek, Teddy" (the longtime former mayor of Jerusalem) to the list with an additional compliment: "A great mayor."

After we had exhausted that topic, Castro asked my permission to pose another question that had disturbed him for some time. He jumped thousands of years back in time: "The Bible says that six hundred thousand Jews left Egypt, and I know that elsewhere it says that only seventy Jews went down to Egypt from Canaan. How was it possible that in four hundred years, seventy people turned into six hundred thousand? Could such a thing really happen?" Castro wondered. I was surprised at such a question, which had bothered him, he said, for some time. "In chapter one of the Book of Exodus," I explained, "the Bible says: *And the children of Israel were fruitful, and increased abundantly, and multiplied, and waxed exceedingly mighty; and the land was filled with them.* Our sages explain that at that time, Jewish mothers regularly gave birth to sextuplets."

Castro was incredulous. "Six babies in one womb?" he asked, waving his hand dismissively, as if he could not believe such a phenomenon. "Can there be such a thing—sextuplets?" he asked. At this point in our conversation, I felt open toward him, and permitted myself to relate that my son was the father of triplets. If triplets were possible today, why should we assume that sextuplets were impossible in ancient times? I added that in Israel, a mother had given birth to quintuplets a few years ago.

Castro was amazed. I think it was the first time he had ever heard of triplets, not to mention quintuplets, and he insisted on pursuing the topic. "You have triplets in your family?" he asked, with a childlike thrill. My wife, who in the meantime had arrived in response to his late invitation, pulled from her purse a picture of our triplet grandchildren and handed it to him. Charmed by the photo, Castro stared at it for a long moment. As he held it, he stroked it between his fingers, murmuring, "It's a miracle. Three in one womb. And they're so beautiful, each one. Interesting that they're not identical."

After returning the photo to my wife, he again focused on the biblical arithmetic problem. He took out a pad of paper and began to make lists and calculations in an attempt to prove the biblical account. From the seventy Jews who went down to Egypt, he made thirty-five couples. He multiplied these by six descendants each, then multiplied several more times. In a few minutes, he gave me a disappointed look and announced that the calculation did not work out. Frustrated, he explained his logic and said he had done me a favor and calculated one generation as twenty years instead of the usual thirty. If thirty-five individuals married at age twenty and began having children, then four hundred years equaled twenty generations. Multiply each generation by six, and the result still did not equal six hundred thousand.

Patiently and carefully, I asked him to try again, but he only became more confused with the numbers. Then I asked why he didn't use a calculator. Castro stared at me angrily. "A calculator? That thing you punch with your fingers? I belong to the generation that thinks with the head, not with the fingers. At any rate, *gran rabino*, the calculation doesn't work out." I felt uncomfortable as I witnessed his efforts and the seriousness that he invested in deciphering this numerical puzzle. I offered him a broad hint: "To solve the problem, I suggest you check another verse in that same book of the Bible: *And a mixed multitude also went up with them.*" Castro gave a sigh of relief, as if I had lifted a burden of many years from his shoulders. "Then how do you know that the Jews in Ethiopia are really Jews?"

I was surprised that Castro connected the Exodus to Ethiopia. I explained that in long meetings with the representatives of Ethiopian Jewry, we had discovered that they had a five-hundred-year Judaic tradition, and that a major halachic authority of the sixteenth century, Rabbi David ibn Zimra (the Radbaz) of Egypt, had determined that they were indeed Jews. They observed many *mitzvot*, such as the laws of Jewish married life. They had always prayed to return to Jerusalem, and had endangered their lives in order to do so. In the early 1900s, a French Jewish professor named Jacques Faitlovitch went to northern Ethiopia to research the issue, leading to the 1908 halachic decision by the chief rabbis of forty-five countries to recognize the Ethiopian Jews as Jewish. In 1921, Abraham Isaac Kook, the first Ashkenazi chief rabbi of the British Mandate for Palestine, also recognized the Ethiopian community as Jews. The Israeli government was able to arrange a small airlift in 1977, and then began smuggling Ethiopians out of the strife-torn, famine-ridden country. Two massive covert airlifts were eventually organized, known as Operation Moses (1984) and Operation Solomon (1991).

I was astonished that Castro knew about the Ethiopian aliya, and that he would be interested in it. When he felt we had concluded that topic, he again switched to another issue, indirectly related. "You know that I hate the Catholic Church, not because of my communist worldview but because of my life history. As a child, I studied in a monastery, and the priests, who were my teachers, taught me to hate Jews. When they taught me English, they told us that the Jews were birds of prey that flew from place to place searching for quarry. Why? Because the Jews have a beard, and they equated 'beard' with 'bird.' From this they concluded that the Jews hunted for prey, like the eagle and the vulture. Since then, for years, each time I saw a vulture, I was sure it was a Jew. As a child, I never thought of Jews as people who walked on two legs. I was sure that Jews were creatures with wings that flew around, preying on carrion. So now, since I know better, I allow no displays of anti-Semitism in my country. That is my reaction to my childhood education in the Church. It's not that I love Jews more than I love other people, but I don't hate any one of them and it's important to me that you know that."

During the course of this entire conversation with Castro, I felt like we were hurtling from one surprise to another. He stunned me yet again with this Jewish-Christian discussion. I decided to take advantage of the new direction in the conversation, and asked his permission to make a request.

"It is now February," I noted. "In two months, Jews all over the world will be celebrating the holiday of Passover. If you know about the Exodus and about the six hundred thousand Israelites who descended from seventy, you must certainly know that Jews are forbidden to eat bread during this holiday. For seven days, they eat only matzah. Perhaps you will allow the Jewish community in Cuba to import matzah?" Castro interrupted me aggressively. "But not from them," he said, pointing in the direction of the United States, toward which he showed such disdain. I promised that Rabbi Brenner would bring matzah from Caracas, and perhaps also from Mexico. Castro agreed, and asked how much we would need. We agreed that Dr. Miller, president of the Jewish community center, would make a calculation, and Rabbi Brenner would ensure that every Jew would be able to eat matzah during Passover.

Encouraged by Castro's cooperation, I dared to make another request: to allow Rabbi Brenner to import kosher meat to Cuba. Again I promised that they would not import it from the United States. I explained to the Cuban leader that Jews were forbidden to eat nonkosher meat, and because Cuba had no rabbis or ritual slaughterers, it was possible that Jews there were violating this prohibition against their will, or else refraining from eating meat. In my mind's eye, I envisioned Getzel Kreplach of Shedlov, for whom such a gesture would mean a quarter chicken once a week and a shank bone for the seder plate.

At this point, Fidel Castro lost his composure, and the anger that flooded his face gave him that fierce, rebellious look for which he was known. In a thundering voice, he replied, "I told you I am fighting against anti-Semitism in my country. Do you want to make my people into anti-Semites? I have no bread to give my own people. Will the Jews in Cuba eat meat while we have a daily bread ration of 150 grams [five ounces]? Is this what you mean? The people will hate them furiously, they will envy them, rob them. My people do not have enough food because Goliath, my neighbor, has cut off all my supply lines. If you import kosher meat for the Jews in this situation, you yourself, *gran rabino*, will be causing the anti-Semitism that I am trying so hard to prevent." I tried to pressure him anyway, reminding him that just a moment earlier he had agreed to import matzah for Passover, but he remained firm, and emphasized,

"Matzah is not food, it's a religious product. There is no way I will ever allow the importation of meat for the Jews," he declared resolutely, and I understood that I had lost the point.

To conclude our meeting, I told Castro that during my visit, I had learned of a Jewish student born in Cuba who had finished medical training at the top of his class. This student wanted to ask for Castro's authorization to undergo specialized training for one year in a hospital in Caracas, where they had advanced medical equipment. Castro listened, then laughed and replied with a decisive "No." He argued that since he finally had a homegrown talent, why should he allow this talent a taste of Western freedom? Who would guarantee that the gifted young doctor would return to Cuba? They needed that one talent in Cuba, so that they would have someone other than second-rate doctors to heal the Cuban people.

I pressed him, asking if he would grant exit visas to Jews who wanted to emigrate to Israel, for the purpose of reunifying Jewish families. He was willing to grant this. "You have seen the situation for yourself," he said with obvious pride. "I brought over a rabbi from Guadalajara; the Jewish community has a leader, Dr. Miller; and I invited you to see all this. You visited the Jewish community center; you met children singing songs in Hebrew and studying the Bible. I do have criticism against your government, but I don't hate any Jew."

Castro insisted on accompanying me to the elevator. On the way, I spoke with him about the Israeli MIAs—air force navigator Ron Arad and the other fighters from the battle of Sultan Yakoub. I asked if he would use his connections with Saddam Hussein and Hafez al-Assad to enlist their help in finding these soldiers. Castro raised his finger and asked if I believed that the soldiers were still alive after twelve years. I told him that five months earlier, the pope had asked me the same question. I had replied by citing Yosef Katz, father of one of the soldiers, who said that if his son was not alive, his only wish was that his son's name would live on. Before he himself went to a better world, he wanted to make sure his son had a grave site and a proper tombstone that bore his name. Despite his severe appearance and army uniform, I found that Castro was really a deeply sensitive person. He replied: "That's it exactly. I understand the principle, and you have convinced me that it is correct. I promise that I will speak with the right people. As I already told you, your enemies are my good friends." It was one o'clock in the morning. Our conversation had lasted for three hours.

About two hours later, we heard a knock on the door of the villa where we were staying. Due to my highly emotional state after the meeting and the thoughts that were spinning through my head, I had not managed to sleep a wink. I opened the door, and in front of me stood several porters carrying two large chests, each one with three drawers full of cigars. The porters said that the delivery was from the Comandante. Castro had added three small envelopes containing his calling card, and had handwritten the names of the recipients on each envelope: "Yitzhak Rabin," "Simon [sic] Peres," and "Teddy Kollek." I took the packages back to Israel with me.

My meeting with Castro revealed a vast gap between the leader's image and his true personality. I discovered a man who lived modestly and unpretentiously, at least as far as the outside world could see. His nation loved him because he saw himself as a personal example of frugality, fairness, and national pride. I also found him a fascinating conversationalist, curious and knowledgeable.

My meeting with the Jewish community was intensely moving. It was amazing to visit Jews who had no school or synagogue, who had not seen a rabbi for years, and whose roots were buried so deeply that they were invisible even to themselves. I was proud to have had the opportunity to tread on the soil of a country that no official representative of the State of Israel had visited for at least thirty-five years.

I thought about Aunt Metta and Uncle Bruno-Berchiyahu, and about the hundreds of Jews in Cuba. No one cared whether they were alive or how they were faring. We had no mail or telephone contact with them. Even at the end of the twentieth century, we were completely cut off. I kept thinking that fifty years after what had happened in Europe, we still had not learned our lesson—we were perpetuating the disconnection with the Cuban Jews. I was glad that during this visit, I had at least made my modest contribution to the return of a few Cuban Jews to the fold of the Jewish people.

. . .

I COULD NOT SAY THIS TO THE JEWS IN CUBA, where I had to be careful about every word I uttered. But I said it explicitly to the Jews of South Africa: "I haven't come to you to ask for donations, but to ask for your souls, or at least the souls of your children." This is what I used to say on my frequent visits to the South African Jewish community. Almost every time I went there, I went in order to recruit people—to gather souls, not money. Certainly, I do not underestimate the importance of donations to fund-raising campaigns, and I am well aware of the economic backing that prosperous Jewish communities such as theirs offer to the State of Israel. I have a warm spot in my heart for the South African Jews, many of whom are Holocaust survivors or left Europe before or during the war.

As a youth, I had heard much about South African Jewry from my teacher Rabbi Yosef Kahaneman, head of Ponevezh Yeshiva. During my years of study there, the yeshiva relied on that community for financial backing. Many Lithuanian Jews had fled to South Africa, and they had known Rabbi Kahaneman from his days as rabbi of the town of Ponevezh, Lithuania. After my yeshiva days, the directors of the aliya department of the Jewish Agency often asked me to visit South Africa on aliya missions, and I was always happy to comply. The South African community is warm, loves Israel, and is strongly Zionist. In 1996, the community organized a large gathering to honor Rabbi Cyril Harris, who had completed ten years of service as their chief rabbi. They invited me, as chief rabbi of Israel, to be the guest of honor. Other participants included Frederik de Klerk, president of South Africa, who had received the Nobel Peace Prize for agreeing to end apartheid. At the airport in South Africa, I was greeted by Rabbi Harris, the leaders of the Jewish community, and Thabo Mbeki, who was then deputy to President Nelson Mandela and was later elected to the post of president. We traveled to Pretoria, capital of the country, where President Mandela received us in his residence, wearing his trademark flowered shirt. From the very beginning, this was the most friendly meeting I can recall among the variety of encounters I have had with representatives of the non-Jewish world, and with leaders in general.

We had no need for empty words to break the ice, because there was no ice to break. At the beginning of the meeting, Mandela embraced me warmly, and we continued arm-in-arm throughout it. The radiance of his face was remarkable. When I presented him with a leather-bound Hebrew-English Bible, I said that I recognized and valued his heroic struggle to take his people from slavery to freedom and to grant them equality and independence. I added that I knew he had sacrificed many years of suffering on the altar of freedom.

I wanted to draw his attention to a verse in chapter 28 of Deuteronomy, which was certain to be meaningful for him: *In the morning, you shall say, 'If only it were evening!' and in the evening, you shall say, 'If only it were morning!' because of the fear in your heart which you shall experience and because of the sights that you shall behold.* For a man sitting in jail, using his fingernails to scratch a mark on the wall to record each passing day, for a person who longs to see the light at the end of the tunnel, this verse is very difficult.

As I explained the verse, Mandela was deep in concentration. He asked to read the verse for himself, in the English translation. Then he nodded his head and marked the page with a bookmark. He said that he knew about my past and my experiences as a child. "Because you know what happened to me, I can tell you that your fate was much more bitter than my own."

I was surprised at his conclusion, since I had suffered for six years during the war, whereas he was a prisoner for twenty seven years. But Mandela knew all the details. He agreed with me on the length of time, but added, "They did not murder my parents, as they did yours." This sentence clarified the reason for his sincere warmth toward me. He knew the intimate details of my personal history during the Holocaust. He knew that Naphtali had hidden me in a sack that he carried on his shoulders and had done everything possible in order to save me, obeying our father's dying wish.

We spoke about the similarities between the fates of our two nations, populated with persecuted minorities—Jews on one hand, blacks on the other—who had been dispersed throughout the world for centuries. I reminded him that the first ones to raise the flag of the rebel exodus from slavery to freedom were Moses and Aaron, who had led the Children of Israel out of Egypt—on the same continent as South Africa. He was excited by the idea that the struggle for freedom had actually begun on this continent thousands of years earlier.

I elaborated. "About thirty-four hundred years ago, a leader of the Jewish Diaspora rose up and said to the oppressive ruler: 'Let my people go.' Our Exodus from Egypt became a model for all the nations of the world," I explained.

"You have enlightened me," Mandela said with thanks. After the warm reception and the unrestrained amity Mandela demonstrated toward me, I felt able to write him a personal letter several years later. "From a former prisoner to another former prisoner, on behalf of prisoners today," I wrote, asking him to act on behalf of the seventeen Jewish prisoners whom the Iranians suspected of spying for Israel and had arrested without trial in Shiraz. I described the terrible tortures they were suffering, such that a youth of sixteen who saw his mother after six months in prison was unable to recognize her. Unfortunately, I never received any reply from Mandela, who was then about to end his term as president, and I do not know if he did anything on behalf of the imprisoned Jews.

In Cape Town, I met with Archbishop Desmond Tutu. Shortly before our meeting, Mandela had appointed him as chairman of South Africa's Truth and Reconciliation Commission for investigating the crimes of apartheid. Concerned with this issue, he asked me how I, as a fellow religious leader, would approach such a role from a religious point of view, considering that his responsibilities included investigating collaborators as well as facilitating a reconciliation between blacks and whites. "As an observer from the sidelines, I clearly see that there is a strong conflict between the search for truth and the pursuit of peace," I said, trying to analyze his situation. I cited a statement by Rabbi Ilai in the Talmud: *We are permitted to depart from the truth for the sake of peace.* In other words, when peace is at stake, it is permissible to alter the truth, for peace is the higher value.

I gave a concrete example from Genesis, chapter 50. After Jacob dies, his sons say to each other: *Perhaps Joseph will hate us and repay us all the evil that we did to him.* Fearing Joseph's revenge, the brothers put words in the mouth of their dead father: *Your father commanded us before his death, saying, "So shall you say to Joseph—Please, forgive now your brothers' transgression and their sin, for they did evil to you."* In the Talmud, Rabbi Ilai explains, "Where is it written that Jacob commanded this? Rather, they altered the facts for the sake of peace." Thirty-nine years after selling him into slavery, the brothers are stricken with the fear of being punished, and so they distort the truth in an attempt to avoid the possibility of Joseph's revenge. But Joseph replies, *Do not be afraid, for am I instead of God? Indeed, you intended evil against me, but God intended it for good, in order to bring about what is at present, to keep a great populace alive.* Joseph says in effect that he was saved from the pit and sold to the Ishmaelites as part of God's plan, so that he would be able to save all the brothers and their families. Even if the brothers' intentions were negative, in the end the result was successful and for the good.

Rabbi Ilai's statement is the first example, I noted to Archbishop Tutu, of the ruling that one may alter the truth for the sake of peace. To this I added the opinion of Rabbi Nathan, who said that not only is it permitted, but it is a positive commandment to make a change for peace. The most outstanding biblical example of this is when the angels come to visit Abraham and inform him that *this time next year* he will have a son. Then *Sarah laughed within herself, saying, "After I have become worn out, will I have smooth flesh? And also, my husband is old."* But God changes her words, asking Abraham, *Why did Sarah laugh, saying, "Is it really true that I will give birth, although I am old?"* She places the blame on Abraham, but God says to him that she blames herself. In other words, Rabbi Nathan says, it is a positive act to modify the truth on behalf of peace; in this case, the peace is that between husband and wife. Desmond Tutu, Nobel Peace Prize laureate, listened intensely, then smiled broadly and took his leave as he praised the Jewish tradition.

Years later, in 2002, we both attended the World Economic Forum. That year, as a demonstration of solidarity after the September 11 disaster, the Forum took place at New York's Waldorf-Astoria Hotel instead of its usual venue in Davos, Switzerland. Tutu commented to me that he had kept these biblical examples in mind when writing the Truth Commission report. I then added the succinct words from the prophet Zechariah: *Therefore love truth and peace.*

CHAPTER 19

PREŠOV—THUS WAS THE CROWN RESTORED TO ITS ANCIENT GLORY

*And it shall come to pass, when many evils
and troubles are befallen them . . .*

DEUTERONOMY 31:21

"I'M GOING TO ASK YOU TO DO SOMETHING VERY UNUSUAL," said Naphtali to the obliging international operator, after she verified that she could look up a telephone number for him in Czechoslovakia, and that she had a telephone directory for the city of Prešov. "Do me a favor," he requested, "and read out the names listed in the directory. All of them, starting from the letter *A*. When I hear you say a name that I am looking for, I'll stop you and ask you for the phone number." The operator may have been surprised, but she cooperated with his unusual request.

It was 1992, and Naphtali had no idea what had happened to the Jewish community in Prešov. He did not know whether any Jews were left there after Hitler, Stalin, and assimilation had taken their toll, but he decided to check. Patiently, the operator read out the list of Slovakian names such as Bobek and Horek until she reached the name Landau, with its Jewish ring. At this, Naphtali asked her to stop and give him the telephone number.

AFTER MY PARENTS WERE MARRIED in prewar Poland, the community of Prešov, near the southern border, offered Father the post of city rabbi (see chapter 2). The large Jewish community there was comprised of

336

German- and Hungarian-speaking Jews. Father, who spoke fluent Polish, Yiddish, and German, served as rabbi for eight years. My brothers Shiko and Naphtali grew up there, and my third brother, Shmuel (Milek), was born in that city and spent his infancy there.

Beginning in 1989, the iron curtain began to fall, and visiting Eastern Europe on an Israeli passport became possible. When the Soviet Union started collapsing, revolution swept Czechoslovakia, which began a course of rapprochement toward the Western world. At that time, Naphtali was director of the Jerusalem office of the United Jewish Appeal, and he felt a yearning to return to his roots, to places that had been part of his childhood in peaceful times. Were any Jews left there? Were there remains of synagogues or tombstones? Such questions gnawed at him until he decided to take action and see if he could make contact with Prešov.

AFTER OBTAINING THE TELEPHONE NUMBER of this person with such an obviously Jewish name, Naphtali phoned right away. A man with an energetic voice answered the call. Naphtali spoke in German, the language of Prešov during his childhood, and asked, "Herr Landau?" The voice on the other end of the line corrected him, saying, "Doctor Landau." Naphtali said to himself that someone who insisted on being called Doctor had to be a Jew. This boosted his self-confidence, and he got straight to the point. He asked if there was a Jewish community in Prešov.

The man did not bother to ask the anonymous caller to identify himself, and his immediate reply was typically Jewish: "Yes—and no. I am the leader of the Jewish community, but I can hardly call it a community, since we have less than a minyan. We are only eight Jews, but the large and well-known synagogue still stands. I clean it every Friday, and it remains as it was before the war. There are two other Jews who come to Prešov from nearby Bardejov—Shapira and Jacobovitch. One of them knows how to lead the prayers and read from the Torah, and the other knows how to blow the shofar. With them, we have a minyan on the High Holy Days."

Naphtali asked if they had a rabbi in the community. "Are you joking?" came the reply. "For whom? Who will support a rabbi? Since the *Oberrabbiner* [chief rabbi] left us before the war, we have never chosen another rabbi. It was hard to find someone like him." When Naphtali asked who that *Oberrabbiner* was, the community president replied: "Oberrabbiner Lau, Moshe Chaim Lau. Haven't you heard of him?" Only at this point in the conversation did Dr. Landau think of asking the identity of the caller.

Naphtali asked him to sit down, and promised to answer his question promptly. After allowing enough time for the doctor to take a seat, Naphtali introduced himself, saying that he was the son of Oberrabbiner Lau. Dr. Landau was skeptical. "I am an elderly man," he said, "and I ask that you respect my age and position and not make fun of me. I know that none of the sons of the *Oberrabbiner*'s family survived."

Naphtali repeated his introduction, using the nickname with which he was known in Prešov: "I am Tulek."

Silence at the other end of the line. "Tulek Lau?" asked Dr. Landau, his voice shaking. "I'm speaking with Tulek Lau?"

"Yes, you are," Naphtali replied, adding that possibly the two of them had played ball together in the courtyard of the synagogue, where our family's apartment stood. When Dr. Landau understood that Naphtali was calling from Jerusalem, he was silent again, then astonished. "I'm speaking with *Jerusalem*?" he asked.

After he calmed down, he asked what had happened to Shiko, our brother. Naphtali informed him that Shiko was alive and well in Jerusalem. Then he asked about Milek, and Naphtali said that he had died along with Father in Treblinka. "But," added Naphtali, "I have another brother whom you never met, since he was born in Piotrków, where Father was rabbi after Prešov. This younger brother survived along with me, and he is still alive today." With this, he informed the doctor of my existence.

Dr. Landau asked whether I also lived in Jerusalem, and Naphtali told him that his younger brother was "the *Oberrabbiner* of Tel Aviv."

Again silence, then amazement: the son of Oberrabbiner Lau was also an *Oberrabbiner*? After the days of Hitler? "Too bad I can't come to see you," Dr. Landau said.

Again, Naphtali surprised him, making a proposal. Their conversation was taking place in May. "In July, on the Shabbat before Tisha b'Av, my brother and I will come to visit you. This is Shabbat Chazon, the 'Sabbath of vision,' when in the synagogue we read the prophecy of Isaiah. Tell the eight Jews of the Prešov synagogue that my brother and I will come to complete your minyan on Shabbat Chazon. I haven't yet spoken about it to my brother, but I'm sure that when he hears it's possible, he'll join me."

Naphtali's choice of Shabbat Chazon for our visit to Prešov was highly symbolic. In the elegies of Tisha b'Av, we mourn a long list of terrible events that befell the Jewish people: among them are the destruction of the First and Second Temples, the killing of the Ten Martyrs by Roman authorities during the time of the Mishnah, the final date for the Expulsion from Spain, and the Chmielnicki pogroms of 1648–49. We mourn the decimated German Jewish communities of Speyer, Worms, and Mainz, and we recite the lament of Rabbi Judah Halevi, *Zion Ha'lo tishali*, the Ode to Zion, which begins with the words, "Zion, will you not ask after the peace of your captives?" When I was chief rabbi of Tel Aviv, I made an addition to the ancient Tisha b'Av liturgy: a booklet with seven laments on the Holocaust composed by modern rabbis. Most of them, such as Rabbi Chaim Michael Dov Weissmandel and Rabbi Shlomo Halberstam (the Rebbe of Bobov), were Holocaust survivors. I had these booklets distributed to seven hundred synagogues throughout the Tel Aviv-Jaffa municipality.

We arrived at our hotel in Prešov on a Friday in the summer of 1992. The bustle at the entrance to the hotel revealed that Dr. Landau had spread the news of our impending arrival. Our hosts escorted us to the meeting hall of the city council, where the mayor of Prešov awaited us. He presented us with a commemorative album of the city. I flipped through the pages, but found not one word about the thousands of Jews who had once populated Prešov. The deluxe album, published during the Stalin era, depicted landscapes and history, but made no mention of Jews at all. I kept my anger to myself.

A woman of about sixty sat in the city council hall, weeping incessantly. At one point she rose, approached Naphtali, and asked whether he remembered that they used to play together. Naphtali did not, and asked who she was. "The daughter of Shloime Schwartz," she replied.

Of course Naphtali remembered Shlomo (Shloime) Schwartz, the *kashrut* supervisor under my father's aegis. He was extremely poor and lived in a single room in the synagogue courtyard, across from our family's home. This woman, my parents' neighbor, had been like part of our family. She was the sole survivor of her own family.

"I heard you were coming," she said to Naphtali through her tears. "There is nothing kosher here, so I baked *birkes* for you for Shabbat." *Birkes* is the vernacular term for challah rolls, since we recite blessings (*berachot* in Hebrew, or *brachot* in Yiddish) over them. Then she continued: "When my father, may God avenge his blood, turned fifty, Rabbi Lau brought him a gift from Kraków: a silver Havdalah spice box, shaped like a tower. I kept it all these years, and today I want to give it to his son, the rabbi of Tel Aviv." A few minutes earlier, this woman had been a complete stranger to us, and here she wanted to give me, whom she had never known, a precious gift.

Today, the spice box that my father carried from Kraków to Prešov is on display in my home in Tel Aviv. This silver piece that my father held in his hands is the only material object I have inherited from him.

We made our way to the synagogue for the afternoon and Shabbat Eve prayers. We anticipated meeting the eight Jews of Prešov, whom Dr. Landau had described in his telephone conversation with Naphtali, but when we entered the synagogue, we discovered that eight Jews had turned into sixty. From May to July, the news of our arrival had spread, causing Jewish seeds that had been buried beneath the ground during the communist era to sprout like buds. One revealed his Jewish identity, another began to look for a Jewish relative, and in the end, dozens of Jews gathered at the synagogue. "You cannot imagine what's going on here," Dr. Landau said in amazement. "It's a real resurrection of the dead."

Those lost Jews were mainly interested in speaking with Naphtali, exchanging memories and asking questions. Their attitude toward me was different, even embarrassing. They gazed at me as though at a statue. With my long black coat and high hat, clothing they had not seen for decades, I must have been a strange sight to them. They did not dare approach or touch me, but gaped at me in astonishment.

I did not remain a spectacle for long. Suddenly I felt their eyes abandoning me. They turned toward the door, through which entered an elderly man, one of the most handsome people I can recall: tall, broad-shouldered, with a beautiful face and a mane of white hair covered with a large, black velvet *kippah* for a striking black-on-white effect. "Herr Professor," the people cried, shocked. "What are you doing here?"

As we learned, this man was Czechoslovakia's best-known cardiologist, head of the cardiology department in a major hospital in the capital of Bratislava (formerly Pressburg, hometown of Rabbi Moshe Sofer, the Chatam Sofer). Although he lived in Prešov, none of the other residents had ever dreamed he was Jewish.

The professor, who knew many of those present, bowed deeply, shaking Naphtali's hand as well as my own. Then he recounted his own moving personal story. He was born in Prešov. The last time he had visited the synagogue was sixty years earlier, for his bar mitzvah. "It was just before Oberrabbiner Lau moved to another town," he recalled. "When he addressed me on Shabbat morning, he stood right here, next to this podium. I stood on his right, and I remember his speech almost word for word, as if it were just a moment ago.

"When the war broke out, I was a university student in Bratislava," he continued. "We hid, but my father did not survive. He perished in Treblinka, along with Oberrabbiner Lau. I became a successful physician, but all these years I never said a word about my Jewish identity. There is no sign of Judaism in my house. The only person who knew about my Judaism was Dr. Landau. Two months ago, he called me and told me about his phone conversation with the son of Oberrabbiner Lau. He said that three of his sons had survived, and two of them would be here today at six in the evening. I had no doubt that at the appointed day and time, I would be inside the synagogue, where I had not set foot for sixty years. Today, I can express to his sons the gratitude I feel toward the departed Rabbi Lau, whose words have echoed in my ears throughout these sixty years.

"All my life, two things reminded me of my origins: his speech at my bar mitzvah and my father's black yarmulke [skullcap], which has been lying in a drawer this whole time. I told myself that when I do go to the synagogue during your visit, I would wear on my head that black velvet yarmulke that I inherited from my father. And if there is a World-to-Come, or a Garden of Eden, my father must be there, deriving satisfaction from his son, who did not sever his roots completely, but wears a yarmulke when he finally returns to synagogue."

The Prešov synagogue was especially beautiful. The entire ceiling was decorated with scenes from Joseph's dreams. In one scene, the sun, the moon, and eleven stars bow down to a representation of the youthful Joseph. In another, the scene of the tribes, his brothers, is based on what Joseph says: *For, behold, we were binding sheaves in the field, and, lo, my sheaf arose, and also stood upright; and, behold, your sheaves stood round about, and made obeisance to my sheaf.*

Drawings on synagogue ceilings are rare, but this practice is not forbidden as long as the images depict objects, such as sheaves and heavenly bodies, not human beings. At the synagogue entrance stood a memorial plaque in German, Slovak, and Hebrew commemorating the Holocaust martyrs of Prešov, who reached Treblinka on the same day that my father arrived with the Jews of Piotrków. On October 11, 1942 (11 Cheshvan 5703), the Jews of Piotrków and the Jews of Prešov descended from the train cars together onto the platform at Treblinka. They did not speak the same language, but they had one thing in common: Rabbi Moshe Chaim Lau. From 1936, after my father left Prešov, until the day of my writing, the city of Prešov has never chosen another rabbi.

In the magnificent synagogue of Prešov, Dr. Landau showed us the podium at which Father used to stand and speak, still covered by the velvet cloth from those far-off days. Each week, Dr. Landau punctiliously brushed the velvet. On the east side, near the podium, stood a leather chair on which my father used to sit, and against the wall were three smaller leather seats. Here, Dr. Landau told us, was where the three sons of the rabbi used to sit: Shiko, Tulek, and Milek. At the sight of these snippets of reality from the lives of our father and family back then, we were speechless.

Dr. Landau broke the silence. He reminded Naphtali of his promise in their first telephone conversation—that his brother, chief rabbi of Tel Aviv, would speak on Shabbat Chazon from the same podium where our

father, Prešov's last rabbi, used to speak, as if history had not been interrupted by a disaster of biblical dimensions.

In my speech, I spoke about the Holocaust and Tisha b'Av. I began
with an evocative story from the Midrash on Lamentations, the scroll of
elegy and destruction, attributed to Jeremiah, prophet of the destruction.
On the Ninth of Av, Nebuchadnezzar ordered his murderous officer
Nebuzaradan to set the Temple on fire. The blood of many of the children of Zion and Jerusalem spilled like water, and their bodies were left
unburied. Then Jeremiah went to Rachel's Tomb in Bethlehem and the
Cave of Machpelah in Hebron to wake the forefathers and foremothers
from their eternal sleep. As the Midrash says, he did this *so that they would
plead for mercy for their sons and daughters who were falling by the sword
and going out to exile, as the Temple was going up in flames.* The Midrash
describes how the prophet awakens the patriarchs and matriarchs from
their deep slumber, ritually washes their hands, and tells them what is
happening to their people.

Abraham is the first to address the Holy One: *Why is this happening
to my people?* God replies, *Your children have sinned.* Abraham then asks,
Who will testify in their case? Paralleling his dialogue with God in Genesis 18, he demands, *Will the Judge of the entire world not do justice?* God
answers: *Let the twenty-two letters of the alphabet, which comprise all the
books of the Torah, come and testify that your children have transgressed what
is written inside it.*

The twenty-two letters went up to the witness stand. First to volunteer
was the first letter, *alef.* Abraham approached the *alef,* but before the letter
opened its mouth, he mocked it, asking whether it was not ashamed. For
it began the very Ten Commandments: Anochi—*I am the Lord your God
Who took you out of the Land of Egypt and the house of slavery.* Abraham
asked, *Who received the Ten Commandments? Who accepted their authority?
My children! But now, when they are in need of a good word, you repay good
with evil and come to testify against them.* Embarrassed, the *alef* slunk off
into a corner.

Then the second letter, *bet,* went up to replace its predecessor. But when
it opened its mouth to testify, Abraham silenced it, saying, Bet, *you should
be ashamed of yourself. The entire Torah begins with you:* "Bereshit—*In the*

beginning God created the heavens and the earth." God presented the Torah to all the nations of the world, asking who wanted to receive it. "What does it say inside?" the nations asked. They examined it: was it worthwhile or not, easy or difficult, desirable or undesirable? Only my children did not ask what it said. Rather, they put action before hearing: "We will do, and we will hear." Today they need encouragement. They need you to speak positively of them. But instead, you, the Hebrew letter bet, come to speak negatively of them. Shame on you. The *bet* was humiliated, and also ran off into a corner. Abraham did the same with the rest of the alphabet, convincing each of the letters of the Torah to retract its testimony.

This episode comes up in Moses's parting speech to the Israelites at the end of Deuteronomy, where he describes the end of days, for, as it says, *There arose not a prophet since in Israel like unto Moses, whom the Lord knew face to face.* Says Moses: *And it shall come to pass, when many evils and troubles are befallen them, that this song shall testify against them as a witness; for it shall not be forgotten out of the mouths of their seed.*

In explaining this verse to those gathered in the Prešov synagogue, I followed the interpretation of my father-in-law, Rabbi Frankel. He said that Moses was really saying: I see with my spiritual eyes a picture that is different from the one Abraham saw. Abraham asked the letters of the Torah to retract their testimony. I, on the other hand, am asking, begging, the Torah to bear witness. This song—the Torah, song of our life—will testify before the Holy One, bearing witness that it will not be forgotten by the nation's children. It will tell how during the Holocaust, Jews ran to the forests to blow the shofar, so as not to miss the mitzvah of Rosh Hashanah; how Jews willingly gave up slices of bread for extended periods so they could exchange them for potatoes for Passover; how they saved bits of margarine and rendered them into oil using a steaming tin mug of tea, then poured the oil into the buttons of their striped uniforms to kindle the Hanukkah lights, pulling threads from their sleeves for wicks. Since they were willing to do all this, did Abraham really need to ask the Torah to refrain from speaking? Rather, *This song will speak up before it as a witness.* What testimony will it give? That *it will not be forgotten from the mouth* of the nation's offspring, even in the most trying times.

To me, this speech in my father's synagogue in Prešov, in which I explained Rabbi Frankel's understanding of the verse from Deuteronomy, meant coming full circle. In my father's synagogue in Prešov, I made the connection to the date of our gathering, the eve of Tisha b'Av: "This week, we read the Scroll of Lamentations. Tonight, we read about the prayers of our forefathers and foremothers. When we look at the vacant rows in the Prešov synagogue, we recall the man who stood beside this podium to speak, and then went to Treblinka carrying the Torah scroll in his arms, so that *it will not be forgotten*. He guarded it as long as he was capable, then recited the *Shema* together with your community, the Jews of Prešov, and his community, the Jews of Piotrków. He said the *Vidui* confessional prayer, and ended with the Kaddish. Do you understand now the meaning of the expression *the eternity of Israel*? And the significance of the phrase *'Am Yisrael Chai*—the Nation of Israel lives'?"

I chose to end my speech with the story of Urke Nachalnik, who jumped into the flames of the synagogue in Zduńska Wola, Poland, in order to save its Torah scrolls. On the eve of Tisha b'Av, in my father's synagogue in the city of Prešov, this story resonated powerfully, as it embodied the living spirit of the verse *It will not be forgotten.* And as Naphtali and I, sons of the last rabbi of the Prešov community, stood inside his synagogue, we felt we were living proof of the eternal nature of the Jewish people.

CHAPTER 20

"IN THE LANDS OF THE LIVING"

I will walk before the Lord in the lands of the living.
PSALMS 116:9

"JEWS, HAVE YOU PAID FOR THE GAS YOU USED IN THE OVENS?" This chilling sentence has burdened me for decades. In July 1982, one month after the Lebanon War broke out, I was invited to give a series of speeches in the Jewish communities of Melbourne and Sydney, Australia, and to meet with survivors of Buchenwald whom I had not seen since the liberation of the camp. While I had made my way to Eretz Israel, they had had no other choice but Australia. On Shabbat Eve, I dined in the home of Rabbi Yitzchok Groner, who lived in the Jewish neighborhood of St. Kilda East in Melbourne.

After the meal, I walked to my lodgings with Heshy Cooper, a lawyer and Chabad member, both of us wearing our obviously Jewish garb of black hat and long black suit coat. We stood in the center of the city, waiting for the light to change, when a luxury car stopped beside the crosswalk. In it were two men in their forties, dressed in suits and ties. They opened the window, and one shouted: "Jews, have you paid for the gas you used in the ovens?" Then they drove off.

We were shocked into silence. To hear such a thing, in Australia, at the ends of the earth, in 1982? It was inconceivable. I looked at Heshy, a native Australian, as if begging for an explanation. He said nothing. I asked if I had heard correctly, and he nodded his head. I asked what he was doing in such a place. He answered, "I often ask myself that same question," but then tried to soften the blow, remarking that this outburst was an exception rather than the norm.

I could not accept his explanation. I reminded him that the two hecklers were about my age, so they had been children during the Second World War, when Jews were butchered in Europe. Australia has a small Jewish population that lives in peace among the general population. If in this place, a young man suddenly gets up to announce that we still haven't paid enough, that the Jews owe the non-Jewish world the price of the gas wasted on them—we can only conclude that no place in the world is ours, except for Eretz Israel.

During my term as neighborhood rabbi in north Tel Aviv, my father-in-law, Rabbi Yitzchak Yedidya Frankel, who then served as rabbi of the southern neighborhoods, asked me to accompany him on a visit to the eminent Yiddish poet Itzik Manger. Rabbi Frankel had told me that this wise man of letters, who was also a dramatist and novelist, was hospitalized in Hartzfeld Geriatric Hospital in Gedera in serious medical condition, and that he might not recover. Rabbi Frankel wanted to perform the mitzvah of visiting the sick by comforting this person in whom the public no longer took an interest, a lonely man at the end of his life.

We went to see Itzik Manger. We entered a dark room, from which emanated fumes of alcohol. Rabbi Frankel took immediate stock of the situation. He opened the window of the room, allowing the fresh autumn breeze to enter and disperse the suffocating haze that hung inside. In the room's only bed lay a man of slight stature, gaunt as a dry twig, eyes closed. He looked lifeless. Rabbi Frankel and I stood on either side of his bed and gazed at him for a while. After a few minutes, I looked at Rabbi Frankel, as if to ask whether our being there might do more harm than good. I feared that, should Itzik Manger suddenly awaken, he might be shocked by our presence, especially by Rabbi Frankel's imposing, patriarchal figure.

Slowly, Manger opened one eye, then the other. His small but sharp eyes recognized my father-in-law immediately. The first thing he said to him, in a Warsaw Yiddish dialect, was the greeting, "*Shalom aleichem,*

Rabbi Frankel. You shouldn't have any complaints or grudges against me. Don't think that something bad has happened. Don't criticize. I am Noah after the flood."

Rabbi Frankel and I exchanged glances. We both thought the man was hallucinating, either because he had been drinking, or because his illness had affected his lucidity. What Manger was saying seemed doubly strange, since he did not ask any of the usual polite questions or inquire after the welfare of his visitors. This sick and lonely man had a powerful need to talk to someone, and that's what he was doing.

We remained silent as he continued: "You know, Rabbi Frankel, ever since my childhood, one question has been bothering me. The verse says, *Noah walked with God*—he was the only one God invited into the ark, in order to save him from the flood. God told him, *For it is you that I have seen as a righteous man before Me in this generation*. The Torah also says of him, *These are the generations of Noah: Noah was a just man and perfect in his generations*. Did the Master of the Universe say such things in praise of any other person?

"I know that some commentators interpret this as criticism of Noah, as meaning that he was righteous only *in his generations*, relative to the generation of the flood. If he had lived in the generation of Abraham, he would not have stood out. There will always be those who will say, 'You're a righteous man in this generation, but compared to other generations you're nothing.' But to remain strong in such a generation, to stay righteous, so that God says you are a *tzaddik* [righteous one]—is that so negligible?

"Noah was an outstanding person, and so God chose to begin the entire world anew with him. Adam had three sons: Cain, Abel, and Seth. Ten generations later, Noah was born, and he also had three sons: Shem, Ham, and Japheth. The world began from Noah. If so, he was truly exceptional. But what happened then? As it says in our sacred Torah, *And Noah began to be an husbandman, and he planted a vineyard; And he drank of the wine, and was drunken; and he was uncovered within his tent*. In other words, Noah was naked inside the tent."

The emaciated, ill poet continued to press his point, as if powered by an internal fire: "How can a *tzaddik* also be a drunk? I always wondered about this, but now I have reached an age and a condition where

I understand Noah. He entered the ark with his wife, his three sons, and their wives. But when he went back home and began to look for his hometown, his *shtetl*—he found nothing. He wanted to visit his neighborhood *shtiebel* [small house of prayer], his study hall, his synagogue, but found not a trace. Where was the corner grocery store? Where was the postman he knew, the wagon driver? No one was left. No house or street, no neighborhood or friends—not a living soul. *And every living substance was destroyed which was upon the face of the ground.* In order to forget his solitude and the destruction of his world, *he drank of the wine and became drunk,*" Manger explained, his voice weak.

Then he spoke forcefully. "I am Noah after the flood," declared Itzik Manger from his bed in Hartzfeld Hospital in Gedera. He continued hurling accusations at the world. "Where is Warsaw? Where is Nalewki, in the old Jewish neighborhood there?" He listed the names of the Chassidic communities and yeshivas in Warsaw, rabbis he had known there, and members of his family. "Of all these, no one is left. I remained alone in the world. So you will excuse me, Rabbi Frankel, if sometimes, in order to forget the horrors, I drink a little."

Itzik Manger, the prominent Yiddish poet and prolific dramatist, lost his entire family in the Holocaust and came to Israel as a lonely old man. When he arrived, his readers and admirers from Poland gave him a royal welcome. But as time went on, his fame subsided and his community of followers dwindled and almost disappeared. Only a few individuals recognized his talent and creativity. This was the fate of the poet, and of Yiddish in general. I cannot judge him for his statement, or criticize him for his choices.

Although I understand Itzik Manger, I choose to identify with those who suffered intensely during the war but who opted to lead their lives in a vastly different mode. The very horrors they experienced pushed them to take advantage of every moment, to live life to the fullest. For them, isolation was not automatically a reason for depression. Instead, loneliness often served as the catalyst for ambition, the desire to accomplish, to come to terms with those terrible years. As Solomon's father, the poet King David, wrote in Psalms: *Make us glad according to the days wherein thou hast afflicted us, and the years wherein we have seen evil.*

. . .

WHEN I WAS CHIEF RABBI OF ISRAEL, the president of Tel Aviv University invited me to speak at a conference there, together with a guest of honor from France, Cardinal Jean-Marie Lustiger. The university planned the conference for the eve of Holocaust Memorial Day, and they asked me to appear at eight in the evening, the same time as the national memorial ceremony in Yad Vashem. I asked the president of the university why he had organized a conference parallel to the national event at the Holocaust museum. He explained that bringing Lustiger to Israel was a significant achievement. In addition, he said that at the exact time of the national ceremony, the cardinal would be speaking about "The Place of God in the Holocaust," and he wanted me to debate him. I refused.

Lustiger was an apostate, a Jew who had converted to Catholicism. His mother had perished in Auschwitz. When he was fourteen, he was baptized as a Catholic in a church in France of his own free will. Aaron Lustiger became Jean-Marie Lustiger.

I refused to participate in the evening at the university, as I would not lend my support to such an example presented before young Jewish students. In my view, Tel Aviv University could certainly find a better way to express identification with the Holocaust. As a resident of Tel Aviv, a citizen of the State of Israel, and a Jew in general, I protested with all my being against the idea of inviting Cardinal Lustiger on that evening.

On that Holocaust Day, I responded to this issue in a speech in the Great Synagogue of Jerusalem, just before reciting the *Yizkor* memorial prayer. I said that Hitler gave us six million reasons to recite Kaddish, but following Lustiger's path would mean that there would be no descendants left to recite Kaddish for those who perished. He defected from the ranks of his people in their darkest hour, when they needed maximum encouragement and support; he deserted the front of the battle for Jewish existence. Not only did he exempt himself from the *Shulchan Aruch* (code of Jewish law) and the "Way of Life," (the first section of the *Shulchan Aruch*, which details the laws of daily life), but his choice to lead a celibate lifestyle and refrain from raising a family resulted in the fact that no one would remain to recite Kaddish for him.

I know that on his father and mother's memorial dates, Cardinal Lustiger removes his Catholic cloak, dons an ordinary civilian suit and a hat, and goes to a synagogue in Paris to recite Kaddish. I am not judging him. There is a Creator, the Judge of the entire world, and He will do justice. But I do judge the person who initiated the outrageous idea of presenting Cardinal Lustiger as a model.

I RECALL ANOTHER STORY, whose beginning is similar but whose ending is completely different.

After the war, the daughter of a rabbi had a child with a non-Jewish man, and she gave up the infant to a Catholic monastery. She also cut herself off from Judaism. A young rabbi who knew her from child-hood, her father's close disciple, attempted to contact her. He tried to find out what had happened to her father, his rabbi, but she avoided him. He decided to go directly to her house. When she saw who it was, she slammed the door in his face, but he did not give up. She opened the door once more, and said quickly and furiously, "I have nothing to do with you people. I've begun a new chapter in my life." He asked for a glass of water. The woman bowed her head, then invited him to come inside. Again the Jew asked to know what had happened to her father, and explained that he had felt like a son to the rabbi, and that he had a responsibility to memorialize him. Finally, the woman recounted her story.

It was morning, after services. Her father was sitting beside the table wearing his tallis and tefillin, studying Talmud. Suddenly they heard a savage pounding on the door. "I opened the door. Three Gestapo men burst into the room. They threw me on the ground. I got up and ran to see what they wanted. They pushed their way into my father's room. He raised his head and gave them a look that I won't forget until my dying day. He stared at them as if to ask, What do you want from me? What can I do for you? That was to be his last look. One of the three slung the rifle off his shoulder and pounded the butt on my father's head with all his might. For a moment, I thought the head tefillin had split his brain. Jets of blood burst from his head. His beautiful white beard reddened, and he fell onto the open Talmud.

"What do you want from me? Can't you understand the source of my bitterness? Can't you understand my anger? That's how they took my father," she ended.

The man sat before her and wept for his rabbi, the daughter weeping along with him. "My sister," he said, "you cannot possibly understand how much I understand you. I also have many questions, but I have no answers. No human being can answer such questions. The Torah cautions that *the secret things belong unto the Lord our God*—we, however, have the responsibility to act. But the revealed things apply to us and to our children forever: that we must fulfill all the words of this Torah.

"Your child's grandfather has only one grandchild," he continued. "A fateful and historic decision now lies in your hands. If he continues in his present direction, you are handing your father's murderers their victory. That is exactly what they wanted—to put out the fire, the flame of Judaism, so that it would never burn again. But if your child follows his grandfather's path, then they have lost the war, and your father has won. Who deserves to win? The key is in your hands. Do you want to finish their work? Will you finish spiritually what they did not finish physically? Or will your father win, and his grandson pick up his grandfather's studies on the very page of Talmud where he left off?"

With these words, the Jew walked out of the house. The daughter was stunned. She ran after him, got into his car, and said, "I want to get him out of there right now." Then she added, "On the condition that you take responsibility for his education. I have no one else who can do it." He agreed, on his own condition: that she assist him, so as not to traumatize the child by the abrupt transition. "You draw him near to you, and through you, I will draw near to him," he proposed.

Today, this child is a *rosh yeshiva* in Jerusalem. He is the only living descendant of the old rabbi from Warsaw.

THIS ANONYMOUS YOUNG RABBI FROM WARSAW, who will never have a street named after him, is one who ensures continued Jewish existence. Itzik Manger was totally immersed in the past and his attempts to dull its pain. The approach of the Jewish cardinal is certainly no way to promise the continued existence of our people. Our way, that of the Holocaust survivors, must be to ensure that the torch of Jewish tradition is passed on, and to do everything so that it will continue to burn. In the spirit of King David's verse in Psalms, *I will walk before the Lord in the land of the living.*

As an example of passing on the torch, I recall the story of the late Reb-betzin Tzila Sorotzkin, my son-in-law's aunt. She was one of the leading educators of the Beit Ya'akov movement—an early-twentieth-century initiative to establish Orthodox elementary and secondary schools for girls—a teacher and a teachers' supervisor, and, mainly, an outstanding person. Mrs. Sorotzkin, who was also a Holocaust survivor, told my daughter Miri: "In all the six years of the war, I cried only once. I was in the most horrible of the camps, and I lost my entire family. I was left all alone in the world, broken in body and spirit—and I didn't cry. I returned to our hometown, and found not a living soul—and still I didn't cry," said Mrs. Sorotzkin. "They told me, 'Go to Łódź, that's where the refugees are gathering, maybe you'll find a relative or an acquaintance.'

"I went to Łódź, totally exhausted. They showed me the area where the Jews were assembling. With my last remaining bit of strength, I walked through the streets in the twilight. Suddenly I recognized sounds coming from one of the windows. As in a trance, as if someone were calling me inside, I opened a gate, entered the courtyard of an ancient building, then opened a door. In the darkness, I made out a row of boys with sidelocks sitting along both sides of a long table. At its head sat an elderly Jew wearing a baseball cap. The children were chanting the *alef-bet,* the Hebrew alphabet, to a tune. I don't remember anything else . . . Then I found myself on the floor of the room, with people standing over me and pouring water on me.

"The teacher tried to revive me, and asked in a worried voice, 'What happened? Can I help you? Sit up. Maybe you'd like to eat something. Who are you? Where did you come from?' Slowly I recovered, and replied: 'This is the first time I've cried in the past six years. But I'm not crying from pain—I'm crying for joy. I wandered far and wide until I reached Łódź, and finally saw Poland as it once was. And if, after all we've been through,' I said to the teacher, 'little boys in sidelocks are sitting here and an elderly teacher is teaching them the Hebrew alphabet—then no one can defeat us. Let me catch my breath; I feel fine. These are tears of joy, not of pain. "

ONE OF THE BLESSINGS IN THE *AMIDAH* PRAYER, which we recite three times a day, addresses the ingathering of the exiles of our people: *Sound the great shofar for our freedom, raise the banner to gather our exiles, and gather us together from the four corners of the earth. Blessed are You, O Lord, Who gathers in the dispersed of His people Israel.* The next sentence reads, *Restore our judges as in former times and our counselors as in the beginning; remove from us sorrow and sighing.* The topics of these two sentences are seemingly unrelated—but only seemingly. In truth, they are inextricably intertwined. When God gathers in the dispersed of His people Israel, we must insist that our judges be restored *as in former times and our counselors as in the beginning,"* in order to *remove from us sorrow and sighing.*

This is the problem inherent in the ingathering of the exiles. We came to Eretz Israel as orphans, from families that were shattered and broken, burdened with difficult questions. Some did not know who was who, or who their parents were, or whether their spouses were still alive. What if a woman were not a widow, as she assumed, but rather still married? Perhaps her prospective husband was also still married, but did not know it. Perhaps a man about to remarry did not know that his first wife had actually been saved from the horrors, and was living in a convent or in some isolated Polish village. If he married again, he would be unknowingly violating Rabbenu Gershom's eleventh-century ban on bigamy.

The aliya of my generation, like all other waves of immigration to Israel, brought with it myriad problems particular to its time. We were the generation of the ingathering of the exiles; we came from 104 different communities, and we desperately needed *the restoration of our judges* as of old. Some of these judges, whom God placed in the right place at the right time, were the Lubavitcher Rebbe, Rabbi Elazar Menachem Man Shach, and Rabbi Ovadia Yosef, each one a world unto himself in terms of leadership. They were vastly different in their personalities and world-views, but all three were spiritual giants of our generation.

•   •   •

HAIM LASKOV WAS A BATTALION COMMANDER at Latrun during Israel's War of Independence, and later became the IDF chief of staff. Although known for his terseness, he always described the fighters at Latrun in warm and sympathetic terms, in vibrant colors. He spoke of those who had come out of the concentration camps directly to the battles for the independence of the State of Israel.

Laskov quoted from David's lament over Jonathan and Saul: *They were swifter than eagles, they were stronger than lions*. Native Israelis often criticized the families and friends of Holocaust survivors for going like sheep to the slaughter. Yet these fighters arrived straight from the illegal immigration boats to the fields of Latrun and attacked their target heroically. They had no identity cards, no reserve-duty call-up notices. They did not even have military identification papers or numbers. But many had a number the Nazis had scorched into their flesh.

These hundreds, like Shalom Tepper, who fell in the battle of Fallujah in the Sinai, did not have time to undergo basic training at military training bases. They arrived from the rickety boats in which they had fled the killing fields directly to the plains of battle, where they took orders from young squad commanders who did not understand their language. And yet *They were swifter than eagles, they were stronger than lions*. They fought for their own home, not a foreign one, one without which the Jewish people have no future. In the war for their own homeland, on their own land, they did not feel they were refugees, but rather proud fighters. Far from behaving like sheep to the slaughter, they revealed nothing of the submissiveness of a flock, but rather courage and strength of character. Military plots in cemeteries and memorials throughout the country are covered with the names of Holocaust survivors whose days in Eretz Israel were numbered, and whose blood spilled onto its ground as they did their part for the establishment of a home for the Jewish people. This, to me, is a miraculous phenomenon.

For the first time after hundreds of years of exile, Jews were fighting for their own flag, their own home, for independence. They were battling for life itself. No one was fighting to gain war spoils, to be decorated for bravery, or to be featured in a victory album. People realized the meaning of a life-or-death war and the full significance of the struggle for survival. For this reason, I think, the fighting of the Holocaust survivors who had just arrived in their homeland was more resolute. For six years in Europe, they had looked death in the face, and with their entire beings, they desired that such an event would never again affect Jews simply because of their Jewishness. They wanted to begin independent lives in their own state. I am certain that this powerful desire that burned within them overcame their lack of military experience, the shortage of weapons, and their ignorance about how to operate them. Theirs was a heroic struggle, inspired by the harsh personal experience they had suffered.

I am not one of those Holocaust survivors who had to decide for themselves which course to take. I was not one who decided for himself whether to follow the path of the poet Itzik Manger, who fell under the influence of alcohol; Ka-Zetnik, who opted to isolate himself; Shalom Tepper, who fought to the death in the fields of Fallujah; or my brother Naphtali, who participated in training exercises for Haganah (the military force that preceded the IDF).

I was practically born here—I came to Eretz Israel when I was eight years old. In the few photographs I have from my childhood, I see a child with an almost constant smile on his face. My memories from the religious school in Kiryat Shmuel, near my aunt and uncle's home, are filled with games of marbles—rose-colored globes of loveliness. I am not an example of the struggle for renewed life, because my future was determined by others. Naphtali decided I would go live with my aunt and uncle, and he and Rabbi Reiner convinced my uncle to send me to Kol Torah Yeshiva. I began to make decisions for myself only at age thirteen and two months, when I came to the yeshiva in Jerusalem. Until then, my world was shaped by others, and so it was easier for me than for adult Holocaust survivors. I did not utter a word of complaint or criticism. My reaction was like the Israelites' acceptance of the Torah: *We will do, and we will listen*.

IN 1988, ABRAHAM HIRSCHSON of the General Federation of Labor (Histadrut) and Dr. Shmuel Rosenman, a former student of mine from *moshav* Chemed, asked me to lead the first March of the Living. Participants in the march walk the 1.8 miles (three kilometers) from Auschwitz to Birkenau, then stand near the bombed-out barracks, where a memorial ceremony for the Holocaust martyrs is held. The goal is to demonstrate to ourselves and the entire world what is written in "Zog Nit Keynmol," or the partisans' anthem: "Beneath our tread the earth shall tremble—we are here!" This is not a declaration of a desire to live in Poland, but rather a statement to emphasize our Jewish stubbornness, perseverance, and power of survival in that very location. Precisely in that place, we must demonstrate that *Am Yisrael Chai*—the Jewish nation lives—and it has a future.

Of course I agreed to Hirschson's request. Seven hundred youngsters from Israel and the Diaspora participated, along with a delegation of adults. Among those representing Israel were minister of education and culture Yitzchak Navon and Knesset members who were also Holocaust survivors. Writer Elie Wiesel came from New York, together with the Israeli ambassador to the United Nations at the time, Benjamin Netanyahu.

We planned to hold the memorial ceremony in the crematorium area, accompanied by speeches and torch-lighting. Cantor Benjamin Muller of Antwerp, who has a remarkable voice, would conduct the ceremony and chant *El Maleh Rachamim*, the memorial prayer. But at the last minute, I felt we needed something else. Someone suggested that we add a musical piece, and all agreed, but we had no idea who might be available to play at such short notice.

A feverish search soon bore fruit. The night before the ceremony, someone brought to my room a Warsaw youth of about fifteen, a talented violinist. Some suggested he might be of Jewish ancestry. We asked him to play something appropriate for Jews. He put his bow to the strings, but none of the melodies he played was appropriate.

We had almost given up hope when I asked him if that was all he knew how to play. The boy replied that at that very moment he remembered one other tune he had heard as a child from his grandmother, who used to sing it softly to him. When the notes of the violin again filled the room, we all shook with emotion: it was the tune to the well-known Yiddish song "Es Brent" ("Brothers, Our Town Is Burning"). The sound of the Polish youth's violin pierced our hearts. The four people in the room sat agape. Slowly we joined in, singing the words in Yiddish: *Es brent! Briderlekh, Es brent!*

But the boy knew not one word of the song, only the melody. After hearing his playing, we realized that his soul must have a Jewish spark. He told us that his grandmother was Jewish. He added that as a child in communist Poland, he had heard her singing this melody very quietly, in secret, and he had remembered it. Placing my hand on his shoulder, I asked him to play this melody the next day, on the scorched earth of Birkenau. In my mind's eye, I could see the hundreds of youths marching up with their backpacks on their backs, looking as if they were on a school trip. But when the boy would stand up to play this familiar melody, he would create the right mood and focus their attention. And this is indeed what happened: at the sound of his violin, there was no need for the usual shouts into the microphone of "Quiet, quiet."

Seven hundred youth from all over the world, accompanied by adults, began their tour of the Auschwitz museum. This was the first time in their lives they had seen the suitcases, hair, and prayer shawls that had belonged to the living human beings who were butchered on that soil. Dr. Alvin Schiff, director of the New York Board of Jewish Education, blew the shofar under the sign reading ARBEIT MACHT FREI (work brings freedom), and then the march began.

Arms linked, without a word, the youngsters and adults marched, wearing sky-blue jackets with white Stars of David on their backs, down the train tracks that had led the trains to Auschwitz. From there we continued to the crematorium of Birkenau, carrying eighteen Israeli flags the whole way. I had objected to the idea that each delegation should march with its own flag. I thought it more appropriate for all of us to walk in unison behind the Israeli flag; it gave a place like Auschwitz a special meaning from our unique perspective. I sensed that we came to this place to demonstrate that the Jewish nation has its own flag— blue and white, like the colors of the tallis, with a Magen David (Star of David) in the center—and there is no other. The delegation accepted my suggestion.

I marched at the head of the line until we reached the ramp across from the place where the accursed Josef Mengele had carried out his selections. All that remained there was a single hut. Someone had affixed to it a photograph of Jewish prisoners standing in line in front of Mengele, his thumb outstretched toward them. That thumb had determined the human fates, signaling who would go to the right and who to the left, who to life and who to death. Then the sound of the violin pierced the air, and all fell silent. Softly, the marchers joined in, singing the words to the song along with the melody of the violin:

> *It is burning, brothers, it is burning.*
> *Our poor little town, a pity, burns!*
> *Furious winds blow,*
> *Breaking, burning, and scattering,*
> *And you stand there*
> *With folded arms.*
> *Oh, you stand and look*
> *While our town burns.*

The voice of the violin shook the souls of all those present. The violinist, who did not even know the words of the song he was playing, the one his Jewish grandmother had sung to him in his childhood, was wearing a blue *kippah* on top of his mane of blond hair. From the top of the ramp, I watched the line as it marched along the barbed wire fence.

All together, we numbered about a thousand people, all wearing blue and white—youngsters, adults, and elderly Holocaust survivors, including Yechiel Reichman of Montevideo, a witness at the Demjanjuk trial, and Chaim Basok, a partisan and fighter in the Vilna ghetto.

In one row, I saw a young man wrapped in his tallis, and as he came closer, I saw that it was yellowed with age. I signaled for him to approach, and asked for his name and hometown. "I'm Mendel Kaplan, from Cape Town, South Africa," he answered. Later he became chairman of the World Jewish Congress. I asked why he had wrapped himself in that tallis. "My father was born in Lithuania," he replied, "not far from here. My father left me with nothing but this tallis and his tefillin. He told me, 'No matter where you go, don't forget that you're a Jew.' This is not the proper time of day to lay tefillin, but I feel an obligation to my father to wrap myself in his tallis in this awful place. I have the feeling that my father is proud, that he knows that with this tallis, I am demonstrating the continuity of Jewish existence."

We arrived in Auschwitz on Yom Hashoah (Holocaust Remembrance Day), 27 Nisan 5748 (April 14, 1988). Snow was falling. Just as we heard the blast of the shofar at the entrance gate, the snow stopped falling and the sun peeked out. When Benjamin Muller began the ceremony by chanting *El Maleh Rachamim*, the snow began to fall once more. Sunshine and snow mingled together, as if the sky were weeping along with us. I went up to the microphone and read from Psalms: *I shall not die, but live, and declare the works of the Lord. God has chastised me, but He has not delivered me to death. . . . For thou hast delivered my soul from death, mine eyes from tears, and my feet from falling. I will walk before the Lord in the land of the living.*

From the corner of my eye, I noticed some eleventh-grade girls taking head coverings and scarves out of their backpacks and covering their heads. They sensed that this was a prayer and thought they were doing the right thing by donning a head covering. Since they were not yet married, this obligation did not apply to them, but I appreciated the emotional power of their spontaneous gesture.

Elie Wiesel led the afternoon service in the Vizhnitz style, as he had learned growing up in Sighet (present-day Sighetu Marmaţiei, Romania). We lit six torches in memory of the victims and ended the ceremony by singing the traditional *Ani Ma'amin* ("I believe in the coming of the Messiah") prayer and "Hatikvah," Israel's national anthem.

Since then, I have participated and led several Marches of the Living. I always speak about the place where we stand as the Jewish people's largest cemetery. I remind the youth that the duration of the March of the Living continues through Israel's Memorial Day for fallen soldiers and its Independence Day. When we return to Jerusalem, I tell them to kiss the ground. Those who go on to Israel from Poland no longer have any doubt in their minds about our right to our own homeland. As we sing in *Lecha Dodi, Arise and depart from the midst of the turmoil / Long enough have you sat in the valley of tears.* From my experience and observation, the Jews who come from other countries around the world to participate in the March of the Living return from it with a deeper commitment to Israel, while the Israelis go home more conscious of their Jewish identity.

•   •   •

IN THE CONTEXT OF HOLOCAUST EDUCATION, I have often heard the expression "to infuse awareness of the Holocaust," and it grates on my consciousness. What do they mean by "infuse"? With a hypodermic needle? By force-feeding? A blood transfusion? I do not understand.

When I was a child, and *The Diary of Anne Frank* was published, I was curious about it. A Youth Aliya psychologist advised my aunt and uncle in Kiryat Motzkin to hide the book from me. She thought a child needed to be born anew. "Let him play with marbles and he'll be like a new child" was her professional advice. But, like the idea of infusing awareness, this concept of forgetting and being reborn is also meaningless.

I was a child, not yet eight, in Buchenwald. Such a child cannot forget Buchenwald. He sees the sights and hears the cries every day of his life. Phrases like "to be reborn" and "to infuse awareness of the Holocaust" are senseless—better to avoid them. I read *The Diary of Anne Frank* when I was twelve years old, while babysitting at a neighbor's house—and I was disappointed. It did not describe the real world. It did not depict the horrors of Buchenwald or my father's humiliation; it did not speak of death, disease, helplessness, or bestial cruelty.

Yet this diary is important because, for the first time, it introduced the world to the sensitive and tragic figure of a Jewish girl of fourteen. It is difficult, even impossible, to comprehend the astronomical number of six million—it is easier to identify with one talented girl who has a name, a family background, and such very human sensitivity. This is the secret of *Anne Frank*, and we can learn a lesson from it.

I remember everything, and if I can also remind—let this be my reward.

To a certain degree, we are all Noah after the flood, like the poet Itzik Manger. Each one of us Holocaust survivors must constantly ask: Why was I chosen to be saved while others were not? Perhaps I have a role, a mission? Maybe I was meant to do something in my own way?

MY OLDEST SON, MOSHE CHAIM, became a bar mitzvah on the Shabbat when we read the biblical account of the Israelites' battle with Amalek. I had not intended to make a speech on this occasion, but the planned speakers pressured me, including my uncle Rabbi Vogelman and my father-in-law, Rabbi Frankel. So I spoke about the last verse in the chapter of Exodus: *The Lord maintains a war against Amalek, from generation to generation*. We cannot fight the enemy Amalek—the nation or the phenomenon—with weapons or with ammunition. Rather, we are obligated to fight this battle in every generation, each generation passing on our heritage to the next. The struggle for the continuity of generations is the true battle, and the great spiritual-divine victory of Israel against the adversary Amalek. Our victory in the war against Amalek is that my son, Moshe Chaim Lau, is continuing the heritage of his grandfather, my father, Rabbi Moshe Chaim Lau, who went up to Heaven in a tempest.

Moshe Chaim is the first candle in the private Hanukkah menorah I have been privileged to create. My wife is the base of that menorah, from which the candles, our eight children, went out into the world. And I am the *gabbai*, whose role is to help light those candles so that they will spread their light and proclaim, each in a special way, the miracle of the victory of eternal Israel.

RABBI ISRAEL MEIR LAU
REMARKS TO PRESIDENT
BARACK OBAMA AT
YAD VASHEM

MARCH 22, 2013

In March 2013, Rabbi Lau gave a historic address to President Obama during his first visit to Israel. The transcript is included here in this first paperback edition.

I WANT TO USE THIS OCCASION, it is an opportunity for me to thank you. On April 11, 1945, in the concentration camp of Buchenwald that you visited, American troops broke in, led by General Patton of the division of General Dwight Eisenhower, and they liberated us. One of the Jewish leaders of the United States, Rabbi Hershel Schachter was [there]. He entered into the barracks and we were there. Crying in Yiddish [he proclaimed] "Jews, you are free!" We didn't believe him. After six years of horror, such a tunnel, we never believed.

This is the opportunity to thank you, to thank the American people, who came finally in 1945 April, to take us out not from slavery to freedom but from death to life.

I want to add one sentence. Two months ago we had a privilege to appear every year at the government's meeting of the International

Commemoration Day of the Holocaust. And I told of a short episode from last year that I experienced in Seattle, the United States. I was in a very small Holocaust museum, one room. At the front stood a brigadier general, an old man, very handsome, in uniform, with all the medals of the United States. He welcomed me with tears in his eyes. He knew that I am a Holocaust survivor, a child from Buchenwald. He shook my hand and said, "Rabbi, I was one of the liberators of Buchenwald. I served with General Patton. When I heard that you are coming to Seattle I asked for permission to meet with you. Before I give back my soul to the Lord of the Universe, me, Leo Hymas, am asking from you forgiveness . . . for being late. We came too late. I saw what we have seen, I understand we were late, forgive me." I told him, "Sixty-seven years you have in your heart, in your consciousness, this worry that you have to ask forgiveness, you must be a great man."

Yesterday, Mr. President, you have promised us that we are not alone. . . . Don't be too late. Remember we need your support; we need your friendship; we appreciate your love to us, to the entire world. We, all together, next week sitting at the night of the Seder, together from all over the countries of the globe, we are asking not only to praise the Lord Almighty for the past, of Exodus, but also we pray for the peace in Israel, in the Middle East, and the entire world. And you will help us together to have the great days of light after the dark tunnel.

Thank you very much.

ACKNOWLEDGMENTS

I AM ETERNALLY GRATEFUL to my brother Naphtali, who risked his life countless times in order to fulfill the dying wish of our father to protect me and thus ensure the continuation of the rabbinic heritage of our family. This book details only the smallest fraction of Naphtali's efforts toward this end. When we came to Israel, we met our oldest brother, Yehoshua, in Atlit. He and Naphtali, together with my uncle and aunt and my teachers, invested much thought in my education, and did everything they could to help me forget the pain of being orphaned at a tender age.

I offer special thanks to my wife, Chaya-Ita, who took upon herself the mission of establishing a home and family with a lifelong partner who did not know exactly what "home" and "family" were. This endeavor demanded great courage and determination on her part, and she met all of our shared challenges admirably.

This book is written especially for my children and grandchildren. Although I have shared some of the journey's hardships with them, I have never told them the entire story. My wife and I have been blessed with children and their spouses, as well as grandchildren, all of whom are God-fearing and graced with precious gifts. They are the fulfillment of our most heartfelt desires, and the result of the remarkable victory against all those who rose up against us. I am confident that when they read this book, they and their contemporaries will understand life's supreme sanctity and the secret of the everlasting glory of Israel.

I offer my thanks and appreciation to the director of Yedioth Ahronoth Books, Dov Eichenwald, who encouraged me to publish my memoirs in the original Hebrew and did not rest until his efforts were rewarded. I am also sincerely grateful to Anat Meidan for her listening and attentiveness, and to Tirtza Arazi for her faultless work and great sensitivity.

THIS ENGLISH-LANGUAGE EDITION is the result of the collaborative efforts of many people.

My distinguished friend Shimon Peres, president of the State of Israel and Nobel Peace Prize winner, who bore a heavy burden on his shoulders, and who carried this burden proudly in his leadership of the people and the nation, found the opportunity to dedicate time to the reading of my book and to the writing of a foreword that is so important for us all. My dear friend from youth Professor Elie Wiesel, an ember rescued from the flames, also a recipient of the Nobel Peace Prize, wrote his foreword with the blood of his heart. I carry the memory of both of these great men in the depths of my heart.

I am thankful to Jessica Setbon and Shira Leibowitz Schmidt for their dedication and commitment in translating the Hebrew edition into English; and to David Szonyi and Dvora Rhein, who edited an early draft of the English translation.

I would like to thank my friend the noted photographer Peter Halmagyi for the pictures he made and contributed to the book.

I extend thanks to OU Press for their cooperation and collaboration with Sterling Publishing, which made this book possible. I express appreciation to my friend Rabbi Menachem Genack, general editor of OU Press, for his commitment to this English-language edition of my memoirs and for his constant encouragement. My thanks go as well to Joelle Delbourgo, my literary agent, for her support and faith in the project. I am also grateful to Rabbi Yigal Sklarin for his invaluable editorial input and advice.

I am deeply indebted to Sterling Publishing for their tireless efforts in bringing this book to the English-language reader, and would like to thank Theresa Thompson, president; Elizabeth Lindy, senior art director, covers; David Ter-Avanesyan, cover designer (back cover); Kevin Iwano, production director; Gavin Aghamore, digital design manager; and Hannah Reich, production editor. I would also like to acknowledge the excellent work of packager Barbara Clark; Robin Arzt, interior designer; and theBookDesigners, Alan Hebel and Ian Shimkoviak, for the front cover design. Barbara Berger, executive editor of Sterling Publishing, put her heart and soul into editing this edition of my memoirs. She was especially motivated because her great-uncle Jack Werber, also a Buchenwald survivor, worked with the camp's underground to hide and save more than seven hundred children there in the last weeks of the war.

Textual Citations

INDEX

Numbers beginning with *p* denote pages containing photographs and captions.

ABOUT THE AUTHOR AND FOREWORD AUTHORS

Ordained as a rabbi in 1961, **ISRAEL MEIR LAU** served as the Ashkenazi Chief Rabbi of Israel from 1993 to 2003. He is currently Chief Rabbi of Tel Aviv and Chairman of the Yad Vashem Council; Yad Vashem is Israel's official memorial organization to the Jewish victims of the Holocaust. In 2005, Lau was awarded the Israel Prize—the country's highest honor—for his lifetime achievements and special contribution to society and the State of Israel. In 2011, France awarded him the Legion of Honor in recognition of his efforts to promote interfaith dialogue.

SHIMON PERES was president of the State of Israel. Mr. Peres served twice as the prime minister of Israel and once as interim prime minister, and was a member of twelve cabinets in a political career spanning more than seventy years. He was recipient of the 1994 Nobel Peace Prize. Mr. Peres was the author of numerous books and writer of hundreds of articles and essays.

ELIE WIESEL was born in Romania, and was fifteen when he was deported to Auschwitz. After the war he became a journalist and writer in Paris, and since then wrote more than 50 books, including the best-selling *Night*. He was the recipient of numerous awards, including the Presidential Medal of Freedom, the French Legion of Honor, an honorary knighthood of the British Empire, and in 1986, the Nobel Peace Price. He was also Andrew W. Mellon Professor in the Humanities and professor of philosophy and religion at Boston University.